A.G. CARUSO
'65-8509

T5-ADN-168

D A T A B ASE PROCESSING
FOR MICROCOMPUTERS

David M. Kroenke and Donald E. Nilson

SRA®
SCIENCE RESEARCH ASSOCIATES, INC.
Chicago, Henley-on-Thames, Sydney, Toronto

An IBM Company

Acquisition Editor Michael J. Carrigg
Project Editor Mary C. Konstant
Compositor The Clarinda Company
Cover and Text Designer Kristin Nelson

Portions of this book have been adapted and/or reprinted by permission from the following texts:

Managing Information with Microcomputers: Featuring R:Base Series Database Management Systems by Donald E. Nilson and David M. Kroenke. Copyright © 1984 Microrim, Inc. World rights reserved.

Database Processing: Fundamentals, Design, Implementation by David M. Kroenke. Copyright © Science Research Associates, Inc. 1983, 1977. All rights reserved.

Illustrations

Figures 1–1 and 1–2 from D. M. Kroenke, *Database Processing*. Science Research Associates, Inc., 1983.

Figures 1–5, 3–9, 12–1, 12–2, 13–1, A–1, A–2, A–3, A–4, A–5, A–6, A–7, A–8 from D. E. Nilson, and D. M. Kroenke, *Managing Information with Microcomputers*, Microrim, Inc. 1984.

Library of Congress Cataloging-in-Publication Data
Kroenke, David.
   Database processing for microcomputers.

   Bibliography: p.
   Includes index.
   1. Data base management.   2. Microcomputers—
Programming.   I. Nilson, Donald E., 1944–
II. Title.
QA76.9.D3K77   1986   005.74   85–27756
ISBN 0–574–21975–7

Copyright © Science Research Associates, Inc. 1986. All rights reserved. No part of this publication may be reproduced, stored in a retrieval system, or transmitted, in any form or by any means, electronic, mechanical, photocopying, recording, or otherwise, without the prior written permission of Science Research Associates, Inc.

Printed in the United States of America.

10 9 8 7 6 5 4 3

CONTENTS

Preface	viii
CHAPTER 1 Introduction	**3**
Preview	3
What Is Database Processing?	4
Advantages of Database Processing	7
Disadvantages of Database Processing	8
Components of Computer-Based Information Management Systems	9
Summary	16
Review Questions	17
CHAPTER 2 Great Plains Music and Video Unlimited	**21**
Preview	21
Great Plains Music and Video Unlimited	22
The Video Rental Information Management System	23
Summary	33
Review Questions	34
CHAPTER 3 Data Models and Their Design	**37**
Preview	37
Data as a Model	38
Designing Data Models	46
Steps in Database Design	48
Summary	51
Review Questions	52
CHAPTER 4 Standards for Database Design	**55**
Preview	55
Problems Resulting from Poor Design	56
Eliminating Modification Anomalies	58
Domain/Key Normal Form: A Design Goal	59

Summary	72
Review Questions	73

CHAPTER 5 Database Design for Great Plains **75**

Preview	75
The Problem	76
Our Approach to Database Design	76
Summary	94
Review Questions	95
Project	96

CHAPTER 6 Database Implementation—
Personnel Data **99**

Preview	99
Database Definition Using the EXPRESS	100
Using the LOAD WITH PROMPTS Command	104
Using SELECT and COMPUTE	105
Changing Data Using the EDIT Command	113
HELP and PROMPT	114
Summary	116
Review Questions	117
Project	119

CHAPTER 7 Database Implementation—
Customer and Sale Data **121**

Preview	121
Adding the CUSTOMER and SALE Tables to the Database Using the R:base DEFINE Mode	122
R:base Rules	124
R:base FORMS	128
Summary	141
Review Questions	143
Project	145

CHAPTER 8 Relational Operations with R:base **147**

Preview	147

Basic Relational Operations	148
Other Relational Operations	148
Relational Operations with R:base	150
Summary	163
Review Questions	164
Project	165

CHAPTER 9   Advanced Report Writing with R:base   **167**

Preview	167
The Problem	168
Begin by Designing	168
Steps in Defining Reports	168
Printing the Report	182
Summary	188
Review Questions	189
Project	191

CHAPTER 10   Menu-Driven Database Applications   **193**

Preview	193
Menu-Driven Applications	194
Developing Menu-Driven Applications	196
Summary	205
Review Questions	206
Project	207

CHAPTER 11   Programming with R:base   **209**

Preview	209
A Note about Files	210
Fundamentals	210
R:base Commands: Processing a Menu	212
R:base Commands Continued—A Special-Purpose Routine	224
Summary	229
Review Questions	230
Project	232

CHAPTER 12 Database Administration	**235**
Preview	235
Lessons Large Corporations Have Learned about Database Administration	236
Database Administration on Microcomputers	237
What is Database Administration?	237
Functions of Database Administration	238
Selecting a Database Administrator	248
Summary	249
Review Questions	250
Projects	251
CHAPTER 13 Data Security	**253**
Preview	253
Data as an Asset	254
Threats to Data	254
Protecting the Database	256
Using R:base for Data Security and Control	264
Summary	273
Review Questions	275
Project	276
CHAPTER 14 Natural Language Processing with CLOUT	**279**
Preview	279
The Power of CLOUT	280
Using CLOUT	282
CLOUT's Special Features	290
Improving Your Communication with CLOUT	298
Summary	304
Review Questions	305
CHAPTER 15 Database Processing on Local Area Networks	**307**
Preview	307
Database and Local Area Networks	308

Design Considerations for Database Applications on LANs 313
A Multi-user Design for Great Plains Music and Video Unlimited 320
Implementing a Multi-user Database with R:base 5000 Multi-user 323
A Multi-user Database Application at Great Plains Music and Video 327
Summary 330
Review Questions 331

Appendix A   Sharing Data Between Computers   **333**

Bibliography **344**

Index **345**

Preface

At this moment there are hundreds of thousands of microcomputer users making needless mistakes. These people, who are users of microcomputer databases, are falling into pitfalls that were discovered by information systems professionals ten to fifteen years ago. The goal of this book is to make the knowledge gained by these battle-scarred database experts available to users of microcomputers.

Background

Although the information systems industry has been fast-paced and continuously changing since its inception in the mid 1950s, nothing prepared the industry for the tornado-like impact of the microcomputer. Micros have changed people's orientation to information systems in ways that will not be fully comprehended for another twenty years.

Among its many effects, the microcomputer threw database technology into a morass of confusion. For example, no knowledgeable database specialist would say that Lotus 1–2–3 is a database management system. Yet, when surveyed, users consistently report Lotus 1–2–3 as their primary database manager. Furthermore, there are today perhaps 10,000 knowledgeable experts in database technology who would say that two million or so users of Lotus 1–2–3 and Pfs:file are misusing the term *database management*. Even more confusing, the most popular micro database management system (in terms of numbers sold) is dBASE II, yet this system falls far short of meeting the definition of a database management system as set out by E. F. Codd (see the bibliography), who is generally recognized as the world's leading database expert.

Meanwhile, oblivious to the experts, millions of people have installed database managers (of some ilk) on their micros and are accomplishing useful and productive work. Unfortunately, since these users are not aware of the technology developed by database specialists, they are needlessly making many of the mistakes that information systems professionals have learned not to make. In writing this book, we have endeavored to bring relevant learnings from mainframe computer databases down to the level of the micro. Our hope is that you will be able to avoid the mistakes that we and others have already made.

Mainframe vs. Microcomputer Databases

There are many differences between a database on a mainframe computer and one on a microcomputer.

Mainframe databases are generally far more complicated in structure and contain considerably more data. A large mainframe database has several billion characters, whereas a large micro database has several million.

Even more important, mainframe databases are shared. They serve a community of users, and consequently, their processing must be standardized and controlled. With the exception of local area network applications (see Chapter 15), micro databases exist on a single computer and have one or at most a few users. Processing can be more informal and less controlled, although, as discussed in Chapter 12 and 13, some controls do need to be placed.

Fundamentally, people build databases because they want to keep track of something. To accomplish this goal, the database must be surrounded by applications that allow the users to enter data, to change data, to answer queries, and to produce reports. For a mainframe database, there is a staff of systems analysts and programmers who construct both the database and the applications. On a micro database, there is generally no such staff. The users must design and implement their own database and build their own applications.

This book is intended to help you do just that.

Learning a Process via R:base 5000

The subject of this book is a *process*—the process of building databases and database applications. It is not the goal of this book to teach you the ins and outs of R:base 5000 or any other database product. From our years in the classroom, however, we know that learning a process requires practice. Perhaps you have heard the adage:

> "I hear and I forget; I see and I remember;
> I do and I understand."

It would be impossible to learn how to make pottery in the abstract. At some point, you have to pick up a pot and examine it; then you need to see a picture of a pot on the potter's wheel; and finally, you have to place some clay on the potter's wheel and work it yourself.

Just the same, you cannot learn how to build databases and database applications in the abstract. Therefore, throughout this text, we have illustrated the process of designing and building databases with a commercial database manager called R:base 5000.

We chose this system for three reasons. First, it is a complete system that is more than adequate for the task at hand. Second, R:base was an efficient choice for us since we already knew and loved it. Finally, we chose this product because Microrim (the publisher of R:base) was willing to arrange with SRA (the publisher of this book) to provide you with a student version of the product. The licensing arragement is as follows: Your instructor has been given a copy of the student version of R:base 5000 along with a license to provide purchasers of this text with a copy of the software. You have a license to use the student version of R:base 5000 as long as you have purchased a new copy of this text.

Using R:base 5000

You will learn the most from this text if you use R:base 5000 to duplicate the examples shown and if you do the exercises and projects at the end of the chapters. If you do not have a computer available, we have included numerous screens to illustrate the development process, but merely reading the material is definitely second choice.

A case example, Great Plains Music and Video Unlimited, is developed throughout the text. Additionally, we have written a second case example for you to build in parallel with the text example. Thus, as we illustrate database design for Great Plains, you can apply the underlying principles to your own case project.

Structure of This Text

The first two chapters provide background information. Chapter 1 defines database processing and compares and contrasts it to file processing. Chapter 2 presents an example of a microcomputer database application. It introduces Great Plains Music and Video Unlimited's video rental club. This example will give you an opportunity to touch and feel a microcomputer database as you assume the role of a user.

The next three chapters deal with database design. Chapter 3 introduces the concept of a database as a model. Chapter 4 provides standards and criteria for evaluating the appropriateness of a database design, and Chapter 5 illustrates the principles of database design by designing a database for the electronic components part of Great Plains' business.

Chapters 6 through 11 illustrate database implementation. We begin in Chapter 6 by implementing one table for the Great Plains database. We show how to define the table and introduce the relational operations of selection, projection, and join. In Chapter 7, we illustrate another method for defining database tables. We also show how to use a forms generator to make data entry easy. In the last part of the chapter, we introduce the use of a report generator to obtain formatted output from the database.

Chapter 8 introduces three additional relational operations: union, interesection, and difference. Chapter 9 deals with advanced report writing concepts and their implementation. Finally, Chapters 10 and 11 conclude the topic of implementation by presenting concepts of menu-driven database applications. Chapter 10 introduces the concept of a command file and shows how to use a program generator to create simple applications. Chapter 11 shows how to use command files to create more complex applications. Some of the command files used to create the sample application from Chapter 2 are used as examples.

Database administration is concerned with the management of database applications. Chapter 12 discusses database administration duties and responsibilities and Chapter 13 considers the important issue of database security. Where appropriate, the chapters illustrate the use of R:base 5000 to implement the concepts discussed.

This text is concluded by discussing ways of increasing the usefulness of the database. Chapter 14 deals with natural language queries. Once again, the Great Plains database is used for illustration. Finally, Chapter 15 presents concepts of multi-user databases using local area networks.

Acknowledgements

Many people have contributed to improve the quality of this book. We especially appreciate the numerous constructive comments of the following reviewers:

Bill Anderson, Montgomery College
Jim Baroff, George Washington University
Harvey Blessing, Essex Community College
Anthony Mann, Sinclair Community College
John Windsor, North Texas State University

Thanks to Caroline Curtis for her efforts in creating the comprehensive instructor's guide. Also, it was Caroline who first expressed the idea that a well-designed database table, like a well-designed paragraph, should have a single theme.

We wish to thank Kent Johnson, president and chief executive officer of Microrim Inc., for his vision in supporting this project. Thanks also to the many other Microrim employees for their help, including Mike Johnson who reviewed the text for technical accuracy; Mike Sherwood who coordinated the production of the student version of R:base 5000; and Wayne Erickson, Fred Gray, and Keith Bangston who modified R:base 5000 to produce the student version.

Finally, a special thanks to the personnel at SRA: to Michael Carrigg for having the courage to sign this project and for his support and encouragement throughout; and to Mary Konstant for her invaluable contributions as project editor.

David M. Kroenke
Mercer Island, Washington
Donald E. Nilson
Fort Collins, Colorado

CHAPTER 1 Introduction

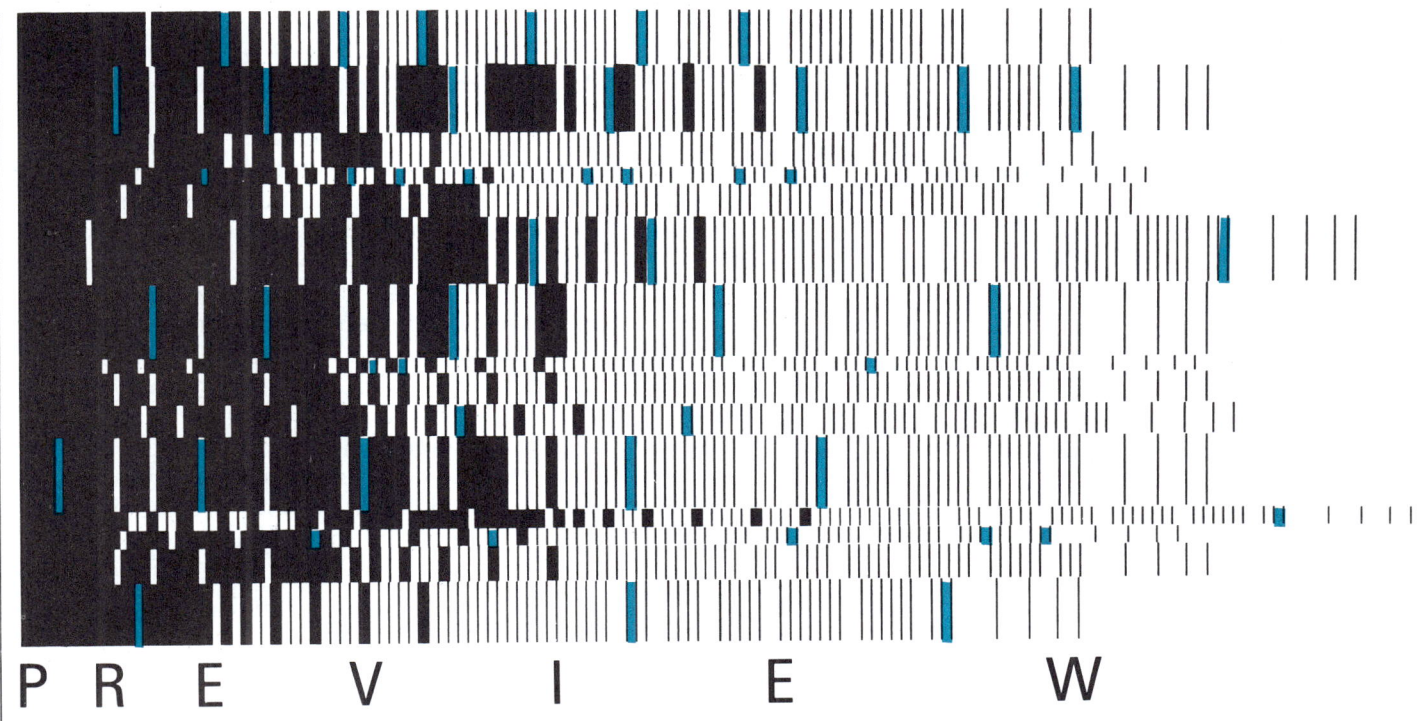

PREVIEW

In this chapter, we'll discuss the concept of database processing as a style of computer processing and its advantages and disadvantages. We'll also explain how database processing differs from file processing. Last, we'll talk about the five components of a computer-based information processing system: people, procedures, data, programs, and hardware.

No matter what the job or profession, information is important to the success of businesspeople. People in marketing need information about products, customers, and sales orders. Production people need information about inventories, purchase orders, shop orders, production machinery, manufacturing costs, and manufacturing capacities. Personnel managers need information about job openings, pay scales, and union contracts.

Information management systems are used to ensure that relevant, timely, reliable information is made available to people who need it. Over the past 30 years or so, organizations which could afford them have used large, expensive mainframe computers in their information management systems. In the process of learning how to use computer technology in information management, data processing professionals in business, academia, and the military developed the technology of *database processing*—a style of processing which allows an enterprise to organize and integrate its data resources.

More recently, microcomputer technology developed in the exploration of space has been applied in the production of inexpensive tools for use in the information management systems of organizations of all sizes. In addition, various vendors of microcomputer software have developed programs which bring database processing technology to the microcomputer environment. That's what this book is about—database processing with microcomputers to manage information.

WHAT IS DATABASE PROCESSING?

Database technology allows data to be processed as an integrated whole. It reduces the artificiality imposed by separate files for separate applications and permits users to access data more naturally.

To appreciate this concept, consider the three information processing systems shown in Figure 1–1. These are *file processing systems;* they are predecessors of database systems. With file processing, each file is considered to exist independently. The payroll system in Figure 1–1 processes only the faculty data file; the class scheduling system processes only class data; and the grade posting system processes only student data. These systems are effective in that they produce the desired results: payroll checks, class schedules, and grade reports.

But suppose someone wants to know the salary paid to each instructor who teaches a class scheduled by the class scheduling system. To obtain this information, a new program must be written to extract data

FIGURE 1-1

Three file processing (pre-database) systems

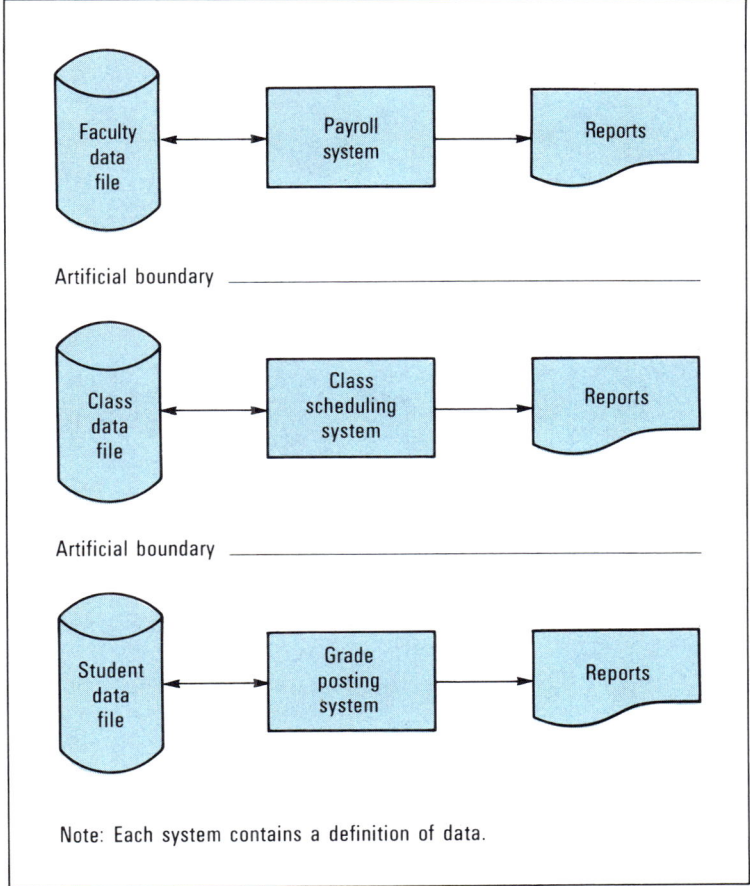

from both the faculty and the class data files. Unfortunately, there is no guarantee that these files are compatible. The faculty data file might be stored in one format, whereas an incompatible record format might be used for the class data file. If so, one file must be converted to the format of the other, and then an extraction program written, tested, and run. This process will take time. Users may decide (as they often do) that responses to new requirements or one-of-a-kind requests are so long in coming that they are not worth requesting.

In some cases, conversion entails so much effort to eliminate incompatibility that it simply cannot be done for a reasonable cost. This leads to the situation in which the user knows that needed information is "in the computer" but, seemingly, no one can get it out.

FIGURE 1–2
Database processing system

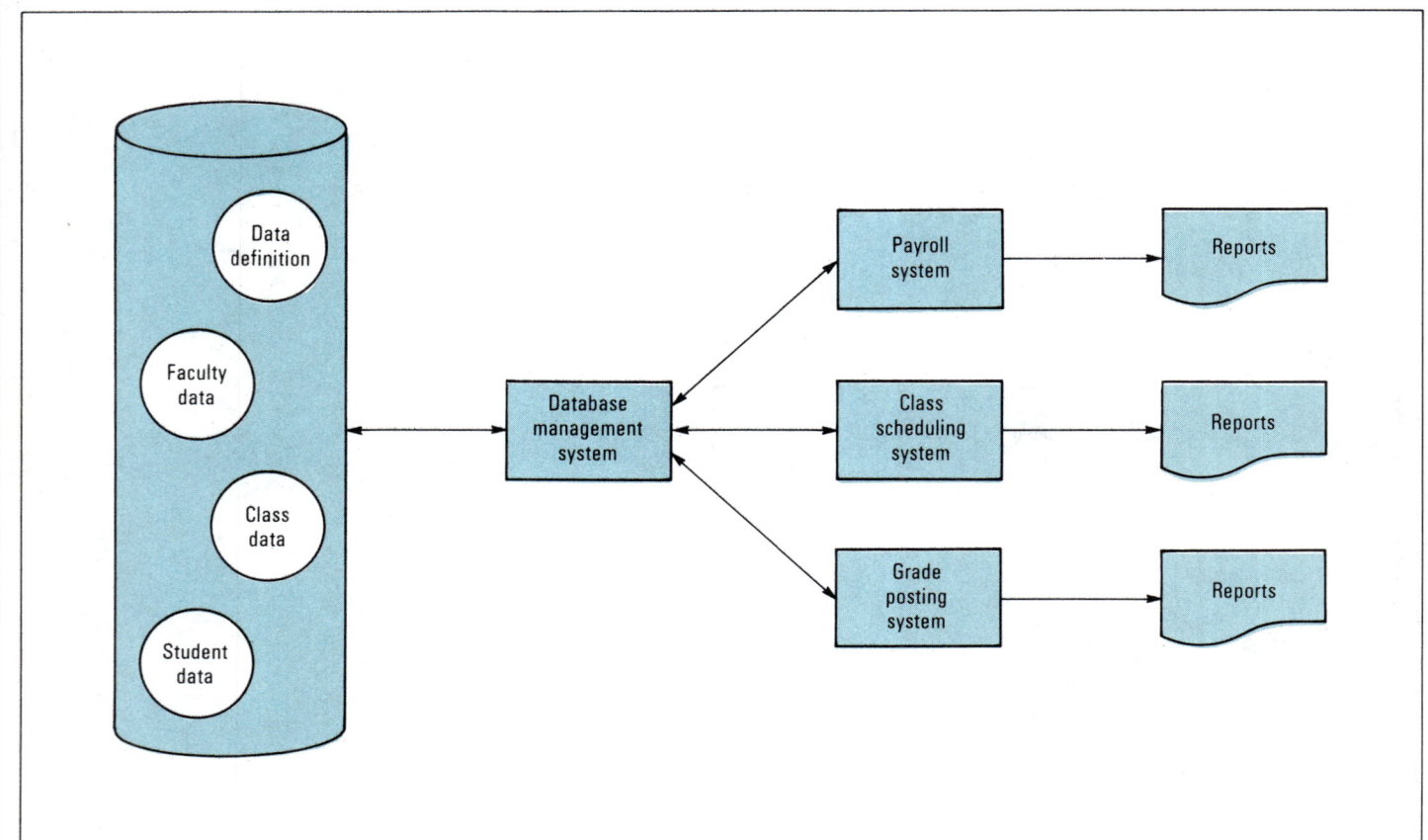

In contrast, Figure 1–2 shows a database processing system. The files in Figure 1–2 have been integrated into a database that is processed indirectly by the application programs. The payroll, class scheduling, and grade posting systems still perform their old functions, but they call on another program, the *database management system* (DBMS), to access the database. The DBMS is a complex program that acts as a data librarian. It stores and retrieves data. For the DBMS to perform its function, it stores not only data, but also a description of the data.

The faculty, class, and student data in Figure 1–2 can be processed as an integrated whole. Since the files have been created by the DBMS, all of the data is compatible. Furthermore, the DBMS may have features to enhance integrated processing. For example, a faculty record can be logically "tied to" several class records to represent the relationship between teacher and class. Thus, database processing is integrated processing. Data integration offers several important advantages.

ADVANTAGES OF DATABASE PROCESSING

Affordable, Sophisticated Programming

Most database management programs for microcomputers cost between $500 and $1,000. While that represents more than just pocket change for the majority of individuals, it is not a significant investment for an average business. What we can buy for less than $1,000 costs the vendor hundreds of thousands of dollars to develop and represents the efforts of some of the brightest programmers available.

More Information from a Given Amount of Data

One important reason why people develop databases is to obtain more information from a given amount of data. Data is facts and figures; information is knowledge derived by processing data. When data is physically partitioned as shown in Figure 1–1, we can get information from faculty data, from class data, or from student data. However, we can't get information from a combination of faculty and class data without additional programming. For example, we can find out average faculty salaries, but not the average salary of faculty teaching the course DAT104. Computing this average would require data from two of the separated files. Segregating data limits the combinations of data to be processed and hence the amount of information that can be obtained.

In contrast to Figure 1–1, the database in Figure 1–2 does not partition the data. We can get answers to questions involving combinations of faculty and class data, or class and student data, and so forth. We can now easily find the average salary of faculty teaching course DAT104.

Elimination or Reduction of Data Duplication

The data integration associated with database processing results in the elimination or significant reduction of data duplication. For example, in the file processing systems in Figure 1–1, it is likely that some student data is recorded in both the class data file and the student data file. In the database, it need only be recorded once. There are two principal benefits of reduced data duplication.

First, reduction of data duplication saves file space and, to some extent, can reduce processing requirements. This, in turn, reduces costs and processing time.

Reduced data duplication also results in improved data consistency. For example, assume that students' last names are recorded in both the class data file and the student data file. If a student's name is changed, it is possible to change the data in one place but not in the other. When that happens, reports produced by the class scheduling system will not agree with reports produced by the grade posting system. Perhaps nothing is more aggravating to users of a system than to be confronted with computer reports that disagree. They soon learn to distrust all computer-generated reports.

Inconsistency cannot arise in the database system of Figure 1-2. Since student names are recorded in only one place, any changes will be immediately reflected in all reports produced by the system.

Program/Data Independence

In Figure 1-1, programs interface directly with data files. Each program must contain a description of the format of the files it uses. As a result, problems arise when the format of a file is changed. For example, if the zip code field is expanded to nine digits, all programs that access a file containing zip codes will need to be modified, even if those programs do not use zip codes.

For the database application in Figure 1-2, however, application programs obtain data from the data librarian, the DBMS. Consequently, the application programs need not contain a description of the format of the data. Only the DBMS needs this information. As a result, to convert to nine-digit zip codes, only the DBMS and those programs that use zip codes will need to be changed. Programs that don't use zip codes will be unaffected by the change.

The advantages of database processing are summarized in Figure 1-3.

DISADVANTAGES OF DATABASE PROCESSING

Increased Vulnerability to Failure

Because database processing is integrated processing, all the data resource eggs tend to be in one basket. A failure in one component of the integrated system can stop the entire system. This event is especially critical if, as is often the case, the operation of the user organization depends on the database. As Mark Twain

FIGURE 1-3

Advantages of database processing

- Affordable, sophisticated programming
- More information from a given amount of data
- Elimination or reduction of data duplication
- Program/data independence

said, "Put all your eggs in one basket and watch that basket!"

Complexity

Database processing tends to be complex. Large amounts of data in many different formats can be interrelated in the database. Both the database system and the application programs must be able to process these structures. This means more sophisticated programming. As you will see in later chapters, database design is critical. This means new and sophisticated skills must be brought to the process of application system design. These skills include conceptualizing and modeling—skills which must be learned. They are not intuitive.

More Difficult Recovery

It is inevitable that, at some point, a failure will occur in any system. To protect themselves against such failures, organizations make periodic backup copies of the programs and data in the system. With these copies, it is possible to return the system to a known point and reprocess transactions which occurred since that point. This process is known as *recovery*.

Backup and recovery are more difficult in the database environment because of increased complexity. Determining the exact state of the database at the time of failure may be a problem. Given that, it may be even more difficult to determine what should be done next.

Figure 1–4 summarizes the major disadvantages of database processing. These disadvantages should be weighed against the advantages discussed in the previous section. Now that we have discussed the concept of database processing as a style of computer processing, let's consider the components of computer-based information management systems.

COMPONENTS OF COMPUTER-BASED INFORMATION MANAGEMENT SYSTEMS

A system is a collection of components working together to perform a task. A computer-based information management system is a collection of five components: people, procedures, data, programs, and hardware (Figure 1–5). These components are designed to work together to collect, organize, and protect data, assemble it into information, and deliver it to people who need it when they need it. Computer-based information management systems may or may

FIGURE 1–4

Disadvantages of database processing

- Increased vulnerability to failure
- Complexity
- More difficult recovery

FIGURE 1-5

Components of a computerized information management system

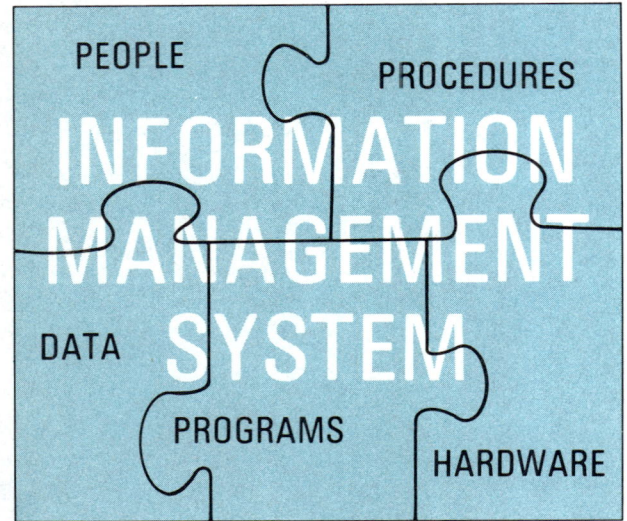

not employ database processing. Since this book is about database processing, let's take a brief look at each of the five components of a database information management system.

Component 1: People

Information management systems exist to serve people. People ask questions, and people design and implement the system which provides the answers. People involved in computer-based information management systems fall into three general categories: decision makers, technical users, and clerical users.

Information management systems exist to answer the questions of decision makers. Such people have a constant need for information. Typically, decision makers may have little interest in and even less time for the technicalities of computing. They usually do have a generous supply of common sense and some understanding of what information they need. Decision makers may occasionally use the system directly to obtain answers to spontaneous *(ad hoc)* questions which arise. Accordingly, the information management system must be responsive, easy to use, and practical.

Technical users may or may not also be decision makers. They are the ones who design and implement the information management system. They must be sure that all five of the components are designed to work well together. Despite recent advances that have made hardware easier to use, every system must have someone who has the time and interest to address the inevitable technical issues of system design, documentation, backup and recovery, and management. If these issues are neglected, the system will fail.

Clerical users deal with the information management system on a detailed level. In a microcomputer environment, the clerical users are the primary operators of the computer. They are responsible for the critical task of data entry. Clerical users can make the difference between a successful system and one that does not function properly.

Component 2: Procedures

Procedures are the lubricants that make the system work smoothly. A decision maker who wants to ask a question needs brief, easy-to-read instructions on how to get the information. Clerical users need instructions on how to turn the computer on, what buttons to push to enter data, how to go about producing monthly reports, and so on. Everyone needs to know what to do if something goes wrong.

Every system fails at some point, and when that happens, everyone needs to know what to do. Users need to know what source documents to save and what transactions can and cannot be processed during a failure. Procedures need to be in place so that business can continue to function even though the primary system is not working. When the system is returned to operation, users need to know what to do to resume processing. For example, how can a user tell how much of the source data gathered during the failure needs to be input before new transactions can be processed? All these issues need to be considered in developing recovery procedures for users.

Such procedures are also important for technical users. When the system fails, technical personnel need to know what to do. What action should be taken to identify the source of the problem and get it corrected? What needs to be done to minimize damage to the database? Who should be called? Once the problem is corrected, how should the database be restored? These actions need to be carefully thought out and documented during the design and implementation of the system. Waiting until a problem arises is far too risky.

Every business is a dynamic activity and business needs will change. When database processing is employed, change must be made very carefully. A change that benefits one user may be detrimental to users in seemingly unrelated departments. Consequently, changes to the database need to be made with a communitywide view. Procedures must be defined and documented to control change to the database.

Developing an information management system without procedures is like giving somebody a camera which has no instructions for its use. Although neither is difficult to use, it is unlikely that either will be used correctly if operating instructions aren't provided. Because procedures are as much a part of the system as the computer, they should be developed with the other components by the person who designs the system.

Component 3: Data

Databases A database is a *self-describing* collection of *integrated files.* The database is self-describing because it contains, within itself, a description of its structure. Database processing differs from file processing, in which the structure of the data files is contained in the application programs. Program/data independence is possible only because the database is self-describing. The database files are integrated because the database contains information about the relationships among records in those files.

According to standard usage in the computer industry, *bits* (1's and 0's) are grouped into *bytes* or *characters, characters* are grouped into *fields,* and *fields* are grouped into *records.* A collection of *records* is called a *file.* It is tempting to continue this progression by stating that files are grouped together to form a database. This statement, however, would be false. A database is more than a collection of files—it is a *self-describing* collection of *integrated* files.

For example, suppose a bank groups customer, checking, and savings files together. If this grouping contains none of the record relationships, it is not very useful. It is also not a database. A database needs two additional ingredients. First, it needs a description of the data which makes the collection self-describing. Second, it needs a way to describe relationships among the records so you will know, for example, that a given checking record corresponds to a particular customer. This ingredient makes the collection of files integrated. Once there is a self-describing collection of integrated files, there is a database.

Component 4: Programs

Several types of programs are used in microcomputer database information management systems. A complete, accurate discussion of these programs is outside the scope of any single volume, but Figure 1–6 shows the approximate relationship. The schematic shows a typical single-user system (Local Area Networks—LANs—are considered in Chapter 15). Through the microcomputer keyboard, the user interacts with the *application programs* and *DBMS utilities.*

Application Programs Application programs perform specific tasks like order entry, inventory accounting, billing, and so forth. They are tailored to a specific business need. Application programs are written in a high-level programming language like BASIC, Pascal, FORTRAN, COBOL, or C. To employ these high-level languages, the DBMS must provide a *programming language interface* (PI) which provides special routines for manipulating the database files.

As you will see in Chapters 10 and 11, many DBMS's for microcomputers include their own built-in programming language which may be used to write application programs. Although these programs do not require a separate PI, the commands must be interpreted by the DBMS each time they are run. As a

FIGURE 1-6

Approximate relationship of the major types of programs in a typical single-user microcomputer database system

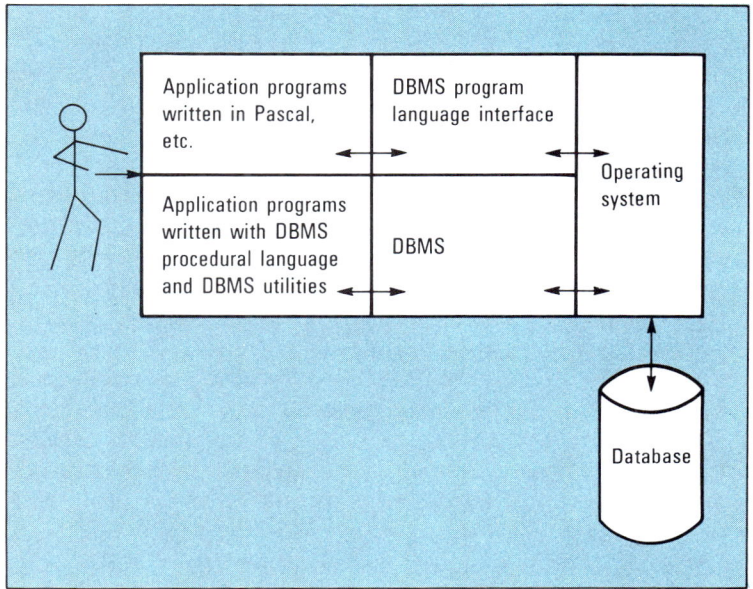

result, they run slower than programs which are written with a PI.

DBMS Utilities These utilities are generally provided with the microcomputer DBMS. Let's look at some of the services provided by DBMS utilities.

Query/update utilities provide generalized retrieval and update of the contents of the database. Since this is a generalized interface, many users can employ the query/update utilities for many different purposes. Since no application program need be involved in this mode, programmers are not required. In Chapter 14, we discuss one product which provides natural language query capabilities with which users can pose questions in their own words—the computer learns to speak the user's language, not vice versa. These utilities free programmers for other activities and give users greater control over the timing and processing of their requests.

Screen utilities provide an easy, graphical means of defining screen forms for data entry and editing. Report writing utilities allow users to specify report formats for obtaining database outputs. Still other utilities create and maintain the database. They generate database structure, unload or reload database data, reformat and clean up database files, and so on.

The DBMS For normal processing, the DBMS receives data and stores it for subsequent processing. Both the application and utility programs call on the DBMS to provide database service. The DBMS acts as a sophisticated data librarian. It allows application programs and utilities a wide variety of access strategies. It also enables these programs to have different views of the same data so that applications can use data in a format that is familiar and useful.

Some microcomputer DBMS's have features to provide security over data; these features ensure that only authorized users can obtain data. Most microcomputer DBMS's include features to provide backup and recovery. More will be said about the important functions of security, backup, and recovery in Chapter 13. DBMS functions are summarized in Figure 1-7.

The Operating System The final program involved in database processing is the *operating system*. This set of programs controls the computer's resources. The DBMS itself does not do data input/output. Rather, it sends requests for input/output services to the operating system. These programs, in turn, cause the service to be performed.

All programs are controlled by the operating system. You can view the operating system as the glue that holds all the other programs together.

Generally, only some of the application programs will be written by end users. Most application programs, and the DBMS, are obtained from software vendors. Usually, the operating system is provided by the hardware vendor.

In this book, we will be primarily concerned with the DBMS, the DBMS utilities, and only those application programs written using the DBMS's built-in language. The operating system and application programs written using the PI are important programs, but they are not our main interest. Consequently, we will consider them only peripherally.

Component 5: Hardware

Contrary to what the television commercials say, the least critical component is the hardware. Buying a computer to solve information management problems is like buying a filing cabinet to solve information management problems. If you buy either one without knowing what information you want to keep and without having procedures to keep it up-to-date and

FIGURE 1-7

Functions of the DBMS

- Define and store database structure
- Load database data
- Provide variety of access methods
- Store and maintain data
- Provide multiple views of the data
- Provide security features
- Facilitate backup and recovery

protected, you've just acquired a very expensive paperweight.

Hardware is the collection of machines that do the work prescribed by the programs. They include a central processing unit (CPU), which is the "brain" of the computer, and some peripherals, such as a keyboard for communicating with the CPU, a display screen, a printer for producing reports, disk drives for storing programs and data, and, perhaps, a plotter for preparing graphics from the data.

SUMMARY

- Businesses use information management systems to provide relevant, timely, reliable information to people who need it.
- Microcomputers are now being used as business information management tools.
- File processing systems are information management systems in which data is artificially partitioned into separate, unintegrated entities.
- Database processing systems are information management systems in which data is integrated.
- A database is a self-describing collection of integrated files. A database management system is a complex computer program that acts as a data librarian.
- The advantages of database processing are:
  - Affordable, sophisticated programming
  - More information from a given amount of data
  - Elimination or reduction of data duplication
  - Program/data independence
- The disadvantages of database processing are:
  - Increased vulnerability to failure
  - Complexity
  - More difficult recovery
- A computer-based information management system is a collection of components designed to work together to collect, organize, and protect data, assemble it into information, and deliver it to those who need it when they need it. The five components are:
  - People
  - Procedures
  - Data
  - Programs
  - Hardware

REVIEW QUESTIONS

1.1
What kind of information would you need if your job were:
- a. Chief executive officer?
- b. Controller?
- c. Marketing director?
- d. Owner of the local paint store?
- e. First-line supervisor?

1.2
Why must information be:
- a. Relevant?
- b. Timely?
- c. Reliable?

1.3
Explain the difference between a database system and a file processing system.

1.4
Summarize the advantages of database processing.

1.5
How does database processing enable a business to get more information from a given amount of data?

1.6
How can reduced data duplication improve the quality of information produced by an information management system?

1.7
How does database processing provide for data and programs to be independent of each other?

1.8
Name and discuss the major categories of programs involved in microcomputer database processing.

1.9
Define *database*.

1.10
Explain the meaning of the term *self-describing*.

1.11
Explain the meaning of the term *integrated files*.

1.12
Is a database a collection of files? Why or why not?

1.13
Describe the system procedures needed by:

a. Decision makers.

b. Technical users.

c. Clerical users.

1.14
Why should we discuss people and procedures in a book about database processing?

1.15
How would you explain the advantages of database processing to the board of directors of a company? Assume these people know very little about data processing.

1.16
Summarize the impact of database processing on security. What aspects of security become easier? What aspects become more difficult? How can security be improved when using database processing?

1.17
Briefly describe actions that should be taken during failure and recovery. Discuss the responsibilities (if any) of decision makers, technical users, and clerical users.

1.18
What is the difference between a database management system and an information management system? What are the components of each?

1.19
Do all information management systems employ database processing? Explain your answer.

CHAPTER 2

Great Plains Music and Video Unlimited

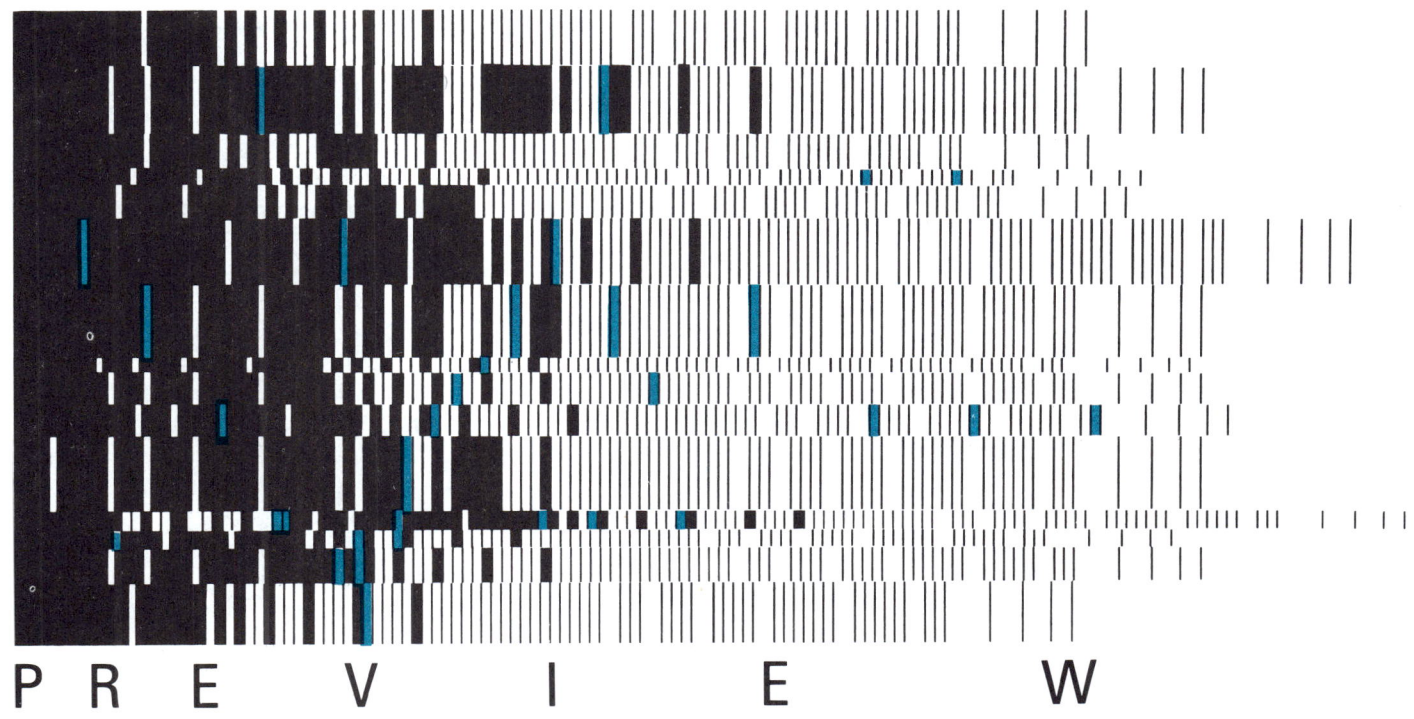

P R E V I E W

In the previous chapter, we discussed the concept of database processing and explored the components of a computer-based information management system. In this chapter, we'll take a look at how those concepts are applied to a realistic business situation. The chapter presents the big picture of database processing with microcomputers: we'll look at the forest before we examine some more of the trees.

GREAT PLAINS MUSIC AND VIDEO UNLIMITED

Great Plains Music and Video Unlimited (Great Plains) is located in a small town near the campus of a large university. It sells electronic components, records, tapes, and compact disks and rents videotapes and VCRs, principally to college students. The business has steadily grown since it was founded about twenty years ago by its owner, Grace Potter. In addition to Grace, Great Plains employs four people full-time and a dozen or so college students as salesclerks.

The business has grown to the point where the manual information management system that supported it in the past is no longer adequate. About a year ago, Grace hired a consultant to help apply computing technology to meet Great Plains' growing information management needs. The consultant approached the job in a phased, organized manner.

First, a project team was formed. The team initially included Grace Potter and two of the full-time employees: Randy Morgan, who is in charge of the video rental part of the business, and Becky Vick, who runs the music portion of Great Plains.

Next, the project team developed a written statement of the specific information management problems of Great Plains. Armed with the written statement of the problems, the consultant interviewed those whose jobs were most critically dependent on receiving relevant, timely, reliable information. The result of these interviews was a statement of the detailed information requirements for Great Plains.

Based on the definition of the requirements, the consultant proposed several alternative systems that would satisfy Great Plains' needs. Each of the alternatives was broken down into the five components we discussed in Chapter 1: people, procedures, data, programs, and hardware. Of all the possible alternatives, only the feasible ones were presented to the project team. Feasibility was determined on the basis of cost, technology, and timing.

On the basis of the work done during this first phase, the project team recommended that Great Plains proceed to automate the information management system. Great Plains decided to accept the consultant's suggestion that they proceed carefully though. The plan was to acquire a microcomputer and automate the video rental portion of the business before proceeding with the rest of the system. That way, they could apply the lessons learned in automating the video rental system to the rest of the business.

The next phase of the consultant's job was detailed

design of each of the five components for the alternative selected. When the design was finished, it was reviewed and approved by Grace and the rest of the project team.

Finally, the automated video rental information management system was implemented. During implementation, the various system components were built or bought and tested. Once everyone was satisfied that the system worked as it was designed to work, the task of converting data from the old manual system was performed.

For one month, the old manual system was maintained along with the new automated one. Periodically, data from the two systems was compared to be sure that the new system was working as it should. The new system has been installed for several months now and, with a few minor changes, everyone is delighted with it. Let's get an idea of how the system appears to the users.

THE VIDEO RENTAL INFORMATION MANAGEMENT SYSTEM

To see how the system works, load R:base. At the R> prompt, type:

RUN INIT IN PROCS.VID

After a short pause, you are presented with the main menu (Figure 2–1). To exit the system, press [ESC]. For an explanation of the choices on the menu, press [F10].

The Main Menu
The system is menu-driven. To make it perform, all you have to do is make choices from the menus which the system puts on the screen. The main menu has three options on it. These options tell the system which functions you want to work with.

Videos (Option 1) This option allows you to enter data about new videos and to print lists of videos.

Members (Option 2) The members option allows you to enter data about new members, change member data, and print a list of members.

Rental Transactions (Option 3) Select this option to record the rental of videos to members, record the return of rented videos, find out whether a video is available for

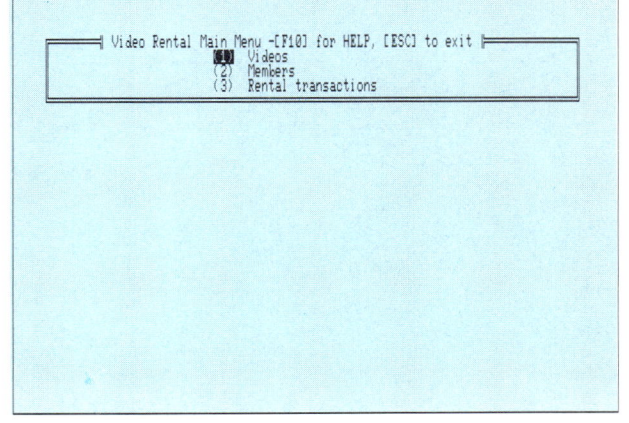

FIGURE 2–1

The video rental information management system's main menu

rental, print a revenue summary, and print a list of overdue videos.

Making choices from the menus is easy. For numbered menus like the main menu, just press the number on the keyboard that matches the number of the option you want and then press [ENTER].

Getting Started

The first thing you want is a video list. To get it, select Option 1, "Videos," from the main menu. The system presents you with another menu (Figure 2–2). Select either Option 2 or Option 3.

The system presents you with another kind of menu (Figure 2–3). You are asked to indicate where you want the report information to go. You can indicate your option in two ways. The easiest way is to type the first letter of the option you want and then press [ENTER]. For example, if you want the price list displayed on the screen, press [S] and then press [ENTER]. The other way to select an option from this kind of menu is to move the highlighted area with the cursor control keys until your choice is highlighted, and then press [ENTER].

When order finishes printing the sample video list (Figure 2–4), it will present you with the video menu again. Press [ESC], and you will receive the main menu.

Now obtain a member list in a similar way. Select Option 2, Members, from the main menu to obtain the member data menu in Figure 2–5. Next select Option 3 from the member data menu (Print a membership list).

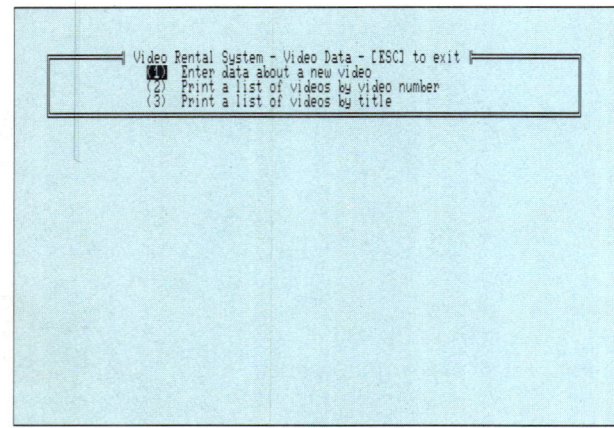

FIGURE 2–2

The Video menu

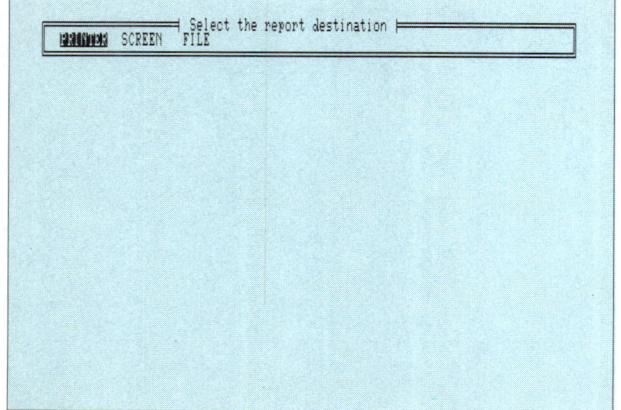

FIGURE 2–3

Menu to choose where information goes

FIGURE 2–4

The sample video list

FIGURE 2–5
The Member data menu

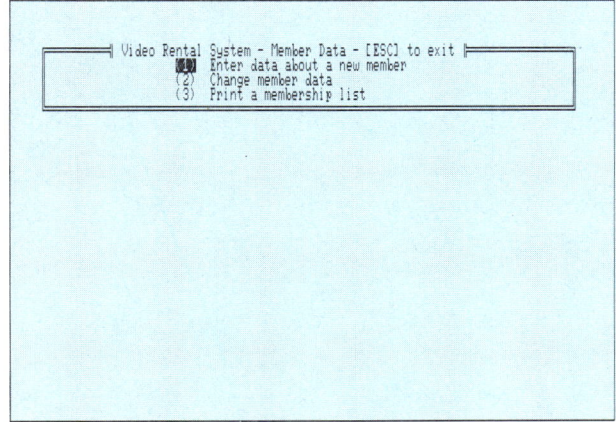

If you have a printer, make sure that the power is on and that the printer has been loaded with continuous form paper. Type [P] and press [ENTER] when you receive the "Select the report destination" menu. If you do not have a printer, select [S] and press [ENTER] when you receive the "Select the report destination" menu. (If you choose [PRINTER] and there is no printer or the power to the printer is off, the computer will wait forever for the printer to respond.) After the report is finished printing (Figure 2–6, a–c), you are asked to "Press any key to continue." You are then returned to the member data menu. Return to the main menu by pressing [ESC].

FIGURE 2–6a
Membership list—report header

Great Plains Music and Video Unlimited
Video Rental Club
Membership List
As Of Sep 2, 1985

FIGURE 2–6b
Membership list

Name	Membership Date	Member Number	Address	Page 1 Phone
Greg Abel	Nov 18,1981	5	394 St. Louis Ave Las Animas CO 92833	233-4984
Stanley Abel	Dec 14,1981	6	9823 Rye Street Las Vegas NV 98203	839-2983
Julie Adams	Sep 19,1985	324526345	234 Bellevue Monte Vista CO 83223	341-3944
Joanne Barnes	Oct 18,1985	235473542	233 Elm Fort Morgan CA 93845	223-3948
Molly Browne	Jul 14,1985	135342565	4860 East 81st Street Malmonte CO 80453	264-5834
David Crumpke	Jul 18,1985	523449586	708 Jule Street Bellevista WA 90812	206-7223
Mike Franzen	Nov 14,1980	7	394 Sailsky Lane Ft. Lake CO 80234	332-9809
Jane Funzy	Jul 18,1985	388383833	123 Elm Ft Morgan CO 80522	333-8165
Merrilee Graceland	Aug 25,1985	329384109	3920 Memphis Street Atlanta GA 92834	234-2849
Gunther MacDonald	Aug 15,1985	423562345	1743 Rose Street Fort Madison WI 39534	223-5678
Jim O'Dell	Sep 6,1972	1	2983 Plumesilver Dillon CA 98234	293-3984
Ronaldo Snupes	Jul 18,1985	233654344	4652 South Mountain Smedley OH 39023	345-2938
Fred White	Nov 12,1985	233759403	2334 Ash Street Bozeman MO 35243	234-5637

FIGURE 2–6c
Membership list—report footer

>   Great Plains Music and Video Unlimited
>   Video Rental Club
>   Membership List
>   As Of Sep 2,1985
>   Total members listed: 13

Entering Data about a New Video

As you can see, getting information from the system is a simple process of selecting menu options. Now try putting data into the database. Record data for a new video by selecting Option 1, "Videos," from the main menu. Next select Option 1, "Enter data about a new video." To record new video information, simply fill in the videotape information form on the screen (Figure 2–7) by following the instructions in the form.

Member Information

Entering Data for a New Member New member data is entered in a similar fashion. Select Option 2, "Members," from the main menu, then Option 1, "Enter data about a new member." This time you are given a member data form to complete (Figure 2–8). As with the videotape information form, you are given instructions with the form. When you have finished entering data for all the new members, leave the form blank and press [ESC]. The system returns to the member data menu.

Changing Member Data To change any piece of data about a member—except the member number, which may never be changed—select Option 2, "Change member data," from the member data menu. You are asked for the member number of the member whose data you wish to change (Figure 2–9). If you have the number,

FIGURE 2–7
The videotape information form

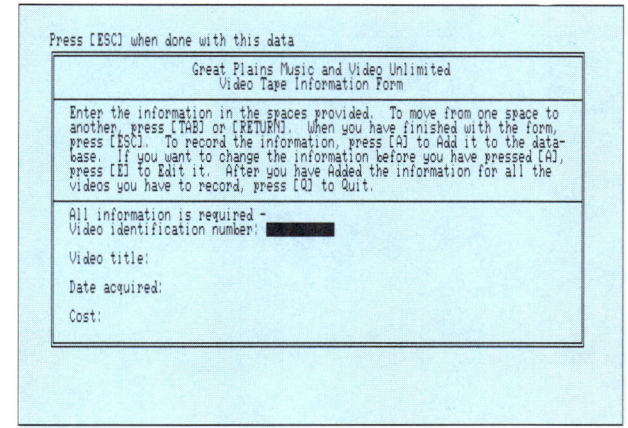

FIGURE 2–8
Member data form

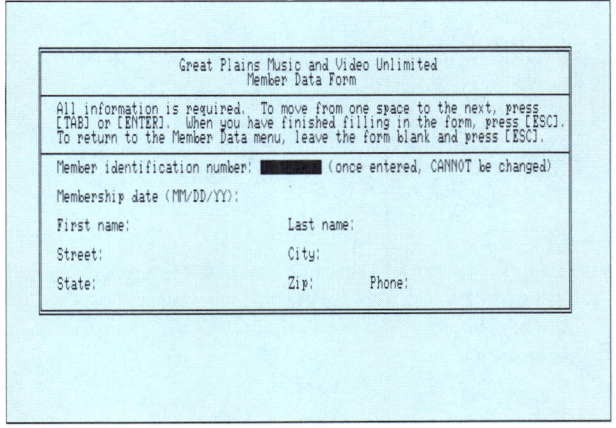

FIGURE 2–9
Request for member number

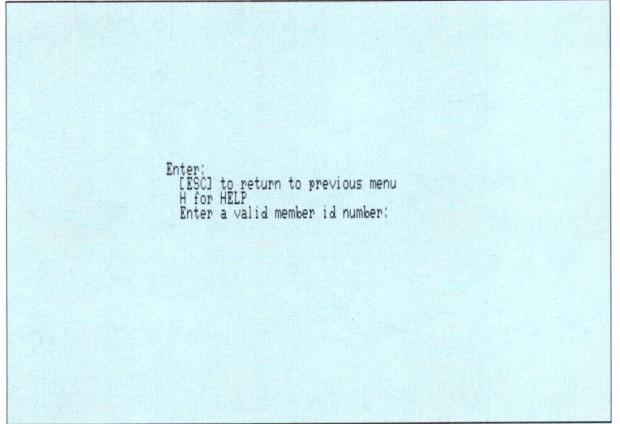

FIGURE 2–10

Help screen for obtaining an unknown member number

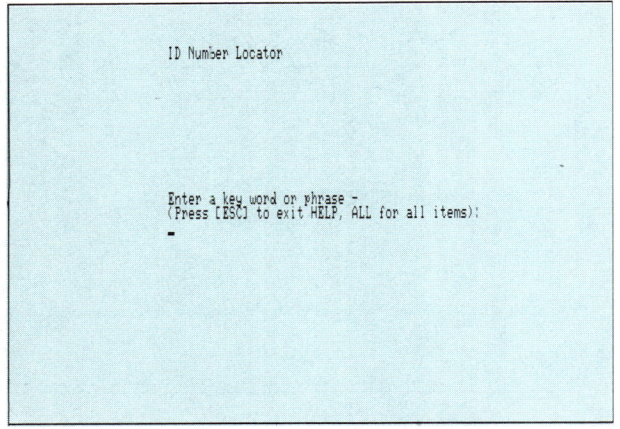

FIGURE 2–11

Crumpke's member number obtained by typing CRUMPKE

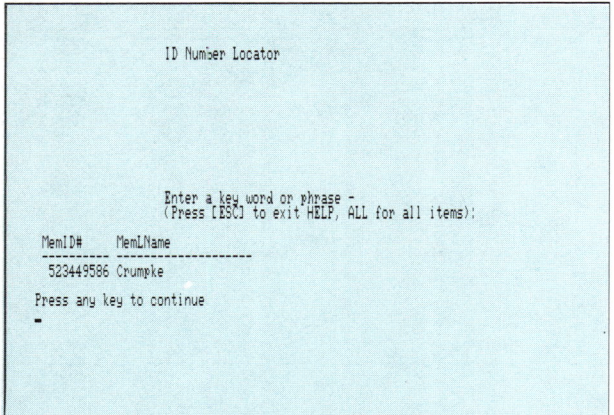

either provided by the member or taken from the member list you printed, enter it. If you do not know the number, you can get help by typing [H] and pressing [ENTER] (Figure 2–10).

If you know the member's last name, enter it. For example, if you want to know the member number of the member whose last name is Crumpke, type:

CRUMPKE

and press [ENTER] (Figure 2–11). If want the member number of all members, type:

ALL

and press [ENTER] (Figure 2–12). Return to the "Enter a valid ID number" prompt by pressing any key.

To change data for Crumpke, enter the member number:

523449586

and press [ENTER]. You are given Mr. Crumpke's member data form. You may move to any space on the form using the [ENTER] or [TAB] key *except* the space for member identification number. As you have seen, the member number is used by the system to identify each member. It is also used to identify which rental transactions each member is associated with. If you were to change the number, the system would

FIGURE 2–12

All members' numbers obtained by typing ALL

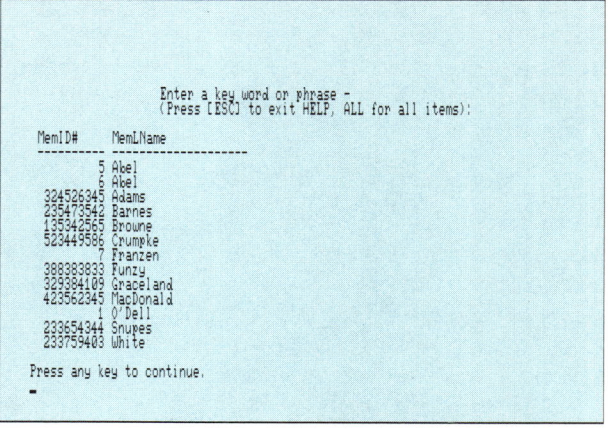

not be able to identify all of Mr. Crumpke's rental transactions.

Change Mr. Crumpke's phone number to 272-8545 by using the [ENTER] key to move to the "Phone" blank. Enter the new phone number, then press [ESC]. The system asks you to wait while the member record is updated. Then it returns you to the member data menu. That's all there is to it. Return to the main menu by pressing [ESC].

Rental Transactions

Select Option 3, "Rental transactions," from the main menu to display the video rental transactions menu (Figure 2–13). This is where most of the work is done. With this menu, you can record video rentals and their return. You can inquire about the status of a particular video. You can print a detailed list of all the rental transactions during any period you choose to specify. You can even print a list of overdue videos, complete with the names and phone numbers of the delinquent members. Let's take a look.

Recording Video Rentals Suppose Molly Browne comes into the store and selects *War Stuff* and *Oceans of the World* for rental. She presents the empty boxes for those two videos to you (you're the clerk at the counter). You obtain the videos from the storage room. To record the rental transaction, select Option 1, "Record video rentals." You are asked to "Enter member ID number" (Figure 2–14). This menu works exactly like the one you saw when you changed Mr. Crumpke's phone number. If you know the number, enter it. If not, you may obtain it by asking for help. Molly knows her number, so type:

135342565

and press [ENTER]. You are asked to wait while the system obtains Molly's data. You are then shown a rental form complete with Molly's name and address. Notice that the invoice number and date have also been provided (Figure 2–15).

To record the rental transaction, simply type the video numbers which are attached to the tapes. The system fills in the video title and the rental amount. When you are finished, press [ESC]. The system totals the rental amount, computes the tax, and calculates the invoice total (Figure 2–16). (Ordinarily, the system would automatically print the invoice. However, because this is only an illustration, the invoices are not printed.)

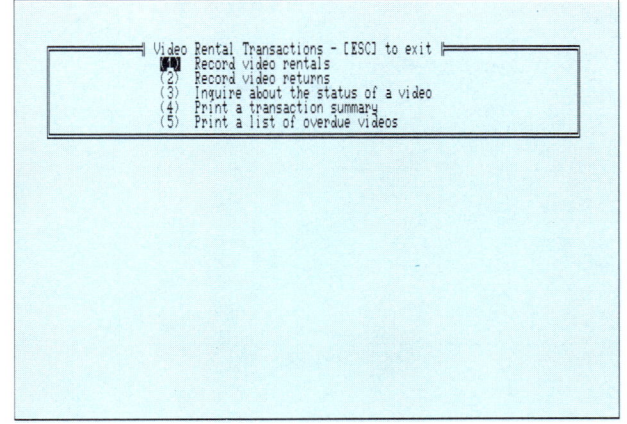

FIGURE 2–13
The video rental transactions menu

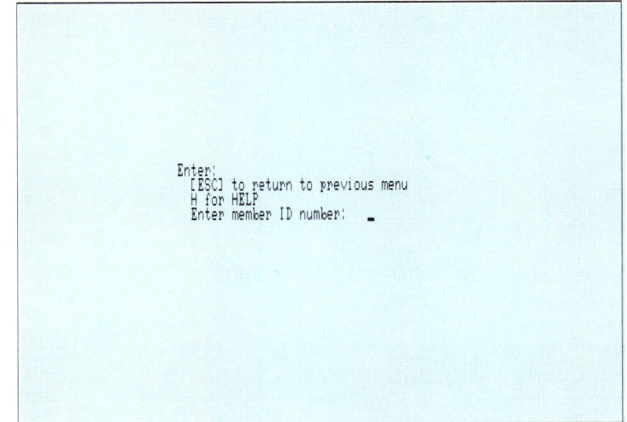

FIGURE 2–14
Prompt for entering member ID number

FIGURE 2–15
Video rental form

FIGURE 2–16
Completed video rental form

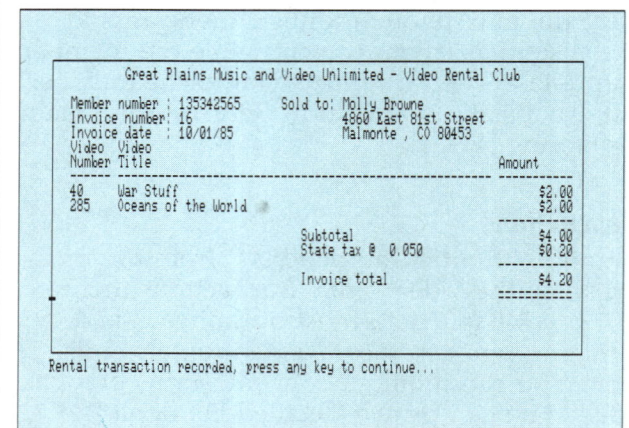

FIGURE 2–17
Rental status of *Never Cry Kumquat*

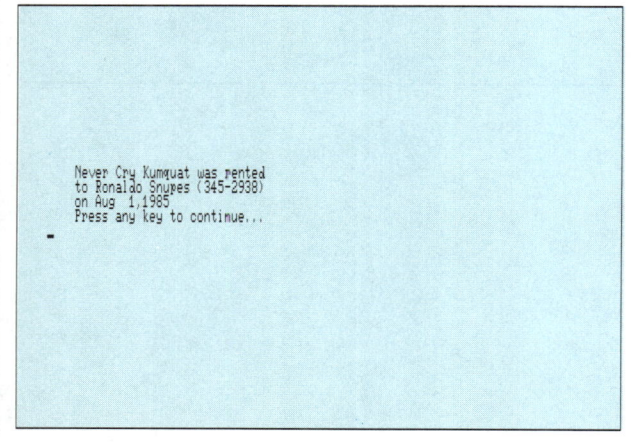

Inquiring about the Status of a Video Next, the phone rings. One of the members wants to know if *Never Cry Kumquat* is available for rental. Select Option 3, "Inquire about the status of a video," from the video rental transactions menu. You are asked to "Enter video number." This menu works like the menus which prompt you for a member number. Look at the video list you printed and see that *Never Cry Kumquat* is video number 287. So type:

287

and press [ENTER]. The system tells us that *Never Cry Kumquat* was rented to Ronaldo Snupes (345-2938) on Aug 1, 1985 (Figure 2–17). You inform the caller that *Never Cry Kumquat* has been rented. If a video is available for rental, the system says so.

Printing a List of Overdue Videos As chief video clerk, it is your job to call members who have not returned rented videos on time. The club rules require that videos be returned by the close of business on the day after they are rented.

To get a list of tapes which are past due, select Option 5, "Print a list of overdue videos," from the video rental transactions menu. After responding to the familiar "Select the report destination" menu, you are given the delinquency list (Figure 2–18).

Recording Video Returns In response to your call, Ronaldo Snupes returns *Never Cry Kumquat* to the store. To record the return, select Option 2, "Record video returns." You are prompted to "Enter member ID number." You request help to obtain Ronaldo's number. Type:

   233654344

and press [ENTER]. You are given a list of all the unreturned videos which the member has. You are asked to make a note of any videos on the list which the member has not returned (Figure 2–19). After pressing any key to continue, you are asked, "Have all tapes been returned?" If you respond by pressing [Y], then [ENTER], the system marks all videos returned. If you respond by pressing [N], the system asks you to enter the number of any tape not returned. In this case, Ronaldo has returned the only tape he had rented, so press [Y] and [ENTER]. That's all there is to it.

Printing a Transaction Summary The accounting department needs a monthly listing of transactions for their bookkeeping purposes. They have asked for a list for the month of August 1985. Select Option 4, "Print a transaction summary," from the video rental transactions menu. You are asked to "Enter the earliest date to be included in the report." Type:

   08/01/85

and press [ENTER]. You are then asked to "Enter the latest date to be included in the report." Type:

   08/31/85

and press [ENTER]. After selecting the report destination, the rental transactions for August 1985 are printed (Figure 2–20). Be patient, this is a complex report and it takes a while for the system to gather everything together. Note that the transactions are grouped by day and by transaction within each day. Return to the video rental transactions menu by pressing any key. Return to the main menu by pressing [ESC].

That completes your tour through the video rental system. By making selections from the system menus, you can perform tasks in minutes which would take you hours to perform by hand.

In subsequent chapters, we'll talk about how to design and use databases to answer questions.

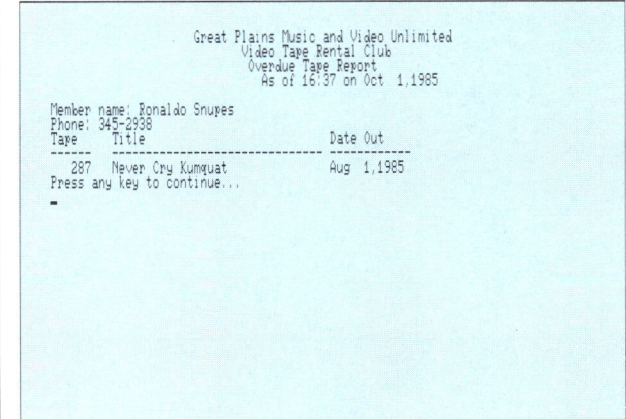

FIGURE 2–18
Overdue tape report

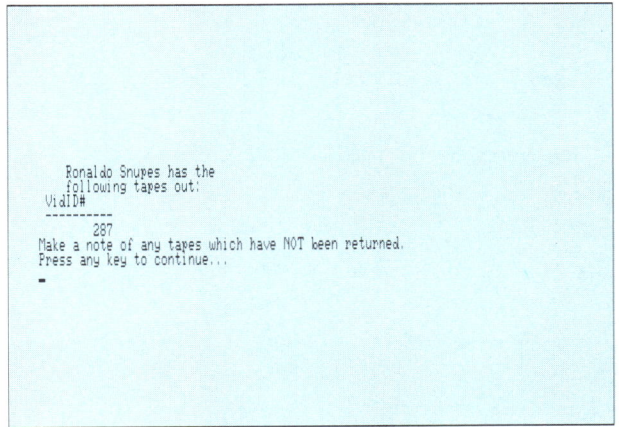

FIGURE 2–19
Request for videos that the member has not returned

FIGURE 2–20
Rental Transactions for August 1985

Great Plains Music and Video Unlimited
Video Rental Club
Transaction Register
From Aug 1,1985 To Aug 31,1985
Printed at 13:17 on Sep 2,1985
Page 1

Date: Aug 1,1985

Transaction number: 13

Member: David Crumpke

Video Number	Title	Amount
284	Space Ace	$2.00
285	Oceans of the World	$2.00
	Transaction total	$4.00

Transaction number: 14

Member: Ronaldo Snupes

Video Number	Title	Amount
287	Never Cry Kumquat	$2.00
	Transaction total	$2.00
	Daily total	$6.00
	Rental amount	$6.00
	Taxes	$0.30
	Total	$6.30

SUMMARY

- Great Plains Music and Video Unlimited is a small business located in a small town near the campus of a large university. It sells electronic components, records, tapes, and compact disks and rents videotapes and VCRs, principally to college students.
- About a year ago, a consultant was hired to automate the information management system. The consultant suggested that the system be automated one part at a time.
- The video rental club was automated first. The processes included the following steps:
  - Requirements definition
  - Alternatives evaluation
  - Detailed design
  - Implementation
- The video rental information system is menu-driven. To make it perform, you make choices from the menus which the system puts on the screen.
- The main menu has three choices:
  - Videos
  - Members
  - Rental transactions
- The video data menu has three choices:
  - Enter data about a new video
  - Print a list of videos by video number
  - Print a list of videos by title
- The member data menu has three choices:
  - Enter data about a new member
  - Change member data
  - Print a membership list
- The video rental transactions menu has five choices:
  - Record video rentals
  - Record video returns
  - Inquire about the status of a video
  - Print a transactions summary
  - Print a list of overdue videos

REVIEW QUESTIONS

Group I Questions

2-1
List the five components of an information management system.

2-2
Which of the five components of an information management system is represented by the description in this chapter?

2-3
Why was the video rental part of Great Plains automated before the rest of the business?

2-4
Why was the new system operated along with the old system for a while?

2-5
Show the command to start the video rental system.

2-6
What are the choices on the main menu?

2-7
Which main menu choice would you select to record a new videotape?

2-8
Which main menu choice would you select to change a member's last name?

2-9
Which main menu choice would you select to find out if the video *War Stuff* was available for rental?

2-10
Which main menu choice would you select to record the rental of a video?

Group II Questions

2-11
Why do you suppose the first step in developing the video rental system was to form a project team composed mainly of Great Plains employees?

2-12
Explain why you think the feasibility of the project was considered on three levels: cost, technology, and schedule?

2-13
Does the video rental system include all the functions you would want if you were responsible for that part of Great Plains' business? (Hint: What would you do about late charges?)

2-14
Suppose you were responsible for the video rental portion of Great Plains' business. Write a report to be given to the data processing consultant which specifies, in detail, how you would want the system changed to accommodate the automatic calculation of late charges.

CHAPTER 3

Data Models and Their Design

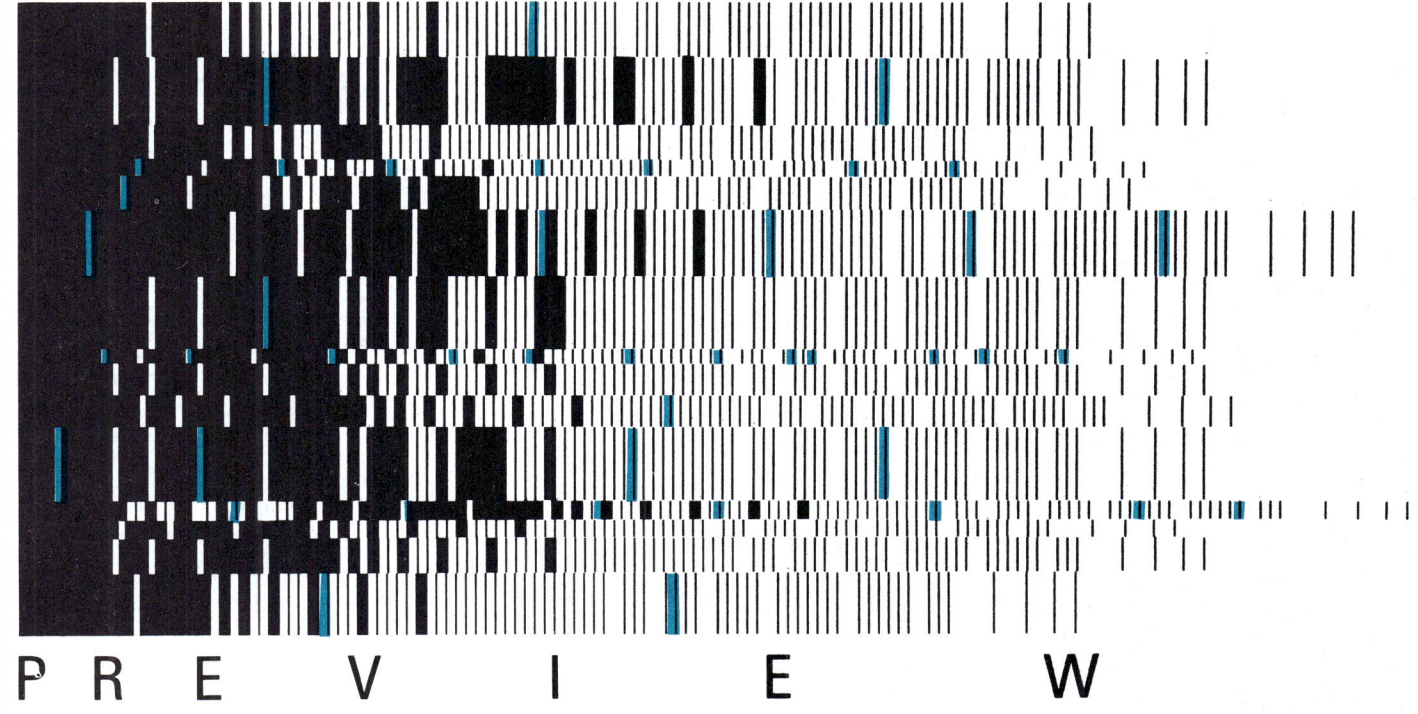

PREVIEW

In this chapter, we will discuss the concept of a database as a model of the work environment, the importance of designing a database before you build it, and the characteristics of the tables which are used in most microcomputer data models. In addition, we will explain the basic terminology which is applied to relational databases, the three basic operations required of a relational database management system, and a simple intuitive approach to database design.

DATA AS A MODEL

A properly designed database is a model of the business as a whole, or at least a segment of it. This model must be dynamic; it must change as the business does. Databases (or data models) exist for one reason: to answer questions. This idea may seem a bit abstract, so let's explore it.

Physical Models

You have probably seen physical models of buildings, airplanes, and cars. Aside from those built by hobbyists for the simple enjoyment of it, why do people build models? Usually, they build them to answer questions.

For example, suppose you are an aerospace engineer working on the design of a new airplane. There are any number of questions which must be answered about your new design. Will it fly? How stable is it? Can it operate from existing airports? Can it withstand the stresses of supersonic flight? It's faster, easier, safer, and far less expensive for you to build a model of the new airplane and run it through a wind tunnel than it is to build a full-size version and test fly it.

Data Models

Data models work the same way. The only difference is that instead of being made of physical material, data models are made of facts about the objects they represent. Thus, if the production manager wants to know the quantity of part number XY-148 in stock, it is faster and easier, and therefore less expensive, to look at the data model of the inventory than it is to go to the warehouse and count the XY-148s.

Consider the example of the video rental segment of Great Plains Music and Video Unlimited from Chapter 2. How could we use data to model that activity? Let's start by listing the objects that make up that activity. To begin with, there are members of the video rental club. Also, there are the videotapes which Great Plains rents to club members. Last, there are rental transactions. Unlike members and tapes, rental transactions are intangible objects. Nevertheless, they are important objects in the data model.

Almost any question that might arise regarding the operation of the video rental activity has to do with these objects. Since it is not practical or economical to keep a copy of all these objects, we build a data model: a dynamic representation made up of facts about the objects.

Figure 3–1 shows a part of the video rental data model (for simplicity, videotapes are not represented).

FIGURE 3-1
Part of data model for video rental business

MEMBER

Member number	First name	Last name	Membership date
7	Mike	Franzen	11/14/80
1	Jim	O'Dell	09/06/72
6	Stanley	Abel	12/14/81
5	Greg	Abel	11/18/81

TRANS

Video number	Member number	Rental date	Return Date	Charge
345	6	05/14/85	05/15/85	$2.00
719	1	05/15/85	05/17/85	$4.00
102	7	05/15/85	05/16/85	$2.00
304	6	05/14/85	05/15/85	$2.00
222	1	05/13/85	05/15/85	$4.00
719	5	05/13/85	05/15/85	$4.00
345	6	05/17/85	05/18/85	$2.00
222	5	05/16/85	05/17/85	$2.00
102	6	05/13/85	05/14/85	$2.00

As you can see, each class of object, MEMBER and TRANSaction in this case, is represented by a table. Each individual MEMBER and TRANSaction is represented by a row in its respective table, and the facts that we want to keep about the individuals are represented by the columns of the tables. (Throughout this book, the names of tables, such as MEMBER, will be capitalized. The names of columns, like First name, will have initial capitals and will be underlined.)

Figure 3-1 tells us that Franzen, O'Dell, and the Abels are all members of the video rental club. The facts we keep in the MEMBER table are Member number, First name, Last name, and Membership date. We keep data about rental TRANSactions in another table. The facts we maintain about TRANSactions include the Video number of the video rented, the Member number of the member who rented the video, the Rental date, the Return date, and the amount of the Charge for the rental.

Even with this simple model, you can answer a number of questions about the video rental activities. Try these:

1. What are the names of the members?
2. What are the rental transactions for May 13, 1985?
3. What is the name of the person who joined the video club on September 6, 1972?
4. What are the names of the members who rented videos on May 15, 1985?
5. What are the names of the members who have rented video number 102?

Characteristics of Tables Used for Data Models

Look again at the MEMBER table in Figure 3–1 and see what we can learn about the characteristics of the tables that are used to build data models with microcomputers. The most obvious thing we can see from the MEMBER table is that it is a rectangle. Why is that? Because every row has exactly the same number of facts in it: Member number, First name, Last name, and Membership date.

Next, notice that each column contains the same type of fact in each row. For example, Membership date for the Franzen row conveys the same fact about Franzen as Membership date conveys about O'Dell.

Also notice that there can only be one entry for each fact. That is, there can only be one Membership date. If one of the members resigns and subsequently rejoins, a policy decision would have to be made. Do we store the original or the most recent date as Membership date? Or do we add another column to the table to store another fact about members: Rejoin date? The answer depends on what we need from the data model.

Another characteristic of the table is that no two rows are exactly the same. Although the rows for Stanley Abel and Greg Abel do have some facts in common, they are different because they have different values for First name, Member number, and Membership date. This very useful characteristic of our table implies another characteristic: the order of the rows is unimportant. To get information about Greg Abel, we do not need to know the location of his row in the table. All we have to know is a fact or combination of facts about him which will identify him. If we know his Member number, we can identify his row whether it is the first or last row in the table. We can do the same if we know his first name and his last name.

The last characteristic of the tables is that the order of the columns is not important. Figure 3–2 is the equivalent of Figure 3–1. Either one may be used to answer questions with equal effectiveness.

Figure 3–3 summarizes the characteristics of tables used for most microcomputer databases. These characteristics come from the relational model first proposed by Dr. E. F. Codd in a paper published in 1970 entitled "A Relational Model of Data for Large Shared Data Banks." The data models, and the tables used to implement them, are based on this relational theory.

Terminology

In our discussion, we have used the terms *table, column,* and *row.* We will continue to use that terminology. Elsewhere, you may encounter other terms for the same things. A *table* may also be referred to as a *file* or a *relation,* a *column* may be referred to as a *field* or an *attribute,* and a *row* may be referred to as a *record* or a *tuple* (some say it rhymes with *couple;* others say it

FIGURE 3–2

Same as Figure 3–1—row and column order make no difference

MEMBER

Membership date	Last name	Member number	First name
12/14/81	Abel	6	Stanley
09/06/72	O'Dell	1	Jim
11/18/81	Abel	5	Greg
11/14/80	Franzen	7	Mike

TRANS

Rental date	Charge	Member number	Return date	Video number
05/14/85	$2.00	6	05/15/85	345
05/14/85	$2.00	6	05/15/85	304
05/17/85	$2.00	6	05/18/85	345
05/15/85	$2.00	7	05/16/85	102
05/15/85	$4.00	1	05/17/85	719
05/13/85	$4.00	5	05/15/85	719
05/13/85	$4.00	1	05/15/85	222
05/16/85	$2.00	5	05/17/85	222
05/13/85	$2.00	6	05/14/85	102

FIGURE 3–3

Characteristics of data model tables
- Rows all have the same number of facts.
- Columns convey the same fact for every row.
- There can be only one entry for each fact.
- Rows are unique.
- Order of rows is not important.
- Order of columns is not important.

FIGURE 3-4
Terminology

English	Data Processing	Relational Theory	What is Represented
Table	Flat file	Relation	Set of objects (e.g., people, places, transactions—not necessarily tangible)
Column	Field	Attribute	Facts about objects (e.g., name, shoe size, date, time, price, color, i.d. number)
Row	Record	Tuple	Individual object (e.g., a person, a place, a transaction)

like *pupil*—take your pick). Don't let it throw you. Although there are technical, theoretical distinctions in some cases, they're basically different names for the same thing. Use whatever you are most comfortable with. Figure 3-4 will help you keep all these terms straight.

Relational Operations

The tables (relations) used in a relational database are used to store data, the raw material from which information is made. To use the data model to answer questions, we must be able to manipulate the tables in various ways. Let's take a look at three of the more important ones: *projection*, *selection*, and *join*.

Projection Projection is an operation that produces a new table which has only the desired columns from the source table. Any duplicate rows created by the operation are eliminated. In other words, projection picks columns out of a table. For example, look again at the MEMBER table in Figure 3-1. The projection of MEMBER on First name and Membership date attributes is shown in Figure 3-5a. This projection is denoted as MEMBER [First name, Membership date].

FIGURE 3-5a
Projection—MEMBER [First name, Membership date]

First name	Membership date
Mike	11/14/80
Jim	09/06/72
Stanley	12/14/81
Greg	11/18/81

The projection MEMBER [Member number, Last name] is shown in Figure 3–5b.

Selection Whereas the projection operation is used to pick columns out of a table, selection picks out rows. Selection produces a new table containing only those rows from the source table whose columns meet conditions prescribed in the selection operation. Selection is denoted by specifying the name of the table, followed by the keyword WHERE followed by a condition involving columns. Figure 3–6a shows the selection, MEMBER WHERE Last name = "O'Dell." Figure 3–6b shows the selection, MEMBER WHERE Member number > 5.

Join The join operation produces a new table which contains combined rows from two source tables. The value of a column in the first table is compared with the value of a column in the second. If the two values have a relationship specified in the join operation, then the rows of the source tables are combined to form a third table. Any duplicate rows created by the operation are deleted. Figure 3–7 illustrates the process. *(results in more attributes)*

TABLE 1 has two attributes, Att A and Att B. TABLE 2 has five attributes: Att B, Att 1, Att 2, Att 3 and Att 4. TABLE 1 has eight rows. In each row of TABLE 1, Att B has a value of X. TABLE 2 has three rows. There is only one row in TABLE 2 where the value of Att B is X.

By joining TABLE 1 and TABLE 2 on matching Att B, we create a new table, TABLE 3, which has eight rows with all the attributes from both TABLE 1 and TABLE 2. Notice that only rows from TABLE 1 and TABLE 2 in which the values of Att B are the same were combined into TABLE 3. The join operation in Figure 3–7 is denoted TABLE1 JOIN (AttB = AttB) TABLE2.

As an example of the join operation, Figure 3–8 contains the join of MEMBER and TRANS from Figure 3–1.

FIGURE 3-5b
Projection—MEMBER [Member number, Last name]

Member number	Last name
7	Franzen
1	O'Dell
6	Abel
5	Abel

FIGURE 3-6a
Selection—MEMBER WHERE Last name = "O'Dell"

Member number	First name	Last name	Membership date
1	Jim	O'Dell	09/06/72

FIGURE 3–6b
Selection—MEMBER WHERE Member number > 5

Member number	First name	Last name	Membership date
7	Mike	Franzen	11/14/80
6	Stanley	Abel	12/14/81

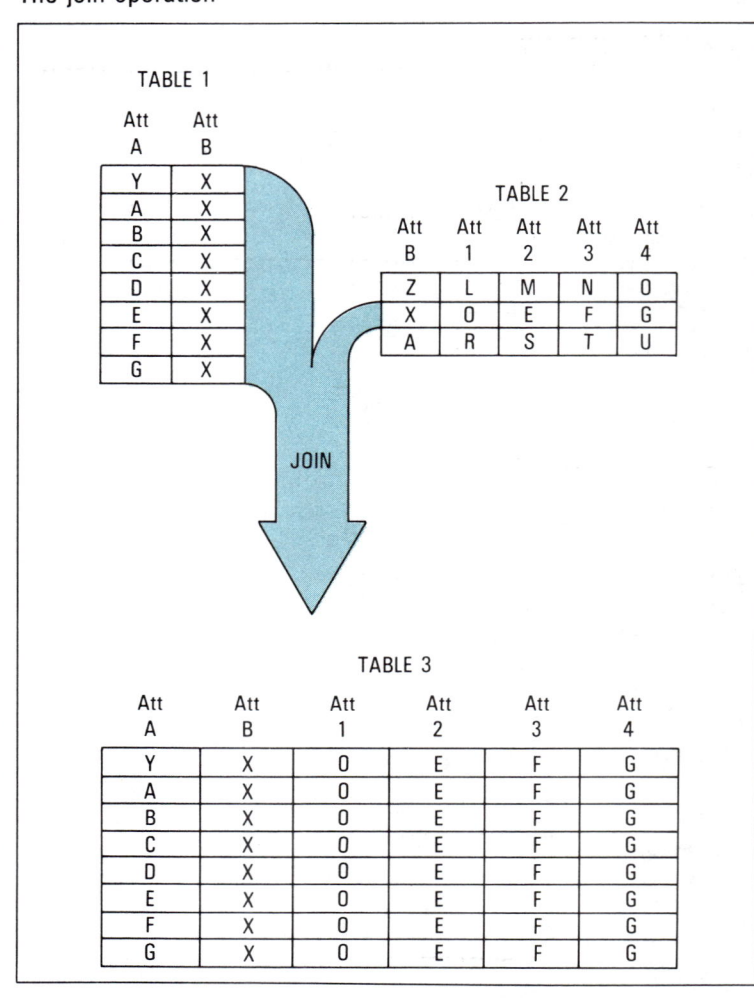

FIGURE 3-7

The join operation

FIGURE 3-8

MEMBER JOIN (<u>M</u>ember number = <u>M</u>ember number) TRANS

Member number	First name	Last name	Membership date	Video number	Rental date	Return date	Charge
7	Mike	Franzen	11/14/80	102	05/15/85	05/16/85	$2.00
1	Jim	O'Dell	09/06/72	719	05/15/85	05/17/85	$4.00
1	Jim	O'Dell	09/06/72	222	05/13/85	05/15/85	$4.00
6	Stanley	Abel	12/14/81	345	05/14/85	05/15/85	$2.00
6	Stanley	Abel	12/14/81	304	05/14/85	05/15/85	$2.00
6	Stanley	Abel	12/14/81	345	05/17/85	05/18/85	$2.00
6	Stanley	Abel	12/14/81	102	05/13/85	05/14/85	$2.00
5	Greg	Abel	11/18/81	719	05/13/85	05/15/85	$4.00
5	Greg	Abel	11/18/81	222	05/16/85	05/17/85	$2.00

Answering Questions with Projection, Selection, and Join

Now let's use the relational operations of projection, selection, and join to answer the questions we asked earlier.

1. What are the names of the members?

    MEMBER [First name, Last name]

    This expression is the PROJECTION of the First name and Last name attributes of the MEMBER table. The result is:

Mike	Franzen
Jim	O'Dell
Stanley	Abel
Greg	Abel

2. What are the rental transactions for May 13, 1985?

    TRANS WHERE Rental date = 05/13/85

    We use SELECTION to pick out the rows we want from the TRANS table. The result is:

222	1	05/13/85	05/15/85	$4.00
719	5	05/13/85	05/15/85	$4.00
102	6	05/13/85	05/14/85	$2.00

3. What is the name of the person who joined the video club on September 6, 1972?

    MEMBER WHERE Membership date = 09/06/72 [First name, Last name]

    Here we use a combination of SELECTION and PROJECTION. We first use SELECTION to pick out the MEMBER row we want. Then we project the result onto the attributes First name and Last name. The result is:

    Jim O'Dell

4. What are the names of the members who rented videos on May 15, 1985?

    TRANS WHERE Rental date = 05/15/85 JOIN (Member number = Member number) MEMBER [First name, Last name]

The answer to this question requires information from both tables. We first select the TRANSactions for May 15, 1985 (TRANS WHERE Rental date = 05/15/85). We JOIN the result with MEMBER, which contains the member names (JOIN (Member number = Member number) MEMBER). The result of this join looks like this:

719	1	05/15/85	05/17/85	$4.00	Jim	O'Dell	09/06/72
102	7	05/15/85	05/16/85	$2.00	Mike	Franzen	11/14/80

The information we need is there. But the question specified the names of the members. The last part of the above expression picks out the First name and Last name attributes. The final result is:

Jim	O'Dell
Mike	Franzen

5. What are the names of the members who have rented video number 102?

TRANS WHERE Video number = 102 JOIN (Member number = Member number) MEMBER [First name, Last name]

This expression is similar to the one used to answer question 4. We first SELECT the rows we want from TRANS. Then we JOIN the result with MEMBER, which has the First name and Last name attributes. Finally, we PROJECT the answer as follows:

Mike	Franzen
Stanley	Abel

You can see that we can answer many questions from a relational data model by using the basic operations of selection, projection, and join. There are other relational operations which we will talk about in other chapters. However, remember that the minimum required for a relational database management system are projection, selection, and join.

DESIGNING DATA MODELS

The tables in Figure 3–1 don't look too complicated. However, good data models don't just happen. They are the result of careful design.

Building a data model is similar in this respect to building a deck for a house. If you simply go to the neighborhood building center and buy lumber, ce-ment, and some hardware and start building, chances are you'll end up with something that you wouldn't find in *Better Homes and Gardens*.

If you are prudent, you will prepare a plan before you build. Think about why you might want to prepare a design before building a deck.

Why Do We Need a Design?

First, the more carefully you design, the closer the result will fit your needs. The design process forces you to give careful consideration to your requirements. If you build your deck with a seating capacity for four and you often have six or eight people for dinner, the deck won't meet your needs. If it doesn't meet your needs, you may not use it. The money you spent to build it would be wasted.

Second, the deck must be constructed to stand up to use. You don't want your favorite aunt falling through the deck because the floor supports were spaced too far apart. You avoid these unhappy surprises by preparing a design that conforms to certain engineering standards.

Third, you want to make use of the standard materials available. These materials have characteristics which must be considered in the design. For example, redwood decking comes in standard dimensions such as 1 1/2 inches thick by 3 1/2 inches wide by 8 feet long. Although you could contract with a lumber mill to cut the decking into different dimensions, why would you?

We design data models for the same three reasons. First, we want to be sure the database accurately models our environment. To achieve that goal, we must be sure that we understand the requirements of the people who are to use the database. The design process forces us to obtain a clear, written understanding of user requirements. If we build a database without careful consideration of user requirements, it is unlikely that it will meet their needs. If users' requirements are not met, they will not use the database.

Second, we want to be sure that there are no unhappy surprises lurking in the database design. As with the construction of physical objects, there are design standards which will help protect the users from having problems with the database. We discuss these design standards in depth in Chapter 4.

Third, we want to build the database using the materials available to us. The materials we want to use for our data models are relations. As with standard materials available to build decks, these tables have characteristics that must be considered in the design.

FIGURE 3-9

A more detailed model enables us to answer more questions, but it takes longer to build and is more expensive

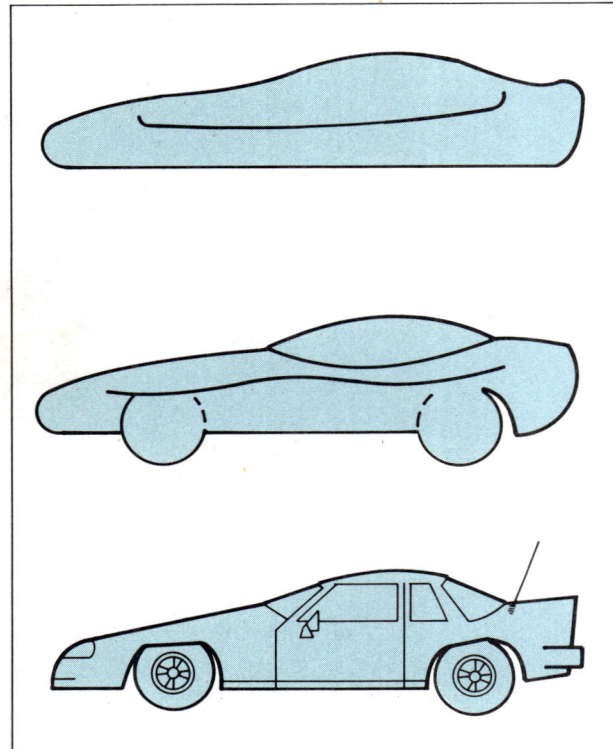

Converting User Requirements to Data Model Designs

To be effective, a database must contain the right facts about the right objects and the right relationships among those objects. Of course, we could try to cover all possibilities by including every conceivable fact about every possible object, but that would be impractical. It would also be a bad design. Data processing professionals have learned from experience that data which is not used will not be maintained.

Models are approximations of what they represent. They should contain only as much detail as they need to serve their purpose. For example, if we need a model car only to test the aerodynamics of the exterior, it is unnecessary and wasteful to represent the texture of the fabric used to upholster the interior. At the top of Figure 3-9 is a very rough approximation of a car. It is unlikely that it would meet the needs of very many users, but it would be inexpensive and easy to build. Progressively more detailed car models are shown in Figure 3-9. The good news is that as we include more detail, we are able to answer more questions about the real car it represents. The bad news is that the more detailed the model is, the longer it takes to build and the more expensive it is.

As you might expect, the same will apply to data models. Database design has two goals. First, we want to include enough detail so that the only question which can't be answered is the question which is never asked. Second, we want to include only those facts which are used frequently so that users will have an interest in helping to ensure that the data is accurate. Sometimes these goals are conflicting. Arriving at the right balance takes judgment.

STEPS IN DATABASE DESIGN

Although there are some technical ways of evaluating a database design which we will discuss in the next chapter, it is not possible to specify a single "correct" way of designing a database. Some computing professionals believe that database design is a science. Some scientific approaches concentrate on analyzing an entity's data. Others suggest that the entity's transactions should be studied. Still others approach scientific database design by looking at the decisions which are made in an entity.

In contrast, another group of computing professionals believe that database design is an art. They approach database design on a largely intuitive basis.

In this book, we suggest one way to approach database design. As you perform database design, you will develop an approach which suits you. We offer the following only as a simple but effective place to start. The approach we suggest emphasizes the concept of the database as a model.

Step 1: List the Objects in the Work Environment

As we have seen, data models are made up of tables which contain facts about objects in our work environment and which allow us to represent the relationships among those objects. A natural way to begin the design of a database is to list the objects in the environment you are modeling. In the example of the video rental segment of Great Plains' business, we decided that the objects in the environment were MEMBER, TRANS, and VIDEO.

RACE (Transaction)
OWNER (member)
HORSE (video)

Step 2: Describe the Relationships among the Objects

The data model must accurately reflect the relationships which the objects in the environment have to one another. Relationships may be one-to-one, one-to-many, or many-to-many. In Chapter 5, we demonstrate a graphical way of portraying these relationships.

Step 3: Decide What Facts about the Objects Are Important

The only reason for having a database is to be able to answer questions about the enterprise or segment which it models. The facts which are maintained about the objects in the model determine which questions you can answer from the database.

Again, there is no single "correct" way of deciding which facts to include. It depends. If the data model is used exclusively to produce routine, periodic reports, then you might analyze the reports which are to be produced. The analysis will tell you what raw material you will need to produce the desired reports.

On the other hand, if the data model is to be used to answer spontaneous, unpredictable questions, you'll have to use other techniques. You may interview the people who will query the database to get an idea of the questions they will ask. In these situations, there is no substitute for a thorough understanding of the business that is being modeled.

Step 4: Designate the Key Columns

We know that each row in a data table must be unique. A key column is a column or combination of columns which uniquely identify each row in the table. To ensure that the tables in the database exhibit this characteristic, we need to designate key columns. We'll look at keys in more depth in the next chapter.

Step 5: Record the Relationships among the Objects

Relationships are represented by the facts the objects have in common. For example, in Figure 3–1, the relationship between the MEMBER table and the TRANSaction table is represented by the Member number of the member—the fact which the two tables have in common. We'll talk more about how to represent relationships in Chapter 4.

Step 6: Evaluate the Design

Once you have an initial database design, you'll want to evaluate it to be sure that there are no unpleasant surprises in store. We'll discuss this topic in detail in Chapter 4.

In Chapter 5, we'll demonstrate how to use these six steps to design a database for Great Plains.

SUMMARY

- A properly designed database is a model of the business.
- Databases exist to answer questions.
- Data models are made of facts about the objects they represent.
- Tables used for microcomputer data models have the following characteristics:
  - Every row has exactly the same number of facts. (*no empty cells*)
  - Every column contains the same facts in each row. (*columns*)
  - There is only one entry for each fact. (*column*)
  - No two rows are exactly the same. (*copies are deleted, not allowed*)
  - The order of the rows and columns is not important.
- Three basic operations used to manipulate tables are:
  - Projection, to pick out columns of a table
  - Selection, to pick out rows of a table
  - Join, to combine data from two tables (*creates more columns, Facts, attributes*)
- Database management systems which store data in tables and which manipulate them using at least projection, selection, and join operations are called relational database management systems.
- It is important to design the data model before you build the database for at least three reasons:
  - To be sure the database accurately models the work environment (*accurate model*)
  - To be sure that the database meets certain design standards which help prevent user problems (*prevent problems*)
  - To be sure that the database can be built using a relational database management system (*make sure it can be relational*)
- To be effective, the data model must contain the right facts about the right objects and the right relationships among those objects.
- The six steps in designing a database are:
  - List the objects in the work environment. (*List objects*)
  - Describe the relationships among the objects. (*Relationships*)
  - Decide what facts are important about these objects. (*Facts of objects*)
  - Designate the key columns. (*Key columns*)
  - Represent the relationships among the objects. (*Linking*)
  - Evaluate the design. (*Evaluate*)

REVIEW QUESTIONS

Group I Questions

3.1
Name three questions which can be answered using a physical model of a building.

3.2
List three ways in which data models are like physical models.

3.3
List three ways in which data models are different from physical models.

3.4
Can you have a data model of an airplane? Explain your answer.

3.5
What is the primary reason for having a database?

3.6
List three questions not already mentioned in the chapter which can be answered using the simple data model in Figure 3–1.

Questions 3.7 through 3.10 refer to the following three tables:

SALESPERSON (Name, Age, Salary)

ORDER (Number, CustName, Salesperson, Amount)

CUSTOMER (CustName, City, Industry)

3.7
Develop sample data for each of these tables. For your data, give an example of:

   a. SALESPERSON [Name, Salary]

   b. SALESPERSON [Age, Salary]

3.8
For your data, show an example of a selection on:

   a. SALESPERSON [Name]

   b. SALESPERSON [Age]

   c. SALESPERSON [Name, Age]

3.9
For your data, show an example of a join of SALESPERSON and ORDER where Name of SALESPERSON equals Salesperson of ORDER.

3.10
With the notations used in the chapter, show how to use projection, selection, and join to answer the following:

a. List the names of all salespeople. *projection*
b. List the names of all salespeople with orders. *projection or join then projection*
c. List the names of salespeople having an order with ABERNATHY CONSTRUCTION. *selection then projection*
d. List the age of salespeople having an order with ABERNATHY CONSTRUCTION. *selection then join then projection*
e. List the city of all CUSTOMERS having an order with salesperson JONES. *selection then join then projection*

Best Sequence of operations
1. Selection
2. Join
3. Projection

3.11
Why is it important to design a database before you build it?

3.12
List the characteristics of tables used for most microcomputer data models.

3.13 *skipped it*
Satisfy yourself that Figure 3–2 is the equivalent of Figure 3–1 by using Figure 3–2 to answer the questions in the chapter about the video rental activities. *Order of rows + columns does not matter*

3.14
The chapter says, "Models are approximations of what they represent." Explain.

3.15
What are the two goals of database design?

3.16 *skipped it*
Do the goals of database design ever conflict? Explain your answer with some examples.

3.17
List the six suggested steps in database design.

Group II Questions

3.18
Suppose you are working on a team to design a database. You have agreed on the objects to be represented in the database and on the relationships among them. It is now time to perform step 3: decide what facts to keep in each table. One member of the team suggests that every report produced during the past year be analyzed to produce a list of all the facts used. What is your reaction to the suggestion? Under what circumstances do you feel the suggested approach might be helpful? When might the approach not work so well?

3.19
Based on what you have learned so far, how would you explain to a businessperson who knows very little about computing what a relational database is and what it is used for?

CHAPTER 4

Standards for Database Design

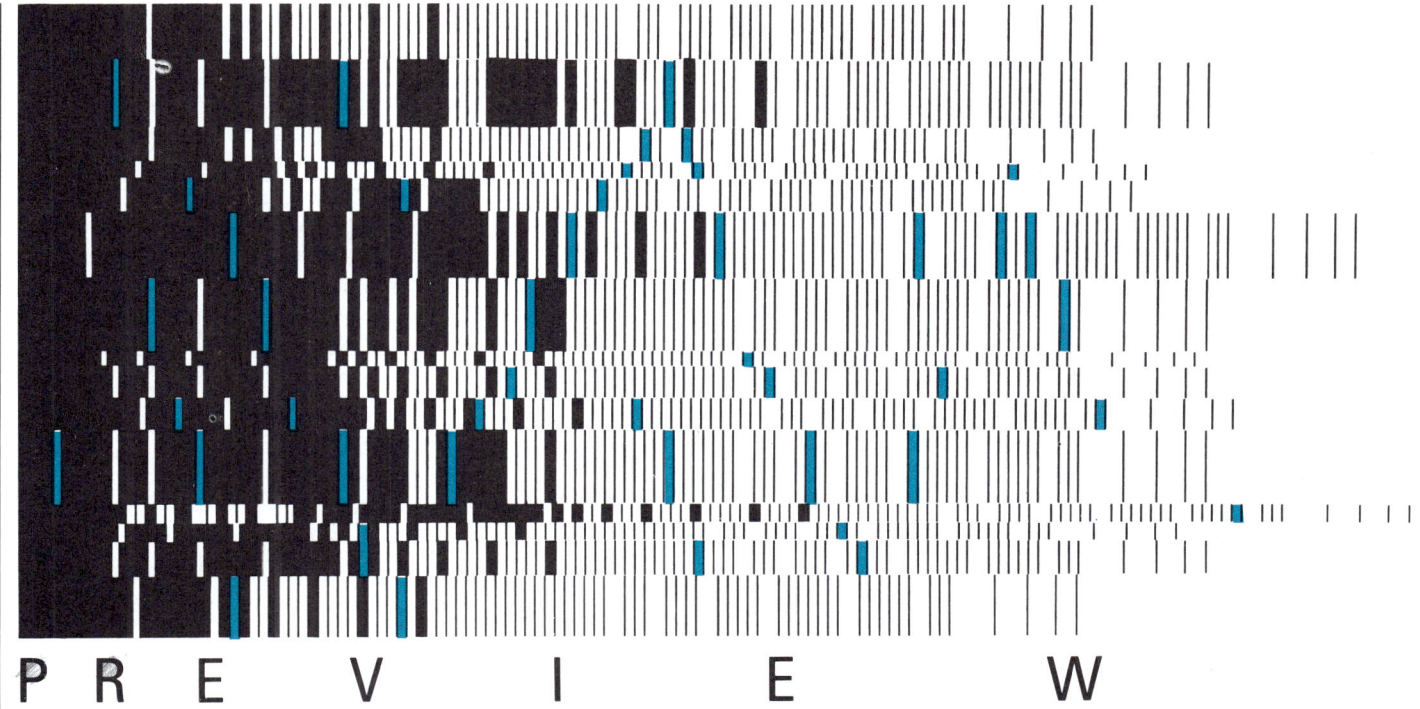

P R E V I E W

The reason for having a database is to answer questions. We want to have a data model of a business or organization that is detailed enough to answer the questions we want to ask. For a given set of questions, however, there are many different ways of designing the database. In this chapter we will consider alternative database designs and formulate several design guidelines.

This chapter shows that well-designed database tables, like well-designed paragraphs, have a single theme. A table should have data about *either* salespeople or orders. It should not have data about *both* salespeople and orders. Additionally, good database designs are convenient to the user; they make intuitive sense.

To help you understand database design, we will first describe several common problems resulting from poor design and present a general rule for eliminating what are called *modification anomalies*. Then we will define some key terms and offer several basic design guidelines.

PROBLEMS RESULTING FROM POOR DESIGN

Suppose Great Plains Music and Video Unlimited wants to keep information about the videotapes it has for rent. For each tape, they need to know the Video number, the Title, the name of the Supplier, and the City where the supplier is located.

To answer questions about videotapes, we define the VIDEO table shown in Figure 4–1. This design is effective in that it provides a way for us to answer our questions. The design has, however, an odd property. To see what that property is, suppose we add a new tape having the following data:

50 Invasion of the Zombies XYZ Boston

We add this video to our table as shown in Figure 4–2a. Can you see that there is now a redundancy in this table? The fact that supplier XYZ is located in Boston is shown in both the first and the last rows. By itself, this is not too serious; we have just wasted file space. Suppose, however, we add another tape:

60 Too Bad   XYZ Boston

The table now appears as in Figure 4–2b. Again, we have duplicated the location of supplier XYZ.

Suppose we now receive a notice that supplier XYZ has moved to Dayton. What do we do? We must find all occurrences of supplier XYZ and change the city to Dayton. Now you can see another disadvantage of the duplicated data: when changes occur, we have to make the change in all copies of the data. Imagine the confusion that would result if we changed only one occurrence.

There are even worse problems. Suppose we get rid of video number 30 and delete its row from the table, as shown in Figure 4–2c. Having done this, consider what will happen when someone asks, "Where is sup-

FIGURE 4–1

Sample data for VIDEO table

VIDEO

Video	Title	Supplier	City
10	Summer of 1885	XYZ	Boston
20	Leaving Home	ABC	Denver
30	That's Not Dancing	JJJ	San Francisco
40	War Stuff	ZZZ	Los Angeles

FIGURE 4–2a
VIDEO table with redundancy in supplier data

VIDEO

Video	Title	Supplier	City
10	Summer of 1885	XYZ	Boston
20	Leaving Home	ABC	Denver
30	That's Not Dancing	JJJ	San Francisco
40	War Stuff	ZZZ	Los Angeles
50	Invasion of the Zombies	XYZ	Boston

FIGURE 4–2b
VIDEO table with more redundancy

VIDEO

Video	Title	Supplier	City
10	Summer of 1885	XYZ	Boston
20	Leaving Home	ABC	Denver
30	That's Not Dancing	JJJ	San Francisco
40	War Stuff	ZZZ	Los Angeles
50	Invasion of the Zombies	XYZ	Boston
60	Too Bad	XYZ	Boston

FIGURE 4–2c
VIDEO table after deletion of video number 30

VIDEO

Video	Title	Supplier	City
10	Summer of 1885	XYZ	Boston
20	Leaving Home	ABC	Denver
40	War Stuff	ZZZ	Los Angeles
50	Invasion of the Zombies	XYZ	Boston
60	Too Bad	XYZ	Boston

plier JJJ located?" We've lost that supplier's address. How? When we deleted the row for video number 30, we deleted the supplier data as well.

Consider one more problem. Suppose a purchasing clerk wants to store the fact that supplier MMM is lo-

FIGURE 4-3
Result of splitting VIDEO table

VIDEO

Video	Title	Supplier
10	Summer of 1885	XYZ
20	Leaving Home	ABC
30	That's Not Dancing	JJJ
40	War Stuff	ZZZ
50	Invasion of the Zombies	XYZ

SUPPLIER

Supplier	City
XYZ	Boston
ABC	Denver
JJJ	San Francisco
ZZZ	Los Angeles

FIGURE 4-4a
EMPLOYEE table

EMPLOYEE

Name	Skill	Child
Jones	Welder	Ann
Jones	Foreman	Ann
Smith	Engineer	Sally
Brown	Pilot	Fred

FIGURE 4-4b
EMPLOYEE table with one insertion

EMPLOYEE

Name	Skill	Child
Jones	Welder	Ann
Jones	Foreman	Ann
Smith	Engineer	Sally
Brown	Pilot	Fred
Jones	Foreman	Robert

cated in Chicago. Unfortunately, this fact cannot be stored until we have a tape from this supplier in inventory.

Computer scientists call problems like these *modification anomalies*. This strange term simply means three things. First, when we add data, we must specify facts about two or more different objects. Second, when we change data, we may need to make changes in more than one place to ensure that the data is consistent. Third, when we delete data, we delete too much.

ELIMINATING MODIFICATION ANOMALIES

Do you recall from writing classes that a paragraph should have a single theme? Well, the same is true of database tables. Each table should have a single theme. The problem with the table in Figure 4-2 is that it has two themes. One theme concerns tapes and the other concerns the location of suppliers.

To correct this problem, we can split the combined table into two separate tables, each with a single theme. This has been done in Figure 4-3. The table named VIDEO has data about videotapes, and the table named SUPPLIER has data about suppliers.

The database in Figure 4-3 does not have the problems we described. We can add tapes without duplicating the location of suppliers. We can change the location of a supplier by changing only a single row in the SUPPLIER table. We can delete tape number 30 without losing the location of supplier JJJ. Finally, we can add supplier MMM in Chicago to the SUPPLIER table before we have any videotapes from them.

What have we lost by doing this? Nothing really. Although the data about tapes and suppliers is no longer stored together, this is not a problem. When we need to, we can form a new table having all the data by performing a relational JOIN operation. (Basic relational operations are discussed in Chapter 3.)

To see another type of problem, consider the table in Figure 4-4a. The EMPLOYEE table has an employee name, the name of a skill the employee possesses, and the name of an employee's child. The database designers didn't know, however, that employee Jones is pregnant. When she has a son named Robert, what happens to the database? Suppose we add one row as shown in Figure 4-4b. As it stands, this table seems to imply that employee Jones has a daughter and a son when she works as a foreman, but only a daughter when she works as a welder. Clearly, this is nonsense. To keep this table logically consistent, we have to add two rows when employee Jones has her son. This is shown in Figure 4-4c.

The table in Figure 4-4 is effective in that it allows us to answer questions about employees' skills and the names of their children. It is ineffective, however, in that it also has anomalies. We can fix this problem by splitting the table into the two tables shown in Figure 4-5. The first table has data about skills, and the second contains data about children. (separate themes)

The tables in both Figures 4-2 and 4-4 have modification anomalies. These anomalies, however, stem from different causes. Computer scientists have classified tables according to the anomalies to which they are susceptible. There are tables in first normal form, second normal form, and so on, to fifth normal form. Some tables are in Boyce-Codd normal form and other, even more strangely named forms.

Fortunately, you do not need to learn all of these forms. In 1981, a mathematician, R. Fagin, showed that if a table was put into what he called *domain/key normal form*, it would not have modification anomalies.

DOMAIN/KEY NORMAL FORM: A DESIGN GOAL

Definitions

Before we can explain domain/key normal form, you need to understand the meaning of four terms: *dependency*, *key*, *domain*, and *restriction*. These definitions may seem a bit stuffy, but be patient. We will eventually arrive at a logical and easily understood conclusion.

Dependency A *dependency* may exist between two columns of a table. For example, let's look at the EMPLOYEE table shown in Figure 4-6. Assume that we assign unique employee numbers to each employee.

In this table, Name is dependent on Number. This means that the employee Number determines the employee Name. Or, in other words, if we know the Number, we can obtain the Name. Similarly, Department is dependent on Number. If we know the Number, we know the Department.

Are there other dependencies in this table? Is Department dependent on Name? No. To see why, suppose we are given the employee name Jones. We cannot determine the Department from this value. It could be either Accounting or Management.

As another possibility, is Name dependent on Department? If we are given the Department, can we determine the Name? This question raises a very important point. For the data shown in Figure 4-6, Name

FIGURE 4-4c
EMPLOYEE table with two insertions

EMPLOYEE

Name	Skill	Child
Jones	Welder	Ann
Jones	Foreman	Ann
Smith	Engineer	Sally
Brown	Pilot	Fred
Jones	Foreman	Robert
Jones	Welder	Robert

FIGURE 4-5
Splitting the EMPLOYEE table to eliminate modification anomalies

SKILL

Name	Skill
Jones	Welder
Jones	Foreman
Smith	Engineer
Brown	Pilot

CHILD

Name	Child
Jones	Ann
Smith	Sally
Brown	Fred
Jones	Robert

FIGURE 4-6
Example of column dependencies
Number can have only one dept.

EMPLOYEE

Number	Name	Department
100	Jones	Accounting
200	Parks	Sales
300	Jones	Management

Name is dependent on Number.
Department is dependent on Number.

FIGURE 4–7

EMPLOYEE data illustrating that Name is not dependent on Department

EMPLOYEE Number	Name	Department
100	Jones	Accounting
200	Parks	Sales
300	Jones	Management
400	Franklin	Sales

appears to be dependent on Department. For this data, if we are given a Department, we can determine a unique Name. However, for dependencies to work, they must hold for all possible data values. The apparent dependency of Name on Department only exists for the data we happen to have. In general, Name is not dependent on Department because departments can have more than one employee. Figure 4–7 shows data for the EMPLOYEE table that illustrates that Name is not dependent on Department.

To determine if a dependency exists, then, we need to think about the work environment which we are representing with the data model. We must ask, "In our environment, does the value of one column determine the value of another?" If so, a dependency exists.

Key A column is a *key* if it uniquely determines a row. Another way of saying this is that a column is a key if all other columns in a row are dependent on it. For example, in the EMPLOYEE table in Figure 4–6, Number is a key. This is true because the other columns, Name and Department, are dependent on Number.

Sometimes no single column is a key. Sometimes, a combination of columns is the key. In some cases, all of the columns in the table make up the key. In Figure 4–8a, the ACCOUNT table holds data about customers, salespeople, and commissions to date. A customer may have several salespeople, and a salesperson may have many customers. Therefore, neither Customer nor Salesperson can be the key. Neither, by itself, determines Commission. The combination of columns Customer and Salesperson,

FIGURE 4–8a

Relation with two-column key

ACCOUNT Customer	Salesperson	Commission
ABC	Jones	$5,768
ABC	Smith	$ 789
DEF	Jones	$1,239
XXX	Parks	$ 458
XXX	Jones	$ 228

Key of ACCOUNT table is Customer, Salesperson

FIGURE 4-8b
Table with three-column key

AD

Product	Publication	Date	Cost
Desk	TV Guide	07/04/85	$ 2,289
Chair	Vogue	07/04/85	$28,976
Table	TV Guide	08/27/85	$ 1,798
Chair	New Woman	07/04/85	$17,658
Desk	TV Guide	08/27/85	$ 2,289

Key of AD table is Product, Publication, Date

however, does determine Commission. Thus, the key of this table is Customer, Salesperson.

Figure 4-8b shows AD, a table of advertisements. Each row represents the fact that a given product was featured in a given magazine on a given publication date. None of the three columns in this table is a key. Furthermore, no set of two of these columns is a key. Product, Publication is not a key because a product may be advertised in the same magazine on different dates. Product, Date is not a key because a product may be advertised on a given date in two or more publications. Finally, Publication, Date is not a key because several products may be featured in a magazine on the same date. Thus, the key of this table is the combination Product, Publication, Date.

Domain A *domain* is a set of values that a column can have. Each column of a table will have a domain. To understand this concept, consider Figure 4-9 which shows a database definition for the table in Figure 4-8a. Customer is defined as TEXT 20. Because of this definition, the domain of Customer is the set of all possible customer names with 20 characters or less. Similarly, the domain of Salesperson is the set of all possible salespersons' names with 20 characters or less, and the domain of Commission is the set of all possible commissions expressed as integers (whole numbers).

A domain, however, is more than just a physical description. It is both a physical and a logical description. The domain of Customer is a set of all customers' names (the logical part of the definition) of length 20 or less (the physical part).

Why is this important? The physical forms of both Customer and Salesperson are the same. This does not

FIGURE 4-9
Database definition for ACCOUNT table in Figure 4-8a

Column	Description
Customer	TEXT 20
Salesperson	TEXT 20
Commission	INTEGER

FIGURE 4–10

Domain is a logical description as well as a physical description

EMP (Ename, Number, Dept-no)
DEPT (Num, Dep-name, Location)
Number, Dept-no and Num are all defined as INTEGER

Only Dept-no and Num arise from the same domain since Number has a different logical definition.

mean, however, that their domains are the same. Consider the value "Franklin." Is the value "Franklin" in the domain of Customer? To be in this domain, it must be less than 21 characters *and* it must be the name of a customer. It is less than 21 characters, so if "Franklin" is also the name of a customer, then this value is in the domain of Customer.

Is "Franklin" in the domain of Salesperson? Again, to be in this domain, it must be less than 21 characters and it must be the name of a salesperson. It is less than 21 characters, so if "Franklin" is the name of a salesperson, then it is also in the domain of Salesperson. If "Franklin" is not the name of a salesperson, then it is not in the domain of Salesperson, regardless of the fact that it fits the physical description. Domain is both a physical and a logical description.

Consider the tables in Figure 4–10. Suppose that the columns Number, Dept-no, and Num are all defined as INTEGER. Do these columns have the same domain? Another way of asking this question is, "Do these columns have the same physical *and* logical definition?" They do have the same physical definition, but they do not have the same logical definition. Dept-no and Num are both numbers of departments. Number, however, is the number of an employee.

Restriction The last of the four terms we need to define is restriction. A restriction is a limitation, of some type, on the values in a table. The meaning of the term is intended to be very general.

Dependencies are one type of restriction. When we say that Name is dependent on Number, we are stating a restriction. Specifically, we are saying that one and only one value of Name can be paired with a given value of Number. If employee number 100 is Jones, then only the name Jones can be paired with employee number 100.

Consider another example of a dependency restriction. Suppose that Location is dependent on Dep-name. If the accounting department is located in building A-200, then whenever Dep-name and Location appear in the same table, the value "A-200" must be paired with the value "Accounting."

Keys are another type of restriction. When we say that a column is a key, we are saying that all the other columns in the table will depend on the key. (Remember, the key may be composed of more than one column.)

Domains are a third type of restriction. When we define a domain, we are defining the physical format, logical meaning, and restrictions on the values of the column. Saying that Department is to have INTEGER department numbers between 001 and 999 is a domain restriction.

There are many other kinds of restrictions. Consider the table AD with the following attributes: Product, Publication, Date, and Cost. Some restrictions on this table are as follows:

- The combination Product, Publication, Date is the key.
- Cost must have a dollar format with values between $1.00 and $99,999.99.
- Date must be of the form yymmdd.
- Prod must begin with the digit 1.
- If the value of Publication is "HOLIDAY MAILER," then the middle two digits of Date must be 11 or 12.

We will consider the implications of these restrictions in the next section. For now, realize that the term *restriction* simply means a limitation of some sort on the values in a table. The four definitions we have discussed are summarized in Figure 4–11.

Achieving Domain/Key Normal Form

We can now use the terms we've defined to explain how to evaluate database tables to determine if they are in domain/key normal form. To begin, consider the following statements, which were developed by Fagin:

- A relation (table) is in domain/key normal form if all the restrictions are logical consequences of key and domain restrictions.
- A table that is in domain/key normal form cannot have modification anomalies. Also, a table that has no modification anomalies is in domain/key normal form.

What do these statements mean? They mean that if we can design tables so that the only restrictions they have are key restrictions and domain restrictions, then the table will not have modification anomalies. Thus, we want to design databases with tables that are in domain/key normal form.

Unfortunately, putting tables into domain/key normal form is more an art than a science. It is currently impossible to specify a sequence of steps for transforming a table into domain/key normal form. The process must be done by trial and error. Still, domain/key normal form is a useful standard by which we can evaluate the quality of our designs.

To illustrate the process of evaluating the design of database tables, let's consider a few examples.

FIGURE 4–11
Summary of definitions

- **Dependency** A relationship between two columns such that the value of one column determines the value of the second.
- **Key** One or more columns that uniquely identify a row. Equivalently, one or more columns in a row that determine the values of all the other columns in that row.
- **Domain** The physical and logical description of a column.
- **Restriction** A limitation on the data values of a table.

EXAMPLE 1

EMPLOYEE (<u>Number</u>, Name, Dept, Tpay)

(When used in the above way, column names will still have initial capitals but only key attributes will be underlined.)

Restriction	Type of Restriction		
	Domain	Key	Other
1. <u>Number</u> is INTEGER	X		
2. Name is TEXT 20	X		
3. Dept is TEXT 10	X		
4. Tpay is DOLLAR	X		
5. <u>Number</u> is key		X	

This table is already in domain/key normal form. The only restrictions on the values of this table are domain or key. Since this table is in domain/key normal form, it cannot have modification anomalies. Notice that the table maintains facts about only one object—employees.

EXAMPLE 2

PRODUCT (<u>Number</u>, Name, Quantity, Supplier, City)

Restriction	Type of Restriction		
	Domain	Key	Other
1. <u>Number</u> is INTEGER	X		
2. Name is TEXT 10	X		
3. Quantity is INTEGER	X		
4. Supplier is TEXT 10	X		
5. City is TEXT 10	X		
6. <u>Number</u> is key		X	
7. City is dependent on Supplier			X

This table is not in domain/key normal form. Restriction 7 is not a key or domain restriction. It is a dependency restriction, but it is not a key restriction. Therefore, this table will have modification anomalies. In fact, this table is similar to the one we used to illustrate anomalies in Figure 4–2. The designer of this table got into trouble by trying to store facts about two different objects, PRODUCTs and SUPPLIERs, in one table.

To convert this table to domain/key normal form, we

must make restriction 7 into a key restriction by making Supplier a key. To do this, we have to create a new table that has Supplier as key and City as a column that is dependent on Supplier. Thus, we create two tables, as follows:

PRODUCT (Number, Name, Quantity, Supplier)
VENDOR (Name, City)

Restriction	Type of Restriction		
	Domain	Key	Other
1. Number is INTEGER	X		
2. Name (of PRODUCT) is TEXT 10	X		
3. Quantity is INTEGER	X		
4. Supplier is TEXT 10	X		
5. Name (of VENDOR) is TEXT 10	X		
6. City is TEXT 10	X		
7. Number is key of PRODUCT		X	
8. Name is key of VENDOR		X	

Now we have two tables and each of them is in domain/key normal form. Notice that the design also now makes sense. There are two tables with facts about two different objects.

EXAMPLE 3

EMPLOYEE (Name, Skill, Child)

Restriction	Type of Restriction		
	Domain	Key	Other
1. Name is TEXT 20	X		
2. Skill is TEXT 4	X		
3. Child is TEXT 20	X		
4. Name, Skill, Child is key		X	
5. Name determines a set of skills (each employee may have many skills)			X
6. Name determines a set of children (each employee may have many children)			X

This is the same table as presented in Figure 4–4. EMPLOYEE is not in domain/key normal form. Why? Remember that a table is in domain/key normal form if all the restrictions are domain or key restrictions. Neither restriction 5 nor restriction 6 is a key or domain restriction. To put this data into domain/key normal form, we create the following two tables:

EMP-SKILL (<u>Name</u>, <u>Skill</u>)
EMP-CHILD (<u>Name</u>, <u>Child</u>)

Restriction	Type of Restriction		
	Domain	Key	Other
1. <u>Name</u> is TEXT 20	X		
2. <u>Skill</u> is TEXT 4	X		
3. <u>Child</u> is TEXT 20	X		
4. The combination of <u>Name</u> and <u>Skill</u> is key of EMP-SKILL		X	
5. The combination of <u>Name</u> and <u>Child</u> is key of EMP-CHILD		X	

All of the restrictions are either domain or key restrictions. Consequently, we know that both tables are in domain/key normal form.

EXAMPLE 4

AD (<u>Prod</u>, <u>Pub</u>, <u>Date</u>, <u>Cost</u>)

Restriction	Type of Restriction		
	Domain	Key	Other
1. <u>Prod</u> is TEXT 10	X		
2. <u>Pub</u> is TEXT 20	X		
3. <u>Date</u> is yymmdd	X		
4. <u>Date</u> must be 85mmdd	X		
5. <u>Cost</u> is DOLLAR	X		
6. <u>Cost</u> must be < $10,000	X		
7. <u>Prod</u>, <u>Pub</u>, <u>Date</u> is key		X	
8. If the value of <u>Pub</u> is "HOLIDAY MAILER" then the middle two digits of <u>Date</u> must be 11 or 12			X

Since there is a restriction which is neither a domain restriction nor a key restriction, the table is not in domain/key normal form. Restriction 8 poses a problem. Unfortunately, there is no practically useful way to put this table into domain/key normal form. One possibility is to define two tables as follows:

AD (Prod, Pub, Date, Cost)

Restriction	Type of Restriction		
	Domain	Key	Other
1. Prod is TEXT 10	X		
2. Pub is TEXT 20	X		
3. Date is yymmdd	X		
4. Date must be 85mmdd	X		
5. Cost is DOLLAR	X		
6. Cost must be < $10,000	X		
7. Prod, Pub, Date is key		X	
8. The value of Pub may not equal "HOLIDAY MAILER"	X		

SPEC-AD (Prod, Pub, Date, Cost)

Restriction	Type of Restriction		
	Domain	Key	Other
1. Prod is TEXT 10	X		
2. Pub is TEXT 20	X		
3. Date is yymmdd	X		
4. Date must be 85mmdd	X		
5. Cost is DOLLAR	X		
6. Cost must be < $10,000	X		
7. Prod, Pub, Date is key		X	
8. The value of Pub must equal "HOLIDAY MAILER"	X		
9. Date must have either the form yy11dd or yy12dd	X		

These two tables are now in domain/key normal form since all restrictions are either domain or key restrictions. However, the design is highly contrived and inconvenient to use. For this example, domain/key normal form may not be worth the effort. It would probably be easier to enforce the non-domain/key restriction with procedures or programs than to attempt to work with the artificial restructuring.

EXAMPLE 5
EMPLOYEE (<u>Name</u>, Sal-code, Salary)

Restriction	Type of Restriction		
	Domain	Key	Other
1. <u>Name</u> is TEXT 10	X		
2. Sal-code is TEXT 2	X		
3. Salary is DOLLAR	X		
4. <u>Name</u> is key		X	
5. Sal-code determines Salary			X

Some data for this table is shown in Figure 4–12a. This table is not in domain/key normal form because of restriction number 5. Again, the solution is to split the table in two. Suppose we define the following:

EMP-CODE (<u>Name</u>, Sal-code)
EMP-SAL (<u>Name</u>, Salary)

Restriction	Type of Restriction		
	Domain	Key	Other
1. <u>Name</u> is TEXT 10	X		
2. Sal-code is TEXT 2	X		
3. Salary is DOLLAR	X		
4. <u>Name</u> is key of EMP-CODE		X	
5. <u>Name</u> is key of EMP-SAL		X	

Figure 4–12b shows the result of the projections EMPLOYEE [<u>Name</u>, Sal-code] and EMPLOYEE [<u>Name</u>, Salary]. These two tables are both in domain/key normal form. However, this design is a poor one. To see why, use Figure 4–12b to answer the question, "How

FIGURE 4–12a
Data for EMPLOYEE relation (example 5)

EMPLOYEE

Name	Sal-code	Salary
Jones	07	$22,000
Franklin	03	$18,000
Wu	06	$29,000
Martinez	14	$67,000
Parks	03	$18,000
Richards	07	$22,000

FIGURE 4-12b

Poor solution—splitting of dependency between Sal-code and Salary

EMP-CODE	
Name	Sal-code
Jones	07
Franklin	03
Wu	06
Martinez	14
Parks	03
Richards	07

EMP-SAL	
Name	Salary
Jones	$22,000
Franklin	$18,000
Wu	$29,000
Martinez	$67,000
Parks	$18,000
Richards	$22,000

much do we pay our code 07 employees?" You must first find an employee who has a Sal-code of 07 in EMP-CODE and then obtain that employee's salary from EMP-SAL.

Even worse, what happens if you try to change the salary of employees with a Sal-code of 07? You must find each code 07 employee in EMP-CODE and then change the employee's salary in EMP-SAL. These operations are inconvenient, to say the least. Imagine the problems associated with a database which contains data about thousands of employees and hundreds of pay codes.

These problems occur because we have split a dependency. Sal-code determines Salary, but we have placed Sal-code and Salary in different tables. A better design (and one that makes intuitive sense) is the following:

EMP (Name, Sal-code)
PAY-CODE (Sal-code, Salary)

Restriction	Type of Restriction		
	Domain	Key	Other
1. Name is TEXT 10	X		
2. Sal-code is TEXT 2	X		
3. Salary is DOLLAR	X		
4. Name is key of EMP		X	
5. Sal-code is key of PAY-CODE		X	

The only restrictions on these tables are domain and key restrictions, so the tables are in domain/key normal form. Further, the dependency between Sal-code and Salary is contained in a single table instead of being split across two. Consequently, we can now ob-

FIGURE 4-13

Split causes interrelation dependency between EMP and PAY CODE. There must be a Sal-code in PAY-CODE for every Sal-Code in EMP. These simple inclusion constraints are OK.

EMP		PAY-CODE	
Name	Sal-code	Sal-code	Salary
Jones	07	07	$22,000
Franklin	03	03	$18,000
Wu	06	06	$29,000
Martinez	14	14	$67,000
Parks	03		
Richards	07		

tain combinations of Sal-code and Salary without having to jump across two tables. To determine how much we are paying the code 07 employees, we need only access the PAY-CODE table. Also, to change the salary of all code 07 employees, we need change only one value in the entire database.

Intertable Constraints

As we have seen, in many cases, we divide one table into two or more tables to achieve domain/key normal form. When tables are split in this way, we create *intertable constraints*. To see this, consider Figure 4–13, which shows the result of projecting EMPLOYEE (Name, Sal-code, Salary) into the two relations, EMP (Name, Sal-code) and PAY-CODE (Sal-code, Salary).

Suppose we allow a row of PAY-CODE to be deleted—say the row (7, $22,000). After this deletion, we will be unable to recreate the old EMPLOYEE table. The rows in EMP that have a Sal-code value of 07 no longer have a matching Sal-code in PAY-CODE. To prevent this situation from occurring, we must place a restriction on EMP which requires that all of the values of Sal-code in EMP must also exist in PAY-CODE. Such restrictions are called *inclusion constraints*.

Although inclusion constraints are neither domain nor key restrictions, they are, as Fagin says, in the spirit of domain/key normal form and ought to be allowed. Thus, a table may have simple inclusion constraints placed on it and still be in domain/key normal form.

Enforcing Database Restrictions

Restrictions of any type are of no use unless they are enforced. For example, if our design specifies that column X is the key to table R, that restriction must be enforced. By some means, we must be assured that every value of X which is entered in table R is unique. Said another way, no value of X must be allowed to be entered twice. Unless this is done, X will not uniquely identify a given row in the table and, therefore, cannot be a key.

How do we enforce database restrictions? There are three possibilities. First, database restrictions can be enforced using procedures. For example, we could provide a procedure by which a manual list of key values is maintained and somebody would be responsible for making sure that key values are not duplicated. This approach is least desirable because it is the least reliable. Procedures are too easy to misunderstand or ignore.

Second, database restrictions can be enforced using programs. For example, we could design the data entry programs in the system to check that key values are unique. With many DBMS's for microcomputers, this is the way most database restrictions are enforced. It is more reliable than manual procedures, but it requires that every operation of the information management system which modifies values in the tables be under the control of a program. Every such program must contain routines to enforce database constraints.

Third, database restrictions can be enforced by the DBMS. For example, the DBMS could have a facility for defining database restrictions. Then, the DBMS automatically applies the prescribed rules to every operation which modifies the database, whether performed by a DBMS utility or an application program. Obviously, this is the most desirable alternative. It is faster and easier than writing program routines to enforce the restrictions. Therefore it is much less expensive. Also, because the DBMS is in charge of manipulating the database, we have the most assurance that the restrictions will be enforced—whether we use DBMS utilities or not.

Elimination of anomalies is reason enough for designing tables in domain/key normal form. However, there is another benefit. The only restrictions on values in tables which are in domain/key normal form are domain restrictions, key restrictions, and simple inclusion constraints. Because these restrictions are not very complex, they are relatively easy to enforce. If our database design is not in domain/key normal form, we are likely to have any number of more complex restrictions to try to enforce.

SUMMARY

- There are many different ways of designing a database.

- Well-designed databases are easy to work with, they do not have *modification anomalies*, and they are convenient to the user. They make intuitive sense.

- Modification anomalies have three serious implications:

  - When we add data, we must specify facts about two or more different objects. As a result, we may be prevented from recording facts about one of them until we have facts to record about the others.

  - When we change data, we must make changes in more than one place to ensure that the data is consistent.

  - When we delete data, we delete too much.

- We are assured that a database table is free of modification anomalies if the table is in domain/key normal form.

- To understand domain/key normal form, you must understand the definitions of four terms: dependency, key, domain, and restriction

- A table is in domain/key normal form if the only restrictions on the values in the table are:

  - Domain restrictions
  - Key restrictions
  - Simple inclusion constraints

- To be of any use, all restrictions on the database must be enforced. Restrictions may be enforced using one of the following (in order of preference):

  - Procedures
  - Application programs
  - DBMS

- Because the restrictions on database tables in domain/key normal form are few in number, domain/key normal form makes enforcing database restrictions easier.

- A good database design has the following attributes:

  - The tables have a single theme.
  - The tables are in domain/key normal form.
  - Dependencies are intact.
  - The only intertable constraints are simple inclusion constraints.
  - The database is easy to use.

REVIEW QUESTIONS

Group I Questions

4.1
Define the term *modification anomaly*.

4.2
Give an example of each of the three problems which are caused by anomalies: (a) when adding data (b) when changing data (c) when deleting data

4.3
What does it mean to say, "Department number determines department name"?

4.4
Define the term *key*.

4.5
If SID is a key of a table, can there be more than one occurrence of a given value of SID in the table?

4.6
Define *domain/key normal form*. Why is it important?

4.7
Classify the following restrictions as domain, key, or other:

  a. StudentID is TEXT 9

  b. StudentID determines a set of Majors

  c. If Grade equals "Junior" then Class-code must < 400

  d. Class-code must be an INTEGER between 100 and 699

  e. StudentID in CLASS must equal StudentID in STUDENT

4.8
Give an example of an inclusion constraint. Why are such constraints important?

Group II Questions

4.9
Transform the following table into domain/key normal form. Make appropriate assumptions about dependencies and domains. State your assumptions. List the restrictions and indicate the type of each—i.e., domain or key.

HARDWARE (Manufacturer, Model, Memory Size, Site Number, City, State, Zip)

4.10
Apply the instructions in question 4.11 to the following table:

INVOICE (Number, Customer Name, Customer Number, Customer Address, Item Number, Item Price, Item Quantity, Salesperson Number, Tax District, Tax, Total Due)

CHAPTER 5

Database Design for Great Plains

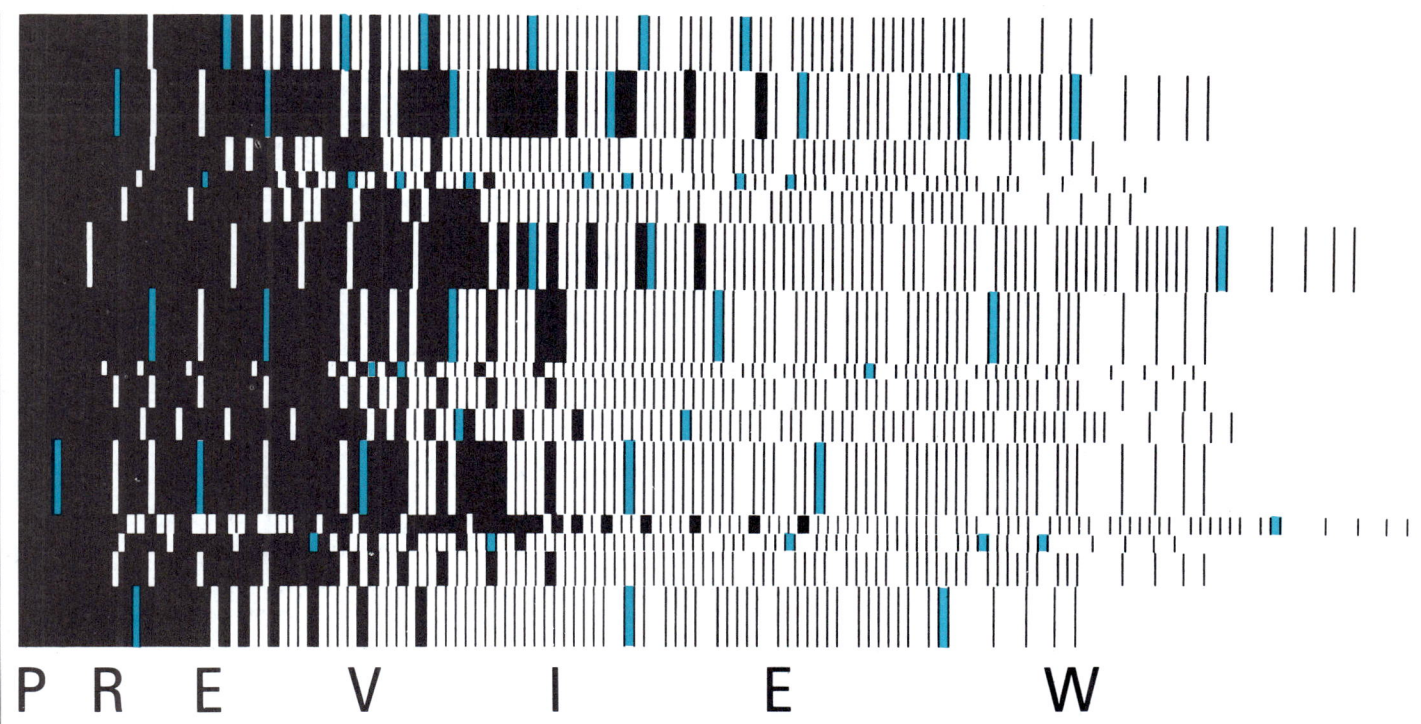

PREVIEW

In the previous chapters of this section, we have talked about databases as models, suggested an approach to database design, and discussed formal ways to evaluate a database design. In this chapter, we will illustrate these concepts. First, we will illustrate the design approach suggested in Chapter 3 by walking through the process of designing a database for Great Plains Music and Video Unlimited. Then we will evaluate our design using the material from Chapter 4.

THE PROBLEM

Recall from Chapter 2 that Great Plains Music and Video Unlimited hired consultants to help apply computing technology to meet their growing information management needs. At the suggestion of the consultants, Great Plains decided to automate the video rental portion of the business before proceeding with the rest of the system.

Now, management of Great Plains has decided to automate the Electronic Components Department. We have been hired as consultants to design the database. It should be an interesting project, so let's get started.

OUR APPROACH TO DATABASE DESIGN

In Chapter 3, we suggested one approach to database design. Recall that the basic steps were:

1. List the objects in the work environment.
2. Describe the relationships among the objects.
3. Decide what facts about the objects are important.
4. Designate the key columns.
5. Record the relationships among the objects.
6. Evaluate the design.

Let's follow these steps to prepare a design for Great Plains.

Step 1: List the Objects in the Work Environment

If we were employees of Great Plains, we would know the details of its business operations. We would have an intuitive knowledge of the objects in the work environment. But since we are outside consultants, we need to learn about the work environment of Great Plains by interviewing the people who work there every day.

Information Requirements From those interviews, we learn that the Electronic Components Department of Great Plains sells stereo equipment such as amplifiers, tuners, and compact disc players as well as large-screen televisions, video recorders, and related equipment.

Customers discuss their needs with a Great Plains salesperson. The salesperson helps the customer decide which components to buy to meet their needs. To help in this process, the salespeople would like to be able to call up information about the various components and display it on a computer screen.

Specifically, they want to know each component's item number, description, unit of measure (each, dozen, pint, etc.), quantity on hand, cost, and suggested selling price.

Salespeople periodically want to get a printout of the components' sales prices. They need these printouts listed by item description. They also need a printout which lists the components in order by item number.

The accountant wants the system to be able to print an inventory list of components which shows the quantities in stock and their costs.

Great Plains periodically mails sales literature to its customers. The person in charge of sales would like the computer to be able to print mailing labels for this purpose. Also, the system should be able to answer ad hoc questions about customers, such as "Which customers purchased item number XYZ within the last six months?" and "Which customers have purchased more than $500 in components from us?"

The salespeople are paid a base salary plus commissions on the amount of sales they make. Thus, the bookkeeper requires the system to print a report of sales revenues by salesperson for any given period.

Also, management informs us that they sometimes want employee lists showing the date the employee was hired, the base salary, the commission rate, and the date of the last salary change. For reporting to the IRS, the accountant needs each employee's name, social security number, marital status, withholding exemptions, and year-to-date earnings.

Picking Out Objects from the Requirements Try to identify the objects in the Electronic Components Department from the requirements. One way to do it is to rely on your grade-school English. You were told that nouns were people, places, and things. That's really what objects are. Why not read the information we got from the interviews again and pick out the nouns that seem to represent objects? (Don't confuse objects with facts about objects.)

See if you agree with the following list:

- CUSTOMERs
- INVENTORY
- SALEs
- EMPLOYEEs

The list is fairly straightforward. There is no way to say at this point whether or not it is "correct." The ultimate test will occur when the database is put into

FIGURE 5–1a

Objects in the work environment

use. You will find when you do database designs on your own that you will make several attempts before you get one you are happy with. So don't waste energy trying to get the "correct" one the first time.

Step 2: Describe the Relationships among the Objects

After we've listed the objects in the data model, we need to make sure our database reflects the relationships among the objects. A graphical tool is helpful in depicting the relationships in the database. We'll depict the objects in our model as boxes (See Figure 5–1a). It doesn't matter where we put the boxes. We'll just spread them out so we can connect them in a way that describes the relationships. Now we can take each object in turn and describe its relationship to the other objects.

The first step in describing relationships is to identify them. Then, for each identified relationship, we need to define what type of relationship exists and what constraints apply to the relationship.

EMPLOYEEs

Identifying Relationships Involving EMPLOYEE What relationships are EMPLOYEEs involved in? Only one—the one between EMPLOYEE and SALE. We can show that this relationship exists by drawing a line between the EMPLOYEE and SALE boxes (Figure 5–1b).

FIGURE 5–1b

Connecting EMPLOYEE and SALE

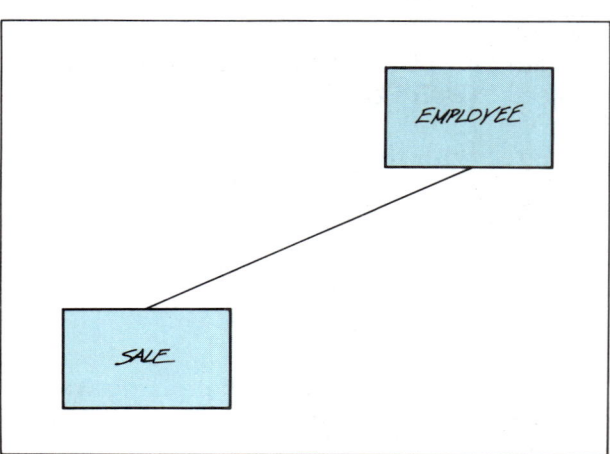

Defining the Type of Relationship There are basically three possible types of relationships:

1. *One-to-one* relationships are those in which there may be only one row in table A for any given row in table B and vice versa. For example, in a monogamous society, the relationship between HUSBAND and WIFE is one-to-one. For every row in the HUSBAND table, there may be only one corresponding row in the WIFE table. Likewise, for every row in the WIFE table, there may be only one corresponding row in the HUSBAND table.

2. *One-to-many* relationships are those in which there may be only one row in table A for any given row in table B but there may be many rows in table B for any given row in table A. That's the kind of relationship that exists between EMPLOYEE and SALE in our Great Plains example. Each SALE can involve only *one* EMPLOYEE, but each EMPLOYEE may be involved in *many* SALES.

3. *Many-to-many* relationships are those in which there may be many rows in table A for any given row in table B and vice versa. For example, the relationship between SALE and INVENTORY is many-to-many. Each INVENTORY item may be involved in many SALEs. Each SALE may involve many INVENTORY items.

We said that the relationship between EMPLOYEE and SALE is one-to-many. We've indicated this by putting a reverse arrow on the "many" side of the relationship line in Figure 5–1c.

Defining Relationship Constraints We have seen that answers often come from more than one table. For example, look at Figure 5–1d. If we need to know the phone number of the salesperson who made sale number 105, we get the Employee name from the SALE table, then look up the phone number from that employee's row in the EMPLOYEE table. The question can be answered only if there is an entry in the EMPLOYEE table for Paige.

To ensure that our model works, we need to express the requirement that no entry may be made in the SALE table if the EMPLOYEE information of the salesperson making the sale has not been entered. We've done that in Figure 5–1e. The small straight line across the relationship line near the EMPLOYEE box indicates that there must be an entry in the EMPLOYEE table for every entry in the SALE table.

The small circle across the relationship line next to the SALE box indicates that there need not be an entry

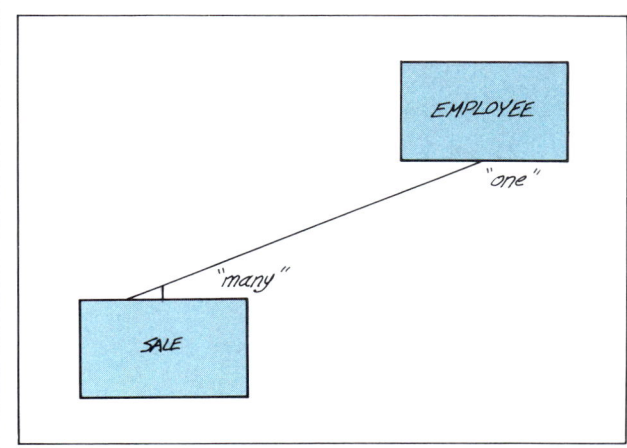

FIGURE 5–1c

Indicating the type of relationship

FIGURE 5–1d

Sample EMPLOYEE and SALE tables

EMPLOYEE

Employee name	Employee phone number
Paige	377-8642
Holly	223-5344
Heather	321-7550

SALE

Sale number	Employee name
101	Paige
102	Holly
103	Holly
104	Heather
105	Paige

FIGURE 5–1e
Indicating relationship constraints

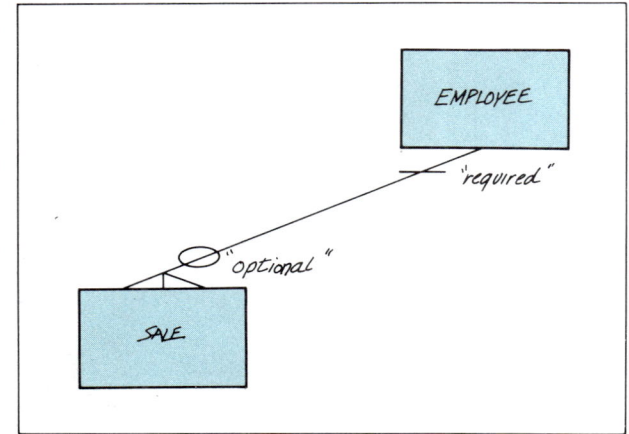

in the SALE table for every entry in the EMPLOYEE table. That way, we can record information about EMPLOYEEs without recording SALEs.

CUSTOMERs

Identifying Relationships Involving CUSTOMER What relationships are CUSTOMERs involved in? Only one—the one between CUSTOMER and SALE.

Defining the Type of Relationship A given SALE may involve only *one* CUSTOMER. However, a CUSTOMER may be involved in *many* SALES. Thus, the relationship between CUSTOMER and SALE is one-to-many. We've drawn the relationship line between CUSTOMER and SALE in Figure 5–1f.

Defining Relationship Constraints Next we decide about the constraints on this relationship. Will we require that every entry in the CUSTOMER table have a corresponding entry in the SALE table and vice versa? It's clear that we should require every entry in the SALE table to have a corresponding entry in the CUSTOMER table: we can't make a sale to a nonexistent customer. However, we should be able to record information about CUSTOMERs before we make any sales to them. We have indicated this constraint in Figure 5–1g.

FIGURE 5–1f
Adding the CUSTOMER/SALE relationship

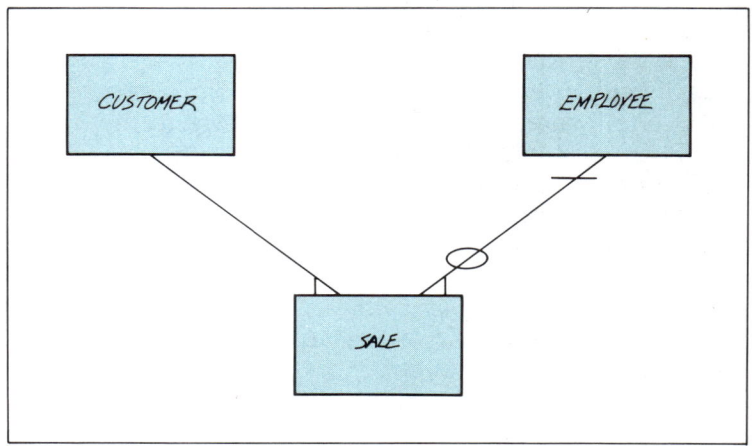

FIGURE 5–1g

Adding the CUSTOMER/SALE relationship constraints

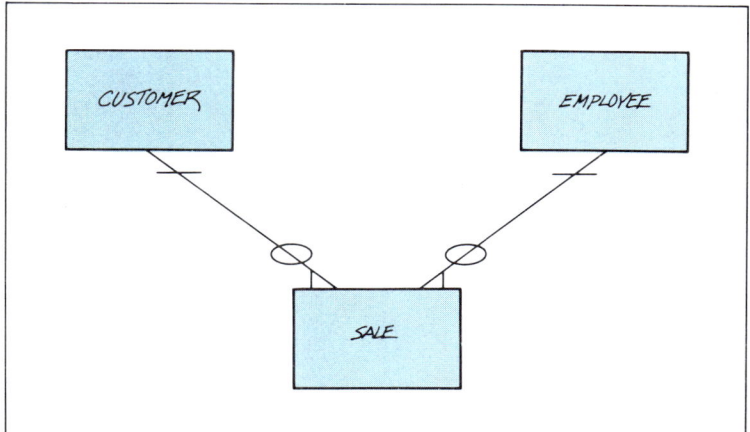

INVENTORY

Identifying Relationships Involving INVENTORY What are the relationships involving INVENTORY? INVENTORY items are related to SALEs.

Defining the Type of Relationship The relationship between INVENTORY and SALE is *many-to-many*. Why? An item of INVENTORY may be involved in *many* SALES. For example, there will be (we hope) *many* SALES of a particular make and model of amplifier. Similarly, any given SALE may involve *many* items of INVENTORY. For example, a single sale may involve a tuner, an amplifier, and a tape player.

Defining Relationship Constraints Finally, we need to define any constraints that exist on the relationship between INVENTORY and SALE. Can there be a sale without an INVENTORY item? Clearly the answer is no. Thus, we will require that there be a corresponding row in INVENTORY for every row in SALE. What about the reverse? Will we allow an INVENTORY row without a corresponding SALE row? Yes. Clearly, there will be times when there is information to record about INVENTORY before there are any SALEs of that INVENTORY item. We have added the relationship between INVENTORY and SALE to our design in (Figure 5–1h).

FIGURE 5–1h

Adding the COMPONENT/SALE relationship

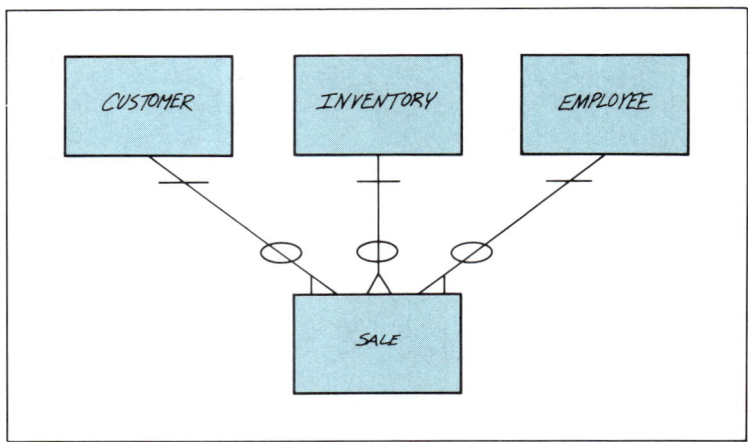

Step 3: Decide What Facts Are Important

Next, we need to decide how much detail the data model will have. Each object has a potentially unlimited number of characteristics we could measure and store in the database. However, as we have said, it is neither necessary nor desirable to make the model too detailed.

CUSTOMERs

Take customers, for example. Think of all the facts we could store about a customer: name, address, phone number, age, height, weight, measurements, shoe size, mother's name, favorite color, religious preference, spouse's name, kids' names, schools attended, favorite food, jobs held; the list is truly unlimited.

Some of these facts are important to us, some are not. While it makes sense to keep track of customers' addresses and phone numbers, it is unlikely that we'll ever need to know their shoe size. The point is, the details we include depend on the information the CUSTOMER table will be expected to produce. Sometimes making these choices is more art than science.

From the description of Great Plains' requirements, it looks like all we need is Customer name and Customer address. But common sense and experience tell us it would be a good idea to include Customer phone as well. We've added these columns to our design in Figure 5–2a.

FIGURE 5–2a

Object/column design—adding CUSTOMER columns

CUSTOMER (Customer name, Customer address, Customer phone)

INVENTORY

Salespeople periodically want to get a printout showing the sales prices of the components. They need these printouts listed by item description. They also need a printout which lists the components in order by item number.

The accountant wants the system to be able to print a list of components in inventory which shows the quantities in stock and the cost.

Look at the requirements. Pick out the facts we need to have in the database about INVENTORY. The salespeople seem to need Item number, Item description, Units, and Price. In addition, the accountant requires Quantity on hand and Cost. We have added these columns to our design in Figure 5–2b.

SALEs

The requirements indicate that the system should be able to produce a list of sales revenues by salesperson for any given period of time. This requirement implies these columns: Sales identification number, Customer, Salesperson, Date, and Amount. These columns have been added to the design in Figure 5–2c.

EMPLOYEEs

As with the other objects in the data model, we examine the information requirements to decide what facts to include about EMPLOYEEs. To meet the information needs of management, we'll need to include Employee name, Hire date, Salary, Commission rate, and Salary review date. In addition, to meet the requirements of the accountant, we'll need Social security number, Marital status, Exemptions, and Total wages. After adding these attributes, our design appears as in Figure 5–2d.

Step 4: Designating the Key Columns

In Chapter 3 we learned that each row in a relational database table is unique. We learned in Chapter 4 that key columns are columns or combinations of columns which uniquely identify each row in the table. To ensure that the tables in the database we are designing exhibit this characteristic, we need to designate key columns. Let's look at each table in the design as it now stands and indicate the key columns by underlining them.

FIGURE 5–2b

Object/column design—adding INVENTORY columns

> CUSTOMER (Customer name, Customer address, Customer phone)
>
> INVENTORY (Item number, Item description, Units, Quantity on hand, Cost, Price)

FIGURE 5–2c

Object/column design—adding SALE columns

> CUSTOMER (Customer name, Customer address, Customer phone)
>
> INVENTORY (Item number, Item description, Units, Quantity on hand, Cost, Price)
>
> SALE (Sales identification number, Customer name, Salesperson, Date, Amount)

FIGURE 5–2d

Object/column design—adding EMPLOYEE columns

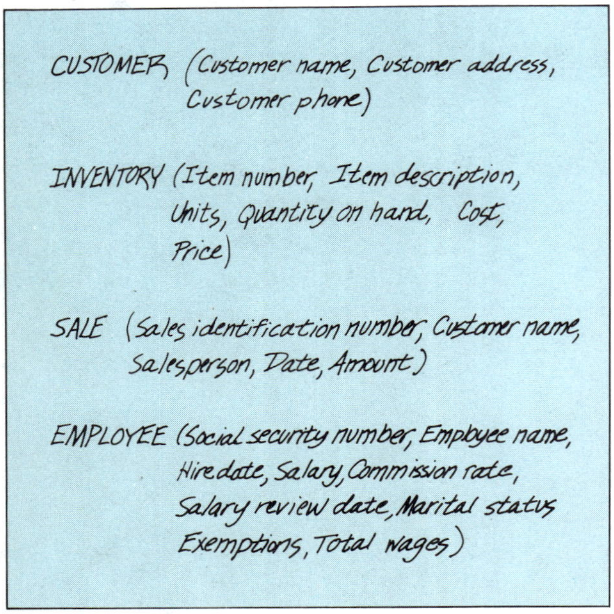

> CUSTOMER (Customer name, Customer address, Customer phone)
>
> INVENTORY (Item number, Item description, Units, Quantity on hand, Cost, Price)
>
> SALE (Sales identification number, Customer name, Salesperson, Date, Amount)
>
> EMPLOYEE (Social security number, Employee name, Hire date, Salary, Commission rate, Salary review date, Marital status, Exemptions, Total wages)

KEY FOR CUSTOMER

To choose a key, we look for a column or combination of columns which will uniquely identify each customer. We have three choices: Customer name, Customer address, and Customer phone. If we choose Customer name, we will not be able to have two customers with the same name in our database. This is a dangerous gamble—one we should not take. If we choose Customer address as the key, we cannot have two customers who live at the same address. It's likely that we may run into this situation, especially with college students. Customer phone has the same limitation.

It appears that none of the CUSTOMER columns alone is a good choice. In this situation, our options are to choose some combination of columns, such as Customer name and Customer phone, or to add a single column which *can* serve as key. Technically, either choice is valid. From a practical standpoint, the database will usually perform better if we choose to add a new column to serve as the key. We'll add Customer identification number to the CUSTOMER table for this purpose.

KEY FOR INVENTORY

Reviewing Figure 5–2d, we can see that the only logical choice as key for the INVENTORY table is Item number. Before making our final decision, we confirm with the users that Item number will always be unique for each component.

KEY FOR SALE

As with INVENTORY, there is a good candidate for the SALE key: Sales identification number.

KEY FOR EMPLOYEE

Here again, we have a logical choice for the key in Social security number.

The design, with the keys designated, is shown in Figure 5–3.

Step 5: Recording the Relationships

Relationships are represented in a relational database by the facts (columns) which the objects (tables) in the relationship have in common. Look at Figure 5–4. It's the same example we used in Chapter 3. Notice that both MEMBER and TRANS contain the column Member number. The relationship between MEMBER and TRANS is represented by the column which the two tables have in common. We'll refer to common columns which are used in this way as *links*.

There are two issues to be addressed when recording relationships in a database design: (1) choosing the column(s) to use as the link, and (2) placing the link.

Choosing the Link Not just any column can serve as a link. In order to serve as a link, the column or combination of columns taken together must uniquely identify a row in the table we're linking to. Sound familiar? That's the definition of *key* we used in Chapter 4.

Why is it important that the link be a key column? Look again at Figure 5–4. Member number is the key of MEMBER. That means that each value of Member

FIGURE 5–3
Object/column design with keys designated

CUSTOMER (Customer identification number, Customer name, Customer address, Customer phone)

INVENTORY (Item number, Item description, Units, Quantity on hand, Cost, Price)

SALE (Sales identification number, Customer name, Salesperson, Date, Amount)

EMPLOYEE (Social security number, Employee name, Hire date, Salary, Commission rate, Salary review date, Marital status, Exemptions, Total Wages)

FIGURE 5–4
Part of data model for video rental business

MEMBER

Member number	First name	Last name	Membership date
7	Mike	Franzen	11/14/80
1	Jim	O'Dell	09/06/72
6	Stanley	Abel	12/14/81
5	Greg	Abel	11/18/81

TRANS

Video number	Member number	Rental date	Return date	Charge
345	6	05/14/85	05/15/85	$2.00
719	1	05/15/85	05/17/85	$4.00
102	7	05/15/85	05/16/85	$2.00
304	6	05/14/85	05/15/85	$2.00
222	1	05/13/85	05/15/85	$4.00
719	5	05/13/85	05/15/85	$4.00
345	6	05/17/85	05/18/85	$2.00
222	5	05/16/85	05/17/85	$2.00
102	6	05/13/85	05/14/85	$2.00

number must be unique. Thus, we are assured that member number 7 will *always* be associated with the values "Mike," "Franzen," and "11/14/80" for First name, Last name, and Membership date, respectively. Whenever the value "7" appears for Member number in TRANS, we are assured that it refers to Mike Franzen. There can be no ambiguity in the information we get from the database. By the way, whenever a key from one table (such as Member number from MEMBER) appears in another table (such as Member number in TRANS), it is known as a *foreign key*.

What would happen if we had chosen Last name as the link between MEMBER and TRANS (Figure 5–5)? Notice we have two MEMBERs with the value "Abel" for Last name. Now, whenever "Abel" appears in TRANS, we do not know whether we are talking about Stanley Abel or Greg Abel. We get ambiguous answers from the database. The lesson is to *always choose keys to serve as links*.

FIGURE 5–5

Using Last name as the link

MEMBER

Member number	First name	Last name	Membership date
7	Mike	Franzen	11/14/80
1	Jim	O'Dell	09/06/72
6	Stanley	Abel	12/14/81
5	Greg	Abel	11/18/81

TRANS

Video number	Last name	Rental date	Return date	Charge
345	Abel	05/14/85	05/15/85	$2.00
719	O'Dell	05/15/85	05/17/85	$4.00
102	Franzen	05/15/85	05/16/85	$2.00
304	Abel	05/14/85	05/15/85	$2.00
222	O'Dell	05/13/85	05/15/85	$4.00
719	Abel	05/13/85	05/15/85	$4.00
345	Abel	05/17/85	05/18/85	$2.00
222	Abel	05/16/85	05/17/85	$2.00
102	Abel	05/13/85	05/14/85	$2.00

Placing the Link We have learned that the link must be a key. The question now arises, "Which table provides the link?" Look again at Figure 5–4. Why did we put the key of MEMBER in TRANS? Would it have been just as well to put the key of TRANS in MEMBER? The answer is no. Where the link is placed depends upon the type of relationship we are attempting to model. Let's see where to place the links in the various types of relationships.

One-to-One Relationships With one-to-one relationships, it doesn't matter theoretically where the key is placed. Choose the most stable of the two keys and place it in the other table. By "most stable," we mean the one which is least likely to change. For example, assume you had a database of spouses with two tables in it: HUSBAND and WIFE. Further assume that, for whatever reason, the key to HUSBAND was Telephone number and the key to WIFE was Social security number. To model the one-to-one relationship between HUSBAND and WIFE, place Social security number of the WIFE in the HUSBAND table.

This choice reflects the relationship we want to model. Also, social security numbers change very infrequently, whereas telephone numbers are often changed. There are no one-to-one relationships in Great Plains' component database.

One-to-Many Relationships To model one-to-many relationships, place the key from the "one" side of the relationship in the table for the "many" side. Why? Let's look at the options. Figure 5–6a contains MEMBER and TRANS tables with no linking columns. What are the options for linking the two tables?

- Option 1: Place a link from TRANS in MEMBER. One way to link MEMBER and TRANS is to put the key of TRANS (the "many" part of the relationship) in the MEMBER table (the "one" side of the relationship). The result is in Figure 5–6b. What happened? Basically, we've converted a table which was in domain/key normal form and created one that isn't. Predictably, in doing so we've created data redundancies and modification anomalies. We're going to waste a lot of storage space by storing redundant data. Why do we need to record Stanley Abel's name and membership date more than once?

    What will we have to do if Mr. Abel changes his

FIGURE 5–6a

MEMBER and TRANS with no linking attributes

MEMBER

Member number	First name	Last name	Membership date
6	Stanley	Abel	12/14/81

TRANS

Video number	Rental date	Return date	Charge
345	05/14/85	05/15/85	$2.00
304	05/14/85	05/15/85	$2.00
345	05/17/85	05/18/85	$2.00
102	05/13/85	05/14/85	$2.00

name? We'll have to search the MEMBER table for every "Stanley Abel" row and change the name in every one. Doing that would be very inconvenient. Also, think of the confusion and frustration that could arise if we missed a row.

Figure 5–6b

Option 1: Place the link in the "one" side

MEMBER

Member number	First name	Last name	Membership date	Video number	Rental date
6	Stanley	Abel	12/14/81	345	05/14/85
6	Stanley	Abel	12/14/81	304	05/14/85
6	Stanley	Abel	12/14/81	345	05/17/85
6	Stanley	Abel	12/14/81	102	05/13/85

TRANS

Video number	Rental date	Return date	Charge
345	05/14/85	05/15/85	$2.00
304	05/14/85	05/15/85	$2.00
345	05/17/85	05/18/85	$2.00
102	05/13/85	05/14/85	$2.00

- Option 2: <u>Place a link from MEMBER in TRANS</u>. Another way to link MEMBER and TRANS is to put the key from the MEMBER table (the "one" side of the relationship) in the TRANS table (the "many" side of the relationship). Look at the result in Figure 5–6c. Is it better than Figure 5–6b? Emphatically yes. Figure 5–6c is in domain/key normal form. Although we haven't eliminated redundant data, we have reduced it significantly. Also, since the table is now in domain/key normal form, we know there are no modification anomalies.

Thus, the best way to represent one-to-many relationships is to put the key from the "one" side of the relationship in the table for the "many" side of the relationship. Let's record the one-to-many relationships in Great Plains' database design.

Employee/Sale Since EMPLOYEE is the "one" side of this relationship, we should put the key of EMPLOYEE (Social security number) in the table for the "many" side of the relationship (SALE). The design currently has Salesperson as a column. All we need to do is change the name of the Salesperson column to Social security number.

Customer/Sale To record the one-to-many relationship between CUSTOMER and SALE, we add the key from the CUSTOMER table (Customer identification number) to SALE.

FIGURE 5–6c

Option 2: Place the link in the "many" side

MEMBER

Member number	First name	Last name	Membership date
6	Stanley	Abel	12/14/81

TRANS

Video number	Member number	Rental date	Return date	Charge
345	6	05/14/85	05/15/85	$2.00
304	6	05/14/85	05/15/85	$2.00
345	6	05/17/85	05/18/85	$2.00
102	6	05/13/85	05/14/85	$2.00

Many-to-Many Relationships A many-to-many relationship between two tables is represented by creating a third table to hold the links. Let's look at an example.

Assume Great Plains wants to keep track of its music tapes and their distributors. Further assume that each distributor can provide many different tapes and that any given tape can be obtained from many distributors. Thus, the relationship between distributors and tapes is many-to-many.

To build a data model of this situation, we begin by identifying TAPE and DISTRIBUTOR as the objects. We'll keep Title, Artist, Price, and Quantity facts in the TAPE table and Name, City, State, Zip, and Phone facts in the DISTRIBUTOR table. Figure 5–7a contains some sample data for these tables without any links. Assume that Great Plains can obtain both tapes from all three distributors.

Figure 5–7b shows the result of adding the key from DISTRIBUTOR to the TAPE table. To record the information that the two tapes can be obtained from all three distributors, we must add two rows for each tape. TAPE is now a nightmare. It is not in domain/key normal form since the key to TAPE is no longer Title. The combination of Title and Supplier now is needed to uniquely identify a given row. The columns Artist, Price, and Quantity are not dependent on the key (Title and Supplier). They are determined by Title, which is only part of the key.

The result of adding the key from TAPE to the DISTRIBUTOR table is left as an exercise to the student.

FIGURE 5-7a

TAPE and DISTRIBUTOR with no linking attributes

TAPE

Title	Artist	Price	Quantity
Beach Stuff	Beach People	$9.95	14
Hard Rock	Stevo	$9.95	12

DISTRIBUTOR

Name	City	State	Zip	Phone
Plains Dist.	Las Animas	CO	80444	366-7011
Lakes Dist.	Ogallala	NE	91442	333-2255
Ocean Dist	Eau Claire	WI	34455	222-6677

FIGURE 5-7b

Attempting to model many-to-many relationship by placing key from DISTRIBUTOR in TAPE

TAPE

Title	Artist	Price	Quantity	Name
Beach Stuff	Beach People	$9.95	14	Plains Dist.
Beach Stuff	Beach People	$9.95	14	Lakes Dist.
Beach Stuff	Beach People	$9.95	14	Ocean Dist.
Hard Rock	Stevo	$9.95	12	Plains Dist.
Hard Rock	Stevo	$9.95	12	Lakes Dist.
Hard Rock	Stevo	$9.95	12	Ocean Dist.

DISTRIBUTOR

Name	City	State	Zip	Phone
Plains Dist.	Las Animas	CO	80444	366-7011
Lakes Dist.	Ogallala	NE	91442	333-2255
Ocean Dist.	Eau Claire	WI	34455	222-6677

Figure 5-7c shows the addition of a new table, SOURCE. The new table has the keys from both TAPE and DISTRIBUTOR. You can see that the information regarding which DISTRIBUTORs supply which TAPEs is now contained in SOURCE. Also, all three tables are in domain/key normal form. The lesson is to *record many-to-many relationships by creating a new table containing the key from each side of the relationship.*

Inventory/Sale The relationship between INVENTORY and SALE in the Great Plains component database is many-to-many. We know we need to create a new table to model this relationship. Let's call the new table COMPONENT/SALE. To complete the recording of the relationship, we add the key from INVENTORY (Item number) and the key from SALE (Sales identification number) to the COMPONENT/SALE table.

An intersection table like COMPONENT/SALE often contains columns other than the columns which link the members of the many-to-many relationship. In this case, individual rows in COMPONENT/SALE represent individual items sold. For example, if a customer were to purchase a tape player, an amplifier, and three tapes, one row would be added to the SALE table and three rows

FIGURE 5-7c

Modeling many-to-many relationship with new table

TAPE

Title	Artist	Price	Quantity
Beach Stuff	Beach People	$9.95	14
Hard Rock	Stevo	$9.95	12

DISTRIBUTOR

Name	City	State	Zip	Phone
Plains Dist.	Las Animas	CO	80444	366-7011
Lakes Dist.	Ogallala	NE	91442	333-2255
Ocean Dist.	Eau Claire	WI	34455	222-6677

SOURCE

Title	Name
Beach Stuff	Plains Dist.
Beach Stuff	Lakes Dist.
Beach Stuff	Ocean Dist.
Hard Rock	Plains Dist.
Hard Rock	Lakes Dist.
Hard Rock	Ocean Dist.

would be added to COMPONENT/SALE: one for the tape player, one for the amplifier, and one for the tapes.

Accordingly, the Amount column which we originally included in the SALE table should now be moved to COMPONENT/SALE. To make the design flexible, we will expand COMPONENT/SALE to include Quantity sold, Selling price, and Sales amount. We complete the design by indicating the key columns of COMPONENT/SALE by underlining Item number and Sales identification number.

The final design is in Figure 5–8. Notice that Customer name no longer appears in SALE. That's because we can now get customer name from CUSTOMER via the link between CUSTOMER and SALE, Customer identification number. Also, the foreign key of EMPLOYEE, Social security number now replaces the Salesperson column in SALE.

Step 6: Evaluate the Design

The last step in database design is to evaluate the design using the standards set forth in Chapter 4. We can evaluate the design by asking the following questions:

- Does each table have a single theme?
- Is each table in domain/key normal form?
- Are dependencies intact?
- Is the database easy to use?

DOES EACH TABLE HAVE A SINGLE THEME?

Look at the table/column design in Figure 5–8b. Every table has only one theme. EMPLOYEE deals only with facts about employees, CUSTOMER deals only with facts about customers, and so forth. We can therefore answer yes to this first question.

IS EACH TABLE IN DOMAIN/KEY NORMAL FORM?

Recall from Chapter 4 that tables are in domain/key normal form if all the restrictions on the table are a logical consequence of domain and key definitions or are the result of simple inclusion constraints.

By carefully reviewing the design, you will see that the tables are in domain/key normal form. The only restrictions we have defined are key restrictions and simple inclusion constraints. We have purposely postponed domain definitions until the next chapter. But domain restrictions cannot violate domain/key normal form. Accordingly, the tables are in domain/key normal form.

ARE DEPENDENCIES INTACT?

By approaching the design of the database in the suggested manner, we have avoided splitting dependencies.

IS THE DATABASE EASY TO USE?

We won't know the answer to this question until we actually implement the design in the succeeding chapters. However, if the design meets the other criteria, the chances are it will be easy to use.

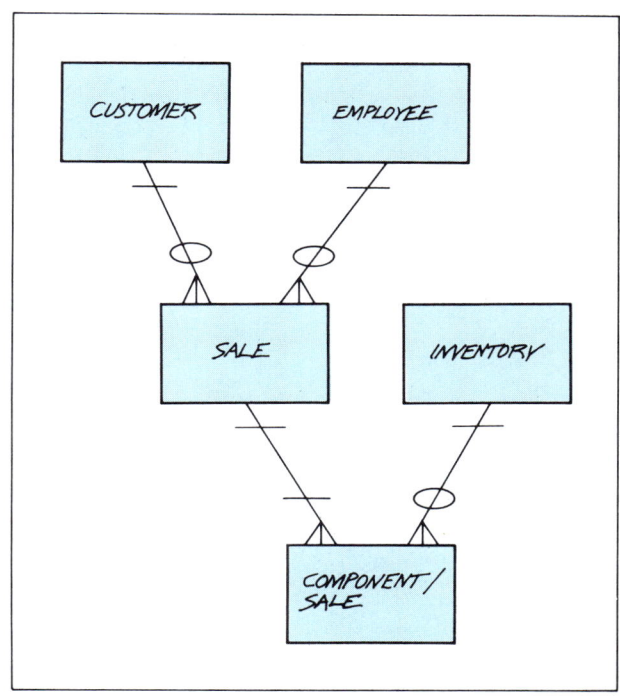

FIGURE 5–8a

Completed design—object/relationships

FIGURE 5–8b

Completed design—table/columns

CUSTOMER (<u>Customer identification number</u>, Customer name, Customer address, Customer phone)
INVENTORY (<u>Item number</u>, Item description, Units, Quantity on hand, Cost, Price)
SALE (<u>Sales identification number</u>, Customer identification number, Social security number, Date)
COMPONENT/SALE (<u>Item number</u>, <u>Sales identification number</u>, Quantity sold, Sales price, Sales amount)
EMPLOYEE (<u>Social security number</u>, Employee name, Hire date, Salary, Commission rate, Salary review date, Marital status, Exemptions, Total wages)

SUMMARY

- We designed a database for Great Plains Music and Video Unlimited by following the suggested approach:
    - List the objects in the work environment.
    - Describe the relationships among the objects.
    - Decide what facts about the objects are important.
    - Designate the key columns.
    - Record the relationships among the objects.
    - Evaluate the design.
- If the database designer is not familiar with the work environment, requirements must be obtained through interviews with the potential users of the database.
- Describing relationships among objects comprises:
    - Identifying the relationships
    - Defining the type of relationship
    - Defining the constraints on the relationship
- There are three possible types of relationships:
    - One-to-one relationships
    - One-to-many relationships
    - Many-to-many relationships
- The facts which are included in the database are dependent on the information which the database will be expected to provide.
- A key column is a column or combination of columns which uniquely identifies a row in the table.
- Relationships are represented in a relational database by the facts (columns) which the objects (tables) in the relationship have in common. These columns are called *links*.
- Only key columns should serve as links.
- A key from one table which appears in another table is known as a *foreign key*.
- The placement of the link depends upon the type of relationship which is being modeled:
    - *One-to-one* relationships: use the most stable key and place it in the other table.
    - *One-to-many* relationships: place the key from the "one" side of the relationship in the table of the "many" side of the relationship.

- *Many-to-many* relationships: create a new table for the relationship which contains the key columns from each side of the relationship.
- Evaluate the database design by asking the following questions:
  - Does each table have a single theme?
  - Is each table in domain/key normal form?
  - Are dependencies intact? *(not separated)*
  - Is the database easy to use?

REVIEW QUESTIONS

Group I Questions

5.1
List the steps in the suggested approach to database design.

5.2
Name the three types of database relationships. Give an example of each. Do not use the examples given in the text.

5.3
What are the steps involved in describing relationships?

5.4
How do relationship constraints relate to domain/key normal form?

5.5
Why do we say that it is not desirable to make the database too detailed?

5.6
Which column(s) would you use as keys for the following: (If you think it is appropriate, create a new column to use for the key.)

  a. FACULTY (First name, Last name, Address, Phone)

  b. STUDENT (Student ID number, First name, Last name)

  c. COURSE (Title, Days held, Time, Credit hours)

  d. TEXT (Author, Title, Edition, Price)

5.7
For the examples you provided in response to Question 5.2, create table definitions and designate the key column(s).

5.8
For the table definitions in Question 5.7, place the links to properly model the relationships among the tables.

5.9
Explain why only key columns should be used to link tables.

PROJECT

Design a database of your academic environment. Your database should allow you to answer questions about the courses you have taken, the grade you received in the course, the rating (from 1 to 10) which you gave the course, the instructors you have had, the textbooks you have used, and the textbooks' publishers and authors.

At a minimum, you should be able to answer questions such as, "In which of the courses I have taken that are rated 8 or more did I receive a grade of A or B?" "Which courses have I taken which were taught by instructor X?" "Which text was used in course ABC?" "Which textbooks have I used which were written by Z?" and "What courses did I take during the fall semester of 1985?" Feel free to add information requirements of your own.

Follow the approach suggested in the text. Your design should include a finished object/relationship plan and a table/column design.

CHAPTER 6

Database Implementation–Personnel Data

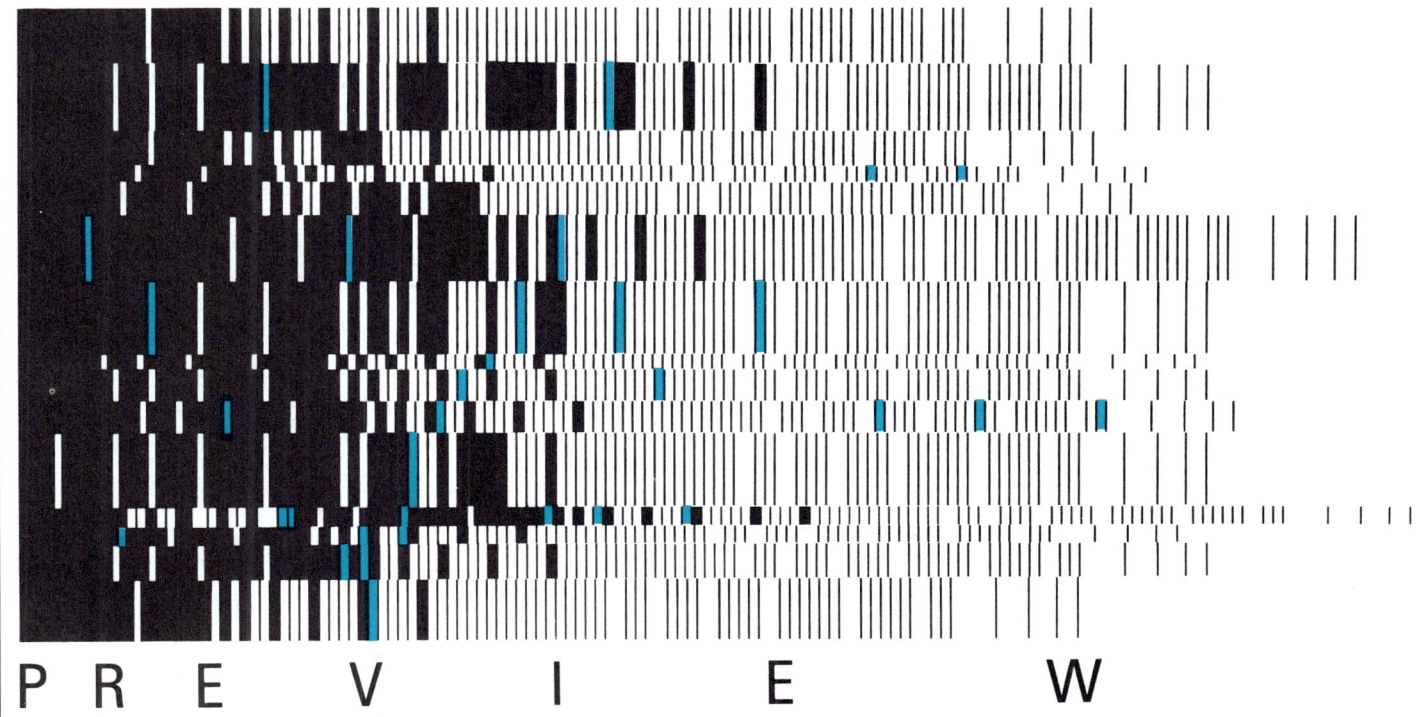

PREVIEW

It is time to implement the design we produced in Chapter 5. In this chapter, we will begin implementation with R:base 5000 by using the Application EXPRESS (the EXPRESS) to define the EMPLOYEE table. We will use the R:base LOAD WITH PROMPTS command to load some data into the EMPLOYEE table. Next, we will illustrate the use of the R:base SELECT and COMPUTE commands to answer questions about EMPLOYEEs. We will then change data using the EDIT command. Last, we will briefly discuss the HELP and PROMPT features of R:base.

FIGURE 6-1
Application EXPRESS main menu

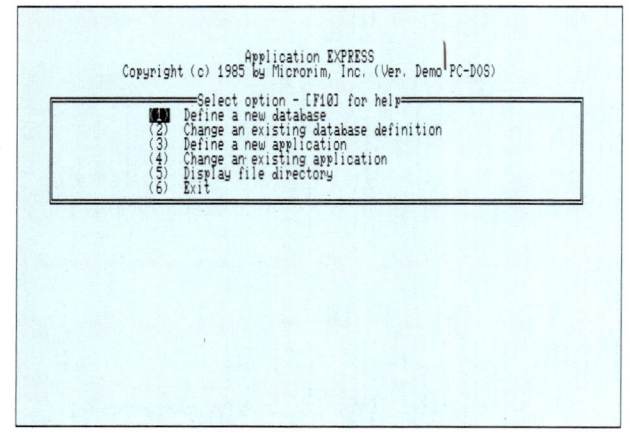

FIGURE 6-2
Providing the database name

FIGURE 6-3
Graphical representation of a blank table

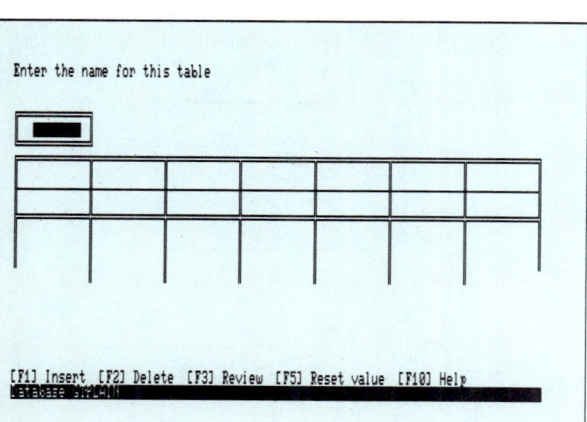

DATABASE DEFINITION USING THE EXPRESS

There are five steps to database definition with the EXPRESS:

1. Load the EXPRESS.
2. Select "Define a new database" from the EXPRESS main menu.
3. Provide the database name.
4. Define the table(s).
5. Exit the EXPRESS.

Let's follow these five steps to begin definition of the Great Plains Music and Video Unlimited database.

Step 1: Load the EXPRESS

Loading the EXPRESS is a simple matter. Detailed instructions for doing so have been provided to your instructor with the master R:base diskettes.

Step 2: Select "Define a new database" from the EXPRESS Main Menu

You are first presented with the EXPRESS main menu (Figure 6–1). Select "Define a new database" by pressing [1].

Step 3: Provide the Database Name

Next, the EXPRESS asks you to "Enter your database name (1–7 characters)." We'll use GTPLAIN as our database name. Enter "GTPLAIN" and press [ENTER]. (See Figure 6–2.)

Step 4: Define the Table(s)

The EXPRESS now presents you with a graphical representation of a blank table (Figure 6–3). You are asked to "Enter the name for this table." (Microrim Inc., the vendors of R:base and the EXPRESS use the terms TABLE, COLUMN, and ROW for the relational database concepts RELATION, ATTRIBUTE, and TUPLE, respectively. We'll use the terms TABLE, COLUMN, and ROW throughout this section of the book.) The name of the table is EMPLOYEE. After you enter the table name and press [ENTER], the first column is highlighted and you are asked to enter the name of the first column (Figure 6–4).

Column Names Column names may contain from one to eight characters. In general, the only other limitation is that you may not use certain R:base reserved words as column names. If you attempt to use a reserved word,

FIGURE 6–4
Ready to enter name of first column

FIGURE 6–5
R:base reserved words

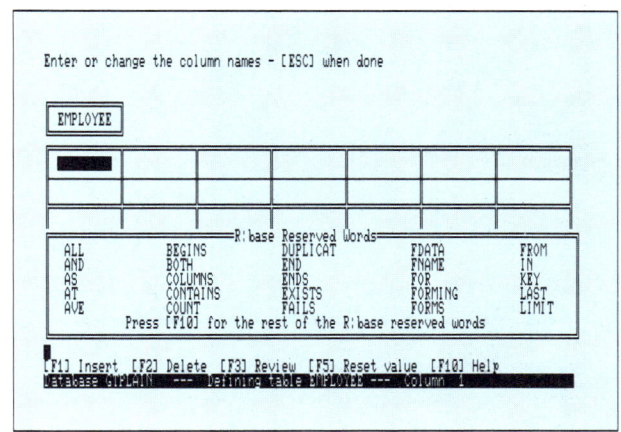

R:base will give you a message to that effect. You can get a list of the reserved words at this point by pressing the [F10] key twice (Figure 6–5). Press [ESC] to resume.

Figure 6–6 contains the final database design we produced in Chapter 5. The first column in the EMPLOYEE table is Social security number. Because that name is longer than eight characters, use EmpID# (Employee identification number) as the name for the column. After entering column name and

FIGURE 6–6a
Completed design—object/relationships

FIGURE 6–6b
Completed design—table/columns

CUSTOMER (<u>Customer identification number</u>, Customer name, Customer address, Customer phone)
INVENTORY (<u>Item number</u>, Item description, Units, Quantity on hand, Cost, Price)
SALE (<u>Sales identification number</u>, Customer identification number, Social security number, Date)
COMPONENT/SALE (<u>Item number</u>, <u>Sales identification number</u>, Quantity sold, Sales price, Sales amount)
EMPLOYEE (<u>Social security number</u>, Employee name, Hire date, Salary, Commission rate, Salary review date, Marital status, Exemptions, Total wages)

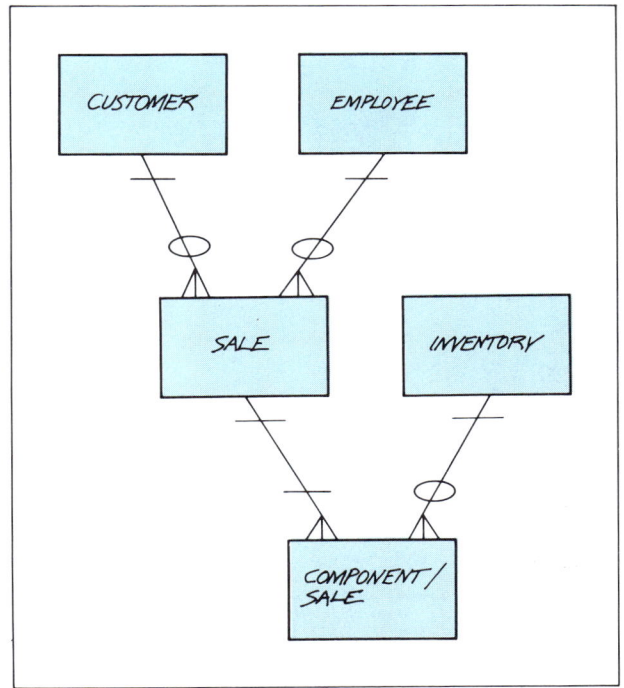

FIGURE 6–7

Selecting a column's data type

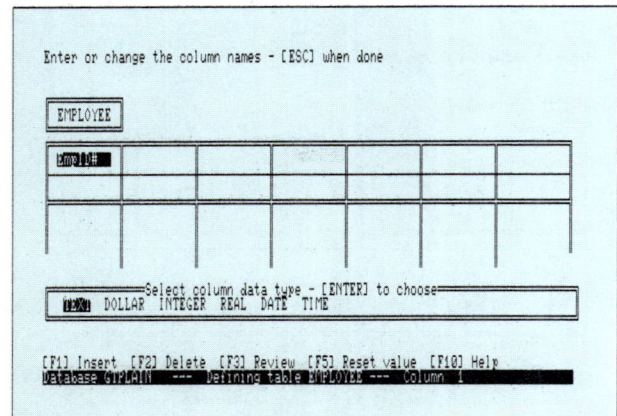

pressing [ENTER], you are asked to select the type of data which the column will contain (Figure 6–7).

Column Data Types R:base provides the following data types:

- TEXT: Text columns are for alphanumeric data such as names, street addresses, descriptions, and comments. R:base TEXT columns may be up to 1500 characters in length.

- DOLLAR: Dollar columns may represent currency amounts of plus or minus $99,999,999,999,999.99.

- INTEGER: Integers are whole numbers such as 1, 43, and −25. In R:base, integers must fall within the range of plus or minus 999,999,999.

- REAL: Real numbers are numbers with fractional parts, such as 2.813 and −6.2. R:base real numbers may be between plus or minus 9×10^{38}.

- DATE: Date columns represent the month, day, and year in any of the following formats:
    mm/dd/yy (default)
    mm/yy/dd
    dd/mm/yy
    dd/yy/mm
    yy/mm/dd
    yy/dd/mm
    mmmddyyyy

    We will use the R:base SET DATE command to change the date format in Chapters 9 and 11.

- TIME: R:base represents the time in hours, minutes, and seconds in the format hh:mm:ss.

You can use either TEXT or INTEGER for the Employee identification number if you do not need to use embedded hyphens (e.g., 523-54-8713). If you need the hyphens, you must choose TEXT. If you anticipate performing any mathematical operations, you must choose INTEGER. For the Great Plains application, it really doesn't matter. Since TEXT is already highlighted, all you need to do is press [ENTER]. To select one of the other options, highlight the option you want by pressing the first letter of the desired option and then press [ENTER]. For TEXT type columns, the EXPRESS prompts you for a column width (Figure 6–8).

Column Width TEXT columns may be from 1 to 1500 characters wide. If you do not enter a width, R:base assigns a width of 8. For Employee identification number, type 9, then press [ENTER].

FIGURE 6–8
Selecting column width

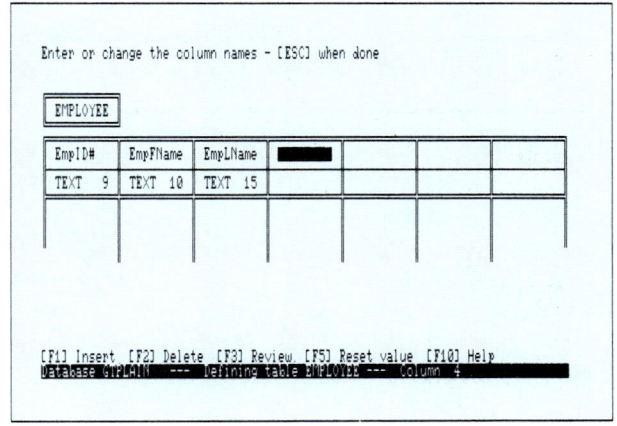

FIGURE 6–9
Definition of all columns

Completing the Definition of the EMPLOYEE Table The other columns in the EMPLOYEE table are defined in the same way: provide the name, type, and width (for TEXT columns). The completed definition is shown in Figure 6–9. We have broken Employee name into EmpFName and EmpLName so the EMPLOYEE table now has ten columns.

Notice the next-to-last line on the screen:

[F1] Insert [F2] Delete [F3] Review [F5] Reset value [F10] Help

This row is a definition of the operations of the function keys normally found in two parallel rows on the left side of the keyboard. The [F1] and [F2] keys are used to insert and delete columns, respectively. Simply move the highlighted area to the desired column using the [TAB] key and the right arrow key located on key 6 of the number pad on the right side of the keyboard. If you wish to insert a column, press [F1]. To delete the highlighted column, press [F2].

The [F3] key is used to display the tables and columns already defined in the database. Since EMPLOYEE is the first table defined for the GTPLAIN database, pressing [F3] at this point will result in a message to the effect that "No tables are defined for this database."

[F5] is used when you have begun to change a column name and change your mind. When you press [F5], the EXPRESS replaces the changes you made with the original entry.

FIGURE 6–10
Menu of table options

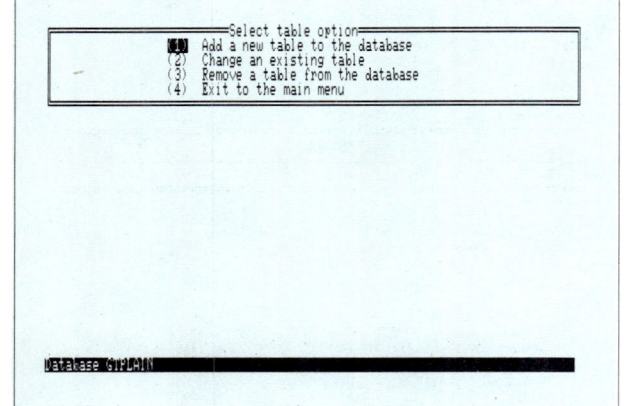

FIGURE 6–11
Menu of R:base options

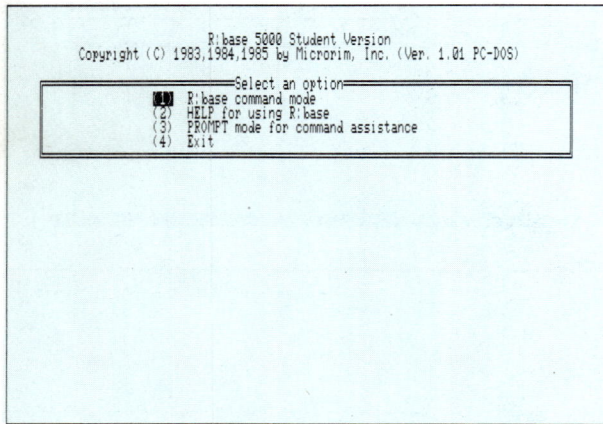

[F10] provides you with a help screen appropriate to wherever you happen to be in the EXPRESS.

To complete the definition of the EMPLOYEE table, press the [ESC] key. The EXPRESS presents the menu in Figure 6–10. Since the only table to be defined at this point is EMPLOYEE, return to the main menu by pressing [4].

Step 5: Exit the EXPRESS

Exit the EXPRESS by pressing [6].

USING THE LOAD WITH PROMPTS COMMAND

Now that you have a database defined, you'll want to enter some data. Follow the instructions provided with the R:base disks to load R:base. After R:base is loaded, you will receive the menu in Figure 6–11. You'll be working with the R:base command mode, so press [1] or [ENTER].

The next thing you have to do is tell R:base which database to work with. To do that, type:

OPEN GTPLAIN

and press [ENTER]. (Note: For the balance of this book, we will omit the words "and press [ENTER].") R:base confirms that the database exists (Figure 6–12).

Take a look at the database defined with the EXPRESS by typing:

LIST EMPLOYEE

FIGURE 6–12
Confirmation that database exists

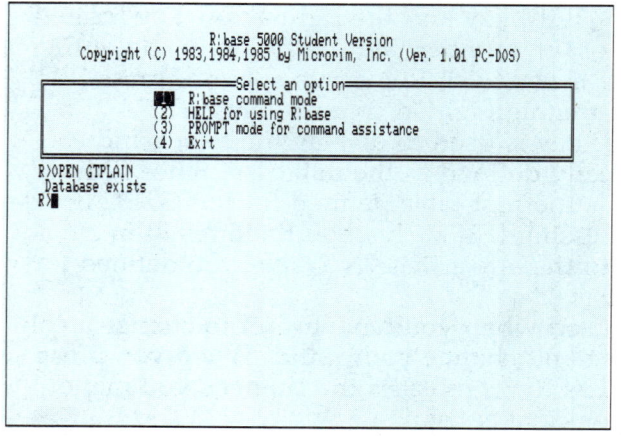

(See Figure 6–13.) Use the LIST (tablename) command anytime you want to see the current definition of any table in the database.

There are a number of ways to load data into an R:base database. One way is to have R:base prompt for the values to be loaded into each column of the table. Type:

LOAD EMPLOYEE WITH PROMPTS

R:base then presents the message "Press [ESC] to end, [ENTER] to continue." Press [ENTER] to load data. Next, R:base prompts for a value for each column in the table. To enter data, type the data value, then press [ENTER]. R:base checks the data for the correct type and, in the case of TEXT columns, length. Figure 6–14 shows what the computer screen looks like after data for Grace Potter is entered.

R:base again presents the message "Press [ESC] to end, [ENTER] to continue." If there are more employees to record, press [ENTER]. Once the last employee record has been entered, press [ESC] to return to the command mode.

USING SELECT AND COMPUTE

(If you want to use the data shown in the screens that follow, load the EMPLOYEE table with the data shown in Figure 6–28. If you have the file CH6.DAT available, you can load the data by typing: INPUT CH6.DAT.) The reason we define a database and load it with data is to be able to answer questions. Two R:base commands can be used to answer a variety of questions from a single table: SELECT and COMPUTE.

Select

The SELECT command is used to display data from a table. With this single command, you can specify which rows and columns are to be displayed and the order in which to display them.

In its simplest form, there are four parts to the SELECT command: the key word SELECT, the list of columns to be displayed (or ALL), the key word FROM, and the name of the table. For example, to display all the columns for all the rows in the EMPLOYEE table, type:

SELECT ALL FROM EMPLOYEE

The result is in Figure 6–15. Notice that only six of the nine columns have been displayed. That's because the computer screen is only wide enough to accommodate the first six columns of the EMPLOYEE table.

FIGURE 6–13
EMPLOYEE table definition

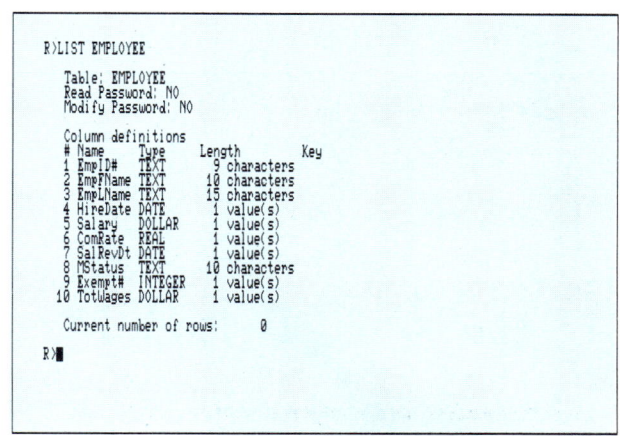

FIGURE 6–14
Using LOAD WITH PROMPTS to load data

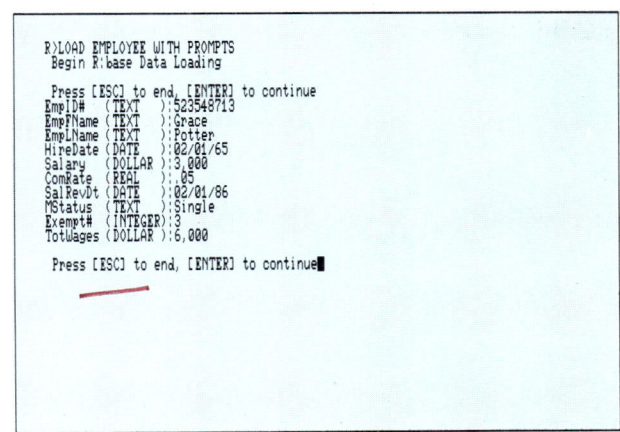

FIGURE 6–15
Displaying EMPLOYEE data with SELECT

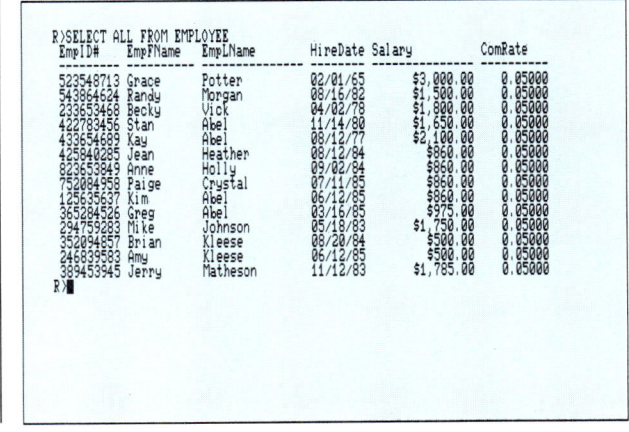

FIGURE 6–16

Displaying EMPLOYEE names with SELECT

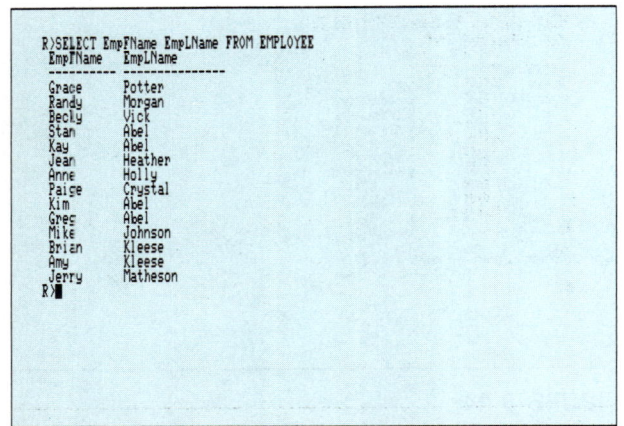

If you want a list of employee names, type:

SELECT EmpFName EmpLName FROM EMPLOYEE

(See Figure 6–16.) Use of SELECT in this way displays data from all the rows in the EMPLOYEE table. Also, the data is presented in the order in which it happens to exist in the table. However, in many cases you'll want to specify the rows from which data is selected or control the order in which the data is displayed. R:base gives you this ability with two optional parts of the SELECT command: the WHERE clause and the SORTED BY clause.

Using the WHERE Clause to Specify Rows The WHERE clause is used to specify the rows which are affected by an R:base command. In this case, it is used to specify the rows which are displayed by the SELECT command. The WHERE clause has two parts: the key word WHERE and a condition list. The condition list describes the rows you want to have displayed.

For example, assume that you want a list of employees whose last name is Abel. Use a WHERE clause to specify the rows in the EMPLOYEE table where the EmpLName column has a value of "Abel" by typing:

SELECT EmpFName EmpLName FROM EMPLOYEE + WHERE EmpLName EQ Abel

as in Figure 6–17. (Use the plus sign [+] whenever

FIGURE 6–17

Displaying EMPLOYEEs named Abel

the command you are entering requires more than one line.) In addition to the EQ(uals) operator, you may use NE (not equal), GT (greater than), GE (greater than or equal), LT (less than), or LE (less than or equal). For example, to obtain a list of employees with last names other than Abel, type:

SELECT EmpFName EmpLName FROM EMPLOYEE +
WHERE EmpLName NE Abel

(See Figure 6–18.) Or, to obtain a list of employees whose last names begin with letters within the range H through K, type:

SELECT EmpFName EmpLName FROM EMPLOYEE +
WHERE EmpLName GE H AND EmpLName LE K

(See Figure 6–19.)

These examples use one of the eight possible types of conditions available with R:base (column name op value—where op means "operator" such as EQ). The other seven are:

- Column name EXISTS
- Column name FAILS
- Column name op column name
- Column name CONTAINS string
- LIMIT EQ value
- COUNT EQ value
- COUNT EQ LAST

Specifying Rows with Column Values That EXIST or FAIL Sometimes you'll want to see all rows in a table where a specified column has been given a value regardless of what the value is. For example, suppose you want to see the names of the employees with any entry in the HireDate column. Type:

SELECT EmpFName EmpLName FROM EMPLOYEE +
WHERE HireDate EXISTS

Conversely, you may want the names of only those employees whose HireDate has not been entered. If so, type:

SELECT EmpFName EmpLName FROM EMPLOYEE +
WHERE HireDate FAILS

FIGURE 6–18

Displaying EMPLOYEEs not named Abel

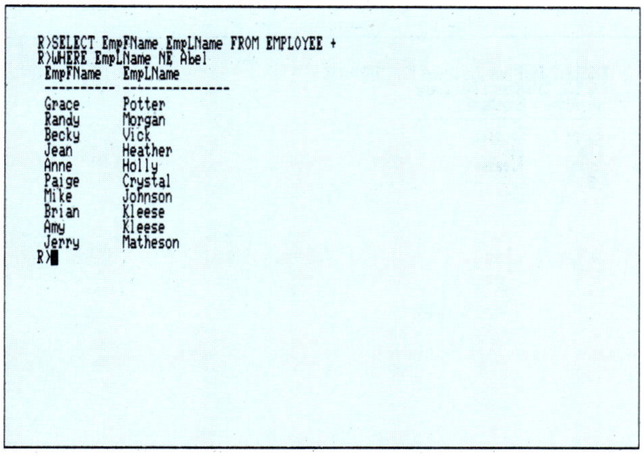

FIGURE 6–19

Displaying names beginning with H through K

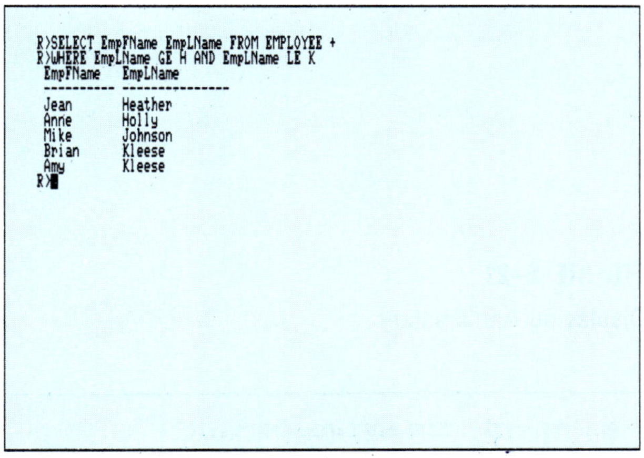

FIGURE 6-20

EMPLOYEEs whose wages are less than $1,000

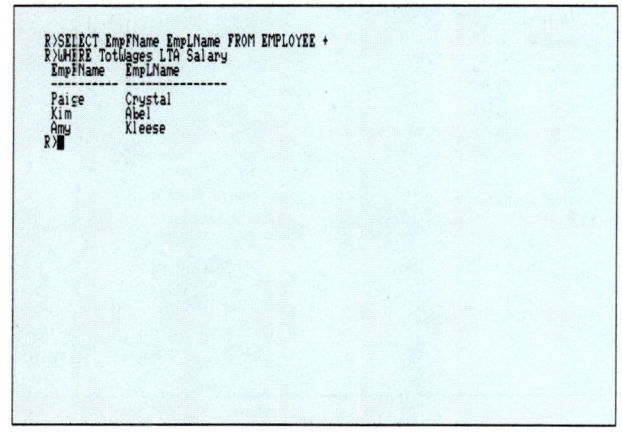

FIGURE 6-21

Displaying Ann's salary

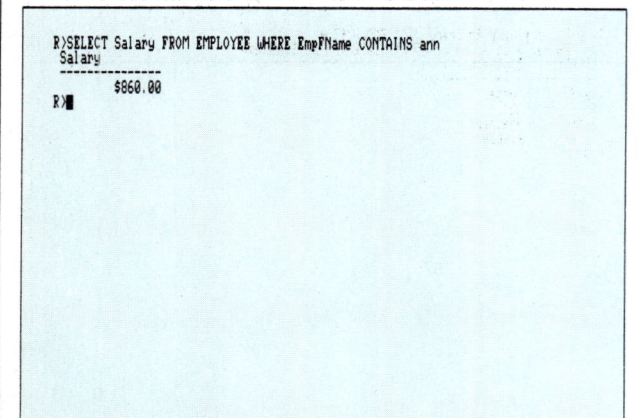

This condition type may be used with any data type column: TEXT, REAL, INTEGER, DOLLAR, DATE, or TIME. Keep in mind that there is a very important distinction between columns with no entry (NULL value) and numeric columns with an entry of zero (0). Zero is a value. A numeric column containing an entry of zero EXISTS. Do not use EXISTS or FAILS to look for columns with a value of zero. Instead, use "column name EQ 0" to find the rows with a value of zero in the specified column.

Specifying Rows by Comparing One Column to Another Instead of comparing a column to a specified value as you did in the first examples of the WHERE clause above, you can compare the value of two columns. For example, to obtain a list of employees whose year-to-date wages are less than their monthly salary, type:

SELECT EmpFName EmpLName FROM EMPLOYEE +
WHERE TotWages LTA Salary

(See Figure 6-20.) For each row in the EMPLOYEE table, R:base compares the value in the TotWages column to the value in the Salary column. If TotWages is less than Salary for the row, R:base displays the value from the EmpFName and EmpLName columns.

You may have R:base determine whether the two columns are equal to one another (EQA), not equal to one another (NEA), the first is greater than the second (GTA), the first is greater than or equal to the second (GEA), the first is less than the second (LTA), or the first is less than or equal to the second (LEA).

Specifying Rows with a Column Value That CONTAINS a String Sometimes you'll want to have data displayed from rows where a TEXT column contains a specified sequence of characters. For example, suppose you want to know the monthly salary of a certain employee. You can't remember her last name or her employee identification number, but you do know that her first name contains the letters, ann. You can get her monthly salary with the command:

SELECT Salary FROM EMPLOYEE +
WHERE EmpFName CONTAINS ann

(See Figure 6-21.) You can use this type of condition to search for a phrase. Whenever you want to specify a string of characters that includes embedded blanks, enclose the string with quotation marks. For example, assume that you have a table called ANYTABLE with a Comments column which is 1500 characters wide. Further assume that you want to see the ID# data from each row in the table where the Comments column contains the phrase, "Now is the time." Use the command:

SELECT ID# FROM ANYTABLE WHERE Comments +
CONTAINS "now is the time"

Limiting the Number of Rows You can limit the number of rows that are displayed by using a LIMIT condition. For example, to get the names of the first three employees in the EMPLOYEE table, type:

SELECT EmpFName EmpLName FROM EMPLOYEE +
WHERE LIMIT EQ 3

Specifying a Row on the Basis of Its Position in the Table In some circumstances, you may wish to see data from the *n*th row in the table. For example, assume you want to select an employee at random. You have chosen 8 as the random number. Now, you want to know which employee data occupies the eighth row in the EMPLOYEE table. Find out by typing:

SELECT EmpFName EmpLName FROM EMPLOYEE +
WHERE COUNT EQ 8

It is an easy matter to find the first row in a table. Simply use either "WHERE COUNT EQ 1" or "WHERE LIMIT EQ 1." But what if you want the last row in the table? That too is a simple matter. R:base includes a special case of the COUNT condition. To obtain the name of the employee whose data occupies the last row in the table type:

SELECT EmpFName EmpLName FROM EMPLOYEE +
WHERE COUNT EQ LAST

Combining Conditions You may combine a maximum of ten conditions in a WHERE clause. For example, to obtain a list of employees whose salaries are due for review in August of 1985, use the command:

SELECT EmpFName EmpLName FROM EMPLOYEE +
WHERE SalRevDt GE 08/01/85 AND SalRevDt LE 08/31/85

(See Figure 6–22.)
   The conditions within a given WHERE clause may

FIGURE 6–22

August 1985 EMPLOYEE salary reviews

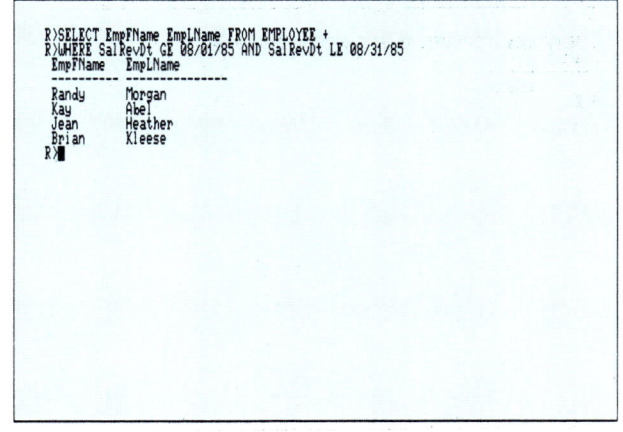

FIGURE 6–23

Using AND with OR in a WHERE clause

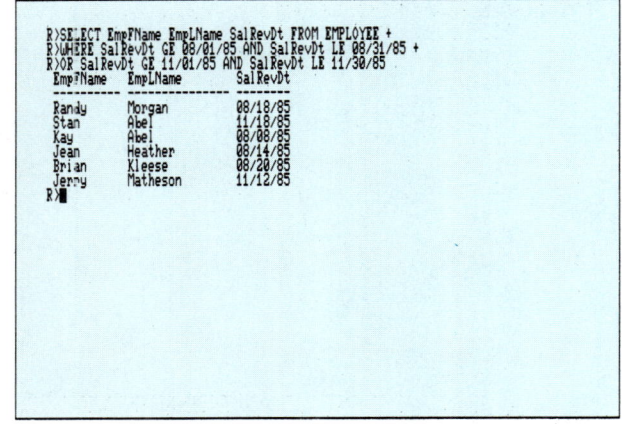

FIGURE 6–24

Using a SORTED BY clause

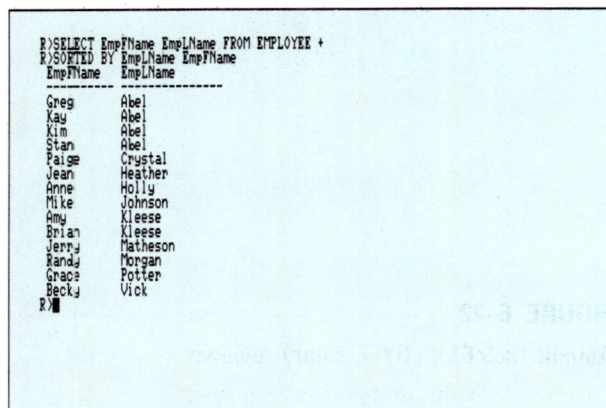

be connected using AND and OR. AND and OR may be combined in the same WHERE clause. For example, to obtain a list of employees whose salaries are due for review in August 1985 or November 1985, type:

SELECT EmpFName EmpLName SalRevDt FROM EMPLOYEE +
WHERE SalRevDt GE 08/01/85 AND SalRevDt LE 08/31/85 +
OR SalRevDt GE 11/01/85 AND SalRevDt LE 11/30/85

(See Figure 6–23.)

Using the SORTED BY Clause to Sort Displayed Data You can use the SORTED BY clause to obtain the display in sorted order. For example, you can obtain an alphabetical list of employees by typing:

SELECT EmpFName EmpLName FROM EMPLOYEE +
SORTED BY EmpLName EmpFName

(See Figure 6–24.)

To obtain a list of employees sorted by their hire date, type:

SELECT EmpFName EmpLName FROM EMPLOYEE +
SORTED BY HireDate

(See Figure 6–25.)

R:base lists the employees with the earliest hire date first. If you do not specify a sorting order, R:base as-

FIGURE 6–25

EMPLOYEEs sorted by hire date

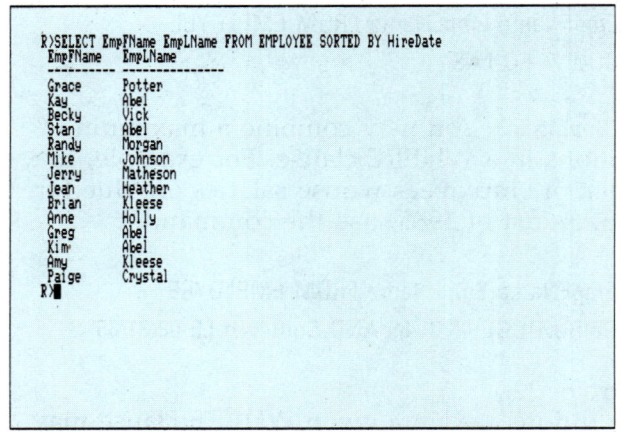

sumes ascending order. If you want the employees with the latest hire date first, type:

SELECT EmpFName EmpLName FROM EMPLOYEE +
SORTED BY HireDate=d

(See Figure 6–26.) The symbols =d tell R:base you want the data sorted by hire date in descending order. You may specify up to ten sort columns in a SORTED BY clause.

Using WHERE Clauses with SORTED BY Clauses A WHERE clause and a SORTED BY clause may be used in the same SELECT command. For example, assume you want a list of employees who were hired prior to January 1, 1983. Assume further that you want them sorted by monthly salary. You can easily obtain this information with the following command:

SELECT EmpFName EmpLName Salary FROM EMPLOYEE +
SORTED BY Salary +
WHERE HireDate LE 01/01/83

(See Figure 6–27). The SORTED BY and WHERE clauses can be on the same line. We used separate lines to make the command easier to read. The SORTED BY clause must precede the WHERE clause, however.

Two Refinements to the SELECT Command There are two refinements to the SELECT command. The first allows you to limit the number of characters displayed for a column value. For example, the EmpFName and EmpLName columns have a combined width of 25 characters. In many cases, most of those 25 characters are blanks. As we have seen, that limits to six the number of columns which can be displayed from the EMPLOYEE table. If you could limit the width of each column, you could be assured that all nine EMPLOYEE columns would be displayed. To do that, type:

SELECT EmpID# EmpFName=5 EmpLName=8 HireDate +
Salary=7 ComRate=5 SalRevDt +
MStatus=7 Exempt#=1 TotWages=7 +
FROM EMPLOYEE

(See Figure 6–28.)
The second refinement allows you to obtain totals of

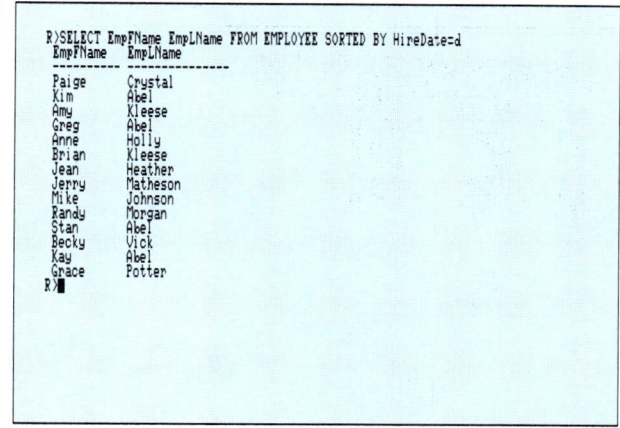

FIGURE 6–26
EMPLOYEEs in descending order of hire date

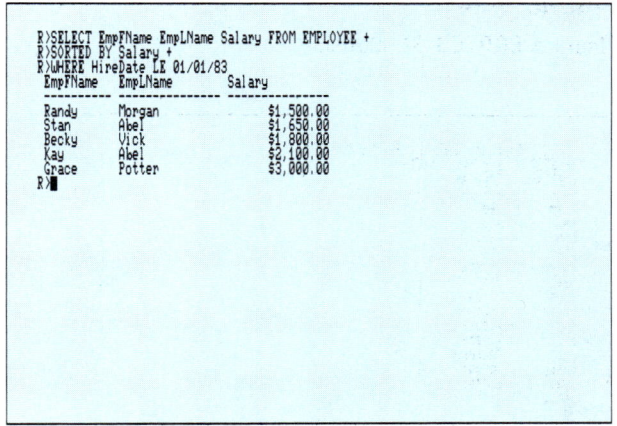

FIGURE 6–27
Combining WHERE and SORTED BY clauses

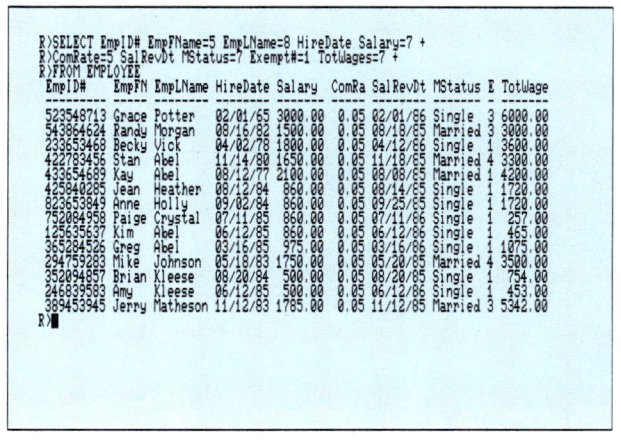

FIGURE 6–28
Limiting the width of columns displayed

FIGURE 6–29

Using =s to summarize wages

```
R>SELECT EmpFName EmpLName TotWages=s FROM EMPLOYEE
EmpFName    EmpLName      TotWages
---------   ---------     ---------
Grace       Potter        $6,000.00
Randy       Morgan        $3,000.00
Becky       Vick          $3,600.00
Stan        Abel          $3,300.00
Kay         Abel          $4,200.00
Jean        Heather       $1,720.00
Anne        Holly         $1,720.00
Paige       Crystal         $257.00
Kim         Abel            $465.00
Greg        Abel          $1,075.00
Mike        Johnson       $3,500.00
Brian       Kleese          $754.00
Amy         Kleese          $453.00
Jerry       Matheson      $5,342.00
                         ----------
                         $35,386.00
R>
```

numeric columns by placing the symbols =s after the column name. For example, to get a total of year-to-date salaries paid to all married employees, type:

SELECT EmpFName EmpLName TotWages=s FROM EMPLOYEE

(See Figure 6–29.)

Compute

My ex: How to figure earnings from purse

Some questions which arise cannot be answered directly from data stored in the database. Instead, the answers must be derived from the data. For example, the answer to the question "What is the average monthly salary?" is not stored in the database. However, it can be derived from data in the database. R:base provides the ability to derive the maximum (MAX) and minimum (MIN) figures as well as the average (AVE) and sum (SUM) of a specified column. To find the average monthly salary, type:

COMPUTE AVE Salary FROM EMPLOYEE

(See Figure 6–30.) In addition, you can determine how many rows are in the EMPLOYEE table with the command:

COMPUTE ROWS FROM EMPLOYEE

(See Figure 6–31.) Or you can find out how many em-

FIGURE 6–30

Display the average salary with COMPUTE

```
R>COMPUTE AVE Salary FROM EMPLOYEE
Salary   Average =          $1,357.14
R>
```

FIGURE 6-31
Display numer of EMPLOYEEs with COMPUTE

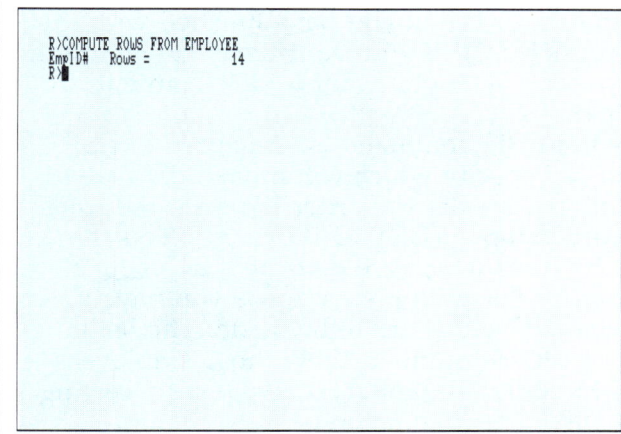

FIGURE 6-32
Showing how many EMPLOYEEs earn less than $1,000

FIGURE 6-33
Computing all salary statistics

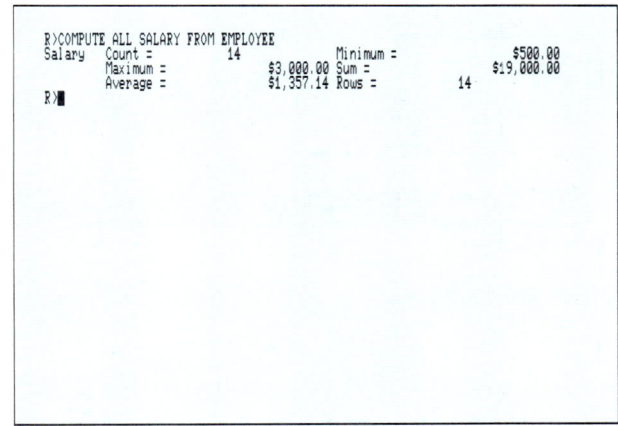

FIGURE 6-34
Editing EMPLOYEE data

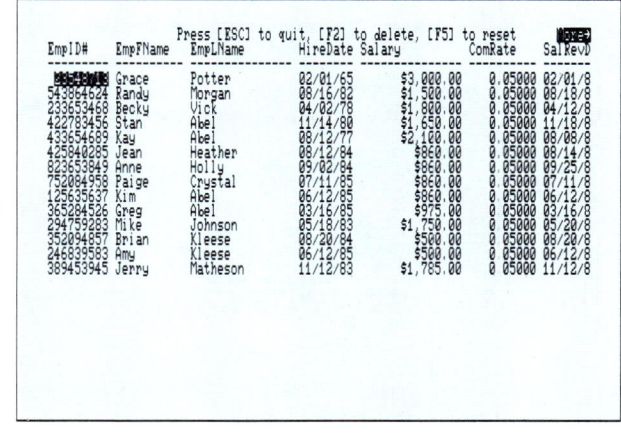

ployees have a monthly salary of less than $1,000 by typing:

COMPUTE COUNT Salary FROM EMPLOYEE +
WHERE Salary LT 1000

(See Figure 6-32.)

You can obtain COUNT, MAXIMUM, MINIMUM, SUM, AVERAGE, and ROWS for the Salary column in the EMPLOYEE table with the command:

COMPUTE ALL Salary FROM EMPLOYEE

(See Figure 6-33.)

CHANGING DATA USING THE EDIT COMMAND

A database is a model. As the environment which it is modeling changes, the database must reflect the change. R:base provides several means of changing database values. One of the most convenient is the EDIT command. You can use EDIT to display data on the computer screen. Then, you can move from data item to data item making changes. The EDIT command is structured like SELECT. To have R:base display all the data from the EMPLOYEE table, type:

EDIT ALL FROM EMPLOYEE

(See Figure 6-34.)

FIGURE 6-35a

First part of a COMPUTE help screen

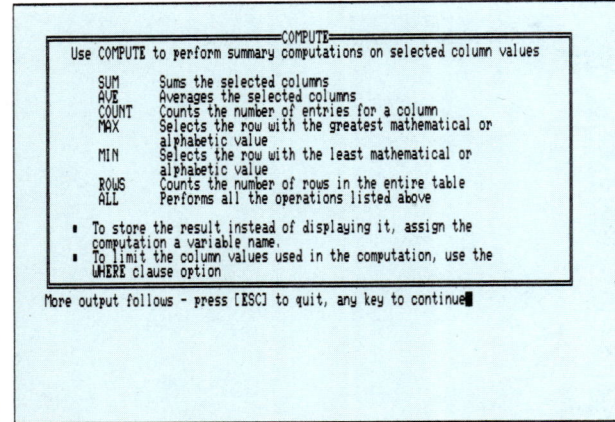

FIGURE 6-35b

Last part of a COMPUTE help screen

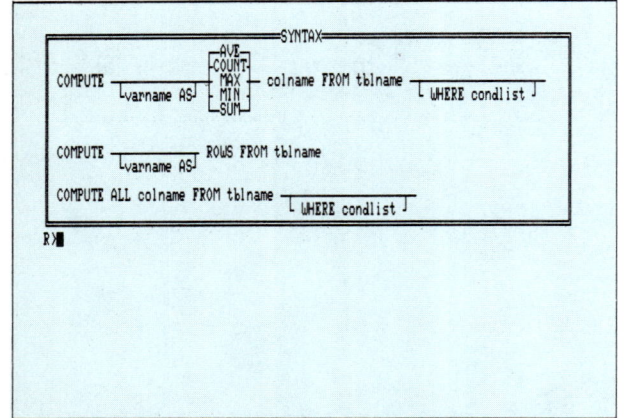

FIGURE 6-36

Main HELP screen

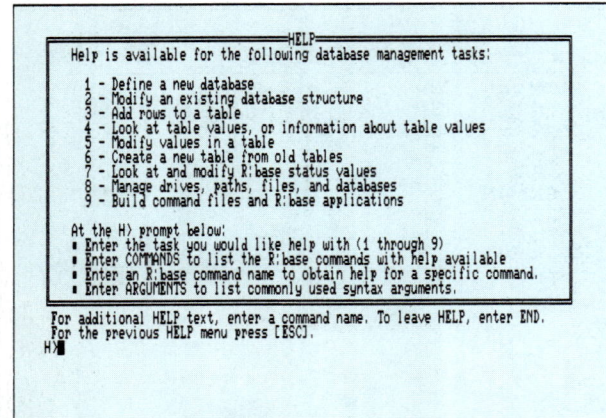

To change data in the highlighted area, simply type in the new value. You can move the highlighted area to the right by pressing the [TAB] key. To move to the left, press the [SHIFT] key while you press the [TAB] key. Use the up arrow and down arrow keys to move between the rows. When you have finished with the changes, press [ESC]. If you want R:base to ignore the changes, press [F5]. If you want to delete an entire row, press [F2].

Because the EDIT command is structured like SELECT, you can specify which columns of data are displayed. You can specify the order in which the rows are displayed using a SORTED BY clause. You can also limit the rows which are displayed by using a WHERE clause. For example, suppose you have a list of salary changes which are to be made. The list is sorted by employee number. Only those employees who were hired before January 1, 1985, are receiving raises. To make the changes, type:

EDIT EmpID# Salary SalRevDt FROM EMPLOYEE +
SORTED BY EmpID# WHERE HireDate LT 01/01/85

HELP AND PROMPT

Whenever you are uncertain about the proper form of an R:base command, there are two very useful features available to help you: HELP and PROMPT.

HELP is used to obtain a brief explanation of the use of a particular command and the proper syntax of the command. For example, suppose you are unsure about the correct syntax for COMPUTE. Simply type:

HELP COMPUTE

and R:base provides the explanation (Figure 6-35). R:base provides an extensive help facility. If you are unsure about what to do next, simply type:

HELP

to receive the task-oriented main HELP screen (Figure 6-36).

R:base goes beyond providing help screens. You can use the PROMPT mode to provide basic information about what it is you want to do. R:base then constructs the proper R:base command, shows you what it is, then executes it. For example, suppose you want to see a list of employee names in alphabetical order. Type:

PROMPT SELECT

then fill in the form which is provided (Figure 6–37). To execute the command, press [G]. R:base builds the correct command (SELECT EmpFName EmpLName FROM EMPLOYEE SORTED BY EmpLName) and then executes it (Figure 6–38).

To obtain a list of R:base commands which may be used with PROMPT, type:

HELP PROMPT

(See Figure 6–39.)

FIGURE 6–37

Filling in the prompt form

```
— Alt menu—Table list—Column list—Go execute—Help—Quit——————
=================================PROMPTS=================================
SELECT
------
Use the SELECT command to retrieve data from a table. Specify
the table and the columns. To display all columns, enter ALL.
To sum a column, add =S to the column name.  To set a display
width for a column, add =w to the column name, where w is a
number from 1 to 256.

Name of table to display : EMPLOYEE
Name(s) of columns to display (or ALL) :
EmpFName EmpLName
Sort order (optional list of column names) :
EmpLName
Condition that selects rows to display (optional) :
```

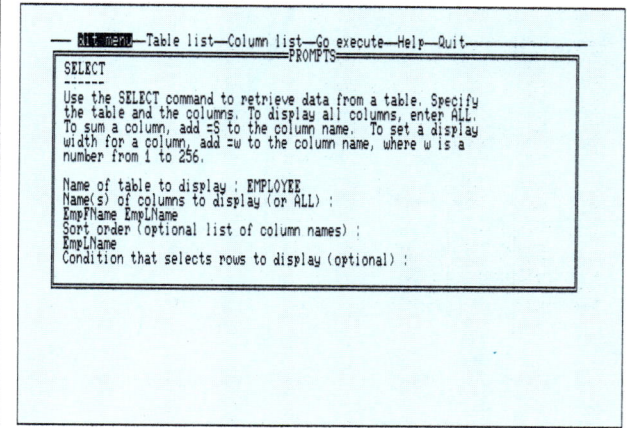

FIGURE 6–38

R:base builds the correct command and executes it

```
Name(s) of columns to display (or ALL) :
EmpFName EmpLName
Sort order (optional list of column names) :
EmpLName
Condition that selects rows to display (optional) :

SELECT EmpFName EmpLName FROM EMPLOYEE SORTED BY EmpLName
 EmpFName   EmpLName
 ---------- ---------------
 Kim        Abel
 Greg       Abel
 Kay        Abel
 Stan       Abel
 Paige      Crystal
 Jean       Heather
 Anne       Holly
 Mike       Johnson
 Amy        Kleese
 Brian      Kleese
 Jerry      Matheson
 Randy      Morgan
 Grace      Potter
 Becky      Vick
R>
```

FIGURE 6–39

The PROMPT help screen

```
=================================PROMPT==================================
Use PROMPT to enter the PROMPT mode.  R:base displays on-line assistance
to help execute any of the following commands:

APPEND   COPY     EXIT      NEWPAGE   RELOAD   SHOW
ASSIGN   DATE     EXPAND    OPEN      REMOVE   SUBTRACT
BUILD    DEFINE   FORMS     OUTPUT    RENAME   TABLES
CHANGE   DELETE   INPUT     OWNER     REPORTS  TALLY
CHDIR    DIR      INTERSECT PACK      RMDIR    TYPE
CHKDSK   DISPLAY  JOIN      PASSWORDS RULES    UNION
CLOSE    EDIT     LIST      PRINT     RUN      UNLOAD
COLUMNS  ENTER    LOAD      PROJECT   SELECT   USER
COMPUTE  ERASE    MKDIR     RBEDIT    SET

To leave the PROMPT mode, enter END at the P> prompt.

=================================SYNTAX==================================
   PROMPT ———————————————
           └ commandname ┘
R>
```

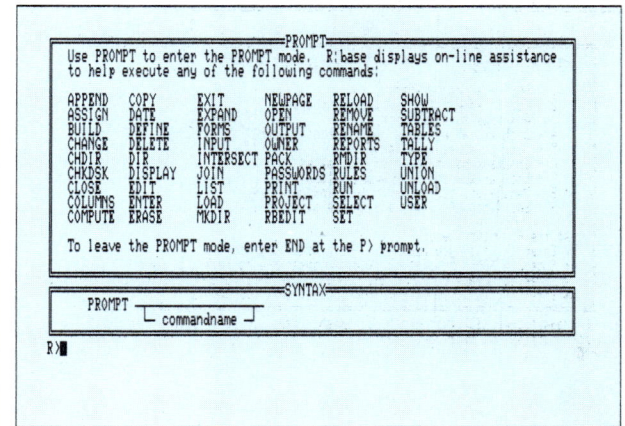

SUMMARY

- There are five steps to database definition with the Application EXPRESS (the EXPRESS):
  - Load the EXPRESS.
  - Select "Define a new database" from the EXPRESS main menu.
  - Provide the database name.
  - Define the table(s).
  - Exit the EXPRESS.
- R:base column names may be from one to eight characters long and may not be R:base reserved words.
- Data types available in R:base are:
  - Text
  - Dollar
  - Integer
  - Real
  - Date
  - Time
- Text-type columns may be from 1 to 1500 characters wide.
- The OPEN command is used to tell R:base which database to work with.
- The LIST command is used to obtain information about a table in the database.
- LOAD table name WITH PROMPTS is one way to load data into an R:base table.
- The SELECT command is used to display data from a table.
- A WHERE clause is used to specify the rows which are affected by an R:base command.
- There are eight types of conditions which may be used in a WHERE clause:
  - Column name EXISTS
  - Column name FAILS
  - Column name op value (op means "operator" and may be EQ (equals), NE (not equal), GT (greater than), GE (greater than or equal), LT (less than), or LE (less than or equal))
  - Column name op column name
  - Column name CONTAINS string

- LIMIT EQ value
- COUNT EQ value
- COUNT EQ LAST
- A WHERE clause may combine up to ten conditions connected with AND and OR.
- A SORTED BY clause is used to obtain the data display in sorted order.
- Both WHERE and SORTED BY clauses may be used in a SELECT command.
- Two refinements to the SELECT command allow you to limit the display width of a column and to obtain the total =s of a numeric column.
- COMPUTE allows you to derive information from data stored in the database:
  - MAX computes the maximum value.
  - MIN computes the minimum value.
  - AVE computes the average value.
  - ROWS computes the number of rows in the table.
  - COUNT computes the number of rows in which the specified column meets the condition in the WHERE clause.
  - ALL computes all of the above for a specified column.
- EDIT is the most convenient way to make changes to database values.
- HELP and PROMPT are available when you are unsure about the proper syntax of an R:base command.

REVIEW QUESTIONS

Group I Questions

6.1
List the three parts to a column definition in R:base.

6.2
What limitations exist for R:base column names?

6.3
What types of data may an R:base column contain?

6.4
What is the maximum width of a TEXT column?

6.5
What is the function of the OPEN command?

6.6
What is the function of the SELECT command?

6.7
What is the function of a WHERE clause?

6.8
What is the function of a SORTED BY clause?

6.9
List the eight types of conditions which a WHERE clause may contain.

6.10
List the six arguments which may be used with the COMPUTE command. Also list their purpose.

6.11
What is the function of the EDIT command?

Group II Questions

If you have R:base available, use the Application EXPRESS to define the EMPLOYEE table in the GTPLAIN database as described in the text.

If you have the student version of R:base, you can load the sample data used in the chapter by typing:

INPUT CH6.DAT

If you do not have CH6.DAT available to you, use LOAD WITH PROMPTS to load the sample employee data from Figure 6–28.

Once you have the sample data loaded, use R:base to answer the following questions about Great Plains' employees. If you do not have R:base available, write the command(s) necessary to answer the questions.

6.12
What are the names of the employees? List them with the most senior employee first.

6.13
What are the employee identification numbers, names, and salaries of the married employees?

6.14
Which employees have more than two exemptions?

6.15
How much has Great Plains paid in total wages?

6.16
Which employee is scheduled for the next salary review? When is it scheduled?

6.17
Which employees were hired in 1982 or 1984?

6.18
What is the average number of exemptions claimed by Great Plains employees?

6.19
How many employees are there?

6.20
Which employee has been with Great Plains the longest?

6.21
Which employee has the highest monthly salary?

PROJECT

Use the Application EXPRESS to define the course table from the academic database you designed in Chapter 5. Use the R:base LOAD WITH PROMPTS command to load data for your last completed semester. Use SELECT and COMPUTE to answer the following:

- What courses did you take?
- List the courses in the order you ranked them.
- List the courses in the order of the grade you earned.
- What was the average rating you gave to the courses?

CHAPTER 7

Database Implementation— Customer and Sale Data

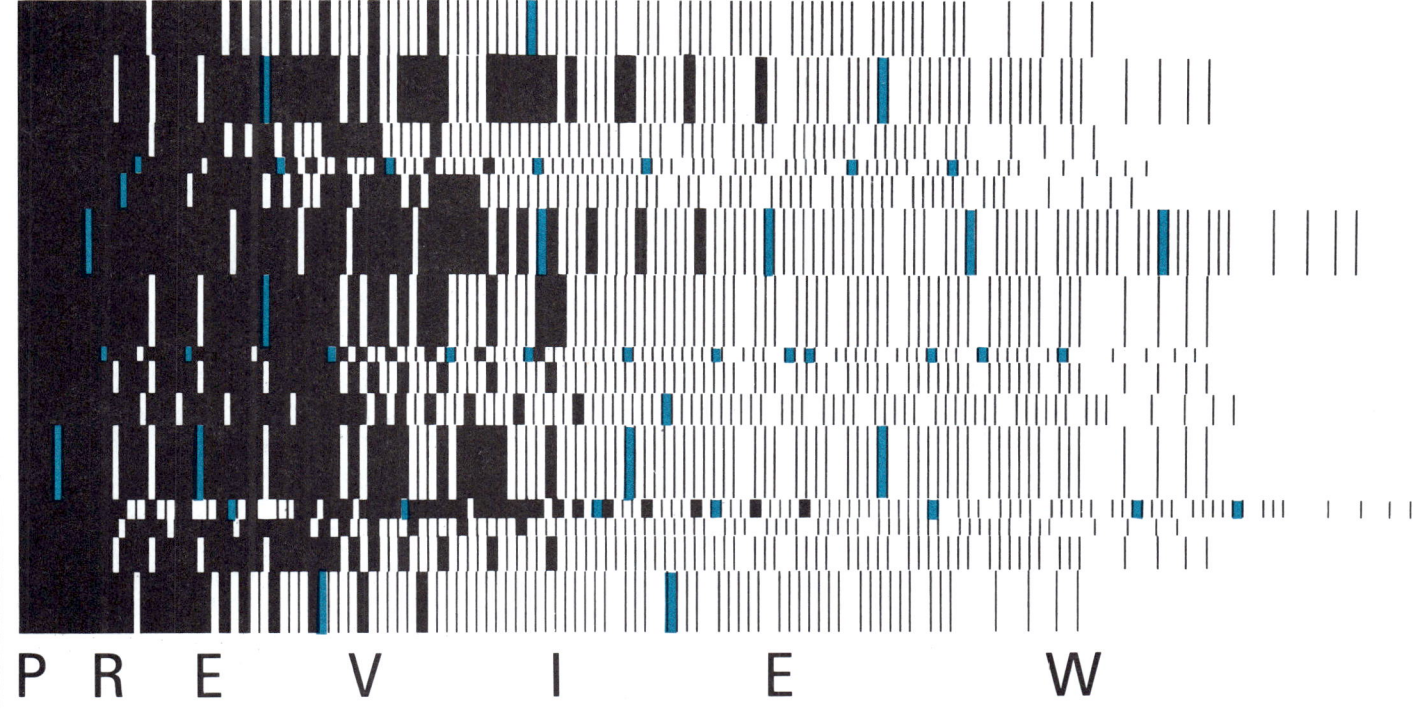

P R E V I E W

In the previous chapter, we began implementation of the Great Plains Music and Video Unlimited database by using the Application EXPRESS to define the EMPLOYEE table. We then used the LOAD WITH PROMPTS command to load data into the EMPLOYEE table. SELECT and COMPUTE were used to answer questions about employees. We demonstrated how to use EDIT to make changes to values in the database. We also showed you how to use R:base HELP and PROMPT when you are unsure about a command.

In this chapter we will continue implementation of the Great Plains database by using the R:base DEFINE mode to define the CUSTOMER and SALE tables. Next, we'll show how to use R:base RULES to enforce simple database constraints. We'll also demonstrate another way to enter data by creating an R:base FORM for use in entering customer data. Last, we'll create an R:base REPORT to print a customer list.

FIGURE 7-1
R:base main menu

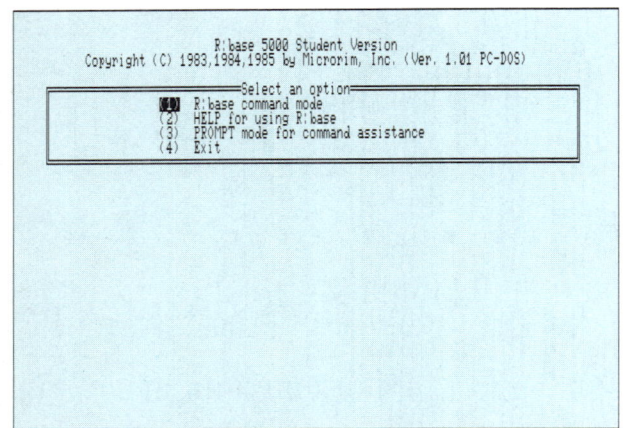

FIGURE 7-2
Enter the DEFINE mode

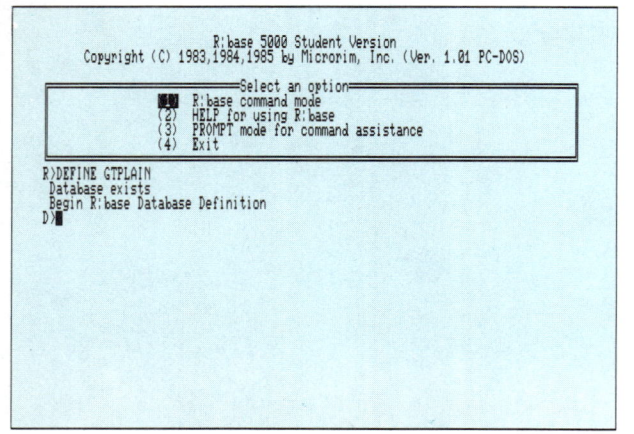

ADDING THE CUSTOMER AND SALE TABLES TO THE DATABASE USING THE R:BASE DEFINE MODE

There are five steps to defining tables using the DEFINE mode:

1. Load R:base.
2. Enter the DEFINE mode.
3. Describe the columns.
4. Define the table(s).
5. Exit the DEFINE mode.

Let's follow these five steps to add the CUSTOMER and SALE tables.

Step 1: Load R:base

Follow the instructions provided with the R:base disks to load R:base. After R:base is loaded, you will receive the menu in Figure 7-1. You'll be working with the R:base command mode so press 1 or [ENTER]. R:base confirms that you are in the command mode by presenting the command prompt (R>).

Step 2: Enter the DEFINE Mode

Enter the DEFINE mode by typing the key word DEFINE followed by a valid database specification in the form, d:path/dbname, where:

- d: = a valid disk drive specification
- path = a valid DOS path (for more details see a DOS manual)
- dbname = a valid R:base database name (any seven characters)

If you do not provide the drive specification, the default drive is assumed. If you do not provide a path, the default DOS directory is assumed. In this case, type:

DEFINE GTPLAIN

R:base confirms that the GTPLAIN database exists. It also confirms that you are in the DEFINE mode in two ways. First, you are given the message, "Begin R:base Database Definition." Second, the prompt is changed from R> to D> (Figure 7-2).

Recall from Chapter 6 that, with the Application EXPRESS, you define a database by defining one table at a time. The DEFINE mode of R:base works differently.

In the DEFINE mode of R:base, you first describe all of the columns in the database, then define the tables. To add the CUSTOMER and SALE tables to the database, we'll describe all of the columns used in CUSTOMER and SALE which have not been previously defined. Then, we'll describe the CUSTOMER and SALE tables. Figure 7–3 contains the final database design we produced in Chapter 5.

Step 3: Describe the Columns

To begin column description, type:

COLUMNS

and press [ENTER]. R:base responds with another D> prompt (Figure 7–4). Recall from Chapter 6 that there are three parts to a column definition in R:base: the column name, data type, and, for TEXT columns, the column width.

Figure 7–5 shows the computer screen after the columns for CUSTOMER and SALE have been entered. Notice that the Social security number column (EmpID#) is not included. That's because it was defined when we defined the EMPLOYEE table with the EXPRESS. Also note that Customer identification number (CustID#) was defined only once, even though it is used twice: once in CUSTOMER and again in SALE. The point is, *a column is defined only once, no matter how many times it is used.*

FIGURE 7–4
Begin column description by typing COLUMNS

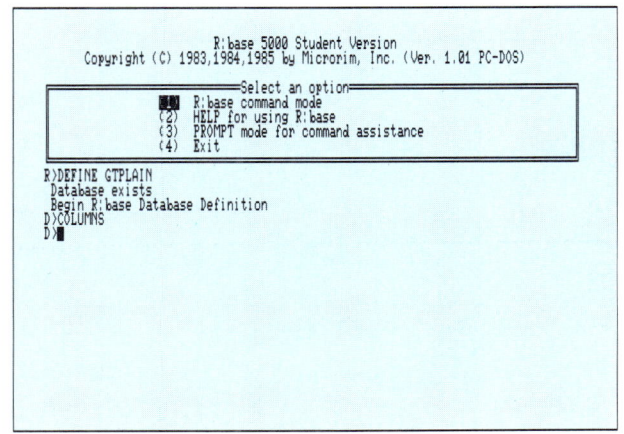

FIGURE 7–3a
Completed design—object/relationships

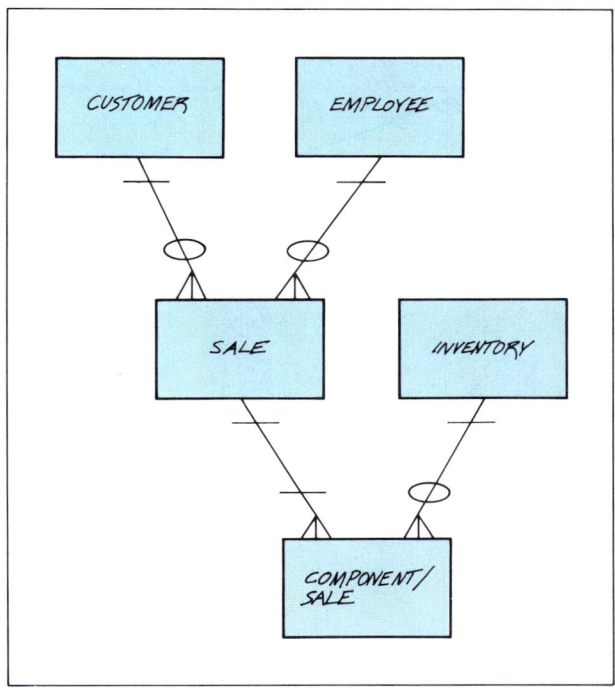

FIGURE 7–3b
Completed design—table/columns

CUSTOMER (Customer identification number, Customer name, Customer address, Customer phone)

INVENTORY (Item number, Item description, Units, Quantity on hand, Cost, Price)

SALE (Sales identification number, Customer identification number, Social security number, Date)

COMPONENT/SALE (Item number, Sales identification number, Quantity sold, Sales price, Sales amount)

EMPLOYEE (Social security number, Employee name, Hire date, Salary, Commission rate, Salary review date, Marital status, Exemptions, Total wages)

FIGURE 7–5

Entering CUSTOMER and SALE column definition

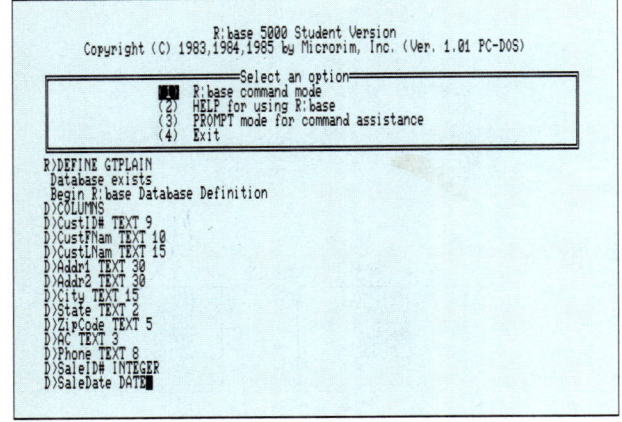

FIGURE 7–6

Prepare R:base to accept table definition

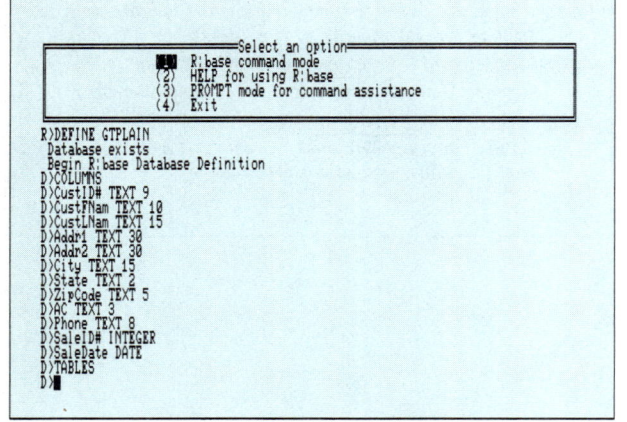

Step 4: Define the Table(s)

Once the columns have all been described, prepare R:base to accept table definitions by typing :

TABLES

(See Figure 7–6). To define database tables, type the table name (any eight characters), the key word WITH followed by the names of the columns in that table. You may separate the column names with commas or simply use spaces as in the definition of the EMPLOYEE and SALE tables depicted in Figure 7–7.

Step 5: Exit the DEFINE Mode

Exit the DEFINE mode and return to the R:base command mode by typing:

END

(See Figure 7–8.)

R:BASE RULES

R:base includes a very useful facility called RULES. With R:base RULES, you may define a condition which must be met by values entered in a particular column.

Whenever an attempt is made to enter or change a value in the column, R:base compares the value to the condition specified in the RULE. If the value meets the condition, R:base enters the value in the column. If

FIGURE 7–7

Complete definition of CUSTOMER and SALE

FIGURE 7–8

Exit the DEFINE mode

```
Begin R:base Database Definition
D>COLUMNS
D>CustID# TEXT 9
D>CustFNam TEXT 10
D>CustLNam TEXT 15
D>Addr1 TEXT 30
D>Addr2 TEXT 30
D>City TEXT 15
D>State TEXT 2
D>ZipCode TEXT 5
D>AC TEXT 3
D>Phone TEXT 8
D>SaleID# INTEGER
D>SaleDate DATE
D>TABLES
D>CUSTOMER WITH CustID# CustFNam CustLNam Addr1 Addr2 City State ZipCode +
D>AC Phone
D>SALE WITH SaleID# CustID# EmpID# SaleDate
D>
D>
D>
D>
D>END
  End R:base Database Definition
R>
```

FIGURE 7–9

Enter the DEFINE mode

```
R>DEFINE GTPLAIN
  Database exists
  Begin R:base Database Definition
D>
```

the value does not meet the condition, R:base displays an error message and the value is not entered. In this way, R:base RULES act as a sort of filter which permits only certain data to be entered into the database.

Specifying R:base RULES

RULES are specified in the DEFINE mode of R:base. There are four steps to specifying RULES:

1. Enter the DEFINE mode.
2. Prepare R:base to accept RULE definitions.
3. Specify the RULES.
4. Exit the DEFINE mode.

Let's look at an example. Suppose we want to specify a RULE for the Great Plains database which will ensure that all entries for sales identification numbers (SalesID#) are greater than zero.

Step 1: Enter the DEFINE Mode Type:

DEFINE GTPLAIN

R:base confirms that you are in the DEFINE mode (Figure 7–9).

Step 2: Prepare R:base to Accept RULE Definitions Next, prepare R:base to accept RULE definitions by typing:

RULES

(See Figure 7–10.)

FIGURE 7–10

Prepare R:base to accept RULE definition

```
R>DEFINE GTPLAIN
  Database exists
  Begin R:base Database Definition
D>RULES
D>
```

FIGURE 7-11

Specifying the RULE

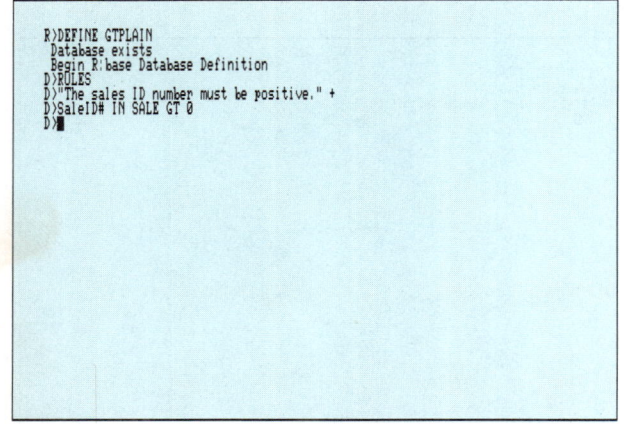

FIGURE 7-12

Attempting to enter a negative sale ID#

FIGURE 7-13

Return to the R:base command mode

Step 3: Specify the RULES There are two parts to each rule:

1. The error message to be printed when the rule is violated
2. The rule condition

Specifying the error message The error message may be any message you choose as long as it contains 40 characters or less. Specify the error message by typing:

"The sales ID number must be positive." +

Specifying the rule condition Next, specify the rule condition for the rule by typing:

SaleID# IN SALE GT 0

(See Figure 7-11. Be sure to type 0 (zero) not the letter "O") Now, if we attempt to enter a negative number into the SaleID# column of the SALE table, R:base displays the error message "-ERROR- The sales ID number must be positive" and the data is not loaded (Figure 7-12).

Notice that the condition in this rule compares the entry value to a constant—an amount specified in the condition itself. This is one of three types of rule conditions. Entries also may be compared to values already in the database. In addition, a rule condition may check to see whether an entry EXISTS or FAILS. You may create complex rule conditions by combining a maximum of ten conditions using AND and OR.

Step 4: Exit the DEFINE Mode Return to the R:base command mode by typing:

END

(See Figure 7-13.)

Enforcing Database Restrictions with R:base

In Chapter 4 we said that the best way to enforce database constraints was to have the DBMS do it for us. You can use two features of R:base for this purpose: automatic data-type checking and RULES.

Recall from Chapter 4 that database tables which are in domain/key normal form will have only the following types of restrictions:

- Key restriction: When a column is designated as a key, values in the column must be unique.

- Inclusion constraint: A value in a given column must have a matching value in another table.
- Domain restriction: A restriction on the values which may be placed in a column.

Let's see how to use R:base RULES to enforce these restrictions.

Enforcing Key Restrictions To ensure that an entry in a column is unique, we define a rule which compares the column entry to all the existing values in that column. For example, to enforce the restriction that EmpID# is the key of the EMPLOYEE table, type:

"This employee number is a duplicate." +
EmpID# IN EMPLOYEE NEA EmpID# IN EMPLOYEE

Enforcing Inclusion Constraints The SALE table includes a column for the identification number of the customer involved in the sale. The database design includes the restriction that entries in the CustID# column of SALE must have a corresponding entry in the CustID# column of CUSTOMER. You can have R:base enforce this restriction with the following RULE:

"Not a valid customer number." +
CustID# IN SALE EQA CustID# IN CUSTOMER

Enforcing Domain Restrictions Recall from Chapter 4 that there are two parts to a domain definition: the physical part and the logical part. To enforce domain restrictions, we must ensure that values entered in a column have the proper physical characteristics (i.e., INTEGER, REAL, DOLLAR, etc.) and that the logical restrictions are met.

The physical part of a domain definition is automatically enforced by R:base. Look at the R:base definition of the SALE table by typing:

LIST SALE

(See Figure 7–14.) Notice that R:base has a permanent record of the Name, Data type, and Length of each column in the table. Whenever an attempt is made to enter or change data in a column, R:base compares the physical characteristics of the new value to the column definition. If the value does not meet the recorded physical definition, R:base presents an error message and the data is not loaded except when TEXT values exceed the prescribed length. In this case, R:base presents us with a warning that the data will be shortened to meet the required maximum length.

FIGURE 7–14

Listing the definition of the SALE table

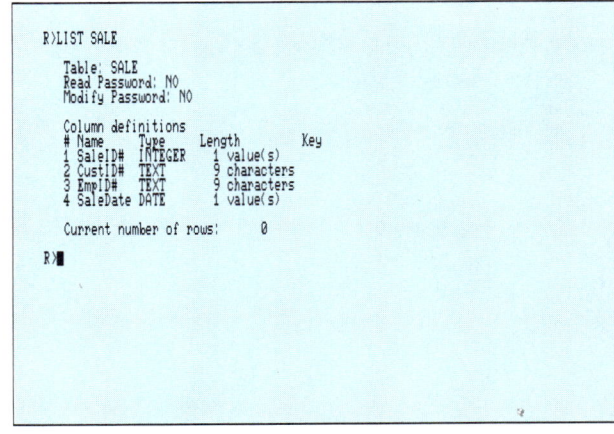

FIGURE 7–15

Attempting to load "A-100" as sale ID#

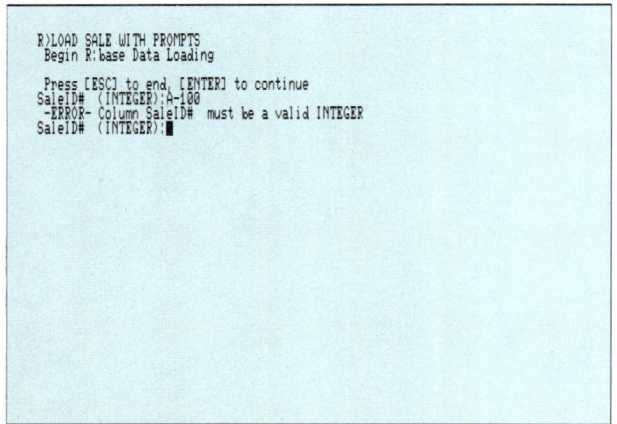

FIGURE 7–16

R:base truncates text items that are too long

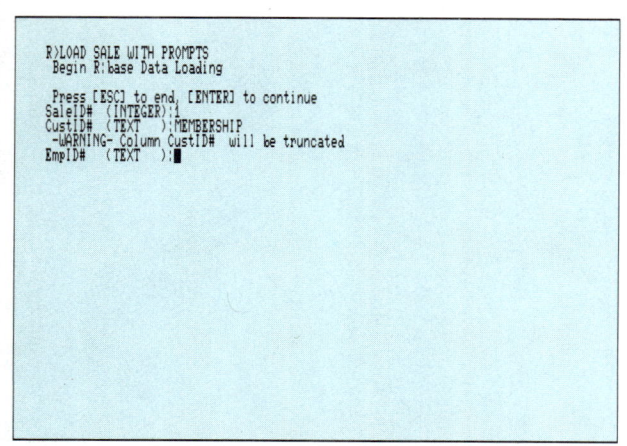

For example, Figure 7–15 shows what happens if we attempt to load the value "A-100" into the SaleID# column of the SALE table using the R:base LOAD WITH PROMPTS command. Because "A-100" is not a valid integer, R:base will not load it into the SaleID# column. Figure 7–16 shows the response if we attempt to load "MEMBERSHIP" (10 characters) into the CustID# column (9 characters). R:base has shortened the value we entered to 9 characters—"MEMBERSHI." Remember, R:base automatically checks the physical definition of data. You do not have to define a RULE to do it.

Enforcing the logical part of a domain definition usually requires the use of RULES. Some domain definitions require value or range checking. For example, assume you have defined a table column called Height to represent the height, in inches, of employees. You have defined the domain of Height as, "INTEGERS in the range from 48 to 84." As we have seen, R:base will automatically ensure that entries in the Height column are INTEGERs. However, you'll need to define a RULE to ensure that entries fall within the specified range. The rule is defined by typing:

"Height must be between 48 and 84." +
Height IN EMPLOYEE GE 48 AND Height IN EMPLOYEE LE 84

Other domain definitions involve interrelation constraints. For example, the SALE table includes a column for employee number (EmpID#). The domain of EmpID# is "A string of 9 characters uniquely identifying an employee." To ensure that an entry in the EmpID# column of the SALE table represents a valid employee number, we define the following interrelation rule:

"Not a valid employee number." +
EmpID# IN SALE EQA EmpID# IN EMPLOYEE

Automatic data-type checking combined with RULES provides an easy, effective way of enforcing database restrictions.

R:BASE FORMS

In the previous chapter, we said that R:base provides a number of ways to load data into the database. Up to this point we have used the most direct way; LOAD WITH PROMPTS. Figure 7–17 shows what's involved in loading a row into the CUSTOMER table using LOAD WITH PROMPTS.

FIGURE 7–17

Using LOAD WITH PROMPTS to load a CUSTOMER record

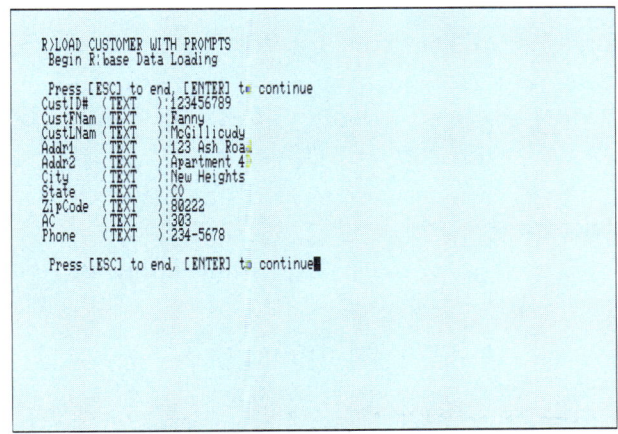

There are several things to notice about Figure 7–17. First, look at the names of the data items. Names like Addr1 and Addr2 are not too descriptive. Users may find them confusing. Also, the data-type names can be threatening to nontechnical users. Finally, there are no instructions about what data to enter. What goes in the item named Addr1? Unless they designed the database themselves or have access to the design documentation, users have no way of knowing.

With R:base FORMS, you can make the computer's screen look like a paper form. You can include comments and instructions and use more descriptive names for the items to be filled in. The user fills in the blanks on the form. R:base takes the data from the spaces in the form and stores it in a row in the table. Let's see how FORMS can be used to enter CUSTOMER data.

Defining FORMS

After loading R:base and OPENing the GTPLAIN database, type:

FORMS

R:base responds with the screen in Figure 7–18, prompting you for the name to be given to the form. Any string of eight or less characters may be used. Type:

CUST

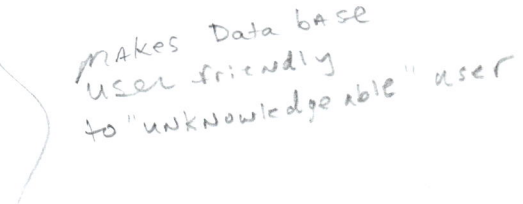

FIGURE 7–18

Beginning FORMS definition

FIGURE 7-19

Providing the FORM and TABLE names

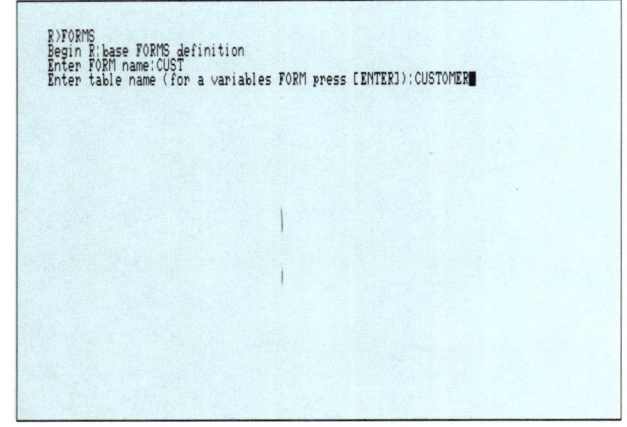

R:base then prompts for the name of the table into which the data is to be loaded. Do not concern yourself with the meaning of the term "variables FORM." Type:

CUSTOMER

This interaction is shown in Figure 7–19. After you press [ENTER], R:base presents you with a menu containing the following choices (Figure 7–20):

- Edit: Use this choice to create or change the way the form looks on the screen.
- Locate: This choice is used to indicate where the data items are to be located in the form.
- Quit: Use this choice to return to the R:base command mode.

To begin, press [E]. R:base presents a screen which is blank except for the following line:

< 1, 1> [F3] to list, [ESC] to exit

The line contains three pieces of information. The first portion (< 1, 1>) tells us that the cursor is located at screen column 1, screen row 1. The second portion ([F3] to list) is telling us that we can get a list of the CUSTOMER columns by pressing [F3]. The third portion is advising us to press [ESC] to exit the EDIT mode.

In the EDIT mode, we may create the form using the full-screen text-editing feature of R:base. Simply type the form on the screen (see Figure 7–21).

FIGURE 7-20

The FORMS definition menu

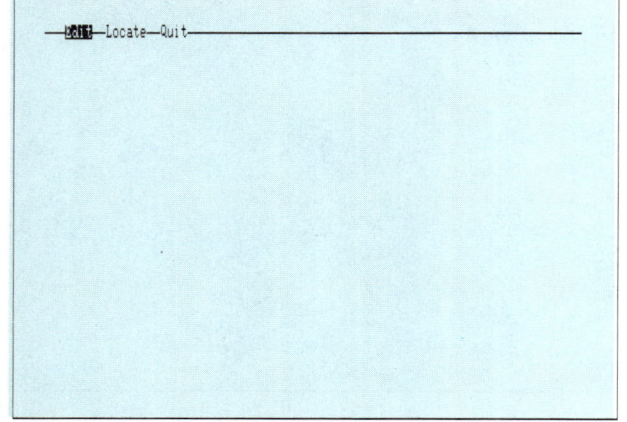

FIGURE 7-21

Type the form on the screen

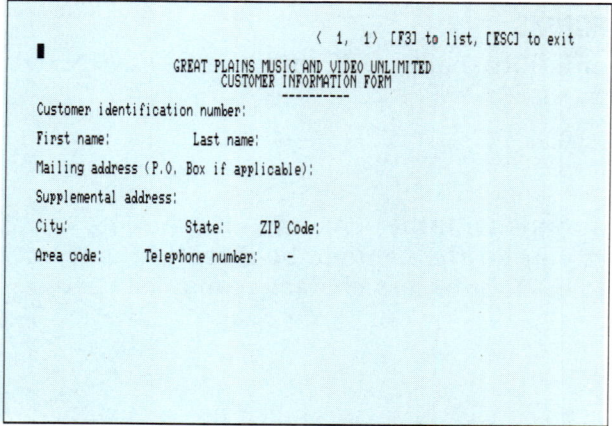

Exit the EDIT mode by pressing [ESC]. Next, choose Locate by pressing [L].

While a form is something that is very familiar to humans (that's the whole point), it means nothing to R:base. To R:base, it represents a place to get data to load into a row in the CUSTOMER table. In the LOCATE mode, you tell R:base the exact location of each data item to be loaded. There are three steps to the location of each item:

1. Type the column name.
2. Mark the starting location of the data item.
3. Mark the ending location of the data item.

Let's follow these steps to locate the customer identification number. Begin by typing the column name. If you do not remember the name, press [F3]. R:base presents the list of column names for the CUSTOMER table (Figure 7–22). We can see that the column name for the customer identification number is CustID#.

After entering the column name, R:base asks that you, "Move the cursor to start location for CustID# and press [S]." On the IBM PC, the cursor is moved by using the arrow keys on the numeric keyboard. We have spelled out "Customer identification number:" in the form. We want the customer number entered beginning immediately after the colon (:), so move the cursor there and press [S] (Figure 7–23). Since CustID# is nine characters wide, R:base moves the cursor nine spaces to the right of the starting location. Press [E] to mark the end of the customer identification number.

These three steps are repeated until we have marked the location for all the CUSTOMER data items. The finished form with all the columns located is shown in Figure 7–24. Exit the LOCATE mode by pressing [ESC]. Return to the R:base command mode by first pressing [Q], then [S] to save the form definition.

If you type:

LIST TABLES

(see Figure 7–25), you'll notice that there are two new tables in the database: RULES and FORMS. R:base stores data for its own use in FORMS, REPORTS, and RULES.

Using the CUST Form

Once defined, the form may be used to enter new data or to change existing data. To enter new cus-

FIGURE 7–22
Press [F3] for a list of column names

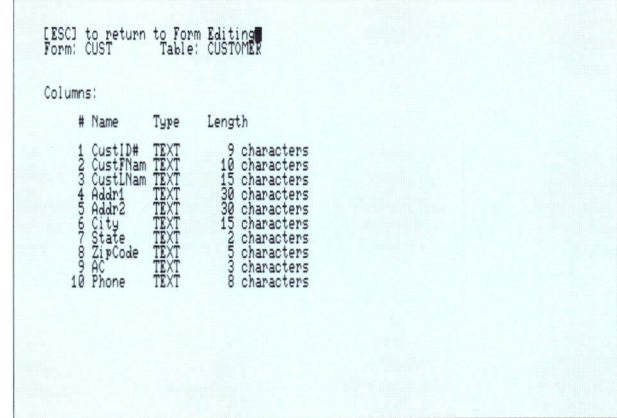

FIGURE 7–23
Mark the start of the field by pressing [S]

FIGURE 7–24
The completed form

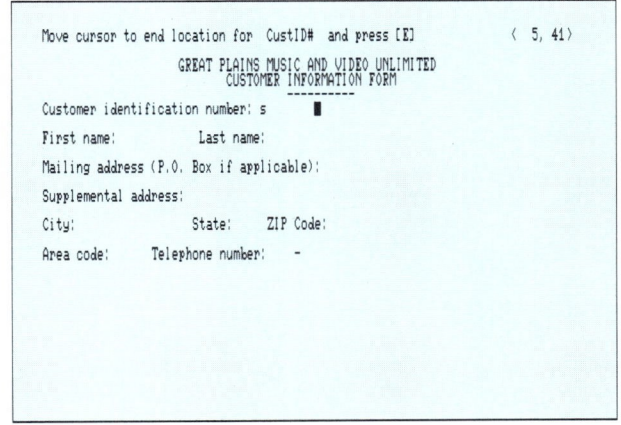

FIGURE 7-25

Use LIST TABLES to get a listing of tables

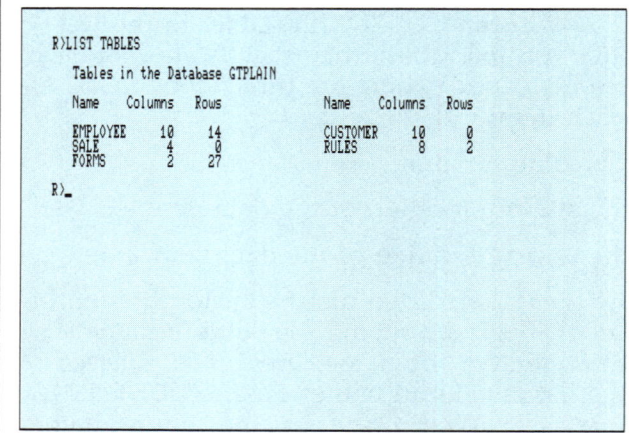

tomer data, type:

ENTER CUST

R:base presents the form we defined (Figure 7-26). R:base has highlighted the space next to "Customer identification number." Simply type in the data. When you're finished entering the customer number, press [ENTER]. R:base moves to the next space. When you are finished entering all the data in the form, press [ESC]. (See Figure 7-27.)

You now have some choices to make.

FIGURE 7-26

R:base presents the form we defined

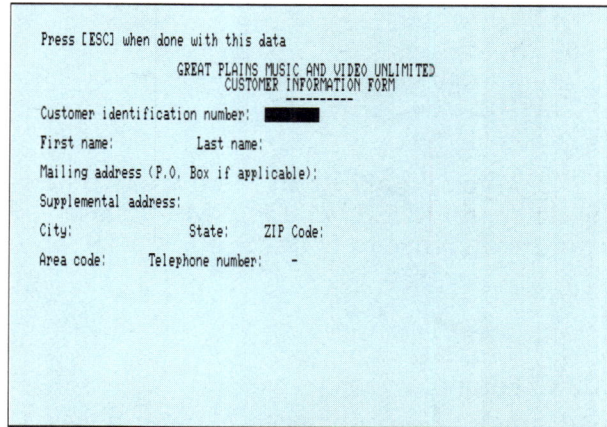

FIGURE 7-27
Customer form filled in

```
┌─Add─Reuse─Edit─Quit──────────────────────────────┐
│         GREAT PLAINS MUSIC AND VIDEO UNLIMITED   │
│                CUSTOMER INFORMATION FORM         │
│                                                  │
│  Customer identification number: 374652948       │
│  First name: Jonah     Last name: Goldstein      │
│  Mailing address (P.O. Box if applicable): P.O. Box 56 │
│  Supplemental address: 124 Ash Street            │
│  City: Denver          State: CO  ZIP Code: 80526│
│  Area code: 203  Telephone number: 233-3984      │
└──────────────────────────────────────────────────┘
```

- **Add**: R:base will take the data from the form and store it in the CUSTOMER table. It clears all the spaces in the form and presents a blank form.
- **Reuse**: R:base will take the data from the form and store it in the CUSTOMER table. It leaves the form filled in so that you do not have to re-enter data that doesn't change.
- **Edit**: This will allow you to change what you have entered.
- **Quit**: Use this choice when you are finished entering data with the form. You must be careful that you add the data for the last form before you quit or the data in the last form will be lost.

To load the data for this customer, press [A]. After adding the data for the last customer, press [Q].

R:base REPORTS

In the previous chapter, we showed how to use the SELECT command to extract data from the database. The SELECT command is useful for answering questions which arise unexpectedly and when the format of the data supplied is not important.

However, there are situations in which you will want the data displayed, either on the computer's screen or on a printer, in a more formal way. R:base REPORTS can be used to meet this need. Let's see how REPORTS can be used to prepare a list of CUSTOMERS.

Figure 7-28 represents a sketch of the customer list which the marketing director of Great Plains Music

FIGURE 7-28
Sketch of customer list

Great Plains Music and Video Customer List

| Customer Number | First Name | Cust. Name | Address | Phone |

FIGURE 7-29

Prompt for name of report

and Video Unlimited would like to have. Let's see how REPORTS can be used to prepare such a list.

Defining REPORTS As with FORMS, you must first prepare the report definition. After loading R:base and OPENing the GTPLAIN database, type:

REPORTS

R:base responds with the screen in Figure 7-29 prompting you for the name to be given to the report. Any string of eight or less characters may be used. Type:

CUSTLIST

R:base then prompts for the name of the table from which the report data will be obtained. Since this report uses customer names and addresses, type:

CUSTOMER

This interaction is shown in Figure 7-30. After you press [ENTER], R:base presents you with a menu containing the following choices (Figure 7-31):

- Edit report: Use this choice to create or change the way the report looks on the screen.

- Define: This choice is used to define or change report variables. We'll discuss report variables in chapter 9.

FIGURE 7-30

Entered table name

FIGURE 7-31

REPORTS main menu

- **Locate:** As with FORMS, this choice is used to indicate where the data items are to be placed in the report.
- **Mark:** This choice is used to mark the location of headings, footings, detail lines, and other parts of the report.
- **Set:** Use this choice to set the number of lines per page.
- **Help:** This choice presents you with more detailed instructions for defining a report.
- **Quit:** Use this choice to return to the R:base command mode.

When defining a new report, you should follow the steps in order: Edit, Define, Locate, Mark, Set, then Quit. Let's follow these steps to prepare the customer list report.

Edit report To begin, press [E]. R:base presents a screen which is identical to the one you received in FORMS definition, except for the reverse video stripe along the left side. This stripe is used later when you "Mark" the various report sections.

At this point, type in everything you want to appear on the report except for the data which comes from the database. This includes report and page headings, total and subtotal captions, and column titles. Figure 7–32 shows the page heading and column titles for the Great Plains customer list as they appear on the screen. Return to the main report definition menu by pressing [ESC].

Define report variables Report variables are variable data items which cannot be extracted from the database. Examples of report variables are subtotals and totals. The Great Plains customer list does not require any report variables.

Locate columns and variables on the report Next, you must indicate where the report variables and data items taken from the database are to be placed on the report. Select "Locate" from the main report definition menu by pressing [L]. You are presented with another menu containing the following options:

- **Locate:** Select this option to locate items which have not been previously located.
- **Relocate:** This option is used to delete or change the location of previously located report variables and data items.

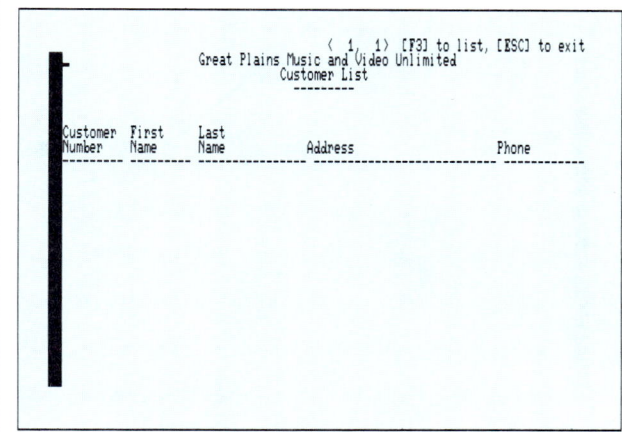

FIGURE 7–32

Page heading and column titles

FIGURE 7–33

Select Locate by pressing [L]

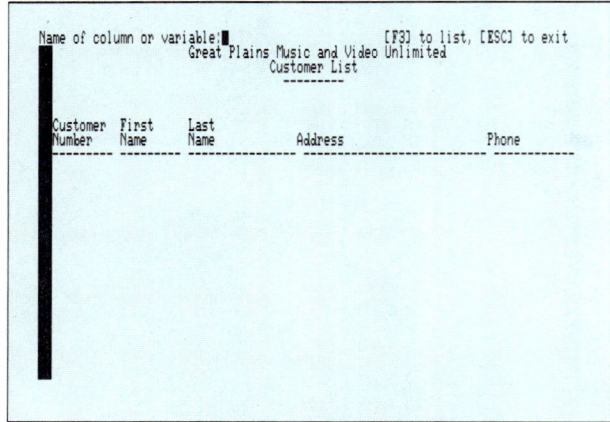

- Help: Select this option to obtain instructions.
- Quit: This option returns you to the main report definition menu.

Since no data items have been located, select "Locate" by pressing [L]. (See Figure 7–33.) Mark the location of data items in a REPORT using the same three steps used to mark data items in a FORM:

1. Type the column name.
2. Mark the starting location of the data item.
3. Mark the ending location of the data item.

The only difference in the "Locate" process between FORMS and REPORTS is in the marking of TEXT items. To see what those differences are, let's locate CustLName—Customer Last Name.

Begin by typing the column name, CustLName. As with FORMS, R:base instructs you to "Move cursor to start location and press [S]." After moving the cursor to the start location in the Last Name column and pressing [S], the screen appears as in Figure 7–34. Notice that the end of the data item can be marked by pressing either [E] or [W].

Use of [W] allows you to create paragraphs from long text items. We will illustrate this feature along with other advanced reporting capabilities of R:base in Chapter 9. Figure 7–35 shows the screen after all data items have been marked. Return to the "Locate" menu by pressing [ESC], then press [Q] to return to the main report definition menu.

FIGURE 7–34

Marking the location of a data item

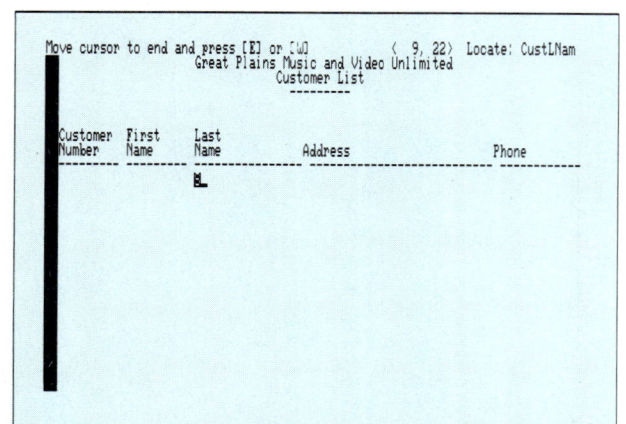

FIGURE 7–35

All data items marked for location

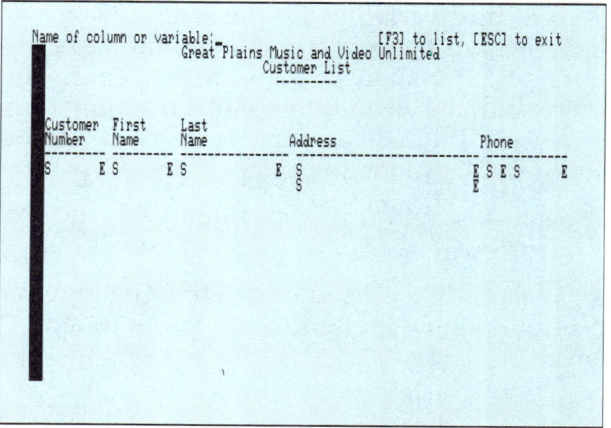

Mark report sections The next step in defining a report is to identify the various report sections. Begin by pressing [M]. You are given another menu with the following choices:

- Report: This choice allows you to mark report heading and footing lines. Report heading lines are printed only once, before the rest of the report is printed. You would use them to print a title page. Report footing lines are also printed once, after the rest of the report has been printed. Use footers to print report summaries.
- Page: Mark page heading and footing lines. Page heading lines are printed at the beginning of each page of the report. Page footing lines are printed at the bottom of each page of the report.
- Detail: There is a detail line in the report for every row in the underlying database table. Mark them using this option.
- Break: You can define 10 levels of control breaks using this option. We'll explain what control breaks are and what they are used for in chapter 9.
- List: This option displays the status of the various report sections.
- Help: Press [H] to obtain instructions for marking report sections.
- Quit: Press [Q] to return to the main report definition menu.

With reports like Great Plains' customer list, you'll only need to mark Page and Detail sections. Press [P] to mark Page sections. R:base presents you with the screen in Figure 7–36. At this point, you can name the report variables which you want reset to zero at the end of each page. Great Plains' customer list has no report variables, so press [Q]. You are then given the screen in Figure 7–37.

We want each page of the customer list to begin as follows:

```
          Great Plains Music and Video Unlimited
                      Customer List
                      -------------

Customer      First      Last
Number        Name       Name    Address                Phone
```

These lines are page heading lines. If the cursor is not on line one, move it there with the cursor movement keys. Mark the heading lines by repeatedly pressing [H] until all of the heading lines are marked. Notice

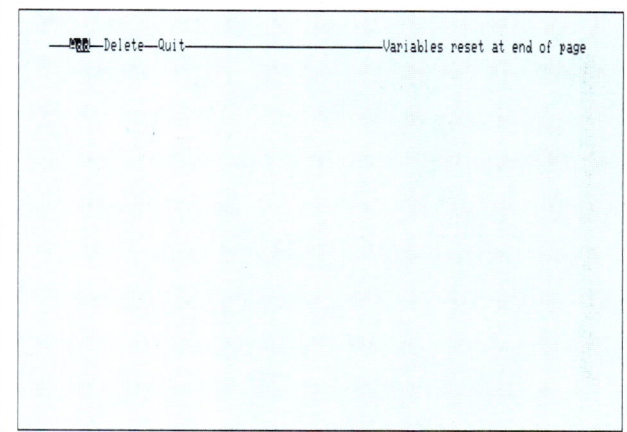

FIGURE 7–36
Screen for naming report variables

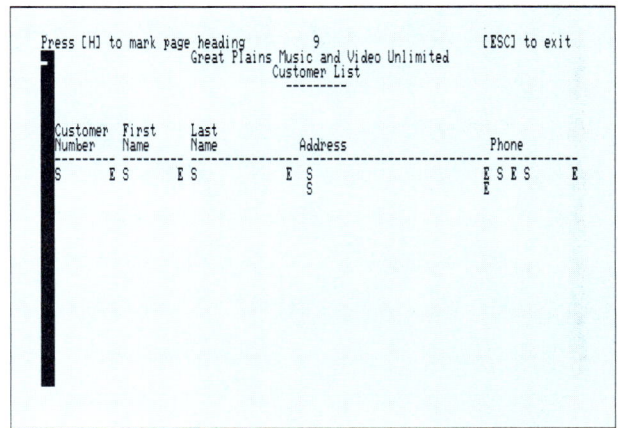

FIGURE 7–37
Screen for marking page headings

FIGURE 7-38

R:base uses the symbol HP to indicate page headings

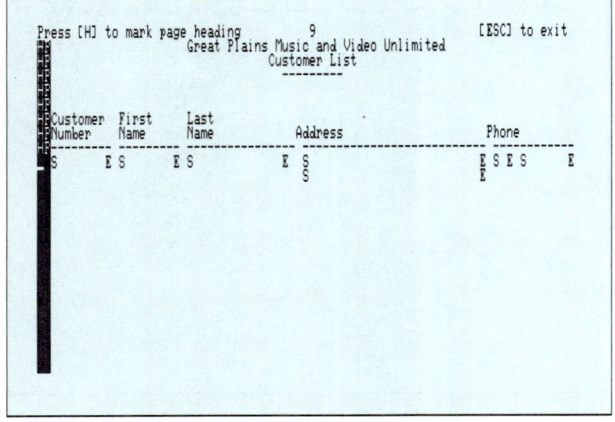

that R:base places the symbol HP in the stripe along the left side of the report. The symbol stands for "Heading — Page" (Figure 7–38). When you have finished marking the page heading, press [ESC] (Figure 7–39).

If the report had footing lines, you would mark them by moving the cursor to the first footing line, then repeatedly pressing [F]. Since there are no footing lines in Great Plains' customer list, press [ESC] to return to the "Marking Sections" menu.

Next press [D] to mark the detail line(s) (Figure 7–40). For Great Plains' customer list, there will be one entry in the report for every row in the CUSTOMER table. Each entry comprises the lines which contain the location of the data items—the ones with all the S's and E's. Move the cursor (if R:base hasn't already done so) next to the detail lines and press [D] twice. If you want the report to be double spaced, press [D] again (Figure 7–41).

Return to the "Marking Sections" menu by pressing [ESC]. Return to the main report definition menu by pressing [Q].

Set number of lines per page R:base assumes that the report will be printed on letter size paper (8 ½" × 11"). For most printers, that means 66 lines per page. If you want to change the number of lines per page, press [S]. (See Figure 7–42.) Enter the new number of lines per page and press [ENTER]. You may enter any number from 0 to 999. Use zero in situations where you do not want any page breaks, such as with continuous form mailing labels.

FIGURE 7-39

Ready to mark footing lines

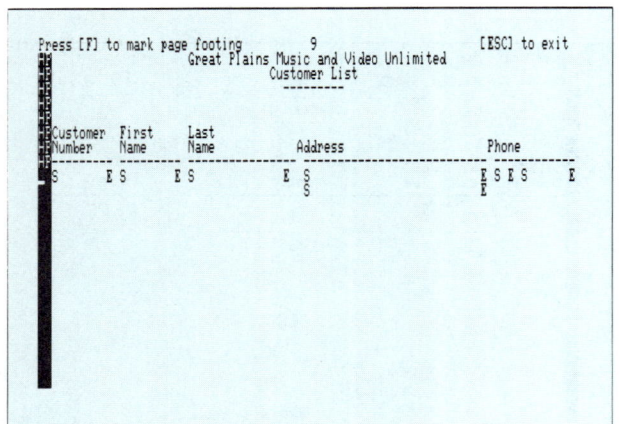

FIGURE 7-40

Ready to mark detail lines

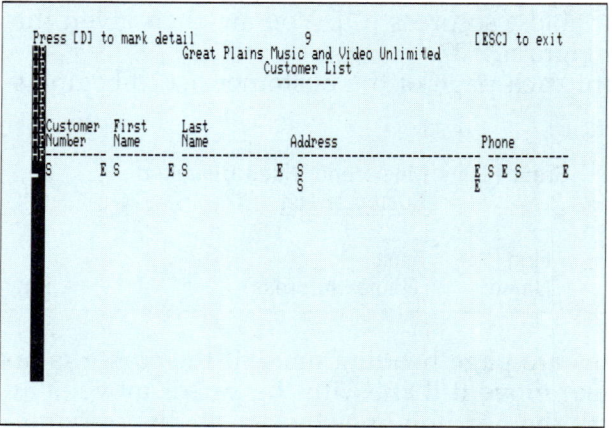

FIGURE 7-41

Indicating detail lines and double spacing

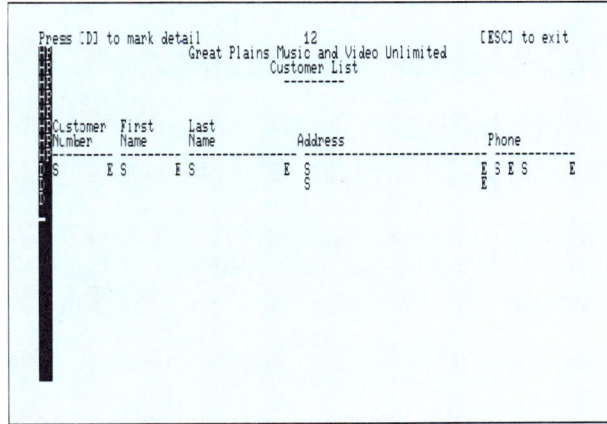

Storing the report definition The definition of Great Plains' customer list report is now complete. Press [Q] (Figure 7-43). R:base gives you three choices:

- Save changes: Press [S] to save the changes you have made and return to the main menu.
- Discard changes: Press [D] to discard the changes you have made and return to the main menu.
- Return: Press [R] to return to the main report definition menu.

FIGURE 7-42

Setting number of lines per page

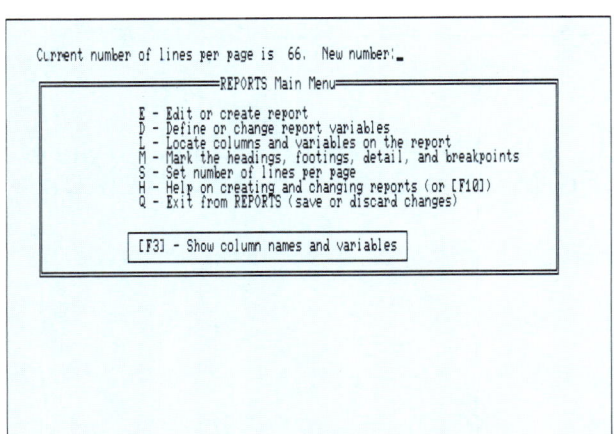

FIGURE 7-43

Storing the report definition

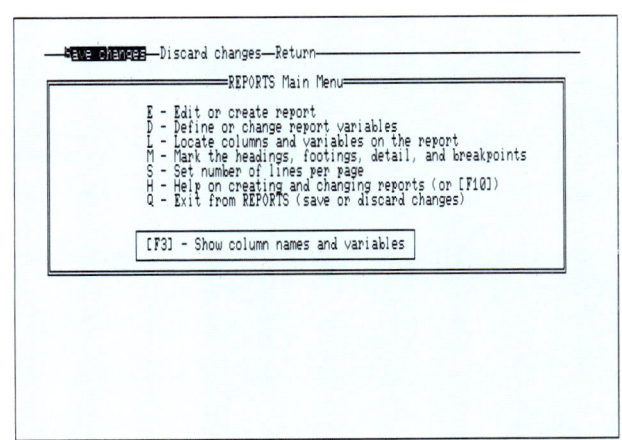

FIGURE 7–44
Press [S] to save the report definition

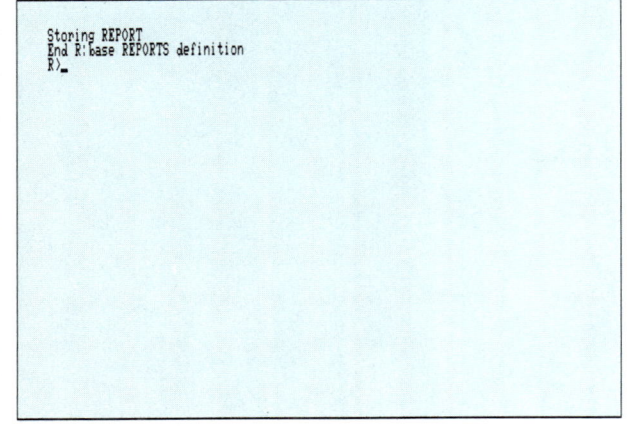

Since you want to save the report definition, press [S]. (See Figure 7–44.)

Printing the report Once a report is defined, it is a simple matter to print it. To display Great Plains' customer list in alphabetical order on the screen, type:

PRINT CUSTLIST SORTED BY CustLNam CustFNam

(The first four customers are shown in Figure 7–45.) If you have a printer and want the list printed type:

OUTPUT PRINTER
PRINT CUSTLIST SORTED BY CustLNam CustFNam
OUTPUT TERMINAL

FIGURE 7–45
R:base displays Great Plains' customer disk

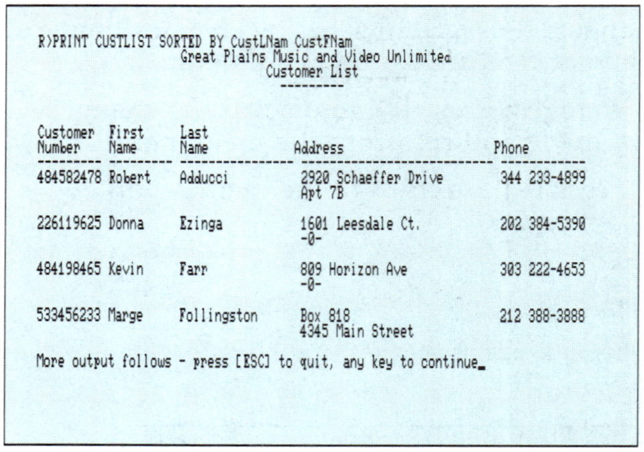

(If you have the file CH7.DAT, you can load the example CUSTOMER data by typing: INPUT CH7.DAT.)

SUMMARY

- There are five steps to defining tables using the R:base DEFINE mode:
  - Load R:base.
  - Enter the DEFINE mode.
  - Describe the columns.
  - Define the tables.
  - Exit the DEFINE mode.
- Enter the DEFINE mode by typing DEFINE followed by a valid database specification.
- A valid database specification has three parts:
  - a valid disk drive specification
  - a valid DOS path
  - a valid R:base database name
- If no disk drive or path is specified, the default drive and path are assumed.
- To describe a column in the DEFINE mode, type the column name followed by the type of data the column is to contain and, for TEXT columns, the column width.
- To describe a table in the DEFINE mode, type the names of the columns which the table is to comprise.
- Exit the DEFINE mode by typing END.
- R:base RULES are used to define conditions which must be met by values entered in a particular column.
- R:base RULES consist of two parts:
  - The error message to be displayed when the RULE is violated
  - The RULE condition
- There are four steps to specifying RULES:
  - Enter the DEFINE mode.
  - Prepare R:base to accept RULE definitions.
  - Specify the RULES.
  - Exit the DEFINE mode.
- RULE error messages can be a maximum of 40 characters.
- A complex R:base RULE condition may combine up to ten simple conditions using AND and OR.
- A properly designed database will have only the following kinds of restrictions:

- Key restriction
- Inclusion constraint
- Domain restriction

- Key restrictions are enforced by defining a RULE which ensures that entries in a key column are unique.
- Inclusion constraints are enforced by defining a RULE which ensures that an entry in a column has a corresponding entry in a column in another table.
- Domain restrictions are enforced by a combination of automatic data-type checking (to verify the physical characteristics of the entry) and RULES (to verify the validity of the value itself).
- R:base FORMS provide a convenient, familiar way for users to enter data.
- There are six steps to preparing an R:base FORM from the R:base command mode:
  - Type the word FORMS.
  - Provide the name of the FORM.
  - Provide the name of the table into which the data from the FORM is to be loaded.
  - Choose "Edit" and type the FORM on the screen.
  - Choose "Locate" and indicate the location of the data items (columns) on the form.
  - Return to the R:base command mode.
- To enter data using a predefined FORM, type ENTER followed by the name of the form to be used.
- After data has been entered in a FORM, you press [ESC] then [A] (Add) or [R] (Reuse) to have the data taken from the form and loaded into the table. If you press [Q] (Quit), the data in the form will not be added to the table.
- There are nine steps to preparing an R:base REPORT from the R:base command mode:
  - Type the word REPORTS.
  - Provide the name of the REPORT.
  - Provide the name of the table from which the data is to be obtained.
  - Choose "Edit report" and type the report on the screen.
  - Choose "Define" and define report variables.
  - Choose "Locate" and indicate the location of the data items (column and report variable names) on the report.

- Choose "Mark" and mark the report sections (Report heading and footing, Page heading and footing, Detail line(s) and control Breaks).
- Choose "Set" and set the number of lines per page.
- Choose "Quit" to return to the R:base command mode.
- To print a REPORT, type PRINT followed by the name of the REPORT and optional SORT and WHERE clauses.

REVIEW QUESTIONS

Group I Questions

7.1
List the five steps to defining database tables using the R:base DEFINE mode.

7.2
Name the three parts of a valid R:base database specification.

7.3
What is the DEFINE mode command which prepares R:base to accept column definitions?

7.4
How are column definitions made in the R:base DEFINE mode?

7.5
What is the DEFINE mode command which prepares R:base to accept table definitions?

7.6
How are table definitions made in the R:base DEFINE mode?

7.7
What is an R:base RULE?

7.8
What are the parts of an R:base RULE?

7.9
How are R:base RULES used to enforce key restrictions?

7.10
How are R:base RULES used to enforce inclusion constraints?

7.11
How are domain restrictions enforced in R:base?

7.12
Explain what an R:base FORM is and what it is used for.

7.13
Explain what an R:base REPORT is and what it is used for.

Group II Questions

7.14
List the R:base database specification for the PEOPLE database to be located:

a. In the root directory of drive A

b. In the PEOPLE directory of drive C

c. In the default directory

7.15
List the R:base command necessary to begin definition of the PEOPLE database located in the root directory of the B drive.

7.16
What would you type to define a column called Name which is to be 15 characters wide?

7.17
What would you type to define a column called Age which is to contain only integers?

7.18
What would you type to define a table called FOLKS which is to comprise the columns Name and Age?

7.19
What would you type to define a table called NAMES which is to comprise only the Name column?

7.20
Once you have prepared R:base to accept RULE definitions, what would you type to define a RULE to enforce the restriction that Name is the key to the NAMES table?

7.21
What would you type to define a RULE to ensure that entries in the Name column of the FOLKS table already appear in the NAMES table?

7.22
What would you type to define a RULE that ensured that entries in the Age column of the FOLKS table were between 0 and 100?

7.23
Explain how you would use R:base to enforce the following domain definition of a column called Height: Integer representing an individual's height, in inches, within the range from 36 to 96

PROJECT

A. Define R:base RULES to enforce the database restrictions on the database you designed of your academic environment in Chapter 5.

B. Create an R:base FORM for the CLASS table in your academic environment database. Use the form to load data about the classes you are currently taking.

C. Create an R:base REPORT for the CLASS table in your academic environment database. Use the report to print a list of classes you are currently taking.

CHAPTER 8

Relational Operations with R:base

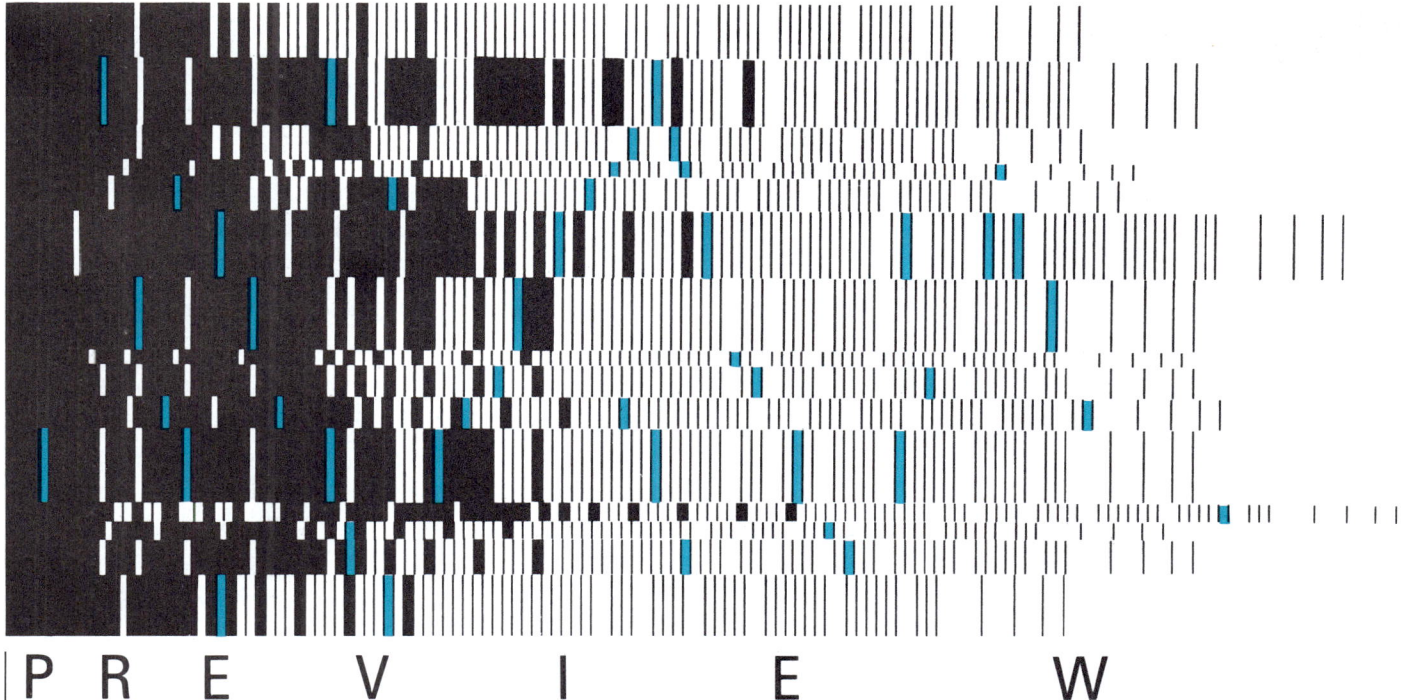

PREVIEW

One of the most important functions of a database management system is to provide a data manipulation language—a collection of operations which can be used to create information from data. In Chapter 3, we discussed three important operations which a relational database must provide: projection, selection, and join. In this chapter, we will briefly review those operations and introduce three additional ones: union, difference, and intersection. In the last part of the chapter, we will show you how to perform relational operations with R:base.

Note: If you want to work the example in this chapter, you will need the CUSTOMER and SALE tables together with the customer data from Chapter 7. In addition, you will need to define the INVENTORY (INV) and COMPONENT/SALE (COMPSALE) tables of the Great Plains database. If you have the files CH8.DAT on your data disk, type: INPUT CH8.DAT at the R:base R> prompt. The GTPLAIN database will be modified for you. If you are not using the student version of R:base and you have the file CH8.DAT on your data disk, type: INPUT CH8.DAT to have the INV and COMPSALE tables and sample data added to the database. Remember to open the database by typing OPEN GTPLAIN after loading R:base.

BASIC RELATIONAL OPERATIONS

In Chapter 3, we discussed the minimum operations required of a relational database management system:

- Projection uses a source table to produce a new table which contains all of the rows from the source table, but only a subset of the columns.

- Selection uses a source table to produce a new table which contains all of the columns from the source table, but only a subset of the rows.

- Join uses two source tables to produce a new table containing all of the columns from both tables. Which rows are included depends on the type of join performed.

If you feel uncertain about these operations, review the complete explanation and examples in Chapter 3.

OTHER RELATIONAL OPERATIONS

As we saw in Chapter 3, projection, selection, and join are very useful operations. However, there are some things you'll want to do which cannot be done using those three operations. Accordingly, most complete relational DBMS products include at least three other relational operations: union, difference, and intersection.

Union, difference, and intersection work with tables that are *union compatible*. Tables are union compatible if they have the same number of columns and the corresponding columns come from the same domain. Consider the following OFFICER and SALESPERSON tables:

OFFICER(EmpID#, Name)

Column definitions:

Column Name	Domain
EmpID#	INTEGER uniquely identifying an employee
Name	TEXT 30 representing the name of an employee

SALESPERSON(Number, EmpName)

Column definitions:

Column Name	Domain
Number	INTEGER uniquely identifying an employee
EmpName	TEXT 30 representing the name of an employee

OFFICER and SALESPERSON are union compatible because they each have two columns and the corresponding columns arise from the same domain. Notice that the column names do not have to be the same. Consider one more table, PEOPLE:

PEOPLE(Number, Name)

Column definitions:

Column Name	Domain
Number	INTEGER uniquely identifying a person
Name	TEXT 30 representing the name of a person

PEOPLE is not union compatible with OFFICER or SALESPERSON because the domain of the PEOPLE columns is different from the domain of the corresponding OFFICER and SALESPERSON columns. Even though the column names are also used in OFFICER and SALESPERSON, they do not represent data about employees, but about people in general.

Now that you understand what *union compatible* means, we can describe the new relational operations—union, difference, and intersection.

Union

The union operation uses two union compatible source tables to produce a new table which contains all of the rows from both source tables. Duplicate rows are eliminated. Sample occurrences of OFFICER and SALESPERSON and the NEWTABLE of their union are shown in Figure 8-1. The union operation has taken the three rows from OFFICER and the two rows from SALESPERSON and placed them in NEWTABLE. Notice that one row [5,Jones], occurs in both tables. If it were included twice in NEWTABLE there would be a duplicate row, which is not allowed.

FIGURE 8-1

Sample occurrences of OFFICER and SALESPERSON and the NEWTABLE of their union

OFFICER

EmpID#	Name
4	Smith
5	Jones
6	Abel

SALESPERSON

Number	EmpName
5	Jones
7	Mason

NEWTABLE

EmpID# or Number	Name or EmpName
4	Smith
5	Jones
6	Abel
7	Mason

You would use union to answer the question "Who is either an OFFICER or a SALESPERSON?"

Difference

The difference operation compares two union compatible tables and creates a third table containing rows which occur in the first table but not in the second. Sample occurrences of the OFFICER and SALESPERSON tables are shown in Figure 8–2a.

As with arithmetic, the order of the subtraction matters. $A - B$ is not the same as $B - A$. Figure 8–2b shows the result of the difference operation—OFFICER minus SALESPERSON. This operation would be used to answer the question "Who is an OFFICER and not also a SALESPERSON?"

Figure 8–2c shows the result of the difference operation—SALESPERSON minus OFFICER. You would use this operation to answer the question "Who is a SALESPERSON and not also an OFFICER?"

Intersection

Intersection uses two union compatible tables to produce a third table containing rows which are common to the tables being intersected. Figure 8–3 shows sample occurrences of OFFICER and SALESPERSON and the result of their intersection. This operation would be used to answer the question, "Who is an OFFICER and a SALESPERSON?"

Figure 8-4 contains a summary of union, difference, and intersection.

RELATIONAL OPERATIONS WITH R:BASE

We have described six relational operations: selection, projection, join, union, difference, and intersection. These descriptions come from the theory of relational algebra. Each DBMS implements the operations within its data manipulation language. Unfortunately, there is not always a one-to-one correspondence between the theoretical operation and the data manipulation language of the DBMS. In this section, we'll explain how R:base implements relational algebra.

The data manipulation language of R:base implements all six relational operations. Learning which R:base commands are used to implement a relational operation can be confusing because an R:base command may not implement the relational operation of the same name. For example, under certain circumstances, the R:base INTERSECT command is used to perform relational join operations. You can minimize confusion for yourself by making sure you are comfortable with the definition of the relational operations

---

FIGURE 8–2a

Tables to be used in difference operation

OFFICER

EmpID#	Name
4	Smith
5	Jones
6	Abel

SALESPERSON

Number	EmpName
5	Jones
7	Mason

FIGURE 8–2b

Result of OFFICER minus SALESPERSON

NEWTABLE

EmpID# or Number	Name or EmpName
4	Smith
6	Abel

FIGURE 8–2c

Result of SALESPERSON minus OFFICER

NEWTABLE

EmpID# or Number	Name or EmpName
7	Mason

before you proceed. We will discuss the most important commands in the R:base data manipulation language and provide examples of how each is used to perform relational operations.

The R:base SELECT Command
The R:base SELECT command is the only command which displays data from R:base database tables. Recall from Chapter 6 that the general form of the command is:

SELECT columnlist FROM tablename WHERE condition

The R:base SELECT command can be used to display the results of either a relational selection operation, a relational projection operation, or a combination of the two. Instead of creating a new table, the R:base SELECT command displays the results of the operation(s) on the screen. Let's look at examples from the Great Plains database.

Performing a Relational Selection Using the R:base SELECT Command The relational selection operation produces a subset of the rows from the source table. This operation is useful in responding to requests like "Show me all of the data for customers with zip code 80526." To respond to this request, use the R:base SELECT command:

SELECT ALL FROM CUSTOMER WHERE ZipCode EQ 80526

This command instructs R:base to display all of the columns from rows in the CUSTOMER table in which the value in the ZipCode column is 80526, as shown in Figure 8–5.

Performing a Relational Projection Using the R:base SELECT Command While the relational selection operation produces a subset of the rows from the source table, the relational projection operation produces a subset of the columns. You can use the relational projection operation to respond to requests such as "Show me the names and phone numbers of all the customers." Use the following R:base SELECT command for this query:

SELECT CustFNam, CustLNam, Phone FROM CUSTOMER

The command instructs R:base to display the contents of the CustFNam, CustLNam, and Phone columns for all the rows in the CUSTOMER table (Figure 8–6).

| **FIGURE 8–3**

Sample occurrences of OFFICER and SALESPERSON and the result of their intersection

OFFICER

EmpID#	Name
4	Smith
5	Jones
6	Abel

SALESPERSON

Number	EmpName
5	Jones
7	Mason

NEWTABLE

EmpID# or Number	Name or EmpName
5	Jones

| **FIGURE 8–4**

Summary of union, difference, and intersection

- **Union** uses two union compatible tables to produce a new table containing the rows from both source tables. Duplicate rows are eliminated.
- **Difference** compares two union compatible tables to produce a new table containing rows from one table which do not appear in the other.
- **Intersection** compares two union compatible tables to produce a new table containing rows which are common to the source tables.

FIGURE 8–5

Using R:base SELECT to perform a relational selection operation

```
R)SELECT ALL FROM CUSTOMER WHERE ZipCode EQ 80526
CustID#      CustFNam   CustLNam     Addr1           Addr2
---------    --------   --------     -----           -----
399453243    George     McGillicuddy P.O. Box 83     59430
                                                     South
                                                     Franklin
                                                     St
374652948    Jonah      Goldstein    P.O. Box 56     124 Ash
                                                     Street
R)
```

FIGURE 8–6

Using R:base SELECT to perform a relational projection operation

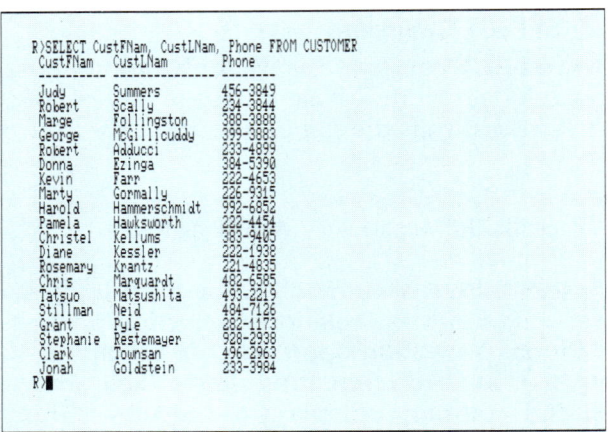

FIGURE 8–7

Using R:base SELECT to combine relational selection and projection operations

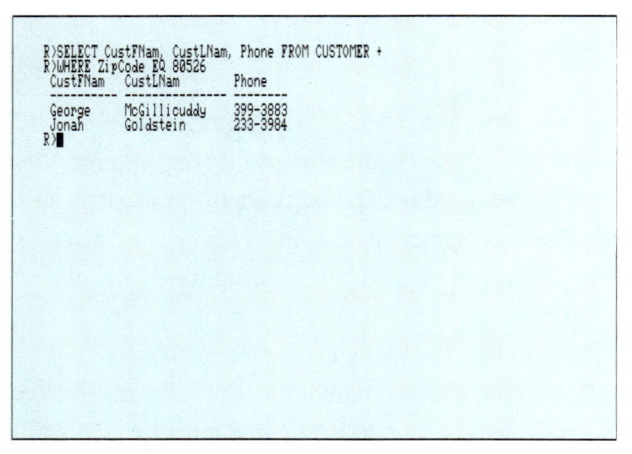

Combining the Relational Selection and Projection Operations Using the R:base SELECT Command What if somebody makes a request like "Show me the name and phone number of customers who have a Zip Code of 80526"? To respond to the request you need to combine the above relational selection and projection operations. You can combine relational selection and projection operations using the R:base SELECT command as follows:

SELECT CustFNam, CustLNam, Phone FROM CUSTOMER +
WHERE ZipCode EQ 80526

Remember that the plus sign (+) tells R:base that there is more of the command on the next line. The command instructs R:base to display the contents of the CustFNam, CustLNam, and Phone columns from the rows in the CUSTOMER table where the value of the ZipCode column is 80526 (Figure 8–7).

The R:base PROJECT Command

R:base PROJECT is similar to R:base SELECT with one important difference. Whereas R:base SELECT displays the results of the operation(s) on the screen, R:base PROJECT creates a new table which contains the results. Like R:base SELECT, the R:base PROJECT command works with only one table at a time. It can be used to perform either a relational selection operation, a relational projection operation, or a combination of the two. Let's look at some more examples.

Performing a Relational Selection Using the R:base PROJECT Command As you know, the relational selection creates a new table which contains a subset of the rows from a source table. Suppose you wanted to create a table called TOPEND which contains the data for inventory items which cost in excess of $400. Use the R:base PROJECT command to accomplish the task:

PROJECT TOPEND FROM INV USING ALL WHERE Cost GT $400

This command instructs R:base to create a new table called TOPEND consisting of rows from the table called INV where the column called Cost contains a value which is greater than $400 (Figure 8–8). The key word USING followed by a column list or the key word ALL tells R:base which columns from the source table to include in the new table. We use ALL in this example since, by definition, the new table which results from a relational selection operation includes all of the columns from the source table. Note in Figure 8–8 that R:base does not display any data resulting from the operation. You are merely given a message to indicate whether the operation was successful and, if so, how many rows are contained in the new table. If you want to see the contents of the new table, you must use the R:base SELECT command:

SELECT ALL FROM TOPEND

(Figure 8–9). Throughout the remainder of this section, we will use SELECT to display the results of the commands being illustrated. Also, don't forget to remove any temporary tables from the database with the R:base REMOVE command as in Figure 8–9.

Performing a Relational Projection Using the R:base PROJECT Command The relational projection operation produces a new table which contains a subset of the columns from the source table. For example, suppose you wanted to create a new table called COSTS which contains only the item number and the cost of all the inventory items. The relational projection operation will accomplish this task. To perform the operation using R:base, use the following R:base PROJECT command:

PROJECT COSTS FROM INV USING Item# Cost

The command instructs R:base to create a new table called COSTS consisting of the values in the Item# and Cost columns from all the rows in the table called INV (Figure 8–10).

FIGURE 8–8

Using R:base PROJECT to perform a relational selection operation

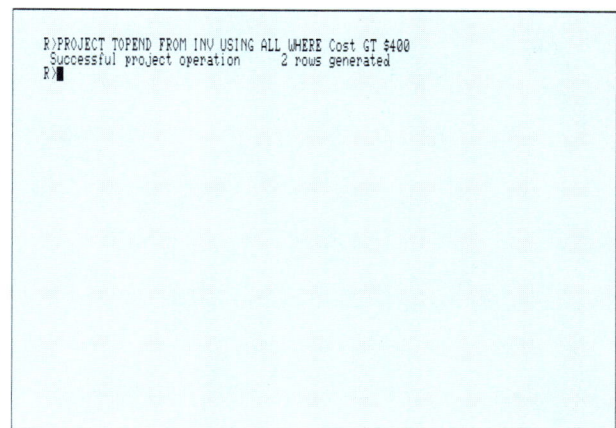

FIGURE 8–9

Display of new table named TOPEND

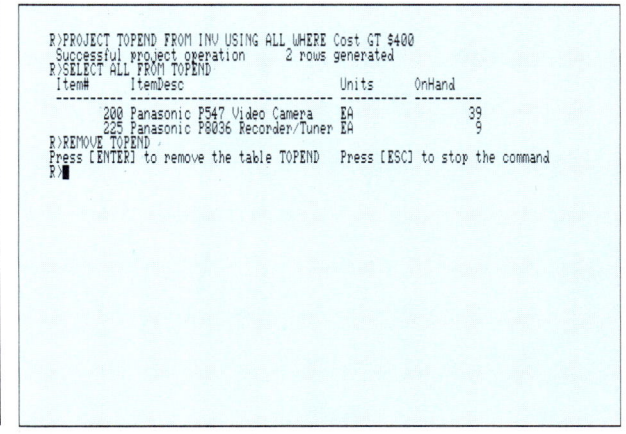

FIGURE 8–10
Using R:base PROJECT to perform a relational projection operation

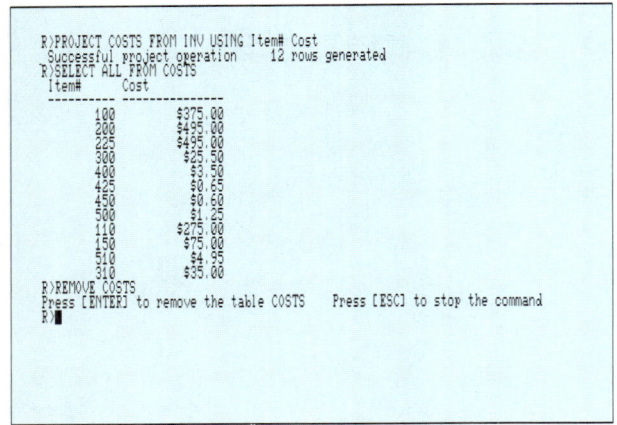

FIGURE 8–11
Using R:base PROJECT to combine relational selection and projection operations

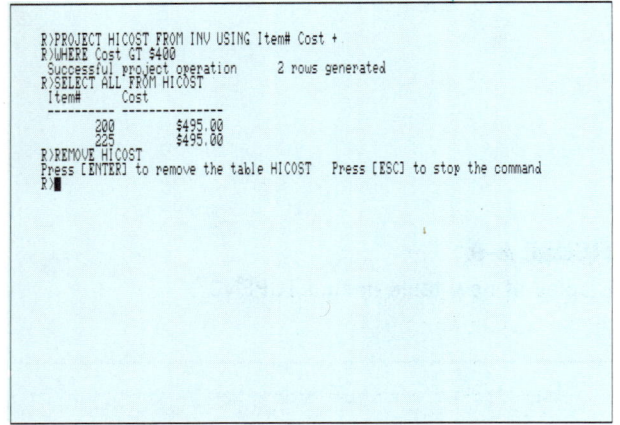

Combining the Relational Selection and Projection Operations Using the R:base PROJECT Command As with the R:base SELECT command, you can combine relational selection and projection operations using the R:base PROJECT command. If you wanted a new table called HICOST which contains only the item number and the cost for inventory items which cost more than $400, you would use the following R:base PROJECT command:

PROJECT HICOST FROM INV USING Item# Cost +
WHERE Cost GT $400

The command instructs R:base to create a new table called HICOST consisting of the values in the Item# and Cost columns from the rows in the table called INV where the value in the Cost column exceeds $400 (Figure 8–11).

The R:base INTERSECT Command

The R:base INTERSECT command is used to create a new table from two source tables. R:base INTERSECT looks for one or more columns in the source tables which have the same name. It then compares the values contained in the common columns. When the values in the corresponding common columns match, it creates a row in the new table. Unless specified in the command, the rows in the new table contain all the columns from both source tables. R:base does not require the source tables to be union compatible.

INTERSECT is used to perform relational intersection operations with union compatible tables or relational join operations with tables which are not union compatible.

Performing a Relational Intersection Using the R:base INTERSECT Command When used with union compatible tables, the R:base INTERSECT command performs a relational intersection operation. Thus, the R:base INTERSECT command can be used to determine which rows two union compatible tables have in common. The general form of the R:base INTERSECT command is as follows:

INTERSECT table1 WITH table2 FORMING table3

The command instructs R:base to create a new table (table3) from two source tables (table1 and table2).

Performing a Relational Join Using the R:base INTERSECT Command Whenever you want to perform a relational join on two tables where the linking columns have the same name, use the R:base INTERSECT command. Recall that the relational join operation uses two source tables to create a new table which contains all of the columns from both source tables. For example, look at the following definition of the INVENTORY and COMPONENT/SALE tables from the Great Plains database:

- INVENTORY (Item number, Item description, Units, Quantity on hand, Cost, Price)

- COMPONENT/SALE (Item number, Sales identification number, Quantity sold, Sales price, Sales amount)

The table (we'll call it NEWTABLE) which results from the join of INVENTORY and COMPONENT/SALE will have the following definition:

- NEWTABLE (Item number, Item description, Units, Quantity on hand, Cost, Price, Sales identification number, Quantity sold, Sales price, Sales amount)

Notice that the key of INVENTORY, Item number, is used as a foreign key in COMPONENT/SALE. Said another way, Item number is used as a link between INVENTORY and COMPONENT/SALE. During the join operation, each row in INVENTORY is compared to all the rows in COMPONENT/SALE. Whenever there is a match between the value in the Item number column of the INVENTORY row and the value in the Item number column of the COMPONENT/SALE row, the two rows are combined and entered as a row in NEWTABLE. This type of join is called a *natural join* because the operation looks for equality between the values in the linking columns and because the linking column appears only once in NEWTABLE.

Whenever you want to perform a natural join on two tables in which the linking columns have the same name, use the R:base INTERSECT command. The following INTERSECT command is used to perform the natural join of the INVENTORY and COMPONENT/SALE tables:

INTERSECT INV WITH COMPSALE FORMING NEWTABLE

(Figure 8–12). Notice that there is no mention of the linking columns in the command. The R:base INTERSECT command automatically looks for columns which the two tables have in common.

FIGURE 8–12

Using R:base INTERSECT to perform a relational join operation

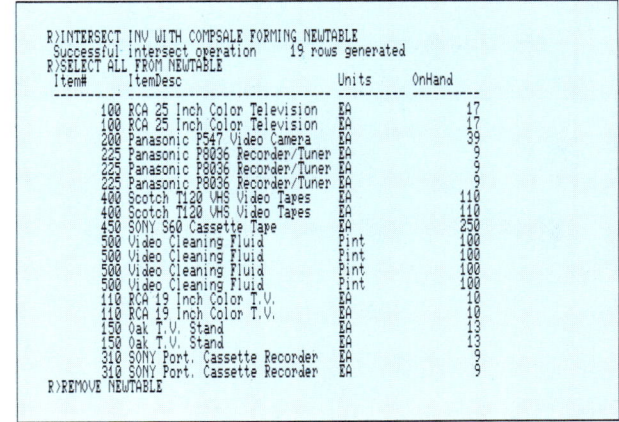

FIGURE 8–13a

Using R:base INTERSECT to perform relational join and projection

```
R>INTERSECT INV WITH COMPSALE FORMING NEWTABLE +
R>USING SaleID# Item# ItemDesc Cost
  Successful intersect operation     19 rows generated
R>
```

FIGURE 8–13b

Display of NEWTABLE containing only sale ID numbers, item numbers, descriptions, and costs

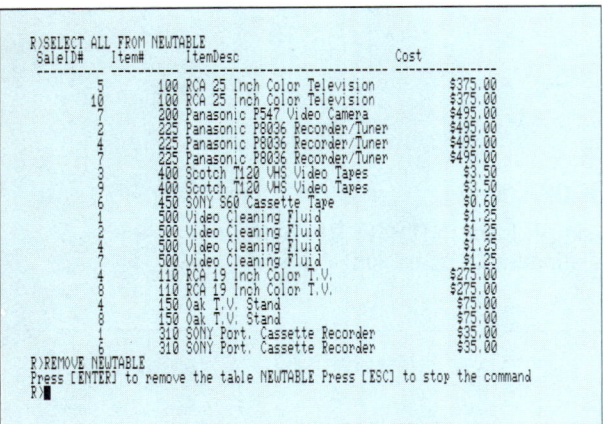

Combining the Relational Projection and Natural Join Operations Using the R:base INTERSECT Command As we saw in the previous section, the relational join operation results in a new table which has all the columns from both source tables. What if you don't want all of the columns? In such a case, use the relational operation which produces a subset of the columns in a table—the relational projection operation. You can have R:base perform a relational projection as part of the INTERSECT command. For example, suppose you want NEWTABLE to contain only the Sales identification number, Item number, Description, and Cost columns from the natural join of INVENTORY and COMPONENT/SALE. Include a USING clause in the INTERSECT command as follows:

    INTERSECT INV WITH COMPSALE FORMING NEWTABLE +
    USING SaleID# Item# ItemDesc Cost

The command instructs R:base to perform the natural join of INV and COMPSALE but to include only SaleID#, Item#, ItemDesc, and Cost columns in NEWTABLE (Figure 8–13). The resulting table is the equivalent of having performed a relational natural join followed by a relational projection.

The R:base JOIN Command

The R:base JOIN command is used to perform relational join operations. It works in accordance with the theoretical definition of the relational operation. R:base JOIN requires that the column which links the tables have a different name in each table.

For example, to use R:base JOIN command to perform the natural join of SALE and COMPSALE, you must first change the name of the linking column in one of the tables using the R:base RENAME command:

    RENAME COLUMN SaleID# TO SaleNum IN SALE

(Figure 8–14). Once the linking columns have different names, the following R:base command will perform the relational join:

    JOIN SALE USING SaleNum WITH +
    COMPSALE USING SaleID# FORMING NEWTABLE

(Figure 8–15).

Recall that a natural join operation creates a row in the new table where the values in the linking columns are equal. You can specify that another type of comparison is to be used by including a unique type of

FIGURE 8–14
R:base command to rename a column

FIGURE 8–15a
Using R:base JOIN to perform a relational join operation

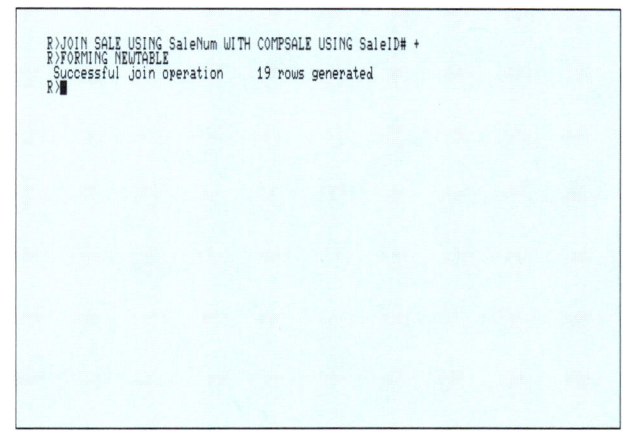

WHERE clause. The general form of the R:base JOIN command which includes a WHERE clause is:

JOIN table1 USING column1 WITH table2 USING column2 + FORMING table3 WHERE logical operator

Logical operator may have a value of EQ (the value assumed if a WHERE clause is omitted), NE (not equal), LT (less than), LE (less than or equal to), GT (greater than), or GE (greater than or equal to). As an example, the R:base JOIN command

JOIN SALE USING SaleNum WITH COMPSALE USING SaleID# + FORMING NEWTABLE WHERE GT

instructs R:base to create a row in NEWTABLE whenever the value of SaleNum is greater than the value of SaleID#. As you might guess, the occasions when you would want to perform a join other than a natural join are rare indeed. Don't forget to rename SaleNum to SaleID# by typing:

RENAME COLUMN SaleNum to SaleID# IN SALE

The R:base UNION Command

The R:base UNION command is used to create a new table from two source tables. When used with union compatible tables, the R:base UNION command performs a relational union operation. When used with tables which are not union compatible, the R:base UNION command creates a new table which has all of the columns and all of the rows from both source tables. See the R:base documentation for more details on

FIGURE 8–15b
Display of NEWTABLE based on natural join of SALE and COMPSALE

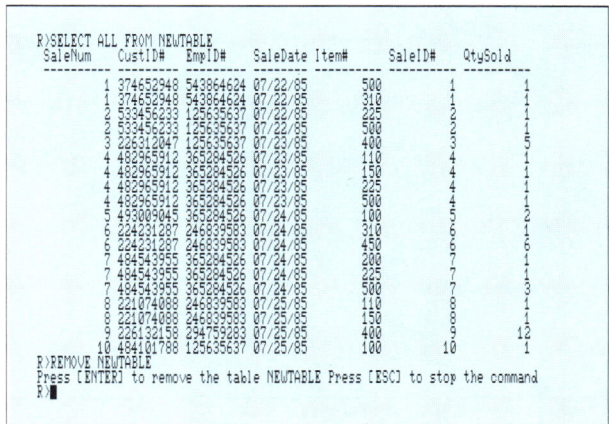

FIGURE 8–16a
Creating a new table that contains the first five rows from CUSTOMERS

```
R)PROJECT NEWCUST FROM CUSTOMER USING ALL WHERE LIMIT EQ 5
  Successful project operation      5 rows generated
R)SELECT CustID# CustFNam CustLNam FROM NEWCUST
  CustID#    CustFNam    CustLNam
  ---------  ----------  ---------------
  374652948  Jonah       Goldstein
  464275330  Judy        Summers
  233542069  Robert      Scally
  533456233  Marge       Follingston
  399453243  George      McGillicuddy
R)
```

FIGURE 8–16b
Display of CUSTOMER

```
R)SELECT CustID# CustFNam CustLNam FROM CUSTOMER
  CustID#    CustFNam    CustLNam
  ---------  ----------  ---------------
  374652948  Jonah       Goldstein
  464275330  Judy        Summers
  233542069  Robert      Scally
  533456233  Marge       Follingston
  399453243  George      McGillicuddy
  484582478  Robert      Adducci
  226119625  Donna       Ezinga
  484198465  Kevin       Farr
  226312047  Marty       Gormally
  226132158  Harold      Hammerschmidt
  223413685  Pamela      Hawksworth
  482965912  Christel    Kellums
  226374325  Diane       Kessler
  493489925  Rosemary    Krantz
  5683644    Chris       Marquardt
  473009045  Tatsuo      Matsushita
  661074088  Stillman    Neid
  224231287  Grant       Pyle
  484101789  Stephanie   Restemayer
  484543955  Clark       Townsan
R)
```

the use of UNION with tables which are not union compatible.

Performing a Relational Union Operation Using the R:base UNION Command There are no union compatible tables in the Great Plains database design to use as an example, so let's make one.

Create a table which is union compatible with CUSTOMER by using the following R:base PROJECT command:

PROJECT NEWCUST FROM CUSTOMER USING ALL +
WHERE LIMIT EQ 5

The command instructs R:base to create a table called NEWCUST which contains the first five rows from the CUSTOMER table. The contents of CUSTOMER and NEWCUST are shown in Figure 8–16. Now perform a relational union operation on CUSTOMER and NEWCUST:

UNION CUSTOMER WITH NEWCUST FORMING TEMP

(Figure 8–17). (If you're using the student version of R:base, be sure to remove NEWCUST before you display the contents of TEMP.) Notice that the R:base UNION command automatically eliminates duplicate rows.

Once you have finished with TEMP, delete it from the database with the R:base REMOVE command:

REMOVE TEMP

The R:base SUBTRACT Command
The R:base SUBTRACT command is useful in comparing two tables to see which items are in one table but not the other. The general form of the command is:

SUBTRACT table1 FROM table2 FORMING table3

The SUBTRACT command instructs R:base to look for columns which the source tables have in common. It then compares the value(s) in the common column(s). The new table contains rows from table2 which do not match rows in table1.

When used with union compatible tables, the R:base SUBTRACT command can be used to perform relational difference operations. The R:base SUBTRACT command does not require the source tables to be union compatible.

FIGURE 8–17a
Using R:base UNION with union compatible tables to perform a relational union operation

```
R>UNION CUSTOMER WITH NEWCUST FORMING TEMP
  Successful union operation    20 rows generated
R>REMOVE NEWCUST
Press [ENTER] to remove the table NEWCUST  Press [ESC] to stop the command
R>
```

FIGURE 8–17b
Display of TEMP based on the union of CUSTOMER and NEWCUST

```
R>SELECT CustID# CustFNam CustLNam FROM TEMP
CustID#    CustFNam    CustLNam
-------    --------    --------
374652948  Jonah       Goldstein
454275338  Judy        Summers
213342069  Robert      Scally
513456233  Marge       Follingston
359453243  George      McGillicuddy
464582478  Robert      Adducci
226119625  Donna       Ezinga
484198465  Kevin       Farr
226312047  Marty       Gormally
226132158  Harold      Hammerschmidt
223413685  Pamela      Hawksworth
482965912  Christel    Kellums
226374925  Diane       Kessler
493489925  Rosemary    Krantz
5683644    Chris       Marquardt
493009045  Tatsuo      Matsushita
221074088  Stillman    Neid
224231287  Grant       Pyle
484101788  Stephanie   Restemayer
484543955  Clark       Townsan
R>REMOVE TEMP
Press [ENTER] to remove the table TEMP    Press [ESC] to stop the command
```

Comparing Tables Using the R:base SUBTRACT Command The R:base SUBTRACT command is a useful one. For example, suppose the management of Great Plains wants to know which inventory items have not had any sales. The following R:base SUBTRACT command can provide the answer:

SUBTRACT COMPSALE FROM INV FORMING NOSALE

(Figure 8–18). Notice that the rows in NOSALE have all the columns from COMPSALE. However, to answer the question "Which inventory items have not sold?", all you need is two columns—Item# and ItemDesc.

FIGURE 8–18
Using R:base SUBTRACT to determine which items have not sold

```
R>SUBTRACT COMPSALE FROM INV FORMING NOSALE
  Successful subtract operation    3 rows generated
R>SELECT ALL FROM NOSALE
 Item#   ItemDesc                      Units    OnHand
 -----   --------                      -----    ------
  300    SONY S210 Portable AM/FM Radio  EA         17
  425    SONY S90 Cassette Tape          EA        250
  510    VHS Video Cleaning Tape         EA          3
R>REMOVE NOSALE
Press [ENTER] to remove the table NOSALE  Press [ESC] to stop the command
R>
```

FIGURE 8-19

Including a USING clause to specify columns to appear in a new table

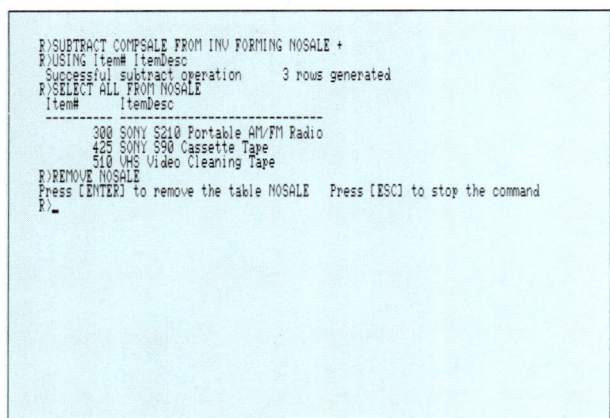

Using a Relational Projection Operation with the R:base SUBTRACT Command You can specify which columns are to appear in the new table by including a USING clause as follows:

SUBTRACT COMPSALE FROM INV FORMING NOSALE +
USING Item# ItemDesc

(Figure 8–19). In effect, the USING clause instructs R:base to perform a relational projection operation as part of the SUBTRACT command.

Figure 8–20 summarizes the relational operations and the R:base commands used to implement them.

FIGURE 8-20

Summary of relational operations and R:base commands

Relational operation	General Form of R:Base Command
Selection	SELECT ALL FROM source table WHERE condition (Displays all of the columns from the source table but only for those rows meeting the WHERE condition.)
	PROJECT new table FROM source table USING ALL WHERE condition (Creates a new table which contains all of the columns from the source table but only for those rows meeting the WHERE condition.)
Projection	SELECT column list FROM source table (Displays the columns listed for all of the rows in the source table.)
	PROJECT new table FROM source table USING column list (Creates a new table which contains the columns listed for all of the rows in the source table.)

Projection and selection combined	SELECT column list FROM source table WHERE condition (Displays the columns listed for the rows in the source table which meet the WHERE condition.) PROJECT new table FROM source table USING column list WHERE condition (Creates a new table which contains the columns listed for the rows in the source table which meet the WHERE condition.)
Natural join	INTERSECT source table1 WITH source table2 FORMING new table (Creates a new table containing all of the columns from both source tables, but only those rows where the common columns have a matching value. Used when the source tables are not union compatible and when the columns which link the source tables have the same name.)
Other joins	JOIN source table1 USING linking column WITH source table2 USING linking column FORMING new table (Creates a new table containing all of the columns from both source tables, but only those rows where the values in the linking columns are equal. Used when the columns which link the source tables have different names.) JOIN source table1 USING linking column1 WITH source table2 USING linking column2 FORMING new table WHERE logical operator (Creates a new table containing all of the columns from both source tables, but only those rows where the values in the linking columns satisfy the comparison listed in the WHERE clause. The logical operator is used to compare values in linking column1 to the values in linking column2 and may be EQ, NE, LT, LE, GT, GE.)

FIGURE 8–20 continued

Relational operation	General Form of R:Base Command
Union	UNION source table1 WITH source table2 FORMING new table (Creates a new table containing all the columns and all the rows from both source tables.)
Difference	SUBTRACT source table1 FROM source table2 FORMING new table (Creates a new table which contains rows from table2 which do not appear in table1.)
Intersection	INTERSECT source table1 WITH source table2 FORMING new table (Creates a new table which contains rows which appear in both source tables.)

SUMMARY

- The minimum operations required of a relational database management system are:
  - Projection, which creates a subset of the columns in a table
  - Selection, which creates a subset of the rows in a table
  - Join, which combines two tables into a new table containing all columns from both tables
- Tables are union compatible if they have the same number of columns and the corresponding columns come from the same domain.
- There are some database operations which require additional relational operations:
  - Union, which creates a new table that contains all of the rows from two union compatible tables
  - Difference, which compares two union compatible tables and creates a new table with rows that appear in one of the source tables but not the other
  - Intersection, which compares two union compatible tables and creates a new table with rows that appear in both source tables
- The R:base SELECT command can be used to display the results of a relational selection operation, a relational projection operation, or a combination of both. R:base SELECT does not create a new database table.
- The R:base PROJECT command can be used to perform a relational selection operation, a relational projection operation, or a combination of both. R:base PROJECT creates a new database table to contain the results of the operation(s).
- The R:base INTERSECT command can be used to perform relational intersection operations on union compatible tables. When used with tables which are not union compatible, R:base INTERSECT is used to perform relational natural join operations. INTERSECT can be used with source tables which have multiple linking columns but requires that corresponding linking columns have the same name.
- The R:base UNION command is used to perform relational union operations on union compatible tables. When used with tables which are not union compatible, R:base UNION creates a new table which contains all of the rows and all of the columns from both source tables.
- The R:base SUBTRACT command is used to perform relational difference operations on union compatible tables.

When used with tables which are not union compatible, R:base SUBTRACT compares values in columns which have the same name in both source tables. It then creates a new table which contains rows from one of the source tables which do not have matching values in common columns in the other source table.

REVIEW QUESTIONS

Group I Questions

8.1
List the three operations required of a minimal relational system. In your own words, explain the function of each.

8.2
Which relational operation(s) is (are) performed with the R:base SELECT command? In what situation(s) would you use the SELECT command?

8.3
Which relational operation(s) is (are) performed with the R:base PROJECT command? In what situation(s) would you use the PROJECT command?

8.4
Which R:base command(s) are used to perform relational join operations? When is it appropriate to use this (these) command(s)?

8.5
What is the function of the relational union operation?

8.6
How are relational union operations performed with R:base?

8.7
What is the function of the relational difference operation?

8.8
How are relational difference operations performed with R:base?

8.9
What is the function of the relational intersection operation?

8.10
How are relational intersection operations performed with R:base?

Group II Questions

If you have the student version of R:base, you can add the remaining tables to your GTPLAIN database and load the data used in the chapter by INPUTing the file CH8STU.VER. Your instructor will provide you with detailed instructions.

Provide the R:base commands to answer the following questions from management of Great Plains Music and Video Unlimited (don't forget about COMPUTE):

8.11
What was the total amount of sales during July 1985?

8.12
What did Tatsuo Matsushita buy from Great Plains in July 1985?

8.13
What is the total amount of sales made by Greg Abel in July 1985?

8.14
How many units of Video Cleaning Fluid have been sold?

8.15
Which inventory items had no sales in July 1985?

8.16
Which sales were made at a discount? (That is, in which sales was the actual selling price less than the suggested selling price?)

8.17
List the dates, salespersons, customers, and item descriptions for all July 1985 sales.

PROJECT

Answer the following questions from your academic database:

- List the names of the instructors of the classes you have rated eight or higher.

- What is the lowest rating you have given any class? What text(s) was (were) used?

- Which publishing company has provided the most texts for the classes you have taken?

CHAPTER 9

Advanced Report Writing with R:base

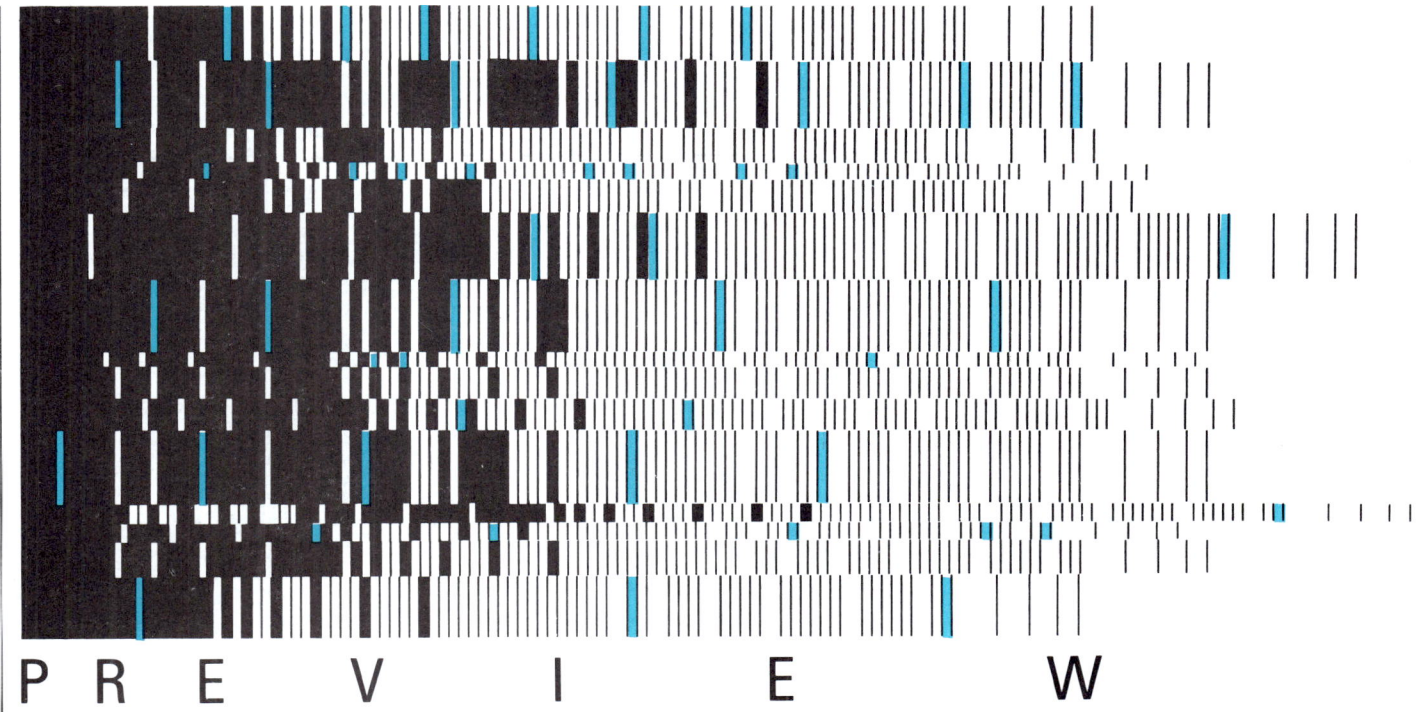

P R E V I E W

In Chapter 7, we created a simple R:base report, a customer list for Great Plains Music and Video. In this chapter, we will create another report for Great Plains, a sales report. This report will illustrate advanced report-writing concepts including report headings and footings, calculations within a report, using system date and time, automatic page numbering, grouping data (control breaks), subtotals and totals, and paragraphing text.

Note: If you want to create the report illustrated in the chapter, you will need the GTPLAIN database created in Chapters 6, 7, and 8. If you have been working along with the examples in those chapters, using the sample data files provided, you can restore the EMPLOYEE table to the database by typing: INPUT EMPLOYEE.DAT. If you have not yet created the GTPLAIN database, you will need to create the EMPLOYEE (Chapter 6), SALE (Chapter 7), COMPSALE, and INV tables and load them with a few rows of sample data. If you have the files CH6.DEF, CH6.DAT, CH7.DEF, CH7.DAT, and CH8.DAT, you can have R:base create the GTPLAIN database by loading R:base and typing:

INPUT CH6.DEF   INPUT CH7.DEF   INPUT CH8.DAT

after you receive the R:base R> prompt.

THE PROBLEM

Management of Great Plains Music and Video has asked that you create a sales report which lists sales broken down by date and transaction. The report is to show the description of the item sold, quantity sold, cost, actual selling price, and gross profit (selling price minus cost). Subtotals should be shown for each transaction and each day. Finally, the report should show grand totals for sales, cost of sales, and gross profit.

BEGIN BY DESIGNING

Before you begin, you should prepare a sketch of the report. This sketch can be used as a communication tool to confirm that you have understood the requirements of management. Once approved, the report sketch can serve as a blueprint to aid in the actual construction of the report. Figure 9–1 contains the design approved by Great Plains management. Items enclosed in square brackets ([]) are the names of data values. These values are extracted directly from the base table in the database or are derived or computed as the report is printed (items marked with *).

STEPS IN DEFINING REPORTS

Follow the steps outlined in Chapter 7 to create the report using R:base:

1. Enter the REPORT DEFINE mode.
2. Edit the report.
3. Define report variables.
4. Locate data items on the report.
5. Mark the report sections.
6. Set the number of lines per page.
7. Save the report definition.

Step 1: Enter the REPORT DEFINE Mode

After loading R:base and opening the GTPLAIN database, type:

    REPORTS

R:base responds with a prompt asking for the name to be given to the report. Any string of eight or less characters may be used. Type:

    SALESREP

FIGURE 9–1a
Sketch of report heading (separate page)

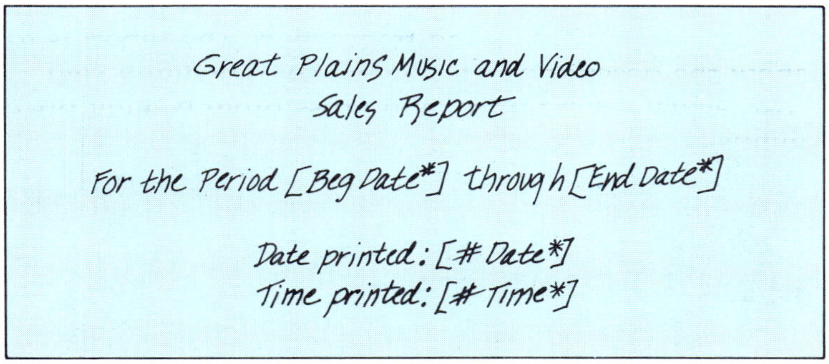

> Great Plains Music and Video
> Sales Report
>
> For the Period [Beg Date*] through [End Date*]
>
> Date printed: [# Date*]
> Time printed: [# Time*]

FIGURE 9–1b
Sketch of report page layout

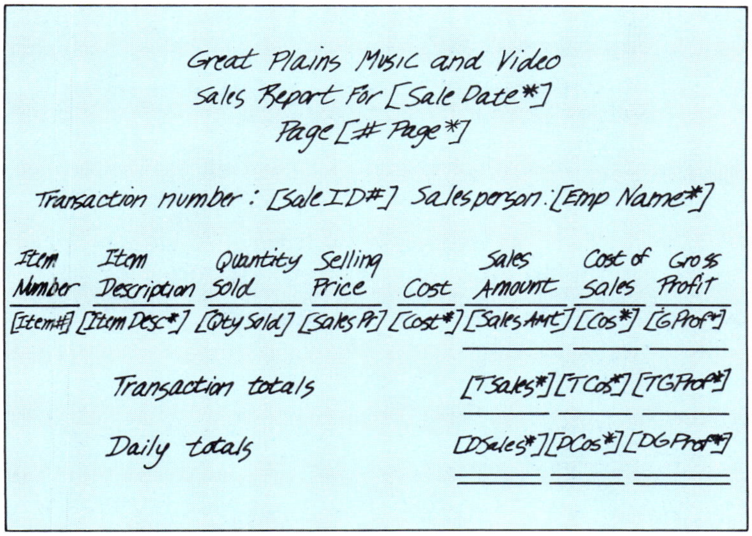

> Great Plains Music and Video
> Sales Report For [Sale Date*]
> Page [# Page*]
>
> Transaction number: [Sale ID#] Salesperson: [Emp Name*]
>
> | Item Number | Item Description | Quantity Sold | Selling Price | Cost | Sales Amount | Cost of Sales | Gross Profit |
> |---|---|---|---|---|---|---|---|
> | [Item#] | [Item Desc*] | [Qty Sold] | [Sales Pr] | [Cost*] | [Sales Amt] | [Cos*] | [GProf*] |
>
> Transaction totals   [TSales*] [TCos*] [TGProf*]
>
> Daily totals   [DSales*] [DCos*] [DGProf*]

FIGURE 9–1c
Sketch of report footing (separate page)

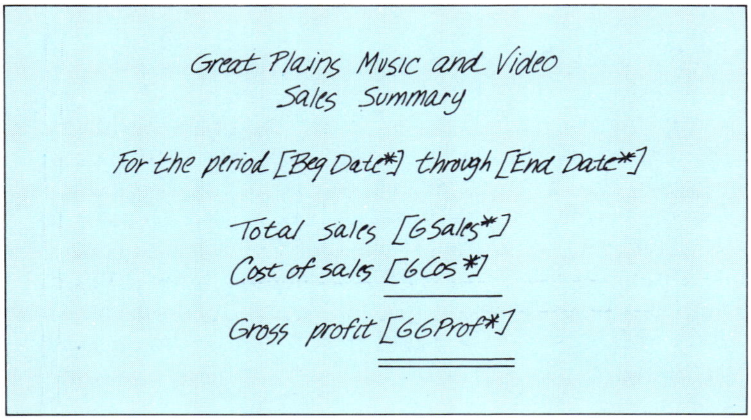

> Great Plains Music and Video
> Sales Summary
>
> For the period [Beg Date*] through [End Date*]
>
> Total sales [GSales*]
> Cost of sales [GCos*]
>
> Gross profit [GGProf*]

FIGURE 9-2a
Completed design—object/relationships

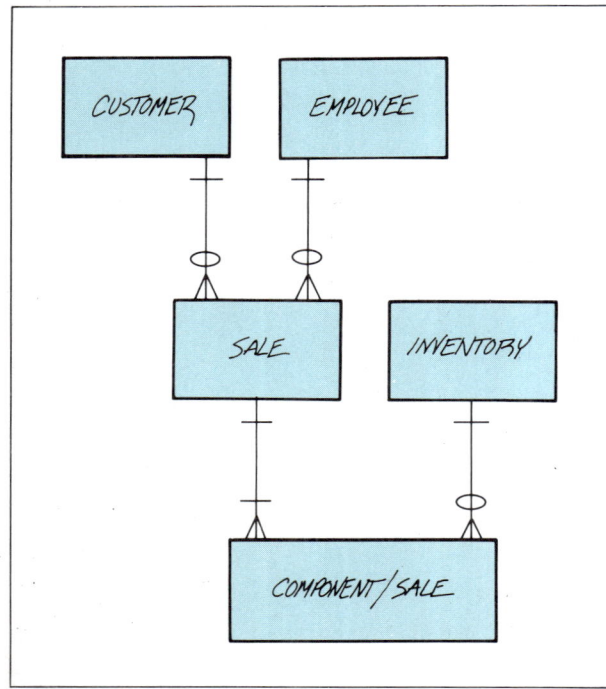

FIGURE 9-2b
Completed design—table/attributes

CUSTOMER (Customer identification number, Customer name, Customer address, Customer phone)
INVENTORY (Item number, Item description, Units, Quantity on hand, Cost, Price)
SALE (Sales identification number, Social security number, Customer identification number, Date)
COMPONENT/SALE (Item number, Sales identification number, Quantity sold, Sales price, Sales amount)
EMPLOYEE (Social security number, Employee name, Hire date, Salary Commision rate, Salary review date, Marital status, Exemptions, Total wages)

R:base then prompts for the name of the table from which the report data will be obtained. Although R:base allows you to obtain data for the report from all tables in the database, selection of the table to use as the base table is crucial. R:base uses the base table to provide most of the data for the detail rows in the report.

Look at the report design in Figure 9-1. The report is based on sales transaction details. Look at the database design in Figure 9-2.

Sales transaction details are kept in the COMPSALE table. Choose COMPSALE as the base table for this report by typing:

COMPSALE

After you press [ENTER], R:base presents you with the menu you saw in Chapter 7:

- Edit report: Use this choice to create or change the way the report looks on the screen.
- Define: This choice is used to define or change report variables.
- Locate: This choice is used to indicate where the data items are to be placed in the report.
- Mark: This choice is used to mark the location of headings, footings, detail lines, and other parts of the report.
- Set: Use this choice to set the number of lines per page.
- Help: This choice presents you with more detailed instructions for defining a report.
- Quit: Use this choice to return to the R:base command mode.

Step 2: Edit the Report

To begin, press [E]. You receive a screen which is virtually blank. At this point, you type in everything from the report design (Figure 9-1) except the data items. This includes report and page headings and footings, total and subtotal captions, and column titles. Figure 9-3 shows the Great Plains sales report as it appears on the screen. The last four lines do not appear because there are not sufficient lines on the screen. Return to the main report definition menu by pressing [ESC].

Step 3: Define Report Variables

Report variables are data items which are not taken directly from the database. They are derived each time the report is printed. Report variables are defined in the form of expressions:

Variable name = definition expression

An R:base report variable may be one of the following types:

- R:base global variables
- System variables: #DATE, #TIME, and #PAGE
- Lookup variables
- Concatenated string variables
- Calculated variables

Great Plains' sales report has at least one of each type. Prepare R:base to accept definition of report variables by selecting [D] from the reports main menu. R:base is prompting you to enter report variable definition expressions (Figure 9–4).

R:base Global Variables — Beginning Date and Ending Date

R:base global variables are scratch-pad data items which exist only temporarily. They are not saved as part of the database. They are lost when you leave R:base. Global variables are used primarily in programming with R:base and are discussed in more depth in Chapter 11, which deals with that topic. We discuss them here because they are one potential source of report variables.

Notice that the sales report header and footer each contain the phrase "For the period [BegDate] through [EndDate]." The data items BegDate and EndDate will take on different values each time the sales report is printed. There is no way to extract these items from the database as the report is being printed. Therefore, the values must be imported into the report.

This is done by setting R:base global variables to the desired values and then assigning report variables equal to the global variables. For example, assume that the report is to be printed for the period April 1, 1985 (BegDate) through April 30, 1985 (EndDate). To get these values into the report, use the R:base SET VARIABLE command to assign the values to R:base global variables before you print the report:

SET VARIABLE BegDate TO 04/01/85

SET VARIABLE EndDate TO 04/30/85

(Don't type these commands yet. Wait until the report is complete and you are ready to print it.)

FIGURE 9–3

Great Plains sales report on the screen

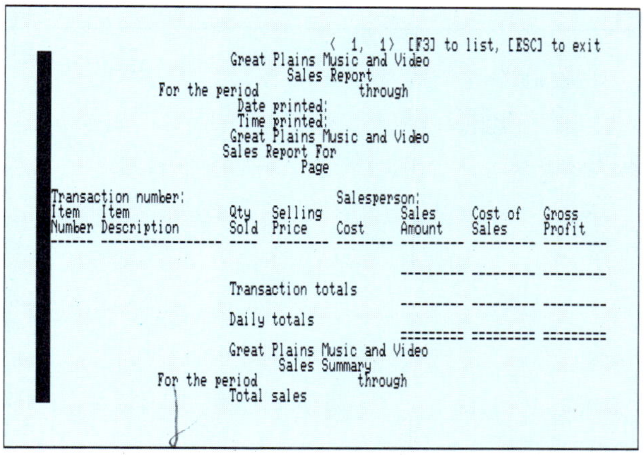

FIGURE 9–4

Enter report variable definition expressions

FIGURE 9–5

Report variables from R:base global variables

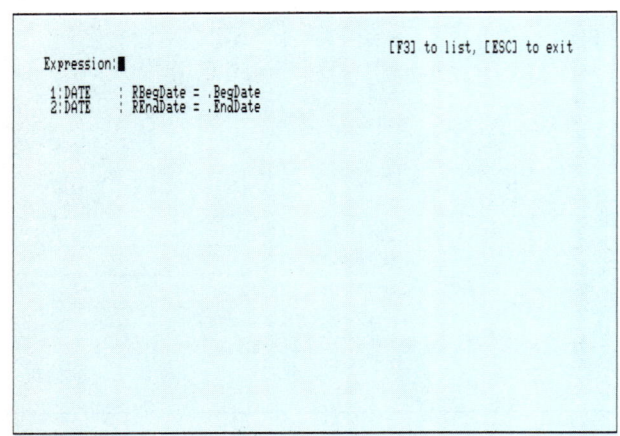

When the report is printed, R:base will look for global variables called BegDate and EndDate and use them in the report. How does R:base know to look for them? Because you have defined report variables by typing:

RBegDate = .BegDate
REndDate = .EndDate

These expressions define two report variables: RBegDate and REndDate. The expressions tell R:base to "Assign the value of the global variable called BegDate to the report variable called RBegDate. Also assign the value of the global variable called EndDate to the report variable called REndDate."

Notice the dot (.) immediately preceding the global variable names. This dot is how R:base knows to assign the value of the global variable called BegDate to the report variable RBegDate. Without the dot, R:base would give the report variables RBegDate and REndDate the literal values "BegDate" and "EndDate" respectively. The report might contain the phrase "For the period BegDate through EndDate" instead of the desired phrase "For the period Apr 1, 1985 through Apr 30, 1985". Because of the use of the dot, R:base global variables are sometimes referred to as *dotted variables*.

Figure 9–5 shows the screen after RBegDate and REndDate have been defined. Notice that R:base has assigned a data type of DATE to the variables. It derived this from the type of global variables which were set before entering the REPORT DEFINITION mode. If the global variables do not exist, R:base will ask you for the data type.

R:base System Variables—Date, Time, and Page To enable users to differentiate versions of the same report, the report header contains the date and time each report is printed. Also, each page of the report is numbered. Here again, these data items are not stored in the database. They are available from the system. The system date and time are based on values entered when you turn on the computer.

To use these system values in a report, you must define report variables. You can define report variables for date, time, and page number as follows:

Rdate = #DATE
Rtime = #TIME
Rpage = #PAGE

(See Figure 9–6.)

FIGURE 9–6

Adding report variables for date, time, and page

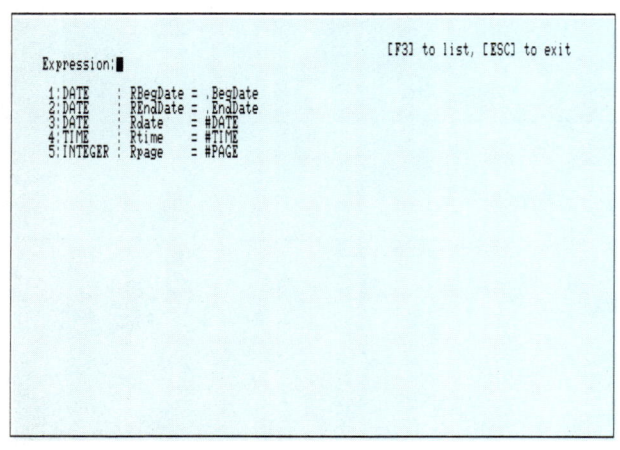

Lookup Variables—SaleDate, Employee Name, Item Description, and Item Cost Each page of the report body begins with the date of the business day for which sales are being reported. However, COMPSALE, the base table for the report, does not contain the date the sale is made. SALE contains that information. You can tell R:base to look in SALE for the needed data by defining a lookup report variable:

RSaleDT = SaleDate IN SALE WHERE SaleID# EQ SaleID#

(See Figure 9–7.) As it prints the report, R:base goes through COMPSALE row by row. Thus, for every row of COMPSALE used in the report, there will be a value for SaleID#. In English, the above definition says,"Set the report variable RSaleDT to the value of SaleDate in the SALE table where SaleID# in the SALE table equals the value of SaleID# in the current row of COMPSALE."

Notice in Figure 9–1b that the sales report contains the name of each salesperson making sales during the reporting period. You'll recall that employee names are broken down into first name (EmpFName) and last name (EmpLName) in the EMPLOYEE table. To obtain EmpFName and EmpLName values for any given employee, you need the employee identification number (EmpID#). To get the EmpID# for the salesperson associated with any given sale, you need to look it up in the SALE table using the transaction number (SaleID#).

First, define a report variable to look up the EmpID# in SALE:

REmpID# = EmpID# IN SALE WHERE SaleID# EQ SaleID#

In English, the expression is saying to R:base "Set the report variable called REmpID# to the value of EmpID# in the SALE table where the value of SaleID# equals the value of SaleID# in the current row of COMPSALE."

Now, look up the salesperson's first and last names in the EMPLOYEE table using the report variable REmpID#:

RFName = EmpFName IN EMPLOYEE WHERE EmpID# EQ REmpID#

RLName = EmpLName IN EMPLOYEE WHERE EmpID# EQ REmpID#

These two expressions define two report variables, RFName (Report First Name) and RLName (Report

FIGURE 9–7

Defining lookup report variables for sale date

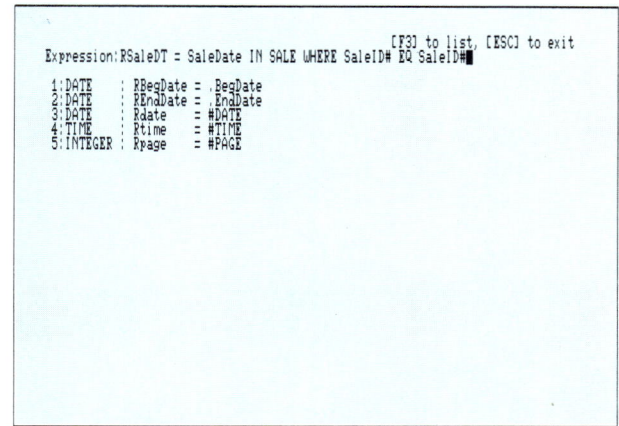

FIGURE 9–8

Defined lookup variables for employee ID number, first name, and last name

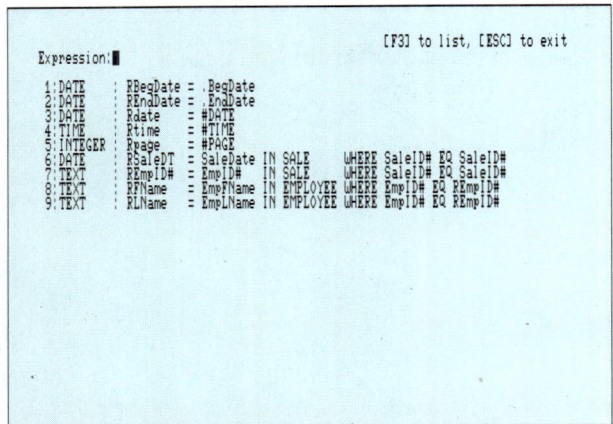

FIGURE 9–9

Defined lookup variables for item description and cost

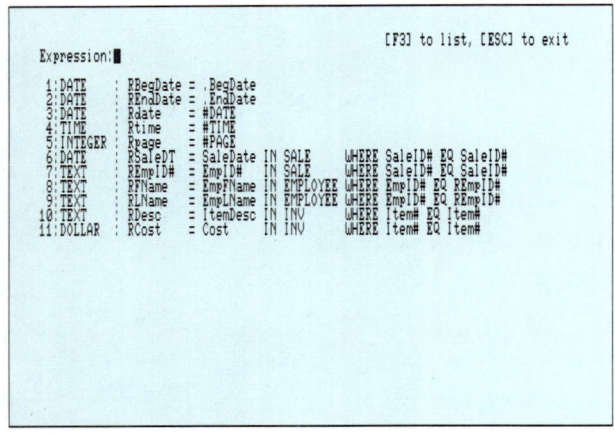

Last Name), which are to be given the values of EmpFName and EmpLName, respectively, from the EMPLOYEE table where EmpID# equals the value of the report variable REmpID#.

Lookup variables allow you to prepare reports using data from any table in the database without having to create temporary tables using relational commands. These lookup variables (Figure 9–8) result in the virtual relational join operation JOIN (JOIN COMPSALE (SaleID# = SaleID#) SALE) (EmpID# = EmpID#) EMPLOYEE.

There are two additional data items for the report which are not stored in the base table: item description and item cost. These two data items are stored in the inventory (INV) table. Define lookup variables for these data items by typing:

RDesc = ItemDesc IN INV WHERE Item# EQ Item#

RCost = Cost IN INV WHERE Item# EQ Item#

(See Figure 9–9.)

Concatenated String Variables—Employee Name At this point you could use the report variables RFName and RLName to print the salesperson's name. If you simply locate RFName next to RLName in the report, Kay Abel's name would be listed:

Kay   Abel

which is accurate but not as readable as if it were printed:

Kay Abel

R:base allows you to combine two text values in this way. To define a report variable called EmpName which combines RFName and RLName, type:

EmpName = RFName & RLName

(See Figure 9–10.) The operator "&" tells R:base to delete the trailing blanks from RFName, skip a space, and then add RLName.

When you do not want a space between the two data items, you can use the "+" operator. If you were to define EmpName as:

EmpName = RFName + RLName

R:base would delete trailing blanks from RFName and immediately follow with RLName; e.g., KayAbel.

Computed Variables—Cost of Sales, Gross Profit, Sub-totals, and Totals Many of the data items in the report are computed from other data items. For example:

- Cost of Sales (COS) is the product of multiplying the Quantity Sold (QtySold) by the Cost of the item (RCost).
- Gross Profit (GProf) is the difference between Sales Amount (SalesAmt) and Cost of Sales (COS).
- Sub-totals and Grand totals are the sum of Sales Amount, Cost of Sales, and Gross Profit.

Cost of Sales and Gross Profit are defined using simple arithmetic expressions as follows:

COS = QtySold × RCost
GProf = SalesAmt − COS

The various totals and subtotals are also easily defined using SUM OF as follows:

TSales = SUM OF SalesAmt
TCOS = SUM OF COS
TGProf = SUM OF GProf
DSales = SUM OF SalesAmt
DCOS = SUM OF COS
DGProf = SUM OF GProf
GSales = SUM OF SalesAmt
GCOS = SUM OF COS
GGProf = SUM OF GProf

The completed definition of report variables is shown in Figure 9–11.

Some Other Points About Report Variables You can change the definition of a report variable by simply retyping the definition. You can delete a report variable by typing:

DELETE variable name

You can change the position of a variable in the variable list by typing "REORDER variable-name position-

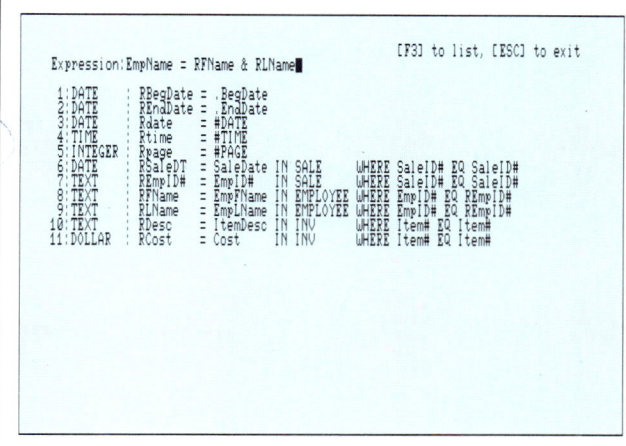

FIGURE 9–10

Defining concatenated variable for employee name

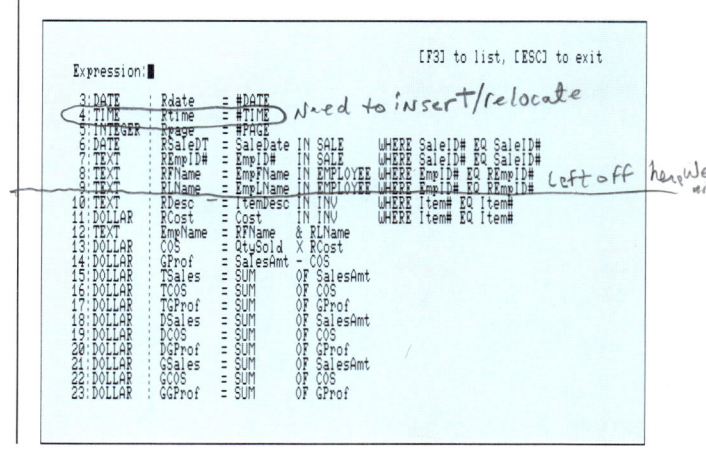

FIGURE 9–11

Complete definition of report variables

number." For example, to change GGProf from position number 23 to position number 14, type:

    REORDER GGProf 14

(If you reorder GGProf, be sure to replace it.) You can change the data type of a report variable by typing "TYPE variable name data-type."

You can use report variables to send special codes to your printer to have the report printed in a special way. These codes, called *escape sequences*, can be sent to the printer by defining report variables in the following format:

    variable name = <escape sequence>

where escape sequence is the decimal equivalent of the ASCII code which you wish to have sent to the printer. For example, some printers interpret:

    ESC -

to mean "Begin/End Underlining." The decimal equivalent of this code is 27 45. You would define a report variable containing this sequence as follows:

    Underln = <27 45>

Locate the variable Underln in the report wherever you want R:base to send the escape sequence to the printer.

We will now resume our discussion of Great Plains' sales report. Return to the reports main menu by pressing [ESC].

Step 4: Locate Data Items on the Report

The next step is to indicate where the data items are to be placed on the report. Select "Locate" from the main report definition menu by pressing [L]. You are presented with another menu containing the following options:

- Locate: Select this option to locate items which have not been previously located.

- Relocate: This option is used to delete or change the location of previously located report variables and data items.

- Help: Select this option to obtain instructions.

- Quit: This option returns you to the main report definition menu.

Since no data items have been located, select "Locate" by pressing [L]. Recall from Chapter 7 that you mark the location of data items in a report using the following three steps:

1. Type the column name.
2. Mark the starting location of the data item.
3. Mark the ending location of the data item.

After the ending location of a DOLLAR type data item is marked, R:base asks if you want the item printed in CHECK format. If so, enter [Y]. Such items will be printed with leading asterisks (such as ****$750.85). If you do not want the item printed in CHECK format, press [ENTER] or [N]. Figure 9–12 shows the sales report after the location of all data items except Item Description. We'll use Item Description to show how to paragraph text data items in a report.

There are 17 characters available for Item Description in the report. However, ItemDesc in INV is defined as TEXT 30. If an item has a description which is 30 characters long, the report would not be very readable if the description were truncated after 17 characters. To solve this problem, you can instruct R:base to "wrap" the item description within the 17-character column allowed.

Begin by typing the column name. Remember, if you can't recall the name of a report variable or column from the base table, press [F3] (Figure 9–13). The data item you want to locate is RDesc. Press [ESC] to return to Locate mode. R:base instructs you to "Move cursor to start location and press [S]." After the cursor is moved to the start location in the Item Description column and [S] is pressed, the screen appears as in Figure 9–14. Notice that the end of the data item can be marked by pressing either [E] or [W]. If you enter [E], the item description will be truncated at that location.

If you enter [W], R:base will wrap the item description. After [W] is pressed, R:base asks you to "Press [T] for end line or [ESC]." If you want to specify a maximum number of lines to be used for the item, you may move the cursor down the maximum number of lines to be printed, then press [T]. In this case, the maximum lines which would be used is two, so you could simply press [ESC] to indicate that there is no maximum.

After [ESC] is pressed, R:base asks you to "Press [I] for indentation or [ESC]." If you want the paragraph to be indented, move the cursor to the column where the paragraph is to begin, then press [I]. In this case, Item Description is not to be indented, so press [ESC].

FIGURE 9–12

All data items located except item description

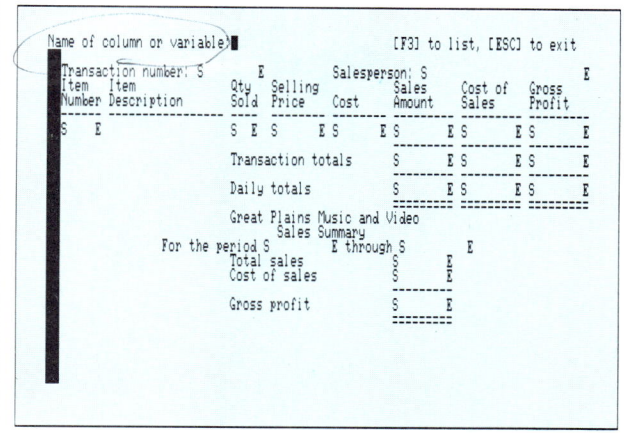

FIGURE 9–13

Press [F3] for a list of all variables

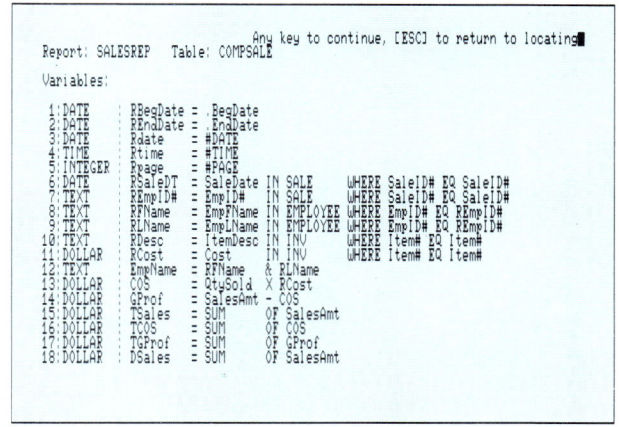

FIGURE 9–14

The end of text items may be marked by pressing [E] or [W]

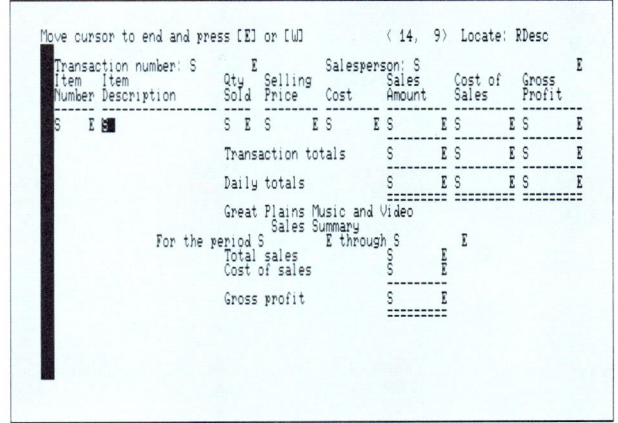

In summary, to build a paragraph out of a large text item, mark the beginning of the column which the paragraph is to occupy with the [S]. Mark the ending of the column (that is, where the item is to wrap) with the [W]. Indicate the maximum number of lines the paragraph is to occupy with [T]. Mark paragraph indentation (or "outdentation" for that matter) with the [I].

As an example, assume you have a text item that is potentially 1000 characters long. If the paragraph is to be 40 characters wide, begin with a 5-character indentation, and occupy a maximum of 6 lines, the location markings would be as follows:

S   I   W

                                                                          T

To make a bibliography entry from the item which is "outdented" and which has no limitation on the number of lines occupied, the location markings would be:

I S   W

The screen appears as in Figure 9–15 after all data items have been located in the sales report. Return to the Locate mode by pressing [ESC]. You can change any data item locations by selecting Relocated (press [R]). R:base shows you the current location of each data item and gives you the opportunity to leave the item location unchanged (Keep), change the location (Change), delete the location definition (Delete), or return to Locate mode (Quit). Return to the reports main menu by pressing [Q].

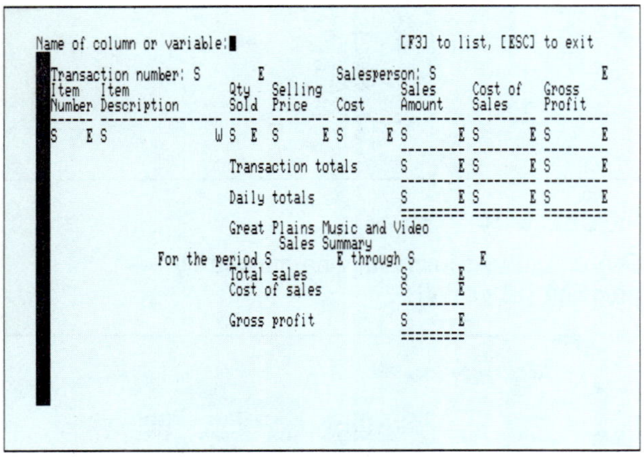

Step 5: Mark the Report Sections

The next step in defining a report is to identify the various report sections. Begin by pressing [M]. You are given another menu with the following choices:

- **Report:** This choice allows you to mark report heading and footing lines. Report heading lines are printed only once, before the rest of the report is printed. You would use them to print a title page. Report footing lines are also printed once, after the rest of the report has been printed. Use footers to print report summaries.

- **Page:** Mark page heading and footing lines. Page heading lines are printed at the beginning of each page of the report. Page footing lines are printed at the bottom of each page of the report.

FIGURE 9–15
All data items located

ADVANCED REPORT WRITING WITH R:BASE   179

- Detail: There is a detail line in the report for every row in the underlying database table. Mark them using this option.
- Break: You can define ten levels of control breaks using this option. Control breaks are used for grouping data on the report.
- List: This option displays the status of the various report sections.
- Help: Press [H] to obtain instructions for marking report sections.
- Quit: Press [Q] to return to the main report definition menu.

You'll need to mark report, detail, and break sections for the sales report.

Prepare to mark report sections by pressing [R]. R:base asks, "Do you want to remove the initial carriage return[NO]?" If you want a blank line to appear before the report begins to print, press [N] or [ENTER]. If you want the report to begin printing on the first line of the page, press [Y].

R:base then asks, "Page eject before report[NO]?" Press [Y] if you want a page eject before the report begins to print, [N] if not. Ensure that the report header is placed on a separate page by pressing [Y] in response to the next prompt, "Page eject after report heading[NO]?" You can also ensure that the report footer is placed on a separate page by pressing [Y] in response to the questions "Page eject before report footing[NO]?" and "Page eject after report footing [NO]?"

You are then presented with the report and asked to "Press [H] to mark report heading." If the cursor is not positioned on line one, move it there with the cursor movement keys. The report heading design is shown in Figure 9–16.

FIGURE 9–16
Sketch of report heading

> Great Plains Music and Video
> Sales Report
>
> For the Period [Beg Date*] through [End Date*]
>
> Date printed: [# Date*]
> Time printed: [# Time*]

FIGURE 9–17
All report heading lines marked

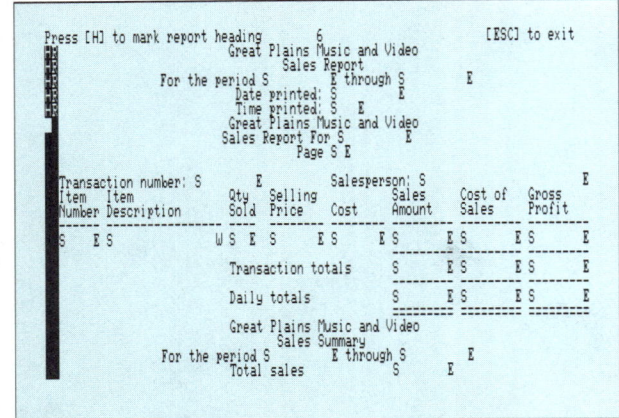

FIGURE 9–19
All report footing lines marked

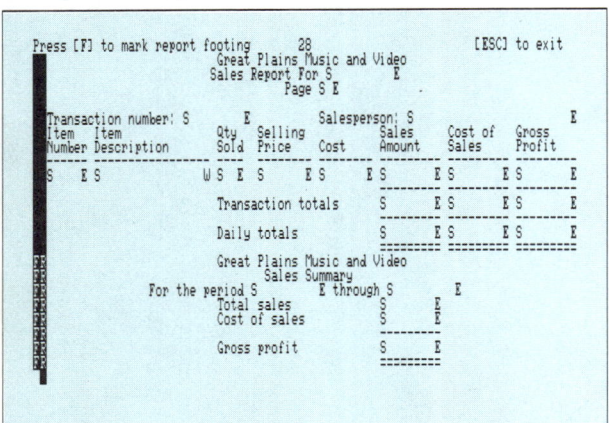

FIGURE 9–20
Report detail line marked

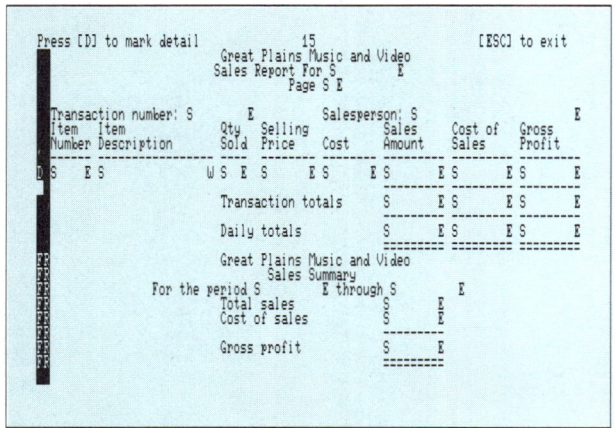

FIGURE 9–18
Sketch of report footing

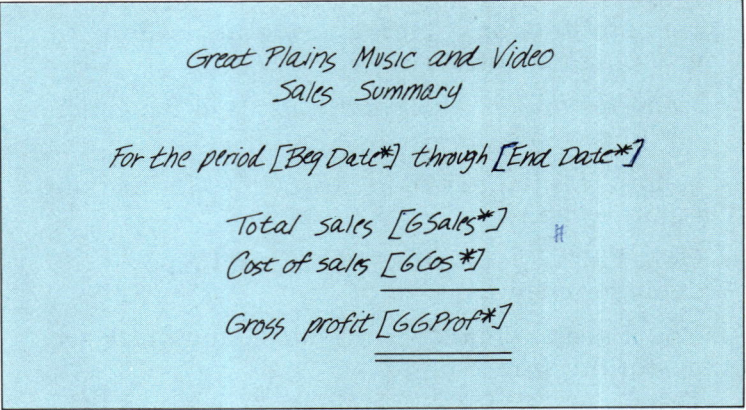

Figure 9–17 shows the screen after the report heading lines have been marked. The symbol HR stands for "Heading—Report." Press [ESC] to indicate that you are finished marking the report heading.

You are then asked to "Press [F] to mark report footing." Move the cursor to the first report footing line using the cursor movement keys. The report footing design is shown in Figure 9–18. Figure 9–19 shows the screen after the report footing lines have been marked. The symbol FR stands for "Footing—Report." Press [ESC] to indicate that you are finished marking the report footing. R:base returns you to the marking sections menu.

The next choice on the menu is P—Set page heading and footing lines. Page headings and footings are not used for the sales report because a new page is to begin with each date reported. As a result, page headings and footings are defined when the breakpoint for sale date is defined.

Select the next choice, D—Set detail lines, by pressing [D]. As with report heading and footing lines, you are presented with the report and asked to "Press [D] to mark detail." Recall from Chapter 7 that a detail line is printed for each applicable row in the base table. Figure 9–20 shows the screen after marking the report detail line. Press [ESC] to return to the Marking Sections menu.

The next choice on the menu is B—Set report breakpoint subheadings and subtotals. What are breakpoints?

Business reports often include many subcategories. For example, in the Great Plains sales report, management wants the details printed for each transaction, then the totals for each transaction, then totals for each date in the reporting period.

To accomplish these subgroupings, the data must be sorted by SaleID# (which implies SaleDate). Then, R:base prints details for a transaction from COMP-SALE until the value of SaleID# changes. When that happens, it is a signal to R:base that all the details for that sales transaction have been printed and it is time to print transaction totals. Transactions are printed in this way until the value of RSaleDT changes. That's a signal to R:base to print daily totals. If there are more transactions to print, R:base is to execute a page eject, then print another page heading. This process continues until the data for the last date in the reporting period is printed.

In this situation, SaleID# and RSaleDT are known as *control variables*. When the values change, a control break occurs. These are also referred to as *breakpoints*. The sales report is said to "Break on RSaleDT and SaleID#." At each breakpoint, there may be a subheading and a subfooting to print. Control breaks are easy to implement in R:base, if you remember one important point.

The breakpoints are numbered from 1 up to a maximum of 10 beginning with the break farthest from the detail line. Thus, breakpoint number 1 in the sales report is based on RSaleDT. Breakpoint number 2 is based on SaleID#. If you reverse the order, the report will not print as you intend it to.

Begin by selecting [B] from the marking sections menu. As shown in Figure 9–21, R:base asks, "Do you want to manually reset break variables[NO]?" To have R:base automatically clear variables, press [N] or [ENTER]. If you respond by pressing [Y], you are given control over which variables are cleared at each breakpoint. This control exacts a price. You must remember to clear all variables cleared at lower breakpoints. For example, if the variables called Sub1, Sub2, and Sub3 are cleared at breakpoint number 4, they must also be cleared at breakpoint numbers 1, 2, and 3. In most cases, you will want R:base to clear the variables automatically.

R:base then prompts for the control variable for breakpoint number 1. Type:

RSaleDt

You are then asked, "Page eject before break heading[NO]?" You want to begin each day on a new page, so press [Y]. You are then given the screen in Figure 9–22. Prepare to enter the names of report variables

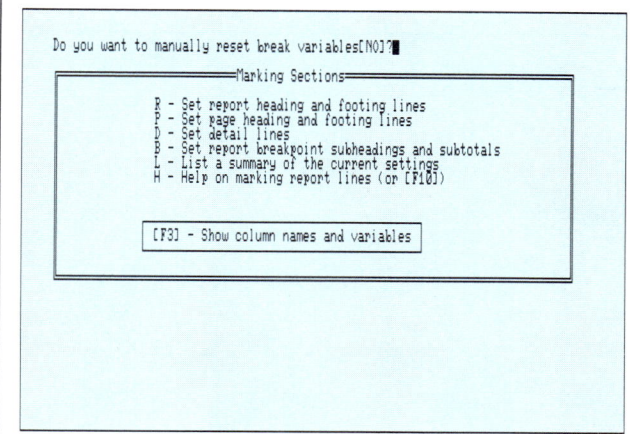

FIGURE 9–21

First breakpoint marking prompt

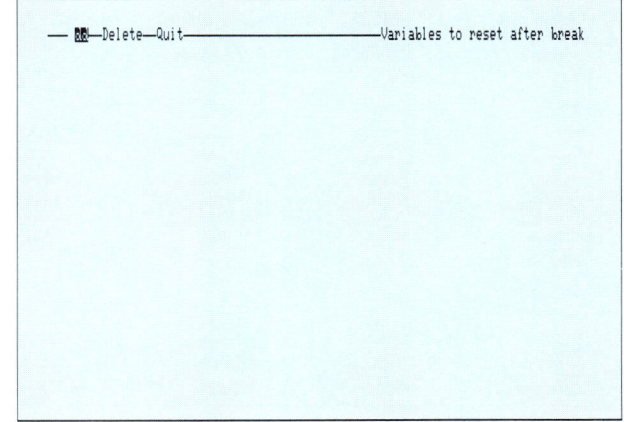

FIGURE 9–22

Press [A] to enter the variables which are to be reset

FIGURE 9–23
Enter the names of the variables to be reset.

FIGURE 9–24
Completed list of report variables to be reset at breakpoint number 2

which are to be reset after RSaleDt changes by pressing [A] (Figure 9–23). After they are printed, you want the daily totals, DSales, DCOS, and DGProf to be reset to 0. Based on the option we chose, R:base will automatically clear the totals for the last transaction of the day, TSales, TCOS, and TGProf. Figure 9–24 shows the screen after DSales, DCOS, and DGProf have been entered. Return to the screen in Figure 9–22 by pressing [ESC]. Then press [Q].

Next, you are asked to "Press [H] to mark break heading." The procedure is identical to that used to mark report and page headings. The break footing is marked in the same way. Figure 9–25 shows the screen after the heading and footing for breakpoint number 1 have been marked. Return to the marking section menu by pressing [ESC].

Breakpoint number 2 is defined in the same way as breakpoint number 1 except that SaleID# is used for the control variable, a page eject is not executed before the heading is printed, and the transaction subtotals (TSales, TCOS, and TGProf) are cleared. Figure 9–26 shows the screen after the heading and footing lines have been defined for breakpoint number 2. Return to the marking sections menu by pressing [ESC]. Return to the reports main menu by pressing [Q].

Step 6: Set the Lines per Page
As we saw in Chapter 7, the default setting is 66, a standard 11" page. Since this suits the requirements, no change is needed.

Step 7: Save the Report Definition
Save the report definition and return to the R> prompt by pressing [Q], then [S].

PRINTING THE REPORT

Once the sales report is defined, there are four steps to print it:

1. Set the R:base global variables BegDate and End-Date.
2. Determine the first and last sales transaction within the range of BegDate and EndDate.
3. Set the date format to mmmddyyyy.
4. Issue the PRINT command.

Step 1: Set the R:base Global Variables
Recall that R:base will be looking for two global variables to use in the report: BegDate and EndDate. If the report is to include sales for the period from July 20,

1985 through July 31, 1985, set the global variables by typing:

SET VARIABLE BegDate TO 07/20/85

SET VARIABLE EndDate TO 07/31/85

Step 2: Determine the First and Last Transactions

You will want to tell R:base which rows from the base table to include in the report. That means you need to know the first SaleID# for July 20, 1985, and the last SaleID# for July 31, 1985. Determine the beginning transaction number by using the R:base COMPUTE command as follows:

COMPUTE BegTrans AS MIN SaleID# FROM SALE +

WHERE SaleDate GE .BegDate

Determine the ending transaction number in a similar way:

COMPUTE EndTrans AS MAX SaleID# FROM SALE +

WHERE SaleDate LE .EndDate

Step 3: Set the Date Format

You want dates in the report to be printed in a more readable format than "07/20/85." You can have dates printed as "Jul 20, 1985" by typing:

SET DATE mmmddyyyy

Step 4: Issue the Print Command

The final step is to instruct R:base to print the report:

PRINT SALESREP WHERE SaleID# GE .BegTrans AND +

SaleID# LE .EndTrans

Be patient, you have just defined a complex report. It takes a while for R:base to format the report, gather all the data, compute the report variables, and print the report. The Great Plains Music and Video sales report is shown in Figure 9–27.

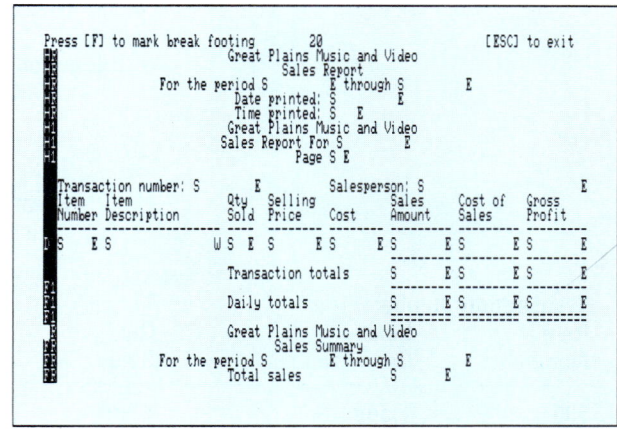

FIGURE 9–25

Heading and footing lines marked for breakpoint number 1

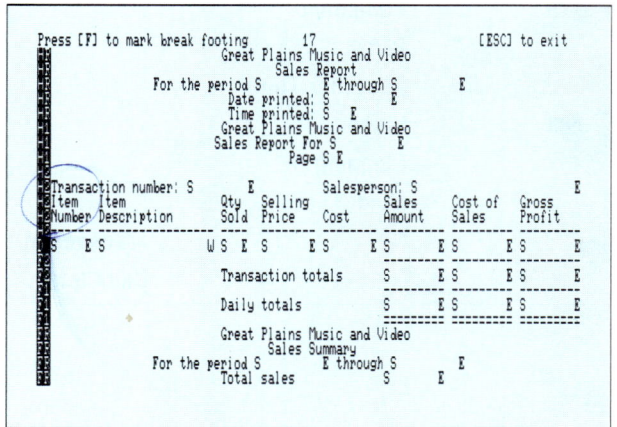

FIGURE 9–26

Heading and footing lines marked for breakpoint number 2

FIGURE 9-27
Great Plains Music and Video July sales report

Great Plains Music and Video
Sales Report
For the period Jul 20, 1985 through Jul 31, 1985
Date printed: Jul 31, 1985
Time printed: 21:34

Great Plains Music and Video
Sales Report for Jul 22, 1985
Page: 1

Transaction number:		1	Salesperson: Randy Morgan				
Item Number	Item Description	Qty Sold	Selling Price	Cost	Sales Amount	Cost of Sales	Gross Profit
500	Video Cleaning Fluid	1	$ 2.50	$ 1.25	$ 2.50	$ 1.25	$ 1.25
310	SONY Port. Cassette Recorder	1	$ 59.95	$ 35.00	$ 59.95	$ 35.00	$ 24.95
		Transaction totals			$ 62.45	$ 36.25	$ 26.20
Transaction Number:		2	Salesperson: Kim Abel				
Item Number	Item Description	Qty Sold	Selling Price	Cost	Sales Amount	Cost of Sales	Gross Profit
225	Panasonic P8036 Recorder/Tuner	1	950.00	$495.00	$ 950.00	$495.00	$455.00
500	Video Cleaning Fluid	1	$ 2.50	$ 1.25	$ 2.50	$ 1.25	$ 1.25
		Transaction totals			$ 952.50	$496.25	$456.25
		Daily totals			1,014.95	$532.50	$482.45

FIGURE 9–27

continued

Great Plains Music and Video
Sales Report For Jul 23, 1985
Page: 2

Transaction number: 3   Salesperson: Kim Abel

Item Number	Item Description	Qty Sold	Selling Price	Cost	Sales Amount	Cost of Sales	Gross Profit
400	Scotch T120 VHS Video Tapes	5	$ 7.95	$ 3.50	$ 39.75	$ 17.50	$ 22.25
			Transaction totals		$ 39.75	$ 17.50	$ 22.25

Transaction number: 4   Salesperson: Greg Abel

Item Number	Item Description	Qty Sold	Selling Price	Cost	Sales Amount	Cost of Sales	Gross Profit
110	RCA 19 Inch Color T.V.	1	433.00	$275.00	$ 433.00	$275.00	$ 158.00
150	Oak T.V. Stand	1	145.95	$ 75.00	$ 145.95	$ 75.00	$ 70.95
225	Panasonic P8036 Recorder/Tuner	1	960.00	$495.00	$ 960.00	$495.00	$ 465.00
500	Video Cleaning Fluid	1	$ 2.50	$ 1.25	$ 2.50	$ 1.25	$ 1.25
			Transaction totals		1,541.45	$846.25	$ 695.20
			Daily totals		1,581.20	$863.75	$ 717.45

FIGURE 9–27

continued

<pre>
                              Great Plains Music and Video
                              Sales Report For Jul 24, 1985
                                      Page: 3
Transaction number: 5   Salesperson: Greg Abel
  Item   Item   Qty   Selling   Sales   Cost of   Gross
  Number   Description Sold   Price   Cost   Amount   Sales   Profit

  100   RCA 25 Inch   2   535.00 $375.00 $1,070.00 $ 750.00 $ 320.00
            Color
            Television
                                 Transaction totals   1,070.00 $ 750.00 $ 320.00

Transaction number: 6   Salesperson: Amy Kleese
  Item   Item   Qty   Selling   Sales   Cost of   Gross
  Number   Description Sold   Price   Cost   Amount   Sales   Profit

  310   SONY Port.   1 $ 67.95 $ 35.00 $ 67.95 $ 35.00 $ 32.95
            Cassette
            Recorder
  450   SONY S60   6 $ 1.75 $ 0.60 $ 10.50 $ 3.60 $ 6.90
            Cassette Tape
                                 Transaction totals $ 78.45 $ 38.60 $ 39.85

Transaction number: 7   Salesperson: Greg Abel
  Item   Item   Qty   Selling   Sales   Cost of   Gross
  Number   Description Sold   Price   Cost   Amount   Sales   Profit

  200   Panasonic   1   895.00 $495.00 $ 895.00 $ 495.00 $ 400.00
            P547 Video
            Camera
  225   Panasonic   1   975.00 $495.00 $ 975.00 $ 495.00 $ 480.00
            P8036
            Recorder/Tuner
  500   Video   3 $ 2.50 $ 1.25 $ 7.50 $ 3.75 $ 3.75
            Cleaning
            Fluid
                                 Transaction totals   1,877.50 $ 993.75 $ 883.75
                                 Daily total   3,025.95   1,782.35   1,243.60
</pre>

FIGURE 9–27

continued

Great Plains Music and Video
Sales Report For Jul 25, 1985
Page: 4

Transaction number:		8	Salesperson: Amy Kleese				
Item Number	Item Description	Qty Sold	Selling Price	Cost	Sales Amount	Cost of Sales	Gross Profit
110	RCA 19 Inch Color T.V.	1	355.00	$275.00	$ 355.00	$275.00	$ 80.00
150	Oak T.V. Stand	1	145.95	$ 75.00	$ 145.95	$ 75.00	$ 70.95
		Transaction totals			$ 500.95	$350.00	$ 150.95

Transaction number:		9	Salesperson: Mike Johnson				
Item Number	Item Description	Qty Sold	Selling Price	Cost	Sales Amount	Cost of Sales	Gross Profit
400	Scotch T120 VHS Video Tapes	12	$ 7.95	$ 3.50	$ 95.40	$ 42.00	$ 53.40
		Transaction totals			$ 95.40	$ 42.00	$ 53.40

Transaction number:		10	Salesperson: Kim Abel				
Item Number	Item Description	Qty Sold	Selling Price	Cost	Sales Amount	Cost of Sales	Gross Profit
100	RCA 25 Inch Color Television	1	465.00	$375.00	$ 465.00	$375.00	$ 90.00
		Transaction totals			$ 465.00	$375.00	$ 90.00
		Daily totals			1,061.35	$767.00	294.35

FIGURE 9–27

continued

Great Plains Music and Video
Sales Summary
For the Period Jul 20, 1985 through Jul 31, 1985

Total sales	6,683.45
Cost of sales	3,945.60
Gross profit	2,737.85

SUMMARY

- There are seven steps to the definition of an R:base report:
  - Enter the REPORT DEFINE mode.
  - Edit the report.
  - Define report variables.
  - Locate data items on the report.
  - Mark the report sections.
  - Set the number of lines per page.
  - Save the report definition.
- Enter the REPORT DEFINE mode by typing the word REPORT and providing the name of the base table.
- The base table is the table R:base uses to provide the detail rows in the report.
- When editing the report, you type the parts of the report which are constant.
- Report variables are data items which are not taken directly from the base table of the database. They are derived each time the report is printed.
- Report variables are defined as expressions:

    Varible name = definition expression
- Report variables may be one of the following types:
  - R:base global variable
  - System variables: #DATE, #TIME, #PAGE
  - Lookup variable
  - Concatenated string variable
  - Computed variable
  - Printer escape sequence variable
- The location of data items in the report is done by moving the cursor to the beginning location and pressing [S], then moving the cursor to the end location and pressing [E].
- By use of [W], [T], and [I], you can create paragraphs when locating large text fields.
- You can mark report headings and footings, page headings and footings, detail lines, and breakpoint headings and footings for your report.

- Breakpoints are used to create subgroupings of data in the report. The key to successful use of breakpoints in R:base is to number the breakpoints from 1 to 10 beginning with the one farthest from the detail line.
- You can have dates printed in the report in the format "mmm dd, yyyy" by typing:

SET DATE mmmddyyyy

REVIEW QUESTIONS

Group I Questions

9.1
List the seven steps to defining an R:base report.

9.2
In your own words, describe what is done when editing an R:base report.

9.3
What is the purpose of R:base report variables?

9.4
How are R:base report variables defined?

9.5
List the various types of R:base report variables and give an example of how each type is defined.

9.6
List the various sections of an R:base report and explain the purpose of each.

9.7
What is a control break?

9.8
What are control breaks used for?

9.9
How many breakpoints may you define in an R:base report?

9.10
What is the key to successful implementation of control breaks in an R:base report?

Group II Questions

9.11
Use R:base to define a report for Great Plains Music and Video which would list sales transactions (no details—just

the transaction number, date, and customer's name). The report is to have a report header listing the company name, title of the report, time period being listed, and the date and time the report was printed.

Each day's transactions are to begin on a new page and are to be grouped by salesperson. Each page of the report is to be structured as follows:

Great Plains Music and Video

Sales Transactions for [Date]

Page [#Page]

Salesperson: [Employee name]

Sales transactions:

Transaction Number	Customer Number	Customer Name
•		
•		
•		

Total number of sales for [Employee name]:

Salesperson: [Employee name]

Etc.

After each day's sales have been listed, the report is to print the following:

Total number of sales for the day:

After all the sales for the period have been printed, a report summary is to be prepared which looks like the following:

Great Plains Music and Video Unlimited

Sales for the period [BegDate] [EndDate]

Total number of sales:

9.12

If you do not have R:base available to you, answer the following questions with respect to the report:

a. Indicate the appearance of the computer screen after the report has been edited.

b. List the report variable definition expressions necessary.

c. On the sketch of the report definition created for part a, indicate the titles of the various report sections. Include the symbols which R:base would insert to mark the various report sections.

d. What data item would serve as the control variable for breakpoint number one?

e. What report variables would be reset for breakpoint number one?

f. What data item would serve as the control variable for breakpoint number two?

g. What report variables would be reset for breakpoint number two?

9.13
List the R:base commands required to print the report for July 1985.

9.14
List the R:base commands to define the global variables required by the report.

9.15
List the R:base command to set the date format so dates will print in the following format:

Jul 31, 1985

PROJECT

Use R:base to create a report of your own design from your academic database. The report should include a report header and footer, report variables of all types, and at least two breakpoints.

CHAPTER 10

Menu-Driven Database Applications

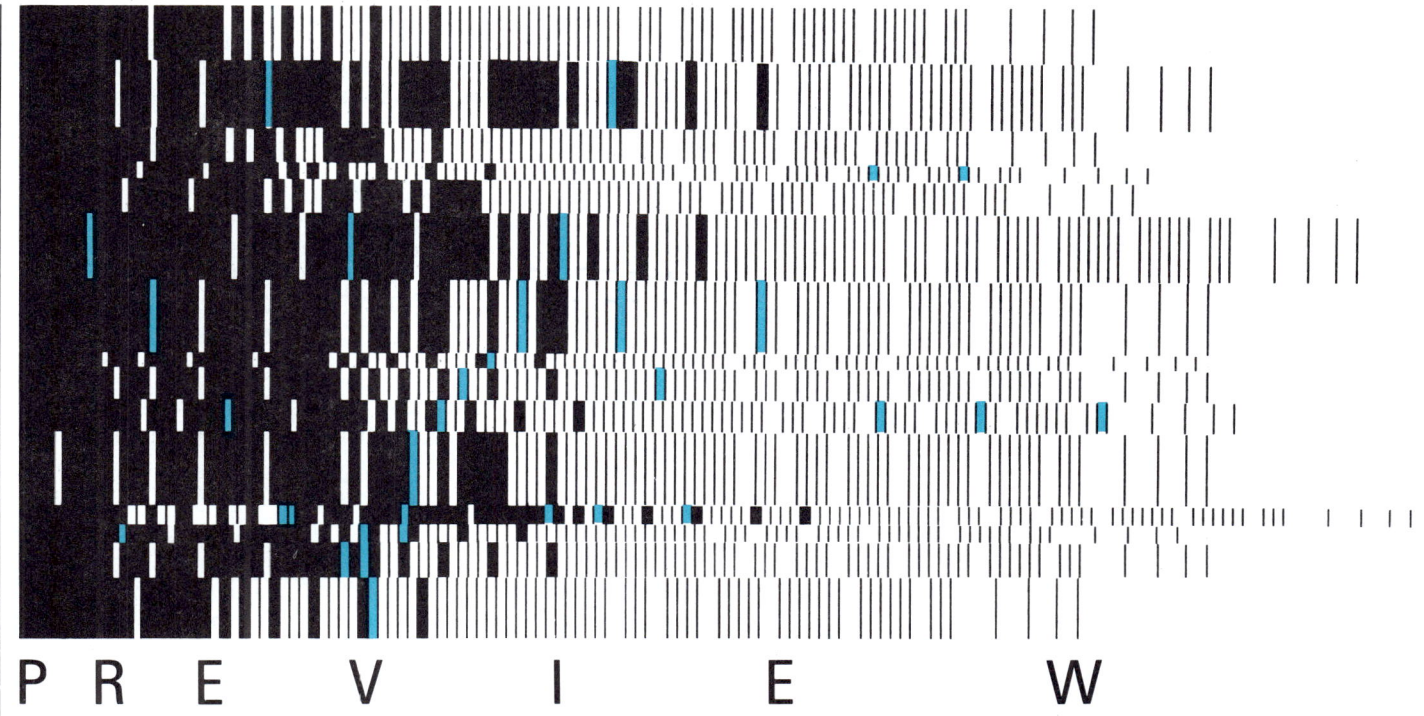

PREVIEW

In previous chapters, we showed how to design and build microcomputer databases. We also showed how to use a database management system (DBMS) to load data into the database and how to manipulate the database using a query language and a report writer to answer questions.

In this chapter, we will discuss menu-driven database applications like the Video Rental system described in Chapter 2. We will talk about what a menu-driven application is and use the Application EXPRESS part of R:base to develop one.

Note: If you want to create the menu-driven database application illustrated in the chapter, you will need the GTPLAIN database created in Chapters 6, 7, and 8. See the preview to Chapter 9 for details. If you are using the student version of R:base, you will need to delete the CUSTOMER table from the database by typing: REMOVE CUSTOMER after loading R:base and obtaining the R:base R> prompt.

MENU-DRIVEN APPLICATIONS

What is a menu-driven database application? Let's look at three terms which we have not yet discussed: *database application*, *menu*, and *command file*.

Database Application

A database application is the use of database processing for a particular purpose. A DBMS is a general-purpose tool. When you use a DBMS to perform a specified set of tasks, you have a database application.

Menu

A menu is a list of choices. An application menu provides the user with a list of the things the application can do. To utilize the application, a user simply makes choices from the application menus.

Command File

A command file is a collection of DBMS commands stored on disk. Instead of getting its commands from the computer's console (keyboard), the DBMS reads them from a command file. For example, suppose management of Great Plains periodically needs the name of the person who made the last electronic component sale. The R:base commands required to open the database, manipulate the database, display the required information, and delete the temporary tables are as follows:

```
OPEN GTPLAIN
PROJECT TEMP FROM SALE USING EmpID# +
WHERE COUNT EQ LAST
INTERSECT TEMP WITH EMPLOYEE FORMING RESULT
REMOVE TEMP
SELECT EmpFName EmpLName FROM RESULT
REMOVE RESULT
```

One way for management to obtain this information is to write down the necessary R:base commands and faithfully type them in each time. However, there is always the risk that the instructions will be misunderstood or a typographical error will be made, resulting in user frustration.

A simpler solution would be to place the commands in a command file. You may use any text editing program to create a command file. R:base comes with a text editor, RBEDIT. To access it, type:

```
RBEDIT
```

FIGURE 10-1
The RBEDIT main menu

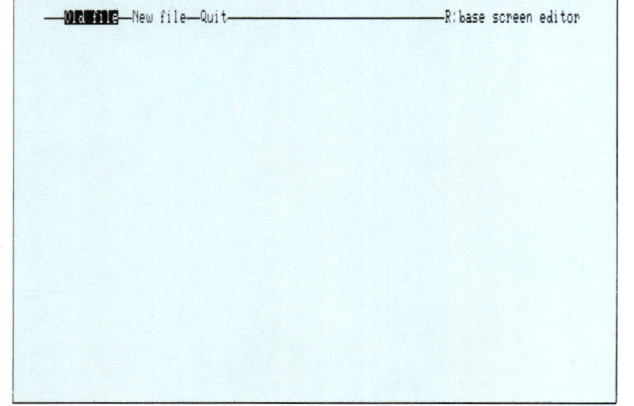

(See Figure 10–1.) You want to create a new file, so press [N]. You are presented with a screen which is blank except for the top line (Figure 10–2).

Since RBEDIT is a full-screen editor, you can move the cursor to any position on the screen with the cursor movement keys. You can use [F1] to insert an entire line any place the cursor is located. [F2] deletes the line on which the cursor is located. Use the [INS] key to insert a character at the cursor location. The [DEL] key is used to delete the character at the cursor location. [HOME] moves the cursor to the first character location in the text. [END] moves the cursor to the last line of text. [PG UP] and [PG DN] move the cursor one page of text up or down, respectively. If pressing the cursor movement keys [INS], [DEL], [HOME], [END], [PG UP], or [PG DN] results in numbers appearing on the screen, press [NUM LOCK] once, then try again.

Press [ENTER] after you type in each of the commands from the previous page beginning with OPEN GTPLAIN and ending with REMOVE RESULT. When you have finished typing the commands, press [ESC]. You are returned to the RBEDIT main menu in Figure 10–1. Save the commands in a file by pressing [S] and entering the file name, LASTEMP.CMD.

Now, to learn the name of the salesperson who made the last sale, simply load R:base and type:

RUN LASTEMP.CMD

(See Figure 10–3.) By using a command file, the answer to the question "Which salesperson made the last sale?" can be obtained with one command, not six. Also, you are assured that the correct commands will be executed in the correct order every time.

AN EXAMPLE

The Video Rental System described in Chapter 2 is an example of a menu-driven database application. To enter data about a newly acquired video tape, the user selects choice 1 (Video data) from the main menu, then choice 1 (Enter new video) from the video data menu. The user need not know anything about database processing in general or about the specific underlying DBMS. That knowledge is incorporated in the design of the database, the application menus, and the command files that make the application work.

What Is a Menu-Driven Database Application?

A menu-driven database application is the use of database processing for a particular purpose. Command

FIGURE 10–2

The RBEDIT screen with cursor at column 1 and row 1

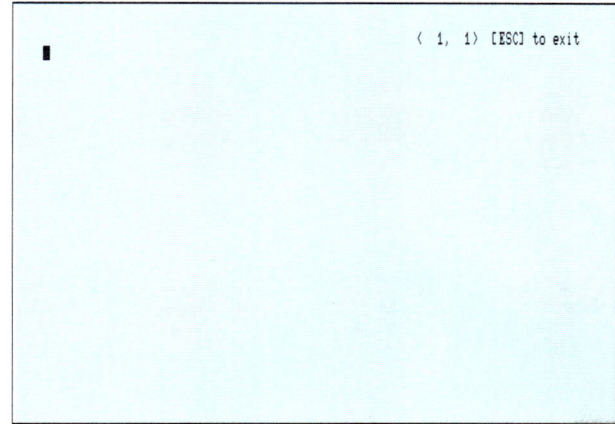

FIGURE 10–3

Using the command file LASTEMP.CMD

files are used to provide the application user with a set of menus, determine which choices the user makes, and perform the related tasks. Instead of having to learn the DBMS commands, the user picks choices from the application menus. The work is performed by the command files.

DEVELOPING MENU-DRIVEN APPLICATIONS

There are presently two ways to develop menu-driven database applications. One way is to use a program generator to create the menus and command files for you. Alternatively, you may create the menus and command files yourself. In this chapter, we will use a program generator. In the next chapter, we will show you how to create menus and command files yourself.

The Application EXPRESS

The Application EXPRESS is a program which builds menu-driven database applications based upon your responses to various questions. For simple applications in which the operations you wish to perform are straightforward, you can create a menu-driven database application complete with menus, help screens, and command files without knowing how to program at all. Let's look at an example.

A New Application

Assume that management of Great Plains Music and Video Unlimited has asked that we make the part of their information management system which deals with employee information menu-driven. If this partial implementation works out, they will want us to make the entire system menu-driven.

Determining User Requirements After interviewing the people involved, we have determined that there only needs to be one menu with the following choices on it:

1. Enter data about a new employee
2. Change employee data
3. Inquire about an employee
4. Print an employee list
5. Show the employee who made the last sale

Creating the Application To begin, load the Application EXPRESS. You are presented with the main menu (Figure 10–4). It's the same menu you saw when you used the EXPRESS to define a part of the GTPLAIN

FIGURE 10–4

Application EXPRESS main menu

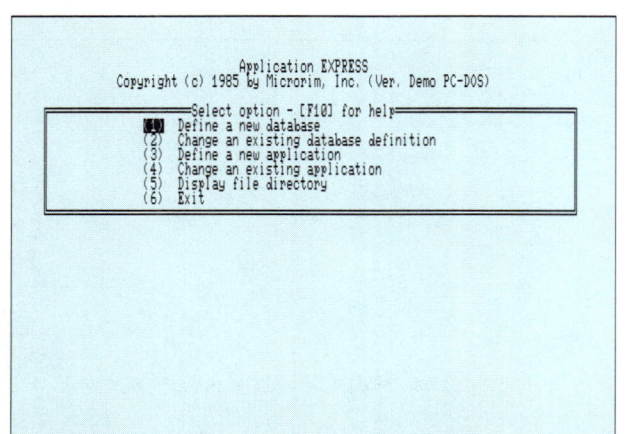

database in Chapter 6. In addition to choices which allow you to exit the EXPRESS and display a file directory, you can create or change a database and create or change an application. Because the GTPLAIN database already exists, choose "Define a new application" by pressing [3].

Select the Database You Want to Use The EXPRESS presents you with a list of all the R:base databases on the default directory (Figure 10–5). In this case, you want to use GTPLAIN. Select it by pressing [G] then [ENTER].

Name the Application You are asked to provide a name for the application. Type:

EMPLOYEE

(See Figure 10–6.)

Name the Main Menu In a similar way, you are asked to provide a name for the main application menu. EX-PRESS suggests the name MAIN. You may enter any eight characters (Figure 10–7).

Select the Menu Type Next you select the type of menu that the main menu is to be: vertical or horizontal (Figure 10–8). The menu you are looking at is a horizontal menu. The choices are presented in rows and columns. Instead of entering a number to select a choice, the user moves the reverse video area using the cursor movement keys until the choice is high-

FIGURE 10–5
List of databases in the default directory

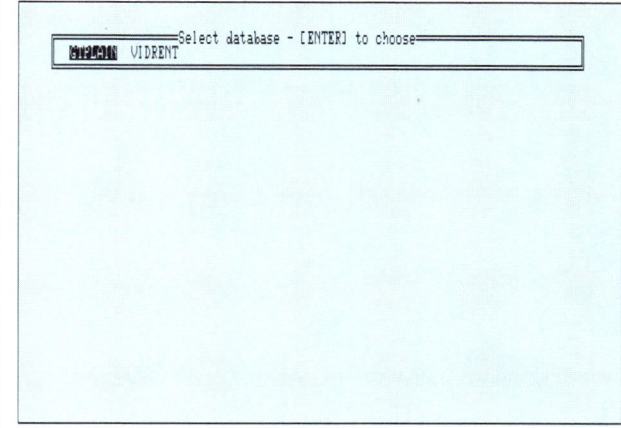

FIGURE 10–6
Entering the name for the application

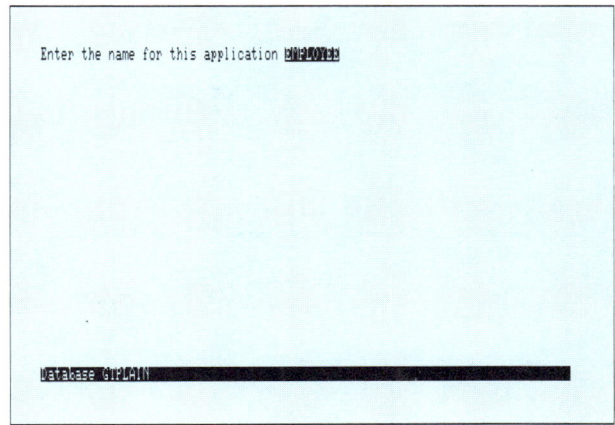

FIGURE 10–7
Entering the name for the main menu

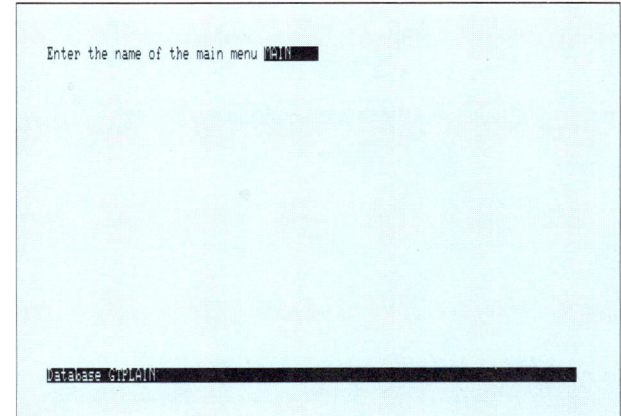

FIGURE 10–8
Choosing between a vertical and a horizontal menu

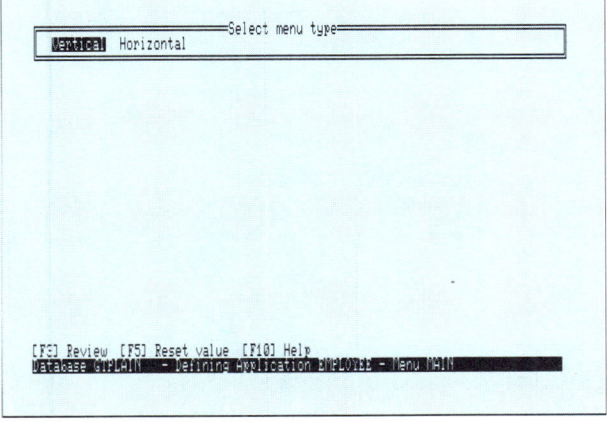

FIGURE 10-9
Skeleton of a vertical menu

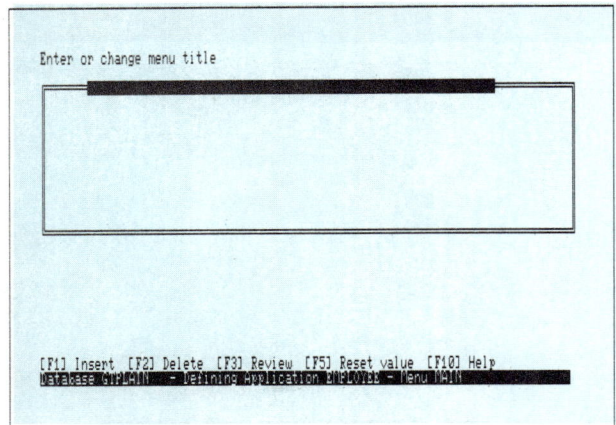

FIGURE 10-10
Entering the menu title

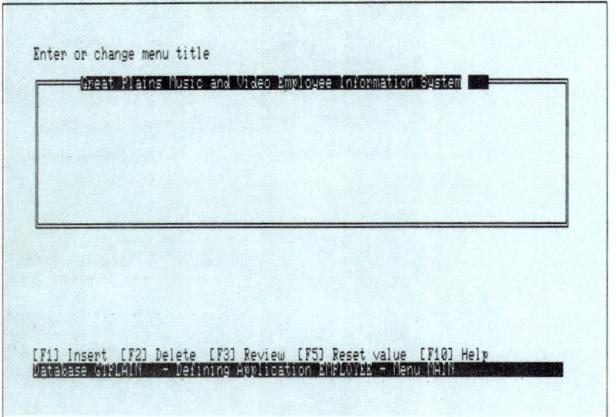

FIGURE 10-11
Ready for entry of menu choices

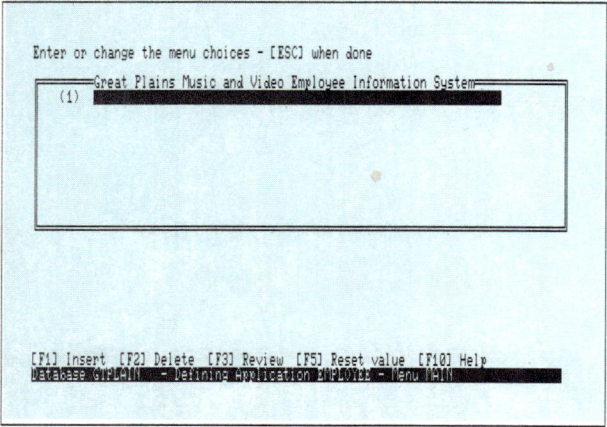

lighted. You may also move the reverse video area by pressing the first letter of the choice you want. The selection is indicated by pressing [ENTER]. In this case, you want a vertical menu, so merely press [ENTER].

Enter a Title for the Menu You are presented with the screen in Figure 10–9. The screen contains the skeleton of a vertical menu. At this point, you are to enter the exact title as you want it to appear to the user of your application. In this case, type:

Great Plains Music and Video Employee Information System

(See Figure 10–10.)

Enter the Menu Choices After you press [ENTER], the screen appears as in Figure 10–11. The EXPRESS is ready for you to enter the choices which are to appear on the menu. Type in the choices from the requirements above (Figure 10–12). When you are finished typing in the choices, press [ESC].

Indicate Whether [ESC] Is Used to Exit the Menu Next, the EXPRESS asks whether you want your user to be able to press [ESC] to exit the menu (Figure 10–13). As a rule of thumb, you should answer yes to this question for all menus in the application. Otherwise, the application user will have no way of getting out of the menu currently in use unless you specify a menu choice for this purpose. To answer yes, press [ENTER].

FIGURE 10-12
After entry of menu choices

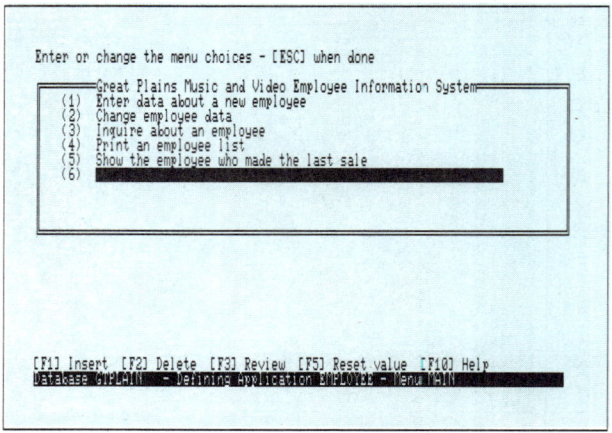

FIGURE 10–13
Decide if [ESC] will be used to exit the main menu

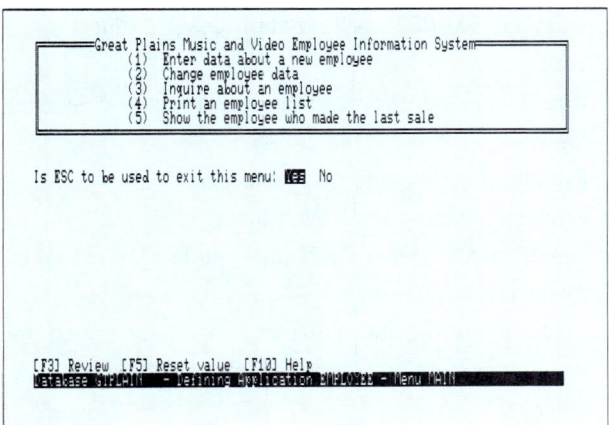

FIGURE 10–14
Decide if a help screen will be available

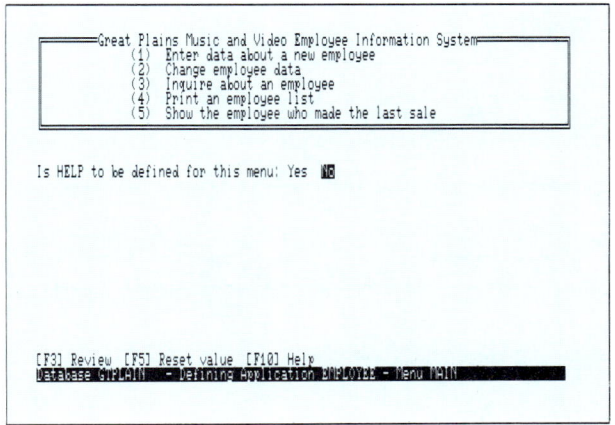

FIGURE 10–15
Naming the help screen

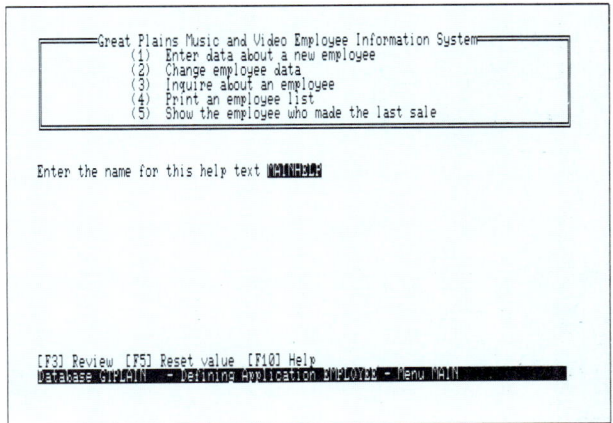

Indicate Whether Help Is to Be Available Next, you are asked whether you want to provide a help screen for this menu (Figure 10–14). If you provide a help screen, the application user can press [F10] to get an explanation of how the various choices on the menu work.

As another rule of thumb, it is difficult to provide too much help to users, so select yes by pressing [Y]. Then enter a name for the help text by typing:

MAINHELP

(See Figure 10–15.) After you press [ENTER] you are given access to RBEDIT. Type in the help screen shown in Figure 10–16. When you are finished, press [ESC].

Define the Actions Associated with Each Menu Selection Now, for each choice on the menu, you must define the actions which R:base is to perform when that choice is selected by the application user (Figure 10–17). The choices are:

FIGURE 10–16
Text for MAINHELP

Action title	Action description
Load	Enter data using an R:base form. If the form is not already defined, the EXPRESS will create a generic one for you.
Edit	Change data using an R:base form.
Delete	Delete data from a table in the database.

FIGURE 10–17

Ready to define actions for the first menu selection

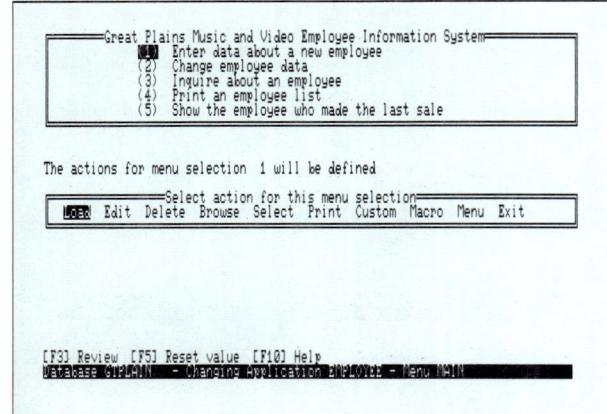

Browse	Look at the rows in a database table.
Select	Perform an R:base SELECT command on a database table.
Print	Print an R:base report. If the report does not already exist, the EXPRESS will create a generic report for you.
Custom	With this choice, you can create your own command file.
Macro	Execute a preexisting command file.
Menu	Process another menu. With this choice, you can "nest" menus within each other, up to a maximum of three deep.
Exit	If you do not provide [ESC] as a means of exiting the menu, you must provide this as one of the menu choices.

CHOICE 1: ENTER DATA ABOUT A NEW EMPLOYEE

When the application user selects this choice, you want the user to be presented with an R:base form for use in loading employee data. Select LOAD by pressing [ENTER].

Select Table to Load As shown in Figure 10–18, the EXPRESS displays the names of all the tables in the database. In this case, EMPLOYEE is the name of the table to be loaded with data. Select it by pressing [E] then [ENTER].

Select Form for Loading You receive a menu of the names of all the forms which have been defined for the database. You want the EXPRESS to define a new form for you so move the reverse video marker to (NEW) using the cursor movement keys, then press [ENTER].

Enter the Form Name The EXPRESS suggests a name: EMPLOYEE. (See Figure 10–19.) That's a good name. Press [ENTER].

Select the Columns to Include in the Form You may now indicate which columns from the EMPLOYEE table you want included in the form (Figure 10–20). To make your selections, use the cursor movement keys to highlight the column of your choice, then press [ENTER]. When all of your selections have been made, press [ESC]. In this case, you want all the columns included, so highlight the (ALL) choice and press [ENTER].

FIGURE 10–18

Selecting the table to load

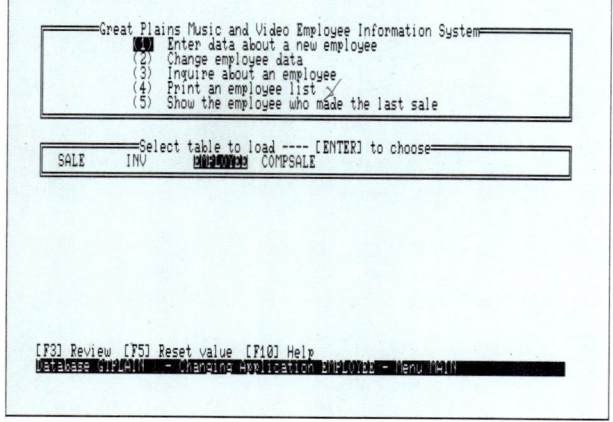

FIGURE 10-19
Naming the new form

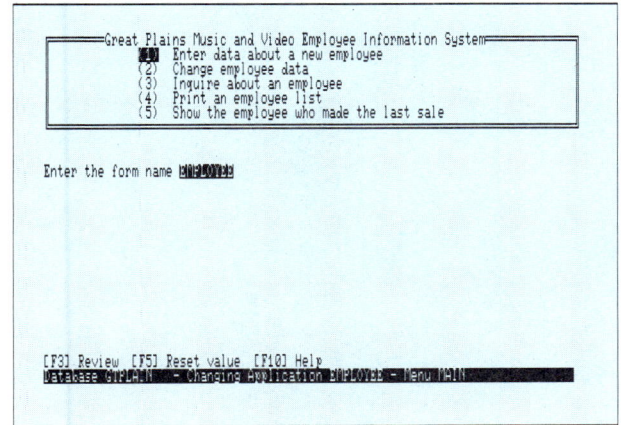

Enter the Form Title At this point, you enter the form title to be displayed to the application user with the form. Type:

Great Plains Music and Video Unlimited Employee Data

(See Figure 10–21.)

Enter Descriptive Column Names In building the generic form, R:base uses column names from the database description (the data dictionary). Names like SalRevDt and Exempt# will not be very meaningful to most application users. The EXPRESS allows you to substitute more meaningful names. Simply type in the names you want used in the form. After you have entered each name, press [ENTER]. (See Figure 10–22.) When you are finished with the names, press [ESC].

Move on to the Next Choice The EXPRESS next asks if you want to define actions in addition to LOAD for choice 1 (Figure 10–23). The only action associated with choice number 1 is LOAD, so enter [N].

CHOICES 2, 3, and 4

Follow similar steps to define the actions associated with the rest of the menu choices. At any point in the definition process, you may review the menus in the application, the choices on the menus, and the actions associated with the choices by pressing [F3]. Figure

FIGURE 10-20
Choosing the columns to include in the form

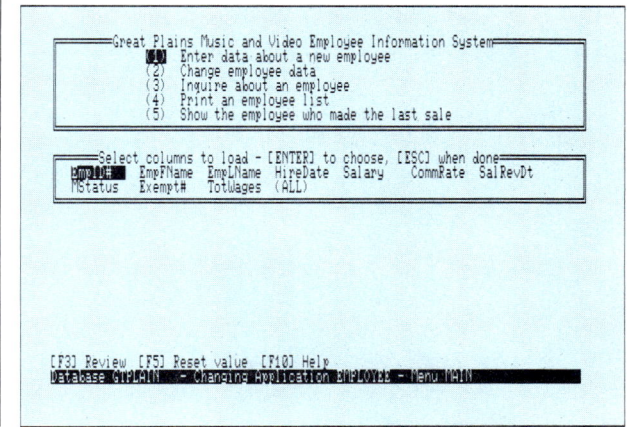

FIGURE 10-21
Entering the form title

FIGURE 10-22
Entering descriptive column names

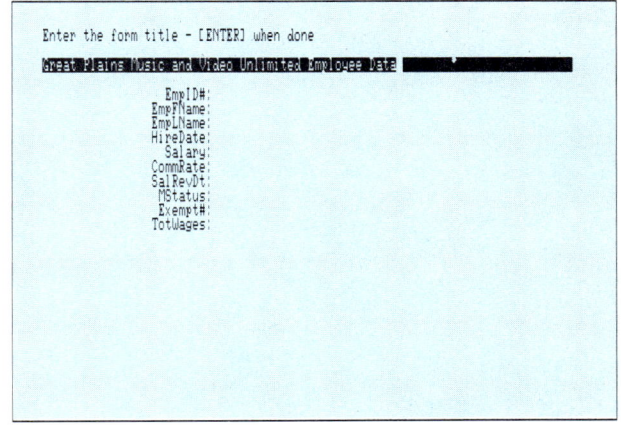

FIGURE 10-23

Press [N] to move on to the next choice

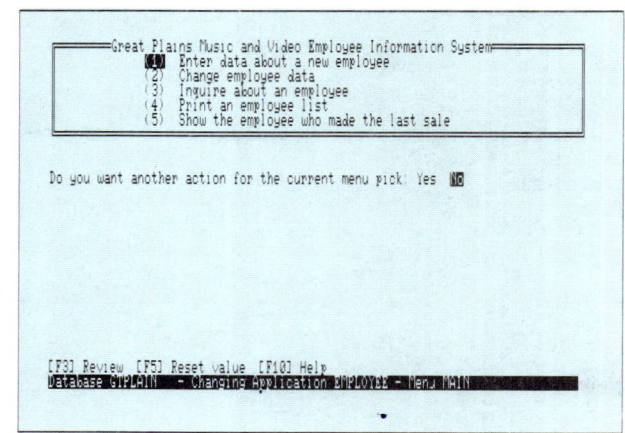

10-24 shows the status of the application after choices 1 through 4 have been defined.

Notice that the actions associated with menu choices 1 through 4 are:

Choice number	Action
1	Load using the form named EMPLOYEE
2	Edit using the form named EDITEMP
3	Select from the EMPLOYEE table
4	Print the report named EMPLOYEE

The process used to define the actions for choices 2, 3, and 4 was similar to the process used to define the action for choice 1 except as follows.

Instead of using the same form for editing data in the EMPLOYEE table as is used to load it, we had the EXPRESS define a new one. For control reasons, we do not want users to be able to change certain items: EmpID#, Salary, etc. Thus, the form used for editing, EDITEMP, contains only name, address, phone number, marital status, and number of exemptions.

With certain actions, including edit, select, and print, you can indicate to the EXPRESS the order in which you want the rows from the table to be processed. You indicate the sort order by making selections from a menu.

In addition to being able to sort the rows which are subject to the action being defined, you can tell the EXPRESS which rows are to be subject to the action. You do that by indicating the name of the column upon which R:base is to select the rows for processing.

FIGURE 10-24

Status of application after choices 1-4 have been defined

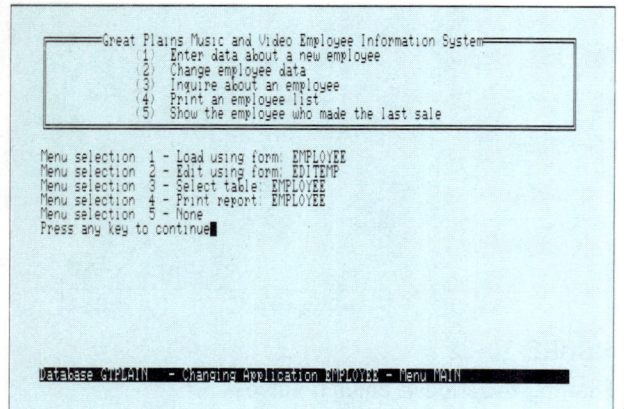

For example, in Options 2 and 3 of the EMPLOYEE application, you want the application user to be able to specify which employee the action is to pertain to. Thus, you can indicate to the EXPRESS that those actions are to apply to rows selected on the basis of the employee's last name (EmpLName). In addition, you can tell the EXPRESS that the application user is to be prompted for the employee's last name at the time the application is being run.

CHOICE 5: SHOW THE EMPLOYEE WHO MADE THE LAST SALE

What happens if you want the application to include an action which is not one of the predefined EXPRESS choices? You can supply your own command file. Recall the command file we wrote to enable management to answer the question, "Which employee made the last sale?" To make life even easier, we can include the command file in a menu-driven application.

To do that, select Macro from the list of action choices provided by the EXPRESS (Figure 10–25). The EXPRESS refers to command files which already exist as macros. Recall that your macro is stored in a file called LASTEMP.CMD, so type:

LASTEMP.CMD

(See Figure 10–26.) Now, when the user selects Option 5 from the menu, R:base will execute the command file you wrote, presenting the user with the name of the salesperson who made the last sale.

After the actions for the last menu choice have been defined, the EXPRESS displays the message:

Writing application files—Please wait.

Then, the program is echoed across the screen as it is written to the disk. When the EXPRESS has finished writing the program, it asks, "Do you want to build the RBASE.DAT file for this application Yes No." You are probably asking yourself, "What is an RBASE.DAT file?" Immediately after it is loaded, R:base looks for a command file named RBASE.DAT. If it finds one, R:base executes the commands in the file. Thus, if you answer yes, the EXPRESS creates the RBASE.DAT file which contains the command required to execute the EMPLOYEE application:

RUN EMPLOYEE IN EMPLOYEE.APX

FIGURE 10–25
Selecting Macro from the list of actions

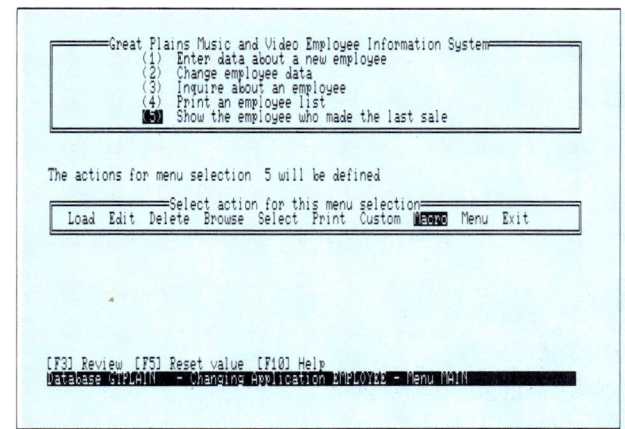

FIGURE 10–26
Entering the name of the macro

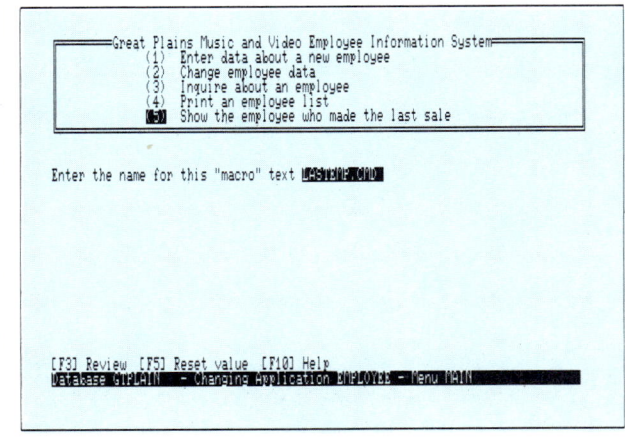

FIGURE 10–27

The application main menu

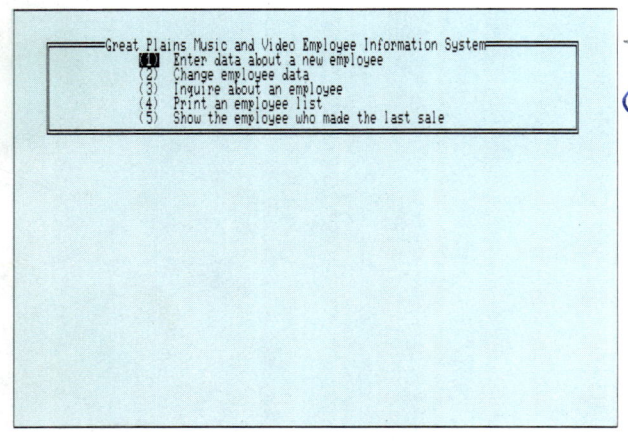

In this way, you can have your application run automatically whenever R:base is loaded.

If you or the EXPRESS creates an RBASE.DAT file and you later change your mind, you can delete it by typing:

DELETE RBASE.DAT

at the R> prompt.

If you simply want to temporarily deactivate the RBASE.DAT file, you can rename it by typing:

RENAME RBASE.DAT RBASE.TMP

at the R> prompt.

When you are ready to reactivate the file, rename it by typing:

RENAME RBASE.TMP RBASE.DAT

at the R> prompt.

Using the Application Now load R:base. If you had the EXPRESS create an RBASE.DAT file, the application menu will automatically appear. If not, type:

RUN EMPLOYEE IN EMPLOYEE.APX

The screen shown in Figure 10–27 will appear. Try each of the menu choices. In a few minutes, you have created what an experienced programmer would take hours to create.

SUMMARY

- A menu-driven database application is the use of database processing for a particular purpose. Command files are used to provide the application user with a set of menus, to help the user determine choices, and to perform the related tasks.
- If a menu-driven database application is provided, the user does not have to learn the database management system (DBMS) commands. Instead, the user picks choices from the application menus. The work is performed by the command files.
- A DBMS is a general-purpose tool. Use of a DBMS to perform a specified set of tasks constitutes a database application.
- An application menu provides the user with a list of the things the application can do.
- To utilize a menu-driven application, the application user makes choices from the application menus.
- A command file is a collection of DBMS commands stored on disk. Instead of getting its commands from the computer's console, the DBMS reads them from the command file.
- A command file can reduce a complex task to one command.
- Use of a command file ensures that a set of procedures is performed correctly each time it is executed.
- Menu-driven database applications can be developed in one of two ways: by using a program generator or by writing the menus, help screens, and command files yourself.
- The Application EXPRESS is a program generator which is provided with R:base.
- The Application EXPRESS uses the following steps to help you build a menu-driven database application:
  - Select the database you want to use.
  - Name the application.
  - Name the main menu.
  - Select the menu type (horizontal or vertical).
  - Enter a title for the menu.
  - Enter the menu choices.
  - Indicate whether [ESC] is to be used to exit the menu.
  - Indicate whether HELP is to be provided (if so, create the help text).

- Define actions associated with each menu selection:

    Load: Enter data using an R:base form.

    Edit: Change data using an R:base form.

    Delete: Delete rows from a database table.

    Browse: Look at the rows in a database table.

    Select: Perform an R:base SELECT on a database table.

    Print: Print an R:base REPORT.

    Custom: Use RBEDIT to create a custom command file.

    Macro: Execute a pre-existing command file.

    Menu: Process a sub-menu.

    Exit: Exit the current menu.

- If an R:base FORM or REPORT is needed for an action such as Load or Print, the Application EXPRESS will create a generic one for you.
- Create the RBASE.DAT file (if you so desire).
- If an RBASE.DAT file exists, the application will be run automatically when R:base is loaded.
- If an RBASE.DAT file does not exist, type:

    RUN (application name) IN (application name).APX

REVIEW QUESTIONS

Group I Questions

10.1
Define the term *application*.

10.2
What is a menu?

10.3
What is an application menu?

10.4
What does it mean to have an application which is menu-driven?

10.5
What is a command file?

10.6
List two advantages of using command files.

10.7
In your own words, define *menu-driven database application*.

10.8
What is the advantage to the user of creating a menu-driven database application?

10.9
List two methods you can use to create menu-driven database applications.

10.10
List the steps used by the Application EXPRESS to help you create menu-driven database applications.

10.11
What command is necessary in order to run an application created by the Application EXPRESS if an RBASE.DAT file exists?

10.12
What command is necessary in order to run an application created by the Application EXPRESS if no RBASE.DAT file exists?

10.13
What command can you use to temporarily deactivate an RBASE.DAT file?

10.14
What command do you use to reactivate a deactivated RBASE.DAT file?

10.15
What command can you use to remove an RBASE.DAT file?

Group II Questions

10.16
What are the advantages to an organization like Great Plains Music and Video Unlimited of creating menu-driven database applications?

10.17
In what way(s) can the use of menu-driven database applications enhance security and control over an information management system?

PROJECT

Use the Application EXPRESS to create a menu-driven database application for your academic environment. Use at least two menus in your application—one for instructor data and one for class data. Your application should include at least one form and one report. Make sure you include help screens. You do not need to include custom command files or macros in your application—yet.

CHAPTER 11

Programming with R:base

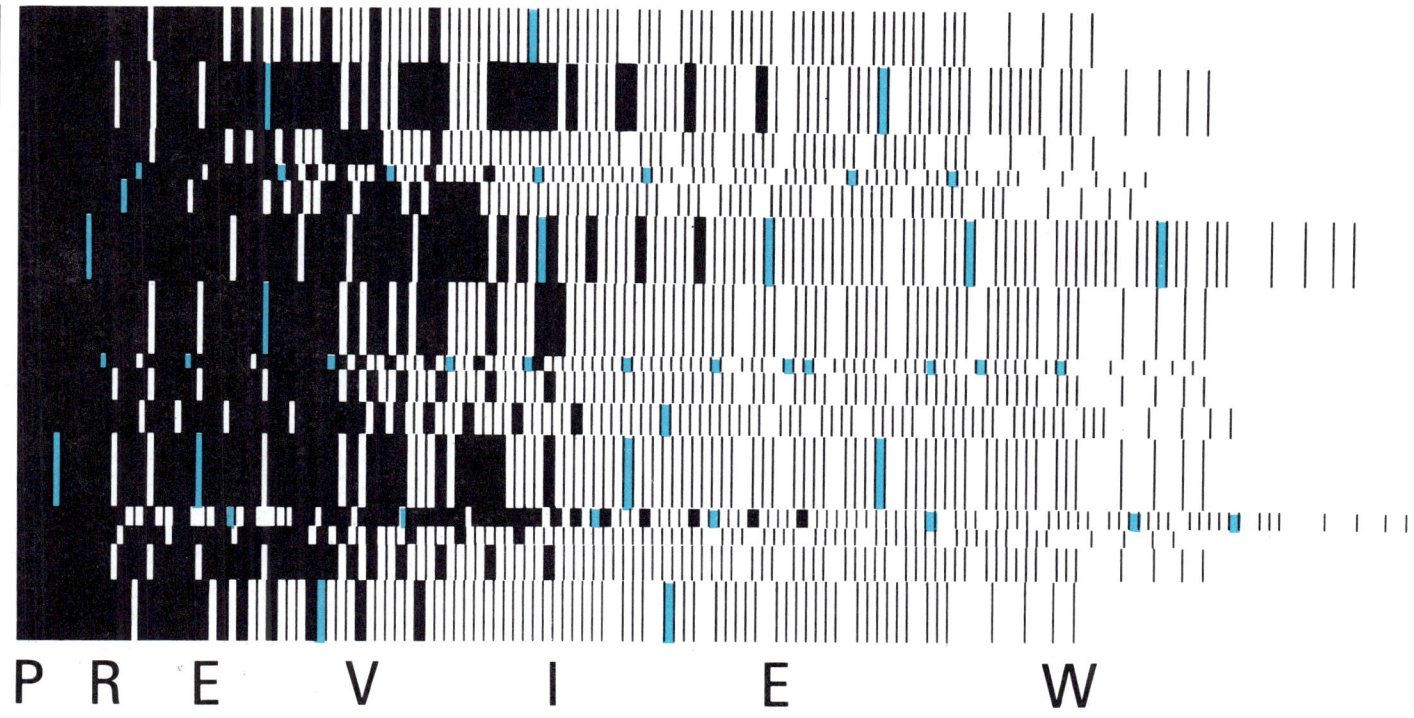

PREVIEW

In the preceding chapter, we showed you how to use a program generator, the Application EXPRESS, to create menu-driven database applications. We observed that these applications are composed of R:base command files, which are collections of R:base commands.

Although the Application EXPRESS is a powerful program, it does not begin to tap the full capability of the R:base command language. If you are familiar with programming, you can write your own R:base command files to accomplish tasks far beyond those possible with the Application EXPRESS. The goal of this chapter is to facilitate your programming by describing and illustrating the use of the most important R:base programming commands.

Because this is not a book on programming, we will not describe ways of developing program structure and logic. Neither will we discuss the theories of structured program design and structured programming. We assume you are already familiar with these topics. If not, see one of the excellent texts on this subject such as 2, 10, or 17 in the bibliography.

To describe the R:base programming commands, we will study example command files from Great Plains'

Video Rental System. These command files illustrate use of the R:base language to solve programming problems typical of many business applications. This chapter will describe three of the command files in that application. The entire collection of programs in Great Plains' Video Rental application is available on disk. See your instructor for details.

A NOTE ABOUT FILES

As shown in this chapter, all of the command files, help screens, and menu files are stand-alone DOS files. That is one way to create an application using the R:base programming language. Another way is to combine all of the files for an application into one or two files using RCOMPILE, a utility program which comes with R:base. The sample application provided on the student data disk which is described in Chapter 2 was prepared using RCOMPILE. Because RCOMPILE is not supplied with the student version of R:base, we will not discuss it further. Refer to the R:base documentation for more information about RCOMPILE.

FUNDAMENTALS

Before discussing R:base commands and their use, we need to review several important fundamentals. Unfortunately, these fundamentals are too broad to discuss comprehensively here. You may want to consult 11 or 19 in the bibliography for more information.

Programming Concepts

A command file is a collection of R:base commands; it is equivalent to a program in COBOL or PASCAL. Not all command files are created equal. Some are simple and straightforward while others are contrived and difficult to understand. Since an application can easily have fifteen or twenty command files, we greatly prefer those which are simple and straightforward. Complexity makes it hard to debug or change the application. Therefore, before discussing R:base commands we will briefly review a few basic principles.

First, a command file should have one and only one function. This statement does not mean that the scope of the command file is necessarily narrow. It means that the command file does ONE task—not half a task or two tasks. The scope, however, may be as broad as

"Process menu number 3" or as narrow as "Get a valid member ID number."

Second, a command file should have sensible and easily understood inputs and outputs that relate directly to its function. A command file should not be given data that it does not use, nor should it be asked to provide data that does not relate to its function.

Third, it has been shown that the logic of any application program can be expressed in three fundamental structures: sequence, alternation, and iteration. The implication of this is that if you know how to express these constructs in R:base, you will know how to express the logic of any application in R:base. Since these constructs are so fundamental, we will briefly review them.

Sequence Sequence occurs when a task is performed by executing one command after the other, in order. In R:base, sequence is determined by the order of the statements in the command file. Unless there are instructions to the contrary, R:base executes the first instruction first, the second, second, and so forth.

Alternation Alternation means to choose the action to take depending on a condition. For example: IF there is valid data, THEN add the employee's record; OTHERWISE print an error message. As you will see, R:base implements alternation with the IF-THEN-ENDIF sequence of commands.

Iteration Iteration means to do a task over and over again. In your programming classes, this construct may have been called the DOWHILE construct. The basic idea is that a set of instructions is performed over and over as long as a particular condition is true. For example, DOWHILE DATA REMAINS means to do a set of instructions until all of the data has been exhausted. As you will see, R:base implements this construct with the WHILE-ENDWHILE sequence of commands.

Menu-Driven Database Applications

The sample applications shown in Chapters 2 and 10 are *menu-driven*. This term simply means that the user is presented with a list of choices, he or she picks one choice from the list, and the program takes some action in accordance with the choice. We have illustrated this type of application because it is the most common type in the business environment. The alternative style, *command-driven applications*, require the user to memorize a set of commands and issue them to the application. This style is uncommon in the business environment, and we will not consider it further.

In general, command files in a menu-driven application fall into one of three basic types. Command files either:

- Process a menu
- Provide a service to other command files, or
- Perform a specific task for the user

When we describe the R:base commands, we will study a command file from each of these categories. These command files are taken from the Great Plains Video Rental application you saw in Chapter 2. Once you have understood them, you will know the majority of the R:base programming commands and realize how these commands are used in a business application.

R:BASE COMMANDS: PROCESSING A MENU

The processing of a menu is conceptually quite simple. Three tasks are involved:

- Present the menu to the user
- Obtain a valid choice from the user
- Perform the task associated with the user's choice

The third task is most generally accomplished by invoking other command files. These subordinate command files either perform the user's work or present another menu. The subordinate menu is processed with the same three tasks in turn.

MEN0PROC—A Menu-processing Command File

We will begin our discussion of R:base commands by examining MEN0PROC, a command file that processes the main menu in the Great Plains Video Rental application.

MEN0PROC has two major sections. The first contains descriptive information that documents MEN0PROC's function and other characteristics. This section will be ignored by R:base: it is there to benefit any programmers who may need to understand the logic of this command file (to debug it [which one hopes will not be required] or to change it when the application requirements change). The second section has two functions. First, the menu is presented and a valid choice is obtained from the user; second, the action corresponding to that choice is taken. Specifically, MEN0PROC consists of the following sections:

- Section 1—Descriptive information
- Section 2—Command file subtasks
    Subtask A—Get the user's choice
    Subtask B—Perform the action associated with the choice

We will examine each of these sections in turn.

Section 1: Descriptive Information The descriptive section contains a brief explanation of the command file's function. In addition, it indicates which command file activates MEN0PROC, and it lists other command files which MEN0PROC will call. Furthermore, the descriptive section lists the inputs that MEN0PROC will receive (parameters expected) and the outputs that it will produce (values returned).

This descriptive section is sometimes called *internal program documentation*. The format shown here is only an example. Some companies have standard formats for such documentation. If your company does, you should follow it instead.

The descriptive section from MEN0PROC is as follows:

```
*(*****************************************************************)
*(                                                                 )
*(Procedure name: MEN0PROC - processes the main menu.              )
*(Implements a DO-WHILE construct by repeatedly RUNning itself.    )
*(Called by          : INIT                                        )
*(Calls              : Other MEN0PROC files                        )
*(Parameters expected: None                                        )
*(Values returned    : None                                        )
*(                                                                 )
*(*****************************************************************)
```

None of these statements is intended for R:base; they are intended for humans instead. To keep R:base from processing these statements, they are preceded by the symbols:

```
*(
```

and terminated by the symbol:

```
)
```

Section 2: Get a Valid Choice and Process It The next section of MEN0PROC is divided into two subsections. First, a valid choice is obtained from the user and then that choice is executed.

Get a valid choice The collection of commands (called *code* in programming terminology) which obtains the user's choice is the following:

```
*(Clear the screen.                                              )
NEWPAGE
*(Initialize choice to a value which ensures that the menu is    )
*(processed.                                                     )
SET VARIABLE choice TO -1
*(The menu will be redisplayed as long as the user asks for      )
*(HELP - choice = -1                                              )
WHILE choice EQ -1 THEN
*(Use the R:base CHOOSE command to display the menu and get      )
*(the user's choice.                                             )
   CHOOSE choice FROM MENU0 AT 1
*(If the user presses [F10], the CHOOSE command returns a        )
*(value of -1.                                                   )
   IF choice EQ -1 THEN
      DISPLAY MEN0HELP
   ENDIF
ENDWHILE
```

MEN0PROC Structure: The Three Programming Constructs Before considering the details of the remaining statements, examine the general structure. You will see an example of each of the three fundamental constructs. First, a *sequence* of instructions is executed. Next, *iteration* occurs starting with the command WHILE and ending with the command ENDWHILE. Finally, *alternation* occurs at the IF and ENDIF statements.

R:base Command Descriptions The first command is NEWPAGE. This command simply clears the screen of any existing characters. The next three commands concern R:base global variables.

R:base global variables Recall from Chapter 9 that R:base global variables are scratch-pad data items that exist only temporarily. They are not saved as part of the database. These variables can be created, accessed, changed, or deleted by any command file. They are global in scope. As you will see, global variables are used extensively in programming. MEN0PROC uses one such variable, *choice,* which is used to hold the numeric value of the user's choice.

Unless you specify it, R:base sets the type of a global variable to match the type of value you assign to it. For example, the command:

SET VARIABLE amount TO $33.15

results in amount being set to DOLLAR. Similarly, the command:

SET VARIABLE message TO "Enter an amount"

results in message being set to TEXT. If you want to ensure that values of a global variable are of a certain type, use the following form of the SET VARIABLE command:

SET VARIABLE variable [TYPE]

For example, the command:

SET VARIABLE blank TEXT

tells R:base that the variable *blank* is to contain only text data. As you will see, the CHOOSE command automatically sets the type of *choice* to INTEGER, thus we need not execute a SET VARIABLE command to change its type.

R:base provides another useful global variable command, SHOW VARIABLE. The command:

SHOW VARIABLE blank AT 1 1

causes R:base to display the value of the global variable *blank* on the screen at line number 1, character position number 1. The line number is first, followed by the position number in the line. Both line and position numbers can also be global variables. For example, if the variable X has the value 1, then the following statement is equivalent to the one above:

SHOW VARIABLE blank AT .X 1

Note that the variable X is preceded with a dot (.) in the above command. The dot tells R:base to use the value of the variable, not the letter X. You may be feeling confused about when to use a dot and when not to use it. Let's look at an example. After the following commands, the global variables *x* and *y* will both have a value of 7:

SET VARIABLE y TO 7
SET VARIABLE x TO .y

Precede the variable name with a dot when you are referring to the *value* which the variable contains. Omit the dot when you are performing an operation on the variable itself. In the above example, the first SET VARIABLE command instructs R:base to place the value "7" in the variable called *y*. The second command instructs R:base to place the value contained in the variable called *y* in the variable called *x*. Consider another example. After the following commands, the global variable x will have the value "y" and the global variable y will have the value "7":

SET VARIABLE x TEXT
SET VARIABLE x TO y
SET VARIABLE .x TO 7

The first SET VARIABLE changes the type of the variable called x to TEXT. The next SET VARIABLE command places the value "y" in the variable called x. Notice the use of the dot in the third command. It instructs R:base to substitute the value contained in the variable called x. Accordingly, R:base interprets the command as if it had been written:

SET VARIABLE y TO 7

Careful review of the above examples should clarify when you use a dot and when you do not.

R:base automatically provides two global variables: #DATE and #TIME. As you can guess, these two variables contain the current date and time, respectively. R:base obtains these values from the operating system based on the values provided by the computer operator when the computer is first turned on. Alternatively, some computers have internal clocks which automatically provide the date and time to the operating system. #DATE and #TIME are used like any other global variable. For example, suppose you have a table called INVOICE in your database. INVOICE contains the columns InvDate, InvTime, and InvAmt. Your command file uses SET VARIABLE to place an appropriate value in the variable called *amt*. You want R:base to load a row into the INVOICE table such that the row automatically includes the present date and time in the InvDate and InvTime columns, respectively. The following commands would accomplish that task:

LOAD INVOICE
.#DATE .#TIME .amt
END

The three lines instruct R:base to add a row to the INVOICE table. The row will contain the current time, the current date, and the value of the variable called amt.

WHILE and ENDWHILE statements MEN0PROC uses the iteration construct to present the menu and obtain a valid choice. When R:base encounters the WHILE command, it looks to see if the variable called *choice* has a value of -1. If so, the commands between the WHILE and ENDWHILE statements are executed. When the ENDWHILE statement is encountered, R:base returns to the WHILE statement and retests the value of *choice*. As long as *choice* has a value of -1, R:base repeats (loops through) the commands between the WHILE and ENDWHILE statements. Such sections of code are called *while loops*.

There are two points to remember about while loops. First, you must ensure that the loop will be executed at least once. In the above example, this is accomplished by setting *choice* to a value of -1 just before the WHILE statement. Secondly, you must ensure that there is a way for the loop to end. In the example, the loop will end when the user selects a choice from the menu other than HELP.

The R:base CHOOSE command CHOOSE is an extremely useful command which displays a menu and obtains a choice from the user. The basic format of this command is

   CHOOSE varname FROM menuname AT rownumber

R:base will look for a file called menuname and display the menu found there on the rownumber row of the screen. It will then prompt the user for a choice and return the value of that choice in the global variable *varname*. The CHOOSE command processes two types of menus, column menus and row menus. MEN0PROC uses a column-type menu. We will explain how row-type menus work when we discuss the PRINTDEV command file.

Column-type menus number the choices from 1 to 9 and list them in order from top to bottom. Accordingly, you can include a maximum of nine choices in a column-type menu. Each choice may be 65 characters in length. The user selects a choice from a column-type menu by pressing the number of the desired choice and pressing [ENTER]. R:base automatically sets the type of the variable used in the CHOOSE command to INTEGER so you do not have to use the SET VARIABLE command to do it.

In MEN0PROC, the CHOOSE command displays the menu contained in the file named MENU0 on line 1 and places a numeric response in the global variable *choice*. MENU0 has the following contents:

```
$MENU
COLUMN Video Rental Main Menu -[F10] for HELP, [ESC] to exit
Videos
Members
Rental transactions
```

The first line of the file identifies it as a menu file. The second line of the file advises R:base that the menu is a column-type menu and provides the text which is to be printed on the top line of the menu. The file then shows the choices which the menu is to contain.

When this menu is displayed, the user can choose one of five actions. He or she can pick the item labeled Videos, pick the item labeled Members, pick the item labeled Rental transactions, press [F10], or press [ESC]. The value returned in the global variable *choice* depends on which action is taken. If the user picks Videos, then *choice* will have the value 1. If the user picks Members, then *choice* will have the value 2, and if the user picks Rental transactions, then *choice* will have the value 3.

If the user presses [F10] or [ESC], then CHOOSE will return special values. CHOOSE is programmed to return the value -1 if the user presses [F10] and the value 0 if the user presses [ESC].

If the user presses [F10] for help, we want to present the help text which we have stored in a file named MEN0HELP. To do this, we use the IF and DISPLAY statements: IF the value of choice is -1, THEN we DISPLAY the contents of the file MEN0HELP. The general format for IF is the following:

```
IF condition THEN
    (one or more R:base commands)
ELSE
    (one or more R:base commands)
ENDIF
```

The ELSE section of the IF statement is optional. In MEN0PROC, we do not need to use it.

The DISPLAY command prints the contents of the named file. The file can be stored in the same way as menufiles described above.

Commands described in this section of the MEN0PROC command file are summarized in Figure 11–1.

A Note on Names

There is a pattern to the names used in this command file. The command file, its menu, and the help text start with the characters MEN0. This is done so that whenever we encounter a file, we can tell where it is used. If we were to use totally arbitrary names, we might forget what is used where. If there are many such files, arbitrary names become very confusing.

MEN0PROC—Processing the User's Choice

The remainder of the code in MEN0PROC concerns the processing of the user's choice. If the user presses [ESC], then he or she has finished processing and wants to exit the application. Otherwise, one of three subcommand files will be called. MEN1PROC processes the Videos choice, MEN2PROC processes the Member choice, and MEN3PROC processes the Rental transaction choice.

The code for these actions is as follows:

```
*(If the user presses [ESC], the CHOOSE  )
*(command returns a value of 0. If the    )
*(user presses [ESC], reset the system    )
*(values and exit to R:base.              )
IF choice EQ 0 THEN
  NEWPAGE
  CLEAR ALL VARIABLES
  SET MESSAGES ON
  SET ERROR MESSAGES ON
  SET ESCAPE ON
  QUIT
ENDIF
*(Determine which selection was made and  )
*(process the appropriate menu.           )
IF choice EQ 1 THEN
  RUN MEN1PROC
ENDIF
IF choice EQ 2 THEN
  RUN MEN2PROC
ENDIF
IF choice EQ 3 THEN
  RUN MEN3PROC
ENDIF
*(When finished, process this menu again. )
RUN MEN0PROC
```

Stopping the Application If the user presses [ESC] at the main menu, then the application is to terminate. The R:base command for this is QUIT. Before this command is issued, however, the application needs to restore the system to its original status. In that way, if another R:base application is started, the system parameters will have their normal settings. This restoration is not required, but it is good programming manners. It's like a professor erasing the blackboard at the end of class so that it will be clean for the next professor.

Examine the MEN0PROC code. If the user has pressed [ESC], then *choice* will be set to 0. In this case,

FIGURE 11–1

Summary of R:base commands introduced

General Form of the Command	Purpose of the Command
*(Comments)	Allows descriptive comments in command files
NEWPAGE	Clears the screen
SET VARIABLE varname TO value	Places value in the global variable called *varname*
SET VARIABLE [TYPE]	Establishes or changes the data type of a global variable
SHOW VARIABLE varname	Displays the value of the global variable called *varname*
WHILE-ENDWHILE	Repeats the commands within the WHILE-ENDWHILE block as long as the WHILE condition is true; used to implement iteration in R:base
CHOOSE varname FROM menu AT rownum	Displays the menu contained in the menu file on row # and places the user's choice in the global variable called *varname*
IF-ENDIF	Executes the commands within the IF block only when the specified condition is true; used to implement alternation in R:base
DISPLAY filename	Displays the contents of filename on the screen
LOAD tablename	Used to load rows into a table

the IF condition will be true, and the commands beginning with CLEAR ALL VARIABLES will be executed.

CLEAR ALL VARIABLES simply erases all global variables except for #DATE and #TIME, the variables which contain the current date and time, respectively.

Next, the two SET commands turn R:base message display back on. The first sets normal messages on and the second sets error messages on. These commands are necessary because message display is set off in the initialization file, INIT. This was done because the programmer wanted to trap errors and process them instead of having them displayed to the user. We will see an example of such error trapping in the next section.

The SET ESCAPE command reestablishes the ability of the user to interrupt R:base processing by pressing [ESC]. It was turned off in INIT so the user cannot cause the interruption of the application by accidentally pressing a key while the application is performing a task.

SET commands can be used to change many of the system default parameters. Special characters can be changed (the dollar sign, for example, can be changed to some other symbol), color can be changed, the bell can be turned off, and so forth. Type HELP SET in R:base to see a comprehensive list of the features available.

Once the system has been restored to its original state, the command file issues the QUIT command. At this point, control is given back to R:base. The user will be presented with the R> prompt.

Processing the Request If the value of *choice* is 1, 2, or 3, then a subcommand file is to be invoked to process the transaction. The remainder of the code simply checks to determine which value *choice* has and to call the appropriate command file.

Continuing the Application The last statement in MEN0PROC tells the system to run MEN0PROC again. This action causes the main menu to be presented again, and the user is prompted for a choice. MEN0PROC is run again and again in this way until the user finishes by pressing [ESC] at the menu choice.

Observe that MEN0PROC is invoking itself. The process of a routine calling itself is known as *recursion*. This is a very powerful action; it enables very sophisticated programming practice. Unfortunately, the subject of recursion is beyond the scope of this book. Be aware, however, that R:base is capable of recursion, and as your programming experience develops you may want to learn more about this important construct.

Commands introduced in this section are summarized in Figure 11–2.

PRINTDEV—A Command File Which Provides a Service to Other Files MEN0PROC calls MEN1PROC, MEN2PROC, and MEN3PROC. All three of these routines, at one time or another, need to ask the user for the name of the device on which to print. Valid choices are the terminal screen, the printer, or a named DOS file. The code necessary for obtaining the printer device could be written into each of these routines. This, however, would be duplicative: the same code would appear in three places. Instead, a general-purpose routine can be written to obtain the name of the printer device. This routine can be called from MEN1PROC, MEN2PROC, and MEN3PROC when necessary.

PRINTDEV is such a command file. It interacts with the user for the name of the device. If a DOS file is named, PRINTDEV attempts to open that file. If the file cannot be opened, PRINTDEV traps the R:base error and sends its own error message to the user. The code is as follows:

FIGURE 11–2

Summary of additional R:base commands used in MEN0PROC

General Form of the Command	Purpose of the Command
CLEAR ALL VARIABLES	Erases all global variables
SET MESSAGES OFF (ON)	Determines whether normal R:base messages will be displayed
SET ERROR MESSAGES OFF (ON)	Determines whether error messages will be displayed
SET ESCAPE OFF (ON)	Determines whether the user will be able to interrupt R:base during processing
QUIT	Returns to R:base
RUN filename	Executes the command file called filename

```
*(***************************************************************)
*(                                                                )
*(Procedure name: PRINTDEV - determines the output device to      )
*(be used.                                                        )
*(Called by         : MEN1PROC, MEN2PROC, MEN3PROC                )
*(Calls             : None                                        )
*(Parameters expected: None                                       )
*(Values returned    : Sets OUTPUT device.                        )
*(                                                                )
*(***************************************************************)
NEWPAGE
CHOOSE device FROM DEVMEN AT 1
NEWPAGE
IF device EQ "PRINTER" THEN
  OUTPUT PRINTER
ENDIF
*(If the user wants the output to go to a DOS file . . .          )
IF device EQ "FILE" THEN
  *(Repeat the file opening procedure until a file is             )
  *(successfully opened.                                          )
  SET VARIABLE valid TO "NO"
  WHILE valid EQ "NO" THEN
    *(Use the WRITE command to erase the message line.            +
    WRITE"                                                        +
                                        " AT 6 1
    FILLIN file USING "Enter valid DOS file designation: " +
      AT 6 1
    *(Attempt to open the file.                                   )
    OUTPUT .file
    *(If the operation is not successful, R:base puts a non-      )
```

```
      *(zero value in the variable ERRVAR.              )
      IF errvar NE 0 THEN
        WRITE "Unable to open that file. Press any key to
continue." AT 7 1
        PAUSE
      ELSE
        *(If the operation was successful, set the variable valid  )
        *(to YES to exit the while loop.                           )
        SET VARIABLE valid TO "YES"
      ENDIF
    ENDWHILE
ENDIF
RETURN
```

Determining the user's choice This routine clears the screen and uses the CHOOSE command to obtain the user's choice. However, this CHOOSE command processes a different kind of menu from that used in MEN0PROC. The menus used in MEN0PROC are column-type menus. In PRINTDEV, the menu is a row-type menu. Row-type menus list the choices side by side in rows. The user selects a choice by highlighting the choice and pressing [ENTER]. You can include a maximum of 40 choices in a row-type menu. Each choice may have as many as twelve characters. Instead of returning the number of the user's choice as with column-type menus, CHOOSE returns the actual text of the user's choice. CHOOSE automatically sets the type of the variable used in row-type menus to TEXT so you do not have to use the SET VARIABLE command to do it.

In PRINTDEV, the CHOOSE command displays the menu contained in the file named DEVMEN on line 1 and places a response in the global variable *device*. DEVMEN has the following contents:

```
$MENU
ROW Select the report destination
PRINTER
SCREEN
FILE
```

Notice that the second line of the file indicates that the menu is a row-type menu.

When this menu is displayed, the user can choose one of five actions. He or she can highlight PRINTER, SCREEN, or FILE; press [F10]; or press [ESC]. The value returned in the global variable *device* depends on which action is taken. If the user picks PRINTER, then *device* will have the value PRINTER. If the user picks SCREEN, then *device* will have the value SCREEN, and if the user picks FILE, then *device* will have the value FILE.

If the user presses [F10] or [ESC], then CHOOSE will return special values. For row-type menus, CHOOSE is programmed to return the value HELP if the user presses [F10] and the value ESCAPE if the user presses [ESC].

Setting the output device PRINTDEV assumes that the output device is SCREEN. Accordingly, it does nothing unless the user chooses PRINTER or FILE. If PRINTER is chosen, PRINTDEV uses the OUTPUT command to set the output device to PRINTER.

If the user chooses FILE, then PRINTDEV must ask the user for the name of the file and use the OUTPUT command to open a DOS file. Something could go wrong. For example, the user might respond with an invalid file name. By using a while loop, PRINTDEV repeats the process until a file is successfully opened. Let's look as the details of the while loop.

Recall the two critical points of a while loop: make sure the loop is executed at least once and ensure that the loop has a way of ending. To ensure that the loop in PRINTDEV is executed once, the variable called *valid* is set to NO. Then, *valid* is used to control the while loop. The loop will be executed as long as valid has a value of NO.

The first command in the while loop is a WRITE command which is used to erase any characters from row number 6 on the screen. The first time through the loop, the command has no effect since the line is already blank. However, if the loop is executed more than once, there will be characters left over from the last time the loop was executed.

Next, a FILLIN command is used to prompt the user for the file name to be used. The general form of FILLIN is:

FILLIN variable USING message AT row column

The FILLIN command displays the message beginning at the specified column in the specified row. The user's response is stored in the global variable specified in the command. In the above example, the message "Enter valid DOS file designation: " is displayed beginning with the first character on line number 6. The user's response is placed in the global variable called *file*.

Next, the command file attempts to open a file with the command:

OUTPUT .filename

This command tells R:base to open a file with a name equal to the value contained in the variable *filename*.

FIGURE 11–3

Summary of additional R:base commands used in PRINTDEV

General Form of the Command	Purpose of the Command
OUTPUT device	Changes the device which R:base uses for output
WRITE "message"	Displays a message on the screen
FILLIN varname USING "message" AT rownum column	Displays message on the screen at row number rownum and column number colnum; obtains a response from the user and places it in the global variable called *varname*
SET ERROR VARIABLE varname	If R:base encounters an error, the error number is placed in the global variable called *varname*
PAUSE	R:base waits for the user to press any key before continuing
RETURN	Returns control to the command file that invoked the command file containing the RETURN command

Remember, the dot (.) tells R:base to use the value contained in the variable. If we forgot to place the dot before the variable name, R:base would interpret the command to mean "Open a file called filename." If you then asked for a directory, a file called FILENAME would appear in the directory.

At this point, the command file uses the error-trapping features of R:base. In the INIT file, display of error messages was turned off and an error variable was defined with the commands:

```
SET ERROR MESSAGES OFF
SET ERROR VARIABLE errvar
```

If the file was successfully opened, R:base will give errvar a value of zero. If not, errvar will have a value other than zero.

If errvar has a value of zero, the job is finished. The variable *valid* is changed to YES so the while loop will be exited.

If errvar has a value other than zero, the WRITE command is used to display the message, "Unable to open that file. Press any key to continue." Since nothing was done to change the value of *valid*, the loop will be repeated.

The special-purpose programming commands introduced in this section are summarized in Figure 11–3.

R:BASE COMMANDS CONTINUED—A SPECIAL-PURPOSE ROUTINE

Most applications require that you create command files that perform a special-purpose task. Let's look at an example from the Video Rental application—determining the rental status of a specified video. The command file which performs that task is called VIDSTAT (video status):

```
*(*******************************************************************)
*(                                                                   )
*(Procedure name: VIDSTAT - determines status of a given tape.       )
*(Called by            : MEN3PROC                                    )
*(Calls                : None                                        )
*(Parameters expected: %1 = VALID video ID number.                   )
*(Values returned     : None                                         )
*(                                                                   )
*(*******************************************************************)
NEWPAGE
WRITE "Please wait . . ."
*(Get the title of the video.
SET VARIABLE title TO Title IN VIDEO WHERE VidID# EQ .%1
*(Initialize the error variable for use with SET POINTER.
SET VARIABLE err INTEGER
```

```
*(Use SET POINTER to see if there is a TRANSaction record for  )
*(the tape where no return date has been recorded.              )
SET POINTER #1 err FOR TRANS WHERE VidID# EQ .%1 AND +
  DateIn FAILS
*(If err has a value of zero, then there is an open TRANSaction )
*(for this tape.                                                )
IF err EQ 0 THEN
  SET DATE MMMDDYYYY
  SET VARIABLE memid# TO MemID# IN #1
  SET VARIABLE dateout TO DateOut IN #1
  *(Get the member information, one piece at a time.            )
  SET POINTER #2 FOR MEMBER WHERE MemId# EQ .memid#
  SET VARIABLE memfname TO MemFName IN #2
  SET VARIABLE memlname to MemLName IN #2
  SET VARIABLE phone TO Phone IN #2
  SET VARIABLE name to .memfname & .memlname
  *(Build the response message in the variable called "message." )
  SET VARIABLE message TO .title & "was rented to"
  SET VARIABLE message TO .message & .name
  SET VARIABLE message TO .message & "("
  SET VARIABLE message TO .message + .phone
  SET VARIABLE message TO .message + ")"
  SET VARIABLE message TO .message & "on"
  SET VARIABLE message TO .message & .dateout
ELSE
*(If the value of err is not 0, then . . .                      )
  SET VARIABLE message TO .title & "is available for rental."
ENDIF
NEWPAGE
*(Display the response to the user.                             )
SHOW VARIABLE message AT 10 5
WRITE "Press any key to continue . . . " AT 13 5
PAUSE
SET DATE MM/DD/YY
RETURN
```

This command file begins by clearing the screen and then displaying the message "Please wait . . . " on the screen. Such messages are appreciated by users. Use them to keep users informed and let them know that the application is responding to their request.

Next, a form of SET VARIABLE is used to obtain the title of the video being processed. There are two things to notice about this SET VARIABLE command. First, instead of providing a value to be placed in the global variable, the command instructs R:base to look up the value in the VIDEO table. The general form of this command is:

SET VARIABLE varname TO column name IN table WHERE . . .

The command instructs R:base to obtain a value for the global variable from the specified column in the row which meets the conditions set forth in the WHERE clause. (You may want to review the discussion of WHERE clauses in Chapter 6.) In the above example, the command:

SET VARIABLE title TO Title IN VIDEO WHERE VidId# EQ .%1

instructs R:base to obtain a value for the global variable title from the Title column in the row where the value of VidId# is equal to the global variable %1. Remember, the "dot" (.) placed in front of the global variable tells R:base to use the value of the global variable in the command.

The second thing to notice about this SET VARIABLE command is the use of a value which was supplied to the command file by the routine which invoked it. Such values are referred to as *parameters*.

Passing Parameters to a Command File

There are two ways to provide data to a command file in R:base. One way is to set a global variable which the command file will look for. Another way is to pass a parameter to the command file as in the above example.

VIDSTAT expects that a valid video number will be provided. This information is passed to the command file as part of the RUN command. For example, assume that a command file wants to RUN VIDSTAT. It would first obtain a valid video identification number and place it in a global variable, say *vidid#*. To run VIDSTAT, the command file MEN3PROC would use the command:

    RUN VIDSTAT USING .vidid#

Internally, VIDSTAT refers to the parameter as %1. You may provide as many as ten parameters to command files in this way.

Using SET POINTER to Process One Row at a Time

Relational database management systems specialize in processing entire tables. However, most business applications are transaction-oriented. That means they deal with one or a few rows at a time. R:base provides a pair of commands which can be used to process tables one row at a time. The commands are SET POINTER and NEXT.

The general form of the SET POINTER command is:

    SET POINTER #n errvar FOR table WHERE . . .

You can establish three pointers in this way. The command sets a pointer to point at the first row in the specified table which meets the condition specified in the WHERE clause. If you include the name of an optional integer global variable to use as an error variable, R:base places a value in the error variable. If a row is found, the error variable is set to zero. If no row meeting the WHERE clause is found, the error variable is set to a nonzero value.

In the example, the command:

    SET POINTER #1 err FOR TRANS WHERE VidId# EQ .%1 AND +
    DateIn FAILS

is used to determine whether there is a row in the TRANS table for the video where no return date has been entered. If a row is found, the error variable, *err*, is set to zero by R:base. In that case, it is assumed that the video has been rented and not yet returned. If no such row is found, *err* is given a nonzero value.

If the video is out on rental, the command file proceeds to get the name and phone number of the member who has it. It does that by setting another pointer into the MEMBER table using the member identification number from the TRANS table. Notice that once the pointer is set, you can refer to the row by substituting the number of the pointer. For example, pointer #2 is pointing at the row of the member who has the video we are interested in. To get the member's phone number, the command file uses this command:

    SET VARIABLE phone TO Phone IN #2

The NEXT Command

The general form of the NEXT command is:

    NEXT #n errvar

It is used to have R:base point to the next row which meets the condition specified in the SET POINTER command. NEXT is not used in the above example since SET POINTER is used only to determine whether the video has been rented.

The NEXT command is useful in a while loop to process all the rows in a table which meet a specified condition. For example, suppose you wanted to perform some action on all the rows in the TRANS table where there is a null value in the DateIn column. You could use SET POINTER and NEXT as follows:

    SET VARIABLE err INTEGER
    SET POINTER #1 err FOR TRANS WHERE DateIn FAILS
    WHILE err EQ 0 THEN
        (commands to process the row)
        NEXT #1 err
    ENDWHILE

FIGURE 11-4

Summary of additional R:base commands used in VIDSTAT

General Form of the Command	Purpose of the Command
SET POINTER #n errvar FOR table WHERE	Establishes a pointer into the specified table. The pointer points to the first row of the table which meets the condition specified in the WHERE clause. If a row is found, the error variable is given a value of zero. If no row is found, the error variable is given a nonzero value.
NEXT #n errvar	Changes the pointer so it points to the next row meeting the condition in the WHERE clause of the SET POINTER command. The error variable is set following the same rules as in SET POINTER.
SET DATE MMMDDYYYY	Changes the date format.
String manipulation operators & and +	Used to concatenate text strings.
RUN command-file USING parmlist	The values listed in the parameter list (parmlist) are passed to the command file being RUN.

Manipulating Text Strings

The remainder of the command file is involved with building a response to the user. The response is contained in the global variable *message*. The text manipulation operators & and + are used to add pieces of the response to *message*. The & operator concatenates (combines end-to-end) two pieces of text together, inserting a space between them. In the above example, the variable *name* is created by combining the member's first and last names as follows:

SET VARIABLE name TO .memfname & .memlname

If memfname has the value "Joanne" and memlname has the value "Browne" then the & operator will cause *name* to have the value "Joanne Browne." If the + operator were used, *name* would have the value "JoanneBrowne."

Once *message* is built, the command file displays the message to the user with the command:

SHOW VARIABLE message AT 10 5

The command file then displays the message "Press any key to continue . . . " and uses the PAUSE command to give the user an opportunity to read the response.

The R:base programming commands introduced in this section are summarized in Figure 11-4.

SUMMARY

- Menu-driven database applications are composed of command files, which are collections of DBMS commands.
- If you are familiar with programming, you can write your own command files to accomplish tasks not possible with an applications generator.
- Simple command files are preferable to complex ones because complexity makes it difficult to debug or change an application.
- A command file should have one and only one function.
- A command file should have sensible and easily understood inputs and outputs.
- A command file should not be given data that it does not use, nor should it be asked to provide data that does not relate to its function.
- The logic of any application program can be expressed in three fundamental structures:
  - Sequence—Execute one command after the other; implemented in R:base by placing the commands in the correct order
  - Alternation—Choose the action to be taken depending upon a condition; implemented in R:base with IF-ENDIF blocks
  - Iteration—Perform a task over and over again; implemented in R:base with WHILE-ENDWHILE blocks
- In general, command files in a menu-driven application fall into one of three basic types. Command files either:
  - Process a menu
  - Provide a service to other command files, or
  - Perform a specified task for the user
- Three tasks are involved in the processing of a menu:
  - Present the menu to the user
  - Obtain a valid choice from the user
  - Perform the task associated with the choice
- The major programming commands available in R:base which are illustrated in the chapter are:
  - CHOOSE varname FROM menufile AT rownum
  - CLEAR ALL VARIABLES
  - *(Comments)
  - DISPLAY filename

- FILLIN varname USING "message" AT rownum colnum
- IF condition THEN commands ELSE commands ENDIF
- LOAD tablename
- NEWPAGE
- NEXT #n errvar
- OUTPUT
- PAUSE
- QUIT
- RETURN
- RUN command-file USING parmlist
- SET DATE MMMDDYYYY
- SET ERROR MESSAGES (OFF) ON
- SET ERROR VARIABLE varname
- SET ESCAPE OFF (ON)
- SET MESSAGES OFF (ON)
- SET POINTER #n errvar FOR table WHERE
- SET VARIABLE varname TO value
- SET VARIABLE [TYPE]
- SHOW VARIABLE varname
- String manipulation operators & and +
- WHILE condition THEN commands ENDWHILE
- WRITE "message"

REVIEW QUESTIONS

Group I Questions

11.1
In your own words, explain what a command file is.

11.2
What is the primary advantage of a program like the Application EXPRESS?

11.3
What is the primary disadvantage of a program like the Application EXPRESS?

11.4
Explain why simple command files are better than complex ones.

11.5
What does it mean when we say that a command file should have one and only one function?

11.6
List the three fundamental programming structures and give a brief explanation of each.

11.7
How is sequence implemented with R:base?

11.8
How is alternation implemented with R:base?

11.9
How is iteration implemented with R:base?

11.10
List the three basic types of command files in a menu-driven application.

11.11
List the three tasks involved in the processing of a menu.

Group II Questions

11.12
Give an example of an R:base comment and explain why they are used.

11.13
What R:base command would you use to clear the screen?

11.14
In your own words, explain what R:base global variables are.

11.15
Which R:base command would you use to create an R:base global variable called *pagenum* and give it a value of 8?

11.16
Which R:base command would you use to create an R:base global variable called *desc* and establish its type as TEXT?

11.17
Which two R:base commands could you use to display the contents of the global variable *desc* beginning at position 15 on line number 10 of the screen?

11.18
Which R:base command would you use to have R:base use the printer as the output device?

11.19
Write the R:base code to clear the screen, display the message "Press any key to continue . . . ," and wait for the user to press any key.

11.20
Write the R:base code to ask the user if he or she wants to continue. If the user wants to continue, display the message "Continuing." If the user does not want to continue, return control to R:base.

11.21
Write the R:base code which will ensure that the user does not see any R:base messages and which will instruct R:base to place any error codes in a global variable called *errors*.

11.22
Using SET POINTER and NEXT, write the R:base code which will display the title of each video which is currently out on rental, together with the name and phone number of the member who rented it.

11.23
Using examples of R:base code, explain what it means to pass parameters to a command file using R:base.

PROJECT

Create a complete, menu-driven application for your academic database using the Application EXPRESS and the R:base programming language.

CHAPTER 12 | Database Administration

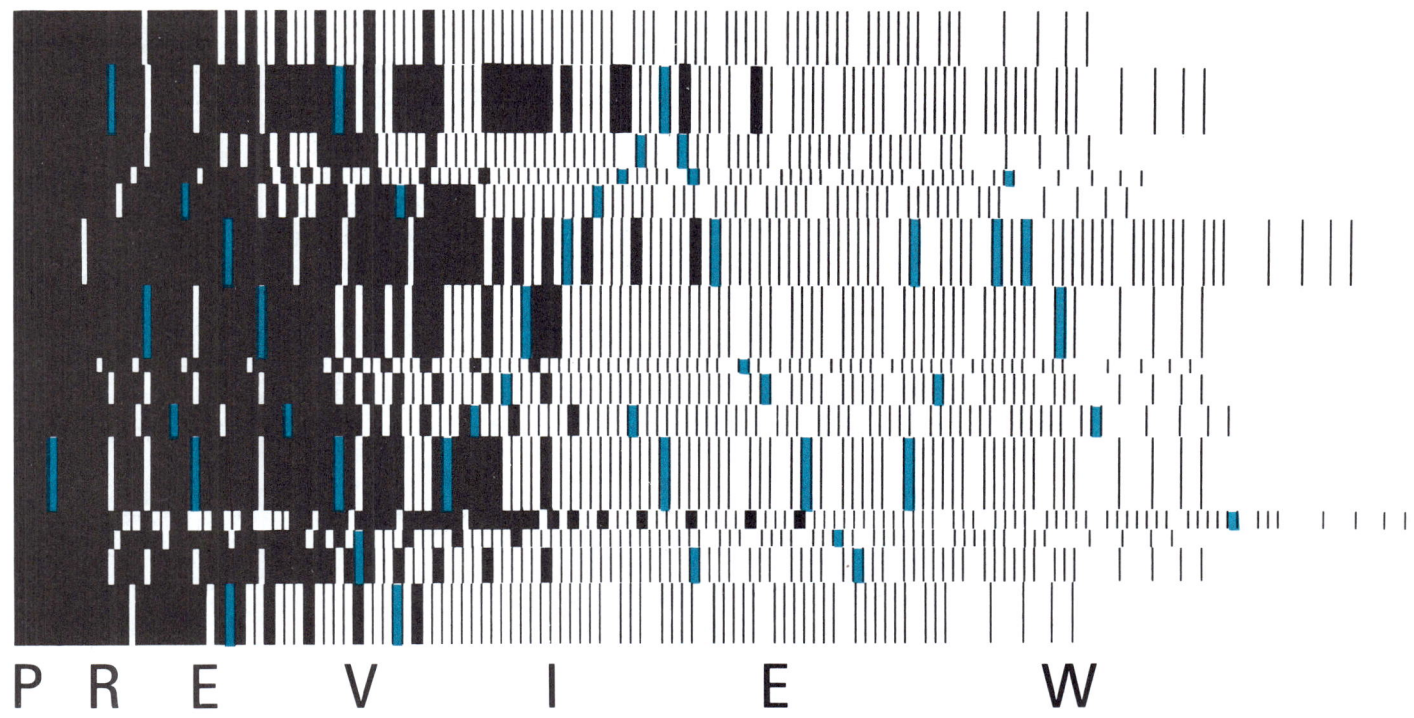

PREVIEW

In this chapter, we discuss the important topic of database administration. In the first part of the chapter, we'll discuss database administration in general terms. Then, we'll describe four specific database administration functions in more detail: processing rights and responsibilities, operations scheduling, data archives, and database configuration control. Finally, we'll present some guidelines for selecting a database administrator.

LESSONS LARGE CORPORATIONS HAVE LEARNED ABOUT DATABASE ADMINISTRATION

In the early 1970s, major corporations began constructing the first large databases. These databases, like the smaller ones discussed in this book, were developed to answer questions. They allowed people to manipulate data in whatever ways were necessary to provide needed information.

As people used these databases, data processing personnel began to hear new types of questions: "What department changes EMPLOYEE data?" "What reports use the Zipcode attribute?" "I don't currently modify the VIDEO data, but I need to. May I?" Such questions were not about the data values stored in the database. Rather, they were about the database itself—about the structure of the data model and the processing of the data.

At the same time, problems were also appearing, because users were sharing the same data. People were changing each other's data incorrectly, arguing about the best way to process the data, and disagreeing over how to design the database.

Companies began to realize that they needed to manage databases differently from the way they had been managing their libraries of data tapes and other data files. Specifically, they needed to put someone in charge of the database. The database needed a custodian, a guardian, someone who viewed the data as a resource for all rather than as a resource for his or her individual group. This situation led to the organization of a new department—that of database administration.

Clearly the databases that you develop on a microcomputer are a far cry from the database that United Airlines, for example, maintains for passenger reservations. Still, as you use your database, you will encounter the same types of questions and problems, only on a smaller scale. While you won't need an entire department of database administration, you probably will need to designate one person to perform many of the same functions.

As large companies have learned, database administration is very important. Unfortunately, the problems that can arise without database administration develop gradually, so the need may not be apparent until the problem is at hand. Happily, we can benefit from the experience of large corporations.

DATABASE ADMINISTRATION ON MICROCOMPUTERS

Suppose you implemented the database for Great Plains Music and Video Unlimited which we have described in this book. Assume that Great Plains has been using the database for several months. How will you respond when someone asks you questions like these:

1. Who deleted the records for our ex-salespeople? Just because they're not with us doesn't mean we don't need their data! I have to send income tax information out to them in January.

2. John is in Mexico for vacation and I want to prepare the cassette tape order for next month. Do you know what he does before he tells me to run the cassette tape order list report?

3. Somebody goofed! The information management system says that we have four compact disc players in stock and I can only find two. Also, according to the computer, we have twelve tape-head cleaning kits and I can only find six. What happened?

4. The IRS called and they're questioning the way we valued our inventory last year. Can you give me the inventory status as of last December 31?

5. We are going to start keeping more information about videotapes we rent. We'll have to change the VIDEO relation. Which employees use that relation? What reports use it? What forms are involved?

These are the types of questions that arise when a database is used over a period of time. They do not involve data directly. They are not questions like, "How many temporary salespeople do we have?" Instead, they are questions about the database itself.

If these questions have been anticipated and if the proper records and procedures have been developed, then they will be easy to answer. If they have not been anticipated, answers may be impossible.

WHAT IS DATABASE ADMINISTRATION?

Database administration is the process by which activities involving the database are planned and controlled to best meet the needs of the user-community. *Activities* is a broad term that means reading and changing data, reading and changing database structure, answering questions about the database, and other similar actions. *User-community* means the group of people who work with the database to accomplish their jobs. This term is used because the needs of one or two individuals must sometimes go unmet for the good of the user-community as a whole.

Database Planning Several types of planning are necessary. First, the design of the database must be planned before the database is implemented. Similarly, changes to the structure of the database must be planned and users of the database given notice of anticipated changes so they can react beforehand.

The ways in which the database will be used must also be planned. Since the database is shared, one user's activities can interfere with another's. Procedures must be developed to maintain the integrity, or correctness, of the database. Finally, methods and procedures for recovering the database in the event of failure must be planned. Once failure has occurred, recovery planning is too late. (Backup and recovery are discussed in the next chapter.)

Database Control Control of database activity involves several functions. First, the rights and responsibilities of users must be defined and enforced. Users must not be allowed to change data at will. If such changes were allowed, other users would be operating with unknown data.

Additionally, the timing of user activity must be controlled. For the Great Plains database, for example, data about cassettes received should be entered into the database before the cassette tape order list report is generated. If not, tapes may be ordered that have already been received. Finally, the structure of the database must be controlled. One user cannot be allowed to unilaterally add a new column or change the structure of an existing column. If such action were allowed, the reports and screens of other users could be unacceptably changed.

FUNCTIONS OF DATABASE ADMINISTRATION

We will now consider these four aspects of database administration more specifically:

- Processing rights and responsibilities
- Operations scheduling
- Data archives
- Database configuration control

Processing Rights and Responsibilities

To prevent chaos and protect the integrity of the database, the rights and responsibilities of users must be defined. Consider question number 1 mentioned earlier. In this situation, the right of data deletion on the EMPLOYEE relation was not clearly defined.

The degree to which processing rights and responsibilities must be defined depends on the manner in which the database is accessed. Let's look at three different types of systems and discuss the processing rights for each.

Single-user Systems At first, you might think that there is no need to define rights and responsibilities for a simple system with only one user. Suppose, however, that the single user is the salesclerk who is responsible for operating the video rental part of the Great Plains system. Most likely, this user will have the right to access TRANSaction data. Other rights are not so clear, however. Should this user have the authority to:

- Add new VIDEOs?
- Delete VIDEOs?
- Change the format of the screens?
- Change the format of reports?
- Add or delete columns from database tables?
- Add new database tables?

Answers to these questions depend on the user's sophistication, other duties and authority within the company, knowledge of the DBMS in use, and other factors. The point here is that whoever designs and develops the database should consider these questions and build in answers before problems arise, not afterwards.

Sequential-user Systems Sequential-user systems are systems in which there are multiple users, and these users access the system one after the other (sequentially). In this mode, one user's action on the database has a direct impact on other users. Consequently, restrictions on activities must be defined and followed.

Consider the Great Plains video rental information management system again. The users of this system are the salesclerk, the accountant, the office manager (who serves as database administrator), and the general manager. We might define the processing rights of these users as follows:

- The salesclerk can read any of the data in the database and may add or modify new MEMBER data. The clerk may not delete any data.

- The accountant may read any of the data in the database but may not modify or delete any data.
- The general manager may read, add to, or modify any of the tables in the database. The general manager may not delete any data.
- The office manager may read any of the data in the database but may not modify any data. At the request of other users, the office manager may delete data, but only in accordance with established procedures that require written approval of all affected users.

These rights must not only be defined, they must also be enforced. Some DBMS's provide facilities that help in this regard. Whoever has the database administration responsibility must see that these rules are followed. Additionally, as the database is used, these rights may need to be changed. The accountant, for example, may want greater authority. The database administrator must be available to consider such requests and make changes when appropriate.

Concurrent-user Systems Companies that have two or more microcomputers connected together (via a local area network or other communications media) can have multiple users accessing the same database concurrently. In this mode, there is a single copy of the database located on one of the microcomputers, which we will call the *database node*. To access the database, users send requests for service to the database node. These requests are processed one at a time.

This system operates so fast that it may appear to two users that their requests are being processed simultaneously. True simultaneous processing is impossible, however, since there is only one copy of the database.

Concurrent-user systems have the same need for control that sequential-user systems do. The processing rights and responsibilities must be defined in a similar way. In addition, concurrent processing introduces special problems, such as the one illustrated in Figure 12–1.

In this example, two users access the same fact in the database at about the same time. As a result, the activity of User A is deleted and an error is introduced into the database—with unhappy results! To prevent this sort of erroneous processing, the record needs to be locked before processing. We will consider this problem further in Chapter 15.

FIGURE 12-1

A potential problem in concurrent-user systems

Time	Number of Beachboys Tapes		User Activities	
	Number Shown in Database	Number Actually in Stock	User A	User B
2:07:00	2	2	Reads database, see 2 tapes in stock, physically removes one	
2:07:30	2	2		Reads database, sees 2 tapes in stock, physically removes one
2:09:00	1	1	Enters in database the new number of tapes; database shows one tape in stock	
2:10:00	1	0		Enters in database new number of tapes; database shows one tape in stock WRONG!
2:37:00	1	0	Reads database, tells customer on phone that tape is in stock	
5:00:00	1	0	Gets chewed out by customer who just drove 120 miles to get the last Beachboys tape!	

242 CHAPTER 12

FIGURE 12-2a
Database design for processing schedule: objects and their relationships

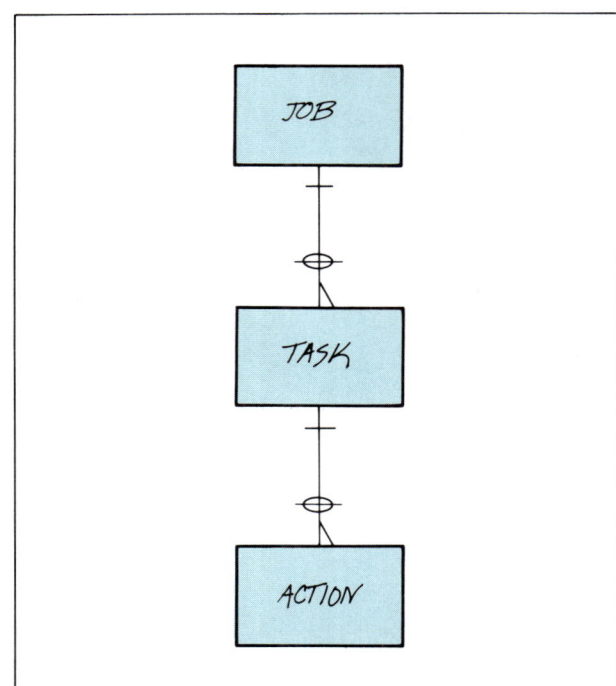

FIGURE 12-2b
Database design for processing schedule: objects and their columns

```
JOB    (Jobname, Dept, When, Freq, JobDescription)
TASK   (Jobname, Taskname, Actor, TaskDescription)
ACTION (Taskname, Actname, Order, ActionDescription)
```

Operations Scheduling

If you were to visit the computer room of any major corporation, you would find that activities are conducted according to a precise and well-defined schedule.

Reasons for Scheduling The schedule is followed for two reasons. First, the action of one job impacts the action of others. For example, one computer program may record sales and a subsequent program may produce bills. If programs are erroneously run in reverse order (if bills are produced before sales are recorded), then the customer bills will be incomplete.

The second reason a schedule is followed is to control processing activity. These companies want to ensure that all work is accomplished on a timely basis. They also want to ensure that only authorized work is performed. For example, the payroll program must be run only once during a pay period.

These same concerns apply to the use of the databases we discuss in this book. Even though microcomputer databases are tiny compared to an airline reservation database, we still need scheduling. We want work done in the proper order, we want all authorized work to be done, and we want only authorized work to be done.

Schedules are useful memory devices. For jobs that are performed infrequently, such as end-of-quarter processing, having a list of tasks can prevent errors and omissions. Employees need not rely entirely on memory.

Questions 2 and 3, mentioned earlier, show the need for proper scheduling for Great Plains. In question 2, somebody needs to know a processing schedule: What needs to be done before producing the cassette tape order list report? Activities might include checking with the office manager to ensure that all deliveries have been entered into the system and checking with the salesclerks to determine that all needs have been entered.

Question 3 indicates that an error has occurred. On investigation, the office manager found that two different employees had entered the same delivery, so the same parts were entered twice.

Building schedules with the database Schedules are an ideal database application. It is simply a matter of deciding what jobs are routinely performed, what tasks are needed to accomplish those jobs, and what actions need to be taken for each task.

Figure 12-2 shows the design of a database that could be used for a processing schedule. The database has three tables: JOB, TASK, and ACTION. Part of the scheduling data for Great Plains is shown in Figure 12–3. When a job is to be done, the clerk prints the tasks and actions that need to be taken for that job. The printout is then used as a worksheet to ensure the job is properly done.

Developing schedules like this is an important way to control the accuracy of database processing. While schedules are mandatory for sequential and concurrent-user systems, they can also be important memory aids for single-user systems.

Data Archives

The Need for a Data Archive Databases can be addictive. If a database enhances productivity, people use it more frequently. As they use it, they generate more and more data, and thus more of the company's records are stored in the database.

Data, like people, ages with time. There comes a point when data items are no longer needed in the database. You'll discover this point in one of two ways. First, the system may begin to run out of disk space and you'll need to unload data to continue processing. Alternatively, data may be updated and overwritten. A table containing orders for the current month will be overwritten at the end of the month. In either of these circumstances, data will be removed from the database.

FIGURE 12–3a

Processing schedule database: sample JOB data

Jobname	Dept	When	Freq	JobDescription
RUN REV REPT	Video rental	Mon	Weekly	Weekly revenue report
VIDEO ORDER	Video rental	Mon	Weekly	Weekly videotape order
CASSETTE ORD	Music	A.M.	Daily	Daily cassette tape order
•				
•				
•				

FIGURE 12–3b

Processing schedule database: sample TASK data

Jobname	TaskName	Actor	TaskDescription
CASSETTE ORD	RUN CASSORD	Becky	Run cassette order report
CASSETTE ORD	CHK INVEN	Becky	Double check inventory levels
CASSETTE ORD	CHK BACK ORD	Becky	Check back orders
CASSETTE ORD	PREP P.O.	Becky	Prepare purchase orders
•			
•			
•			
•			

FIGURE 12–3c

Processing schedule database: sample ACTION data

Taskname	Actname	Order	ActionDescription
RUN CASSORD	Start	1	Turn on computer, printer, start R:base
RUN CASSORD	Open	2	Open database
RUN CASSORD	Paper	3	Mount continuous form paper
RUN CASSORD	Print	4	Type PRINT CASSORD
•			
•			
•			
•			

So far, so good. However, what should be done with this unneeded data? Can it be thrown away? Should it be saved in magnetic form? Should it be printed, and the printed copies saved for some time? Even more importantly, how can we keep track of this data?

To answer questions like number 4, we need a data archive. Unfortunately, the need for such an archive may not appear until it is too late to build one. Here again, we can take a lesson from the experience of large companies.

Building an Archive To build the data archive, we need to determine the archival needs for groups of data in the database. One way to begin is to examine each table in the database and answer three questions about it:

- How long do we need this data to reside in the database?
- How long do we need this data to be kept in some magnetic form?
- How long do we need this data to be kept in printed form?

We need to keep data in magnetic form if we expect we might need to return the data to the database for processing.

Consider the video rental database for Great Plains. To build the archive, we examine each table in turn, asking the same three questions. The results of this process are shown in Figure 12–4.

Once we have determined the form and duration of storage for each table, we then develop procedures to ensure that the data is saved appropriately. If we have developed a processing schedule as discussed in the last section, we can add the task of saving data to this schedule.

FIGURE 12–4

Archive requirements for some Great Plains tables

Relation	How Long Kept in Database?	How Long Kept in Magnetic Form?	How Long Kept in Printed Form?
VIDEO	1 Year	2 Years	Never
MEMBER	1 Year	Never	3 Years
TRANS	1 Month	3 Months	3 Years
SYSPARM	Perpetual	Perpetual	Perpetual
FORMS	Perpetual	Perpetual	Perpetual
REPORTS	Perpetual	Perpetual	Perpetual
RULES	Perpetual	Perpetual	Perpetual

FIGURE 12–5a
Archive database design: objects and columns

MEDIA (<u>Name</u>, Type, Location)
VERSION (<u>Table</u>, <u>Database</u>, <u>Version</u>, Location, Datemove)

FIGURE 12–5b
Archive database: MEDIA data

Name	Type	Location
VIDRENT	DB	System
GTPLAIN	DB	System
D0034	Diskette	Office
D0035	Diskette	Office
D0032	Diskette	Bank vault
File 1	Cabinet	Office
File 2	Cabinet	Office
File 3	Cabinet	Office

For the Great Plains example, we'll want to add to the end-of-month schedule the task of unloading the data which is to be archived monthly. Another task should be scheduled to recycle these diskettes after three months of storage. Still other tasks will be needed to unload other data and print data in accordance with Figure 12–4.

The data archive will be easier to manage if records are kept of the archive contents. Figure 12–5 shows a possible design for a database that keeps archive records. Depending on the size and complexity of your database, you may want to add database columns or tables to this design.

Again, as business activities become more and more dependent on the database, the need for a data archive will increase. However, you may not see the need for an archive until it is too late. If the data you create has any value over time, you will be well advised to develop some type of archival plan when you are designing the database itself.

Database Configuration Control

The last of the four basic database administration functions is control over the database design, sometimes called *configuration control*. Companies with large databases have long realized that since the database is a shared resource, changes to structure must be made very carefully and with the knowledge and concurrence of the entire user-community. Configuration control is also important for companies with microcomputer databases, even though they operate on a smaller scale.

The design of all the elements in the structure of the database must be controlled. Such elements include tables, database columns, reports, forms, rules, and command files. A change to any one of these can po-

FIGURE 12–5c
Archive database: VERSION data

Table	Database	Version	Location	Datemove
TRANS	VIDRENT	MAR86	STORE	APR86
TRANS	VIDRENT	FEB86	D0034	JUN86
VIDEO	VIDRENT	JAN86	STORE	JAN88
VIDEO	VIDRENT	JAN85	D0032	JAN87
MEMBER	VIDRENT	JAN84	FILE1	JAN87

tentially cause problems. To prevent such problems, two types of coordination are important:

- Coordination with other database elements
- Coordination with other database users

Coordination with Other Database Elements Databases are integrated, and a change in one element can have undesirable impacts on other elements. For example, a change in the format of a database column impacts not only the tables in which the database column resides, but also the reports, forms, and other elements. Therefore, when a change is proposed, the first need is to determine the impact of the proposed change throughout the database.

Figure 12–6 shows potential impacts of changes to various elements. When a change to an element is proposed, the potential impacts listed in this figure should be investigated. For example, if Zipcode is changed from five to nine digits, all of the tables, reports, forms, command files, and rules that involve this database column must be examined.

Experience shows that it is much easier to deal with the impacts of change before the change is actually made. If changes are made without anticipating the side effects, the DBMS may detect a problem and send error messages to unsuspecting users. Even worse, the DBMS may be unable to detect the problem and erroneous data will be reported or stored. If this happens, days or weeks may pass before the error is discovered, making correction of the problem that much more difficult.

Coordination with Other Database Users A second type of coordination is necessary when design changes are proposed for databases that have more than one user. Before a change to the database structure is made, everyone who uses the element to be changed should be consulted. One group of users may have excellent reasons for not making a change that seems perfectly innocent and appropriate to another group. The only way to avoid problems is to ask the users.

The way in which this coordination is done depends on the number of users, the size and complexity of the database, and the frequency with which such changes are proposed. If there are only a few users or if the changes are simple or infrequent, an informal survey will suffice. On the other hand, if there are many users, complex changes, or frequent requests, a formal procedure may be necessary. Large companies have regular configuration control meetings for the coordi-

FIGURE 12–6

Potential impacts of changes to database elements

Changes to	Can impact
Table	Columns, reports, forms, rules, command files
Column	Tables, reports, forms, rules, command files
Report	Command files
Form	Rules, command files
Rules	Forms, command files

nation and approval of database changes. An occasional memo or meeting will probably meet the needs of most companies with microcomputer databases. The important point is that all users be consulted, beforehand, about proposed changes to database structure.

SELECTING A DATABASE ADMINISTRATOR

As mentioned at the start of this chapter, large companies maintain a department of database administration, often staffed with many employees. Clearly, such a staff is inappropriate for microcomputer databases. Most likely, one person will serve this function on a part-time basis. The question is, who?

The database administrator (DBA) is like a trustee. The administrator is the guardian of the database and has the responsibility of ensuring that the database is protected and controlled so that it can be used for the purposes for which it was developed.

Consequently, the DBA should be a responsible employee and one who is likely to be with the company for some time. Also, the DBA should have an interest in the database and not view database administration as an optional function to be done when there is nothing else to do. Finally, the DBA should be someone who has the respect of the database users. Much of the DBA function is diplomatic. There is probably no defined line of authority among database users. Therefore, the DBA needs to be a facilitator, not an autocrat.

SUMMARY

- Companies which are designing databases for microcomputers can benefit from the experience of large corporations in solving database administration problems.

- Database administration is the process of planning and controlling activities involving the database.

  - Planning is needed to design the database, anticipate changes in the database structure, determine how the database will be used, and recover the database in case of loss or failure.

  - Control is needed to define the rights and responsibilities of users, schedule the timing of user activity, and protect the database structure.

- Basic database administration functions are processing rights and responsibilities, operations scheduling, data archiving, and database configuration control.

  - Determining who has what processing rights and responsibilities depends on whether the system is for single users, sequential users, or concurrent users.

  - Operations scheduling is needed so that work is done in the proper order, so that all authorized work will be done, and so that only authorized work will be done.

  - A data archive system is used to determine what should be done with data that is no longer needed in the database and when it should be removed from the database.

  - Database configuration control provides for agreement among database users regarding any change in database structure (including tables, database columns, reports, forms, rules, and command files).

- The database administrator should be a responsible employee who is:

  - Likely to be with the company for some time
  - Interested in the task of database administration
  - A skilled communicator and facilitator
  - Respected by all database users

REVIEW QUESTIONS

Group I Questions

12.1
Describe three types of database planning that must be performed.

12.2
Why is it important to define the rights and responsibilities of users?

12.3
Summarize the job responsibilities for the DBA.

12.4
Describe the three ways a database can be accessed.

12.5
Why is operations scheduling important?

12.6
What is a data archive?

12.7
What forms can data archives take?

12.8
What does the term *configuration control* mean?

12.9
Explain what the phrase *coordination with other database elements* means.

12.10
Explain why a DBA should be a facilitator and not an autocrat.

Group II Questions

12.11
Prepare a formal, written recommendation to the owner of Great Plains Music and Video Unlimited discussing who should perform the database administration function at Great Plains.

12.12
Prepare a formal job description for the database administration function at Great Plains.

PROJECTS

A. Design an operations scheduling database for Great Plains. Provide some sample data for the operation of your choice. Implement your scheduling database using R:base.

B. Design an archive database for Great Plains. Implement your archive database using R:base.

CHAPTER 13 | Data Security

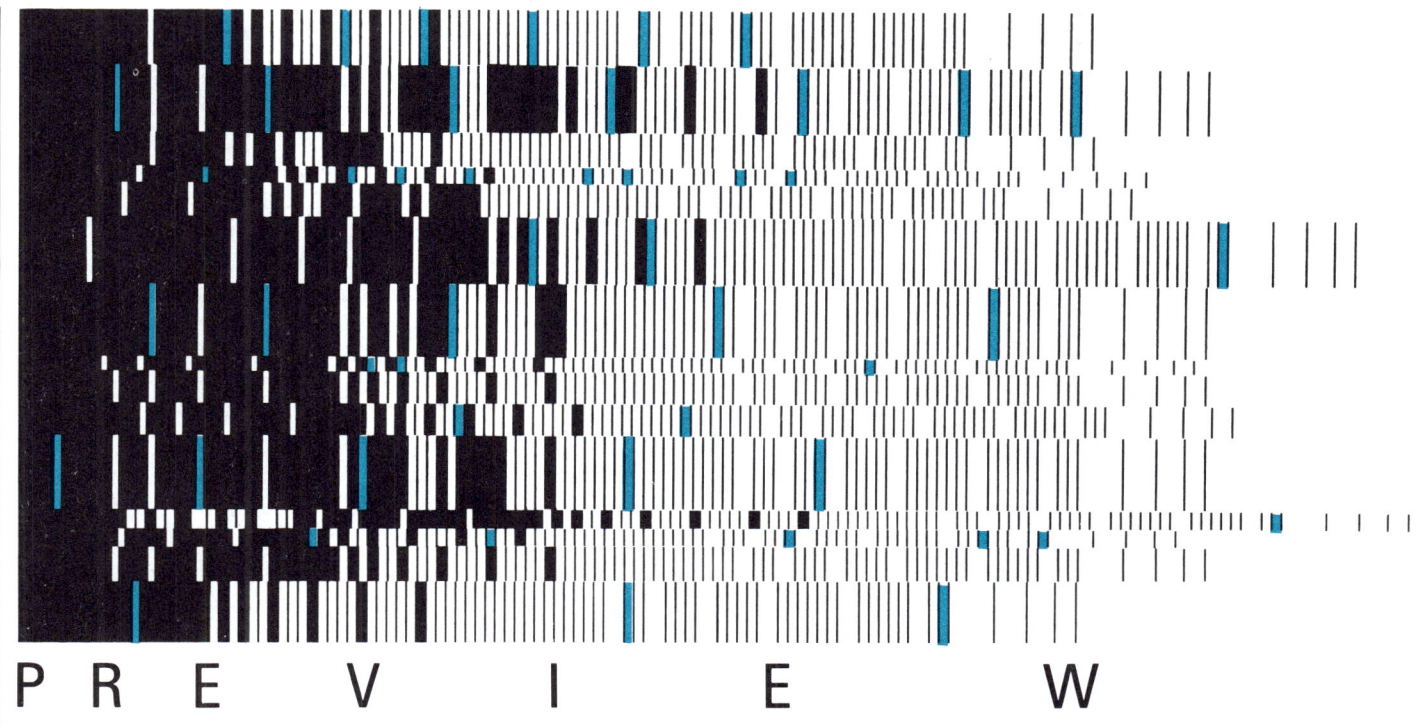

PREVIEW

The purpose of this chapter is to discuss the concept of data as an asset, survey the basic threats to data, and discuss methods, procedures, and techniques for protecting it.

DATA AS AN ASSET

Data is an asset, just like inventory, equipment, and people. As an asset, data has value. If you doubt this, consider what would happen if a company lost its accounts receivable, accounts payable, or customer data.

What is the value of accounts receivable data? If it can't be recreated, then its value is the total amount owed to the company by its customers. In some cases, this could represent a significant percentage of the company's total assets. If the data can be recreated, then its value is the cost of the labor to recreate it, plus the cost of borrowing money to replace the lost collections while the data is being reconstructed.

The value of some data, such as accounts payable, may be difficult to compute. If such data is lost, the company will be unable to pay its debts on a timely basis. The cost will be extra finance charges plus the loss of credibility in the eyes of creditors. That loss will be hard to value, but nonetheless it will be a loss.

Sometimes the value of data is intangible. Suppose a competitor steals a data file containing a list of the company's customers. The theft of data is different from the theft of tangible assets like cash or inventory. With the theft of tangible property, the victim no longer possesses the property which was stolen. When data is stolen, the victim still has the data; the thief merely has a copy. The victim may never know the theft has taken place or how much business has been lost as a consequence.

Protection against theft of data is particularly important for systems that access databases at the company's data processing center. Such data can be especially valuable because it has been generated through the processing of hundreds or thousands of transactions. This data can reflect the condition of the entire company and hence is an especially likely target for theft.

In these situations, the company's data processing department may be most concerned that those who access the central database follow appropriate security measures. This attitude does not reflect rampant paranoia on the part of the computer experts. Their advice and recommendations should be given careful consideration. They earn their livelihood by their ability to process and protect data.

THREATS TO DATA

Threats to the database fall into two major categories:

- Accidents
- Willful abuse

Losses Due to Accidents

Data can be lost or damaged from a variety of accidental causes.

Mistakes During Processing First, people can make mistakes during the processing of data. For example, suppose a clerk wants to delete all of the customer accounts that have a zero balance. Consider the impact if the clerk mistakenly types the following command:

```
DELETE ROWS FROM CUSTOMER WHERE BALANCE GT 0
```

When this command is executed, all customer accounts having a nonzero balance will be deleted. If there are many such accounts, the cost of this mistake will be high. Unfortunately, mistakes such as this are all too easy to make.

Incorrect System Operation A second type of accidental data loss can occur through incorrect system operation. Someone may mount the wrong diskette, for example, and inadvertently change or overwrite a database. Also, a diskette or other data volume can be damaged from careless handling, or diskettes can simply be lost.

Vendors have many sad stories to report about the ways in which data can be accidentally damaged. In one such case, a company employee was packing a microcomputer and related equipment in preparation for a move. Near the end of the day, the employee ran out of storage boxes. There was no time to find another box, so the system diskettes, which contained the company's programs and data, were placed in an empty trash container. During the night, the janitorial service emptied all the trash cans in the room, including the one that contained the diskettes! The diskettes themselves were worth little. But the data and programs stored on them were worth thousands of dollars. Unfortunately, such stories are common. There are endless numbers of ways in which data can be inadvertently lost or damaged.

Natural Disasters Natural disasters are a third way that data can be accidentally lost. Fires, floods, hurricanes, tornados, earthquakes, and volcanos all represent threats to data. Large data processing departments go to great lengths to store redundant copies of critical data in off-premise locations. Some go so far as to store data in such safe and remote locations as caves and abandoned mines.

It is unlikely that microcomputer database data will be so critical that you need to store it in caves.

However, as described later in this chapter, copies of this data can be stored in a separate building. If a company has a data processing department, its members may be willing to store some data in a tape vault or other protected location.

Losses Due to Willful Action

There are several ways that data losses can occur from willful action. The first is theft. Data can be stolen by removing a diskette or other medium that contains data, by copying data onto a second diskette, or by copying data over a communications line. The latter two forms of theft are difficult to detect because nothing tangible is missing.

A second type of willful abuse is malicious destruction of data by a disgruntled employee, thrill-seeker, or paid saboteur.

A final type of willful abuse is unauthorized changes to data. Systems that generate checks or process some form of account balance are the most likely targets for such changes.

Theft or willful abuse of data is a criminal activity. Companies that suspect such activity should contact legal counsel and law-enforcement agencies for advice on how to proceed.

PROTECTING THE DATABASE

Over the years, large data centers have worked with company auditors to develop procedures for protecting data resources. In this section, we'll discuss five categories of procedures, or *controls,* as they are called by auditors:

- Management controls
- Organizational controls
- Resource controls
- Backup and recovery
- Input/process/output controls

Management Controls

Control over the data resource begins at the top. Management must understand the value of data and the need for its control. This understanding should be communicated to employees. If management is not interested in data security, employees will not be interested either. Specific management tasks are:

- Building employee awareness
- Training database users
- Monitoring error reports and user activity

Building Employee Awareness Employees who are assigned microcomputers should understand the need for security and take this responsibility seriously. Such employees should not allow their microcomputers to be used for unauthorized purposes, nor should they discuss processing procedures, controls, and similar topics except in the course of business. A microcomputer is at least as valuable as a cash drawer on a teller line and should be treated with the same respect.

Most first-time computer users think they need to be careful not to damage the computer equipment. This concern is misplaced. Hardware is designed to take care of itself. The typical user would have difficulty causing any serious damage to computer hardware (unless, of course, it came to an attack with bricks and hammers).

Users do need to be careful, however, with data. Data can easily be damaged by executing the wrong commands, operating the system incorrectly, and using incorrect procedures. With a relational DBMS, hundreds of thousands of data items are at the user's fingertips. A database can be ruined with a single command. Employees need to be aware of this fact and realize that they should not execute commands unless they know what they are doing.

Also, insofar as possible, the system should be designed to limit the operations which users can perform on the database. One way of doing this is to have the system present the user with a limited list of options—a menu. Chapters 10 and 11 deal with the topic of creating menu-driven database systems.

In addition to a concern for correct processing, employees need to realize that data is a company asset, to be protected like any other company asset. Diskettes and reports that contain sensitive data should not be made available to unauthorized personnel.

To focus concern on the necessity of protecting data, some managers require their employees to sign letters of understanding at performance reviews. Such letters document the sensitivity of the data that the employee uses and state the need for the employee's cooperation in protecting the data. Company counsel should be involved in preparing these letters because of the potential legal ramifications.

Employee Training The most effective component of a secure system is a well-informed and thoroughly trained staff. Employees are more careful when they understand the value of the data they use. They also make fewer errors if they are adequately trained and can thus easily use the system to accomplish their job. Fewer errors mean less likelihood of catastrophe.

Management should ensure that employees are properly trained. To determine if training is adequate, managers should undergo the same training as their employees and then do the employees' jobs for a short time. Managers should ask themselves, "Could I do this job with this amount of training?" If not, changes to the training program should be made.

Monitoring Error Reports and User Activity If training is inadequate, high error rates will result. Management can determine the appropriateness of training by requesting and monitoring error reports. How often are major mistakes made? How much employee time is lost as a consequence? What can be done to prevent such mistakes in the future? Managers should realize that major mistakes (those that require reloading the database) should occur extremely rarely—once or twice a year at most. If the rate of major errors is greater, either employees need more training or the system design is defective. In either case, management action is called for.

Periodically, managers should monitor user activity. If violations of established security procedures are found, users need to be reminded of their responsibility and given further training, if appropriate. Users who repeatedly violate security procedures should be assigned to new jobs. (Perhaps with a different company!)

Organizational Controls

The three major kinds of organizational controls are:

- Separation of duties and authorities
- Documented definition of responsibilities
- Employee accountability

Separation of Duties and Authorities The consequences of errors vary among systems. Errors in a system that monitors an inventory of nuclear waste are more serious than errors in a system that monitors used auto parts. Errors in systems that produce checks can be serious, as can errors in systems that maintain other financial data, such as account balances or loan payments. Control in such systems can be improved by separating duties and authorities.

For example, consider a system that produces paychecks. Suppose one employee makes changes to pay rates in the database, runs a program that produces payroll checks, puts the checks through the signature machine, records the checks in the cash disbursements journal, and reconciles the bank accounts. Since one employee performs all significant activities, control is poor. Auditors say that this employee has *incompatible functions* since the employee is in a position to both perpetrate and conceal errors or irregularities. As a general guideline, the duties of authorization, custody of assets, and record keeping should be separated.

In our payroll example, a better system would involve three different employees, each performing separate functions. One employee would make pay-rate changes (the authorization function), another would run the program to produce the checks and run them through the check-signing machine (custody of assets), and a third would record the checks and reconcile the bank account (record keeping). As a result, each employee could be held accountable for one portion of the payroll process.

Documented Definition of Responsibility Once jobs are broken into appropriate tasks and the tasks are assigned to different employees, the processing rights and responsibilities for the database should be clearly defined. These restrictions should be documented and enforced, preferably with passwords. We'll talk more about that at the end of this chapter.

Employee Accountability Steps should be taken to hold employees accountable for their actions. One way to increase accountability is to require employees to document their activities. Using payroll as an example, the employee who makes pay-rate changes should do so only on the basis of written authorization from management. The computer program that is used to make the changes should automatically print a report which lists the details of the changes made. The report should identify the employee involved and the values of the columns changed—both before and after the change. This report should then be reviewed by management or by another department. In this example, a payroll clerk might make the changes and an employee in the accounting department might review the changes.

Resource Controls

One of the most important ways of protecting data is to control access to the computer system's resources. Data vulnerability is dramatically reduced if only authorized users can access the system at authorized times.

The three major kinds of resource controls are:

- Limiting physical access to the computer
- Using passwords to limit access to the database
- Unloading critical data and locking the system

Limiting Physical Access to the Computer Physical access to the microcomputer and database should be limited. Ideally, a microcomputer should be located in an out-of-the way office that is locked at night and all other times when it is not being used for authorized purposes. If this is impossible, the microcomputer should be placed in the least visible location available. There are also various locking devices on the market for limiting the use of hardware. At all times, measures should be taken to ensure that only authorized employees use the microcomputer.

Limiting Access to the Database Access to data must also be controlled. Processing rights and responsibilities should be determined and documented. These rights should be enforced with passwords. The last section of this chapter illustrates how to use passwords for this purpose.

Unloading Critical Data If possible, data should be unloaded from the system and stored under lock and key during nonbusiness hours. This will be difficult for large files loaded on microcomputers that have large fixed-disks, such as the IBM PC/XT or PC/AT. If you work with such a system, you should use other measures to make it as difficult as possible for the data to be accessed for unauthorized purposes. For example, as mentioned previously, many companies keep their computers in locked rooms.

Backup and Recovery

Unfortunately, no matter how carefully data is processed and protected, some sort of catastrophic error is bound to occur. There are simply too many things that can go wrong. The only prudent measure is to assume that at some unknown time the database will be lost. When this occurs, it must be recovered.

Large data centers have complex and expensive subsystems for recovering a database as quickly as possible while losing as little data as possible. Imagine the recovery activity that must take place at a large bank when the online account-processing system fails. Clearly, the system must be restored to operation quickly and accurately. The difficulty of recovery is compounded for such systems because many users access the data concurrently.

Backup and Recovery on Microcomputers For microcomputer databases, such sophisticated recovery systems have not yet been developed. In fact, there is some debate over whether such recovery is appropriate on microcomputers. A common procedure for backup and recovery with a microcomputer system is to periodically make a copy of the database on diskettes and keep a record of all transactions that have been processed since the copy was made. When a failure occurs, the old database is restored from diskette and transactions input after the copy was made are reprocessed.

Figure 13–1 shows the situation of a company that unloads, or backs up, its database on diskette at the end of each business day. A system failure (crash) occurs at 9:30 Wednesday morning. The company fixes the problem that caused the crash and restores the database as it existed at the end of business on Tuesday. All changes to the database that had been made between the start of work and 9:30 on Wednesday morning are reentered.

The consequence of this system failure is not too severe. Only an hour or two of processing needs to be repeated. Imagine the unfortunate situation of a company that backs up its database at the end of each month and has a failure occur on March 27! Twenty-seven days of processing must be redone. Reprocessing in this situation will be time consuming, very expensive, and, chances are, inaccurate. The lesson is clear: you must periodically make backup copies of your database.

FIGURE 13–1

Timing of typical database backup, crash, and recovery

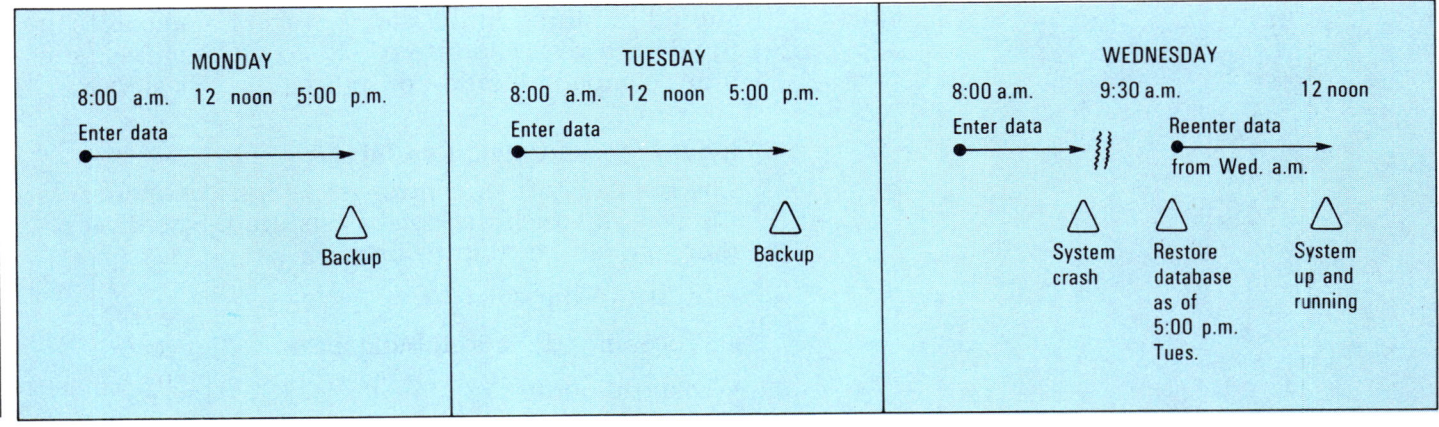

FIGURE 13–2

Summary of Great Plains example

Relation	Frequency of Change
VIDEO	Every Friday, at most
MEMBER	Daily
TRANS	Daily
FORMS	Very seldom
REPORTS	Very seldom
RULES	Very seldom
SYSPARM	Very seldom

How often should you make backups? It depends on how frequently you change your database and how long it takes to make a backup copy. If you change your database frequently, then reprocessing will be time consuming, so you should make backup copies frequently. On the other hand, if changes are infrequent, backups can also be less frequent. Remember, however, that you must keep a record of all changes that have occurred since the backup. Otherwise reprocessing will be impossible.

If your database is large, making backup copies will take time. You may wish to backup only the tables that have been changed. Consider the Great Plains example summarized in Figure 13–2. The VIDEO table is changed once per week, at most. However, TRANS and MEMBER are changed daily. To save time, only these latter tables are backed up daily, Monday through Thursday. The other tables are not copied to diskette because they are not changed. On Fridays, the entire database is copied to diskette.

You will need to evaluate each situation to decide how frequently to make backup copies of your database. In the beginning, it is better to make too many backup copies.

Practice backup procedures Two warnings are in order. First, be certain that you know how to recover your database in the event of a failure. You should practice once or twice to ensure that your procedure works. Do not wait until the database is damaged to learn how to recover it. Second, make certain that the backup copies you are making are valid. One company's employees faithfully followed an invalid backup procedure without testing the backup copies. They did not know their procedure was invalid until they attempted to use the supposed copy of the database. They found nothing had been recorded on the backup diskette. Don't let this happen to you.

Storing backup copies Backup copies of the database should be stored in the data archive. Some copies of the database should also be stored off premises, at another company location or in a safety deposit box.

Input/Process/Output Controls

The last category of control we will discuss concerns the way in which the database is used. Specifically, there should be controls over:

- Inputs to the database
- Processing done to the database
- Disposition of outputs

Input Controls Unfortunately, it is extremely easy to make mistakes while putting data into a computer system. Keying errors are an obvious source of problems. Additionally, transactions can be missed or duplicated. Two documents may stick together and one may be overlooked. An operator who is interrupted in the middle of processing a batch of transactions may process one document twice. Such errors are common. Therefore, special procedures need to be followed to detect input errors.

Transaction counts Transaction counts may be used to detect discrepancies in data entered. To use transaction counts, the number of transactions to be processed are manually counted, then compared to the total produced by the computer system.

Verification of keyed data Keying errors are more difficult to detect. One way to detect them is to have one person key the input data and another person verify the keying by retrieving the new records and comparing them to the source documents. It is important to have a second person do the verification since a person who makes a mistake once is prone to make the same mistake again. Because of this, it is difficult for operators to detect their own errors.

Checks of batch totals Another common input control is to compute and check batch totals on critical fields. For example, suppose an operator is keying orders and wants to be certain that all order amounts are keyed correctly. The operator can divide the orders into batches of, say, 100 each. Then, the operator can manually total the amounts of the orders in each batch and compare the manual totals to totals computed by the computer to reveal any keying mistakes.

Input errors are frequent. Therefore, it is wise to plan for them and build controls into the system operation. Obviously, if erroneous data is keyed into the system, the value of the database decreases dramatically. The responsibility for detecting such errors lies with the system user. Neither hardware nor programs can detect such errors by themselves.

Processing Controls The goal of processing controls is to ensure that all authorized work is performed on a timely basis and that no unauthorized work is performed.

Documented processing schedule Processing cannot be controlled unless a schedule of processing is prepared. This schedule, which itself can be maintained in a database, as shown in Chapter 12, defines the actions to be taken to accomplish various jobs.

Employee checks and balances Better processing control results if two or more employees are involved in system operation. These employees can provide checks and balances for one another. For example, one employee can set up the work to be done in a particular period, and another employee can perform the work. Later, the first employee can check the database to ensure that the work was properly done.

Supervisor review of processing reports Even greater control can be obtained if processing reports are generated by these employees and reviewed by their supervisors. Such a procedure may be cumbersome, but if the system is critical, it may be worth the effort.

Output Controls The goal of output controls is to ensure that outputs are delivered to appropriate users on a timely basis and that unneeded outputs are properly destroyed.

Documentation of reports and authorized users To make sure that outputs are promptly delivered to the appropriate persons, a list of outputs and their authorized users must be compiled. Then, as part of processing, the system operator produces the output and delivers it to the user. If the data is particularly sensitive, logs can be kept of the outputs produced and the employees who received them.

Careful destruction of reports Printed reports will most likely outlive their usefulness. When this occurs, the reports must be destroyed. In most cases, the reports can simply be thrown away. But some reports may contain sensitive data and should be destroyed more carefully, perhaps by shredding. This precaution may seem unnecessary. However, in several documented computer crimes, the criminal obtained crucial information from company waste containers.

Careful destruction of storage media Diskettes and other forms of computer data storage eventually wear out. When this occurs, these media should be erased and then destroyed. Even though the operating system may be giving you disk error messages, a knowledgeable hacker equipped with the right utility programs can still glean a lot of data from a "bad" disk.

USING R:BASE FOR DATA SECURITY AND CONTROL

R:base provides several features to help the user protect the database. *Passwords* can be used to enforce data processing rights and authorities. UNLOAD,

LOAD, RELOAD, and other commands can be used to archive data as well as to provide backup for recovery.

R:base Passwords

R:base supports three types of passwords. Each database has one and only one OWNER password. The user of this password can access and modify any table, and change database structure as well. Each table may have two passwords—RPW and MPW. RPW, which stands for *read password,* only enables the user to read the data in the table.

MPW, which stands for *modify password,* enables the user to change, delete, and read the data in the table. Without the MPW, a user cannot use EDIT, EDIT WITH FORMS, CHANGE, ASSIGN, DELETE ROWS, DELETE COLUMNS, EXPAND, REMOVE, or any other command which modifies the table.

A user provides a password value to R:base with the USER command. For example, if your password is ABC, enter it by typing:

USER ABC

When a database is first created, all the passwords are set to NONE. Passwords can be assigned or changed by entering the DEFINE mode of R:base. For the GTPLAIN database, we set the owner password to XYZ by typing:

DEFINE GTPLAIN
OWNER XYZ
END

Once the owner password is established, only the owner can assign or change passwords. Thus, to change the owner password from XYZ to MMM, the following commands are necessary:

USER XYZ
DEFINE GTPLAIN
OWNER MMM
END

Read and modify passwords are also set in the DEFINE mode. For example, to establish passwords for the VIDEO and MEMBER tables in Great Plains' VIDRENT database, type:

USER MMM
DEFINE VIDRENT

```
PASSWORDS
RPW FOR VIDEO IS APPLE
MPW FOR VIDEO IS ORANGE
RPW FOR MEMBER IS BERRY
MPW FOR MEMBER IS PEAR
END
```

Figure 13–3 summarizes the processing authorities described for the VIDRENT database.

Notice that we distinguish between adding/modifying and deleting data. Unfortunately, R:base makes no such distinction. Therefore, if we give a user permission to add or modify data, that user will also have permission to delete data. Personnel who are not supposed to delete data will have to be trained not to do so. Also, perhaps their activity will have to be monitored.

Assigning Passwords

There are two ways we can assign passwords. First, we can give every table an RPW and an MPW. In Figure 13–3, however, you can see that all personnel can read VIDEO data. Therefore, it makes no sense to define an RPW for VIDEO. Such a password would just be cumbersome. Therefore we could decide to assign read passwords to the other tables and modify passwords to all tables. This requires a total of five passwords.

FIGURE 13–3

Great Plains' VIDRENT database processing rights

Relation	Read	Add/Modify	Delete
VIDEO	Salesperson Rental mgr. Accountant Office manager	Rental mgr.	Office manager
TRANS	Salesperson Rental mgr. Accountant	Salesperson Rental mgr.	Office manager
MEMBER	Salesperson Rental mgr. Accountant	Salesperson Rental mgr.	Office manager

A second approach is to assign passwords to groups of people. Notice in Figure 13-3 that the people who can read TRANS are the same people who can read MEMBER. Therefore, we can assign the same RPW to TRANS and MEMBER and give it to the members of this group. Let's call it PW1. A second group of people may modify TRANS and MEMBER. We can assign a second password, PW2, to this group. In this way, we can assign unique passwords to each group of users that have the same authorities. Figure 13-4 gives a list of the passwords needed. Using this second approach, we only need three passwords.

Passwords need to be changed periodically, but not necessarily on a regular basis. For example, the owner of the database might establish new passwords every three to six weeks. Security will be better if passwords are not changed in a regular pattern.

Respect for Passwords

Regardless of the approach used, passwords should only be assigned if they are going to be respected. *If the data does not actually need this degree of protection, or if employees take security lightly, the passwords will become a joke.* In one company, employees commonly shout passwords to one another across the office. If this occurs, the security system will be worse than no security at all.

Database Backup

When a database is defined, three files are created to store the database structure, data, and indexes. Names of these files are formed by adding 1, 2, or 3 plus the suffix .RBS to the name of the database. Thus, when you defined the GTPLAIN database, the files GTPLAIN1.RBS, GTPLAIN2.RBS, and GTPLAIN3.RBS were created. R:base provides three commands which you can use to backup R:base databases: RELOAD, COPY, and UNLOAD. Let's see how each of these is used.

Reload The primary function of the RELOAD command is not related to backup and recovery—its primary function is to recover unused disk space. When you use the DELETE ROWS command to remove data from a table or the REMOVE command to delete a table from the database, the database files do not get smaller. The disk space occupied by the "deleted" data is trapped and is not reused by R:base.

Consequently, over time, the database files will be larger than they need to be. In fact, if you perform many relational operations on the database (such as we did in Chapter 8), the database files can easily

FIGURE 13-4

Sample passwords for the VIDRENT database

Relation	Read Password	Modify Password
VIDEO	None	PW3
TRANS	PW1	PW2
MEMBER	PW1	PW2

grow to fill the disk. The RELOAD command is used to recover the trapped disk space. This process is sometimes referred to as *packing* the database. RELOAD functions by creating new database files, omitting deleted data. Since it creates new database files, RELOAD creates a backup copy of the database as it packs it.

The general form of the R:base RELOAD command is:

RELOAD dbname

where dbname is any string of up to seven characters. The name used must be different from the name of the database being reloaded. For example, to reload the GTPLAIN database, type:

RELOAD GBACKUP

At this point, two copies of the database exist. The unpacked database is available under the name GTPLAIN. The packed database is available under the name GBACKUP. To save the backup, you can copy the three GBACKUP files to a separate diskette. Then, to operate with the packed files, you can close the unpacked database, erase the three GTPLAIN files, then rename the GBACKUP files as follows:

CLOSE GTPLAIN
ERASE GTPLAIN*.RBS
RENAME GBACKUP*.RBS GTPLAIN*.RBS
OPEN GTPLAIN

While we are on the subject of database packing, R:base provides one more command which can be used for that purpose. The R:base PACK command packs the currently open database. Unlike RELOAD, PACK does not create a duplicate copy of the database. For example, the commands

OPEN GTPLAIN
PACK

result in the same three file names which previously existed: GTPLAIN1.RBS, GTPLAIN2.RBS, and GTPLAIN3.RBS.

Copy The easiest way to make a backup copy of the database is to use the R:base COPY command to copy the three database files to the backup device. For example, the command:

```
COPY GTPLAIN*.RBS A:
```

will create a copy of the GTPLAIN database files on the disk in drive A.

Unload You can backup all or part of a database using the UNLOAD command. There are two things to remember about UNLOAD.

First, UNLOAD is not related in any way to RELOAD, so don't confuse the two. RELOAD stands on its own and is used to pack databases as described above.

Second, UNLOAD is a complicated command with three major functions:

- To create a file of R:base commands and data. This file can be input directly to R:base to reconstruct the unloaded table(s) using either the INPUT or the RUN command.

- To create a file of data values only. This file, which has no R:base commands, can be saved and reread into the database using the LOAD command.

- To create a file for transferring data to other software packages such as Lotus 1-2-3. We will not be concerned with this third purpose here since it has nothing to do with backup and recovery.

The best way to learn the various forms and purposes of UNLOAD is to consider some examples.

Unloading commands and data You can use the UNLOAD command to make a copy of the contents of a table or to make a copy of the structure of a table as well as the contents.

For example, to make a copy of only the contents of the VIDEO table, type:

```
OUTPUT VIDEO.DAT
UNLOAD DATA FOR VIDEO
OUTPUT SCREEN
```

At this point, the VIDEO table still contains the data. To remove it, type:

```
DELETE ROWS FROM VIDEO WHERE VidID# EXISTS
```

If you want to reload the archived data, type:

```
INPUT VIDEO.DAT
      or
RUN VIDEO.DAT
```

R:base looks to VIDEO.DAT and finds commands to instruct it to load the VIDEO table. It also finds the data. By the way, if any of the rows in VIDEO.DAT duplicate rows which exist in VIDEO, they will be added to the table.

Sometimes, you'll want to save the structure of the table as well as the contents. For example, suppose you want to temporarily delete the VIDEO table from the database. You'll want to have a copy of the structure of the table as well as the data it contains so you can later restore it to the database. The following commands will allow you to do this:

```
OUTPUT VIDEO.DAT
UNLOAD ALL FOR VIDEO
OUTPUT TERMINAL
REMOVE VIDEO
```

The commands necessary to define the VIDEO table, along with the VIDEO data, are now contained in a file called VIDEO.DAT. To restore the VIDEO table to the database, type:

```
INPUT VIDEO.DAT
```

Unloading data only You can use the UNLOAD command to unload data only. To save a copy of the VIDEO data in a file called VIDEO.DAT, type

```
OUTPUT VIDEO.DAT
UNLOAD DATA FOR VIDEO AS ASCII
OUTPUT TERMINAL
```

ASCII stands for American Standard Code for Information Interchange. Data is unloaded in the standard ASCII form. No R:base commands are included.

At this point, the unloaded data still resides in the database. You can remove it with the following command:

```
DELETE ROWS FROM VIDEO WHERE VidID# EXISTS
```

Since the file contains only data, you can restore the data to the database by typing:

```
LOAD VIDEO FROM VIDEO.DAT
END
```

Notice that LOAD returns to the terminal when it reaches the end of VIDEO.DAT. You must terminate the load by typing END after receiving the L> prompt.

To review, if you use the UNLOAD DATA command without specifying AS ASCII, R:base will unload both data and R:base commands. Either the R:base INPUT command or the RUN command is used to retrieve the data and commands. If you use UNLOAD DATA with the AS ASCII clause, only data is written to the file. In this case, you retrieve the data using LOAD.

Reasons for unloading data In case you've forgotten, let's review why you want to unload data in the first place. As mentioned in the previous chapter, you need to unload data when any of several situations occur. First, the database can become too large for the available disk space, so some of the data must be removed. If the data may be needed sometime in the future, you cannot simply delete it. Instead, you must first unload an archive file and then delete it from the database.

A second reason for unloading data is that you may need to delete unused data from the database. If the MEMBER table is supposed to contain data only for members who have rented videotapes within the last month, you will need to unload MEMBER data at the end of each month.

A third reason for unloading data is security. Passwords are effective, but it is possible for someone to learn your password or to learn the owner password. The best security is to remove the data from the database. This can be done by unloading the data to diskettes, removing the diskettes from the system, and locking them in your own safe.

A final reason for unloading data is for backup and recovery. In general, it is better to make backups with the COPY command or the RELOAD command than with UNLOAD. With COPY or RELOAD, you automatically save the structure of the entire database as well as important utility tables including FORMS, REPORTS, and RULES.

However, if your database is kept on a fixed disk, and the backup files become too large to fit on a single diskette, then you may prefer to backup the database by unloading it one relation at a time. If you make backups in this way, be sure to use the UNLOAD ALL form of the command so that you also save the database structure. Also, don't forget to make copies of the utility tables.

Recovery

Recovery in microcomputer database systems is a two-step process. First, the database must be restored from a backup copy. Then all processing that was done since the backup was made must be redone.

Restoring from the Backup Restoring from the backup depends on how the backup copy was made. If the backup copy was made with UNLOAD, then the restore can be done with the RUN, INPUT, or LOAD commands as illustrated above. If the backup copy was made with COPY or RELOAD, then the restore is done with the COPY command.

Repeating Recent Processing Once the backup has been restored, all processing since the backup must be repeated. Herein lies a problem: How do you know what has been done? One way is to keep a log of processing activity. R:base can help keep this log. You start by creating a file named GTPLAIN.LOG. When you sign on to the database, execute the following command:

OUTPUT GTPLAIN.LOG WITH TERMINAL

Once this command has been executed, R:base will record your activity in the log file. Unfortunately, there are two important restrictions. First, whenever you load R:base, it will begin recording on this file at the beginning. Thus, if there is valid data on the log file, R:base will write on top of it. Consequently, you must empty the log to another file every time you start R:base.

The second restriction is more of a problem. R:base will not record any interactive processing on the log. Thus, work done with ENTER and EDIT commands will not be recorded on the log.

Because of these restrictions, you should keep a manual log of processing activity. This manual log should show what work has been done and in what order. If reliable recovery is important to your application, a manual log is a necessity.

SUMMARY

- Data is a company asset and should be protected. Its value depends on the cost to the company if the data were lost or stolen.
- Data can be destroyed by accident in the following ways:
  - Mistakes during processing
  - Incorrect system operation
  - Natural disaster
- Data can be willfully destroyed in the following ways:
  - Theft
  - Malicious destruction
  - Unauthorized changes
- Five categories of procedures for protecting the database are:
  - Management controls
  - Organizational controls
  - Resource controls
  - Backup and recovery
  - Input/process/output controls
- Management must take data security seriously if any controls are to be effective. Specific management tasks are:
  - Building employee awareness of the value of the data and need for security
  - Training database users to reduce errors and the potential for data loss
  - Monitoring error reports and user activity
- Three major kinds of organizational controls are:
  - Separating duties and responsibilities so no single employee can both perpetrate and conceal an error or irregularity (eliminate incompatible functions)
  - Documenting definition of responsibilities
  - Holding employees accountable
- Resource controls ensure that only authorized users can access the system. Such controls include:
  - Limiting physical access to the computer
  - Using passwords to limit access to the database
  - Unloading critical data and locking the system when not in use and during nonbusiness hours

- Procedures for backup and recovery are essential, since even the most careful planning cannot prevent all catastrophic errors or accidents.
  - On microcomputers, the general backup and recovery procedure is to periodically copy the database on diskettes or tape and keep a paper record of all transactions processed after the copy is made.
  - Backup procedures should be practiced before disaster strikes.
  - Backup copies of the database should be stored safely.
- Input/process/output controls:
  - To detect input errors, typical procedures include keeping a manual count of all transactions, verifying keyed data, and checking batch totals.
  - Processing controls aim to ensure that all authorized work is performed on a timely basis and that no unauthorized work is ever performed. Procedures include keeping a processing schedule, having employees check each other's work, and generating reports for review by supervisors.
  - Output controls are designed to make sure outputs are delivered on a timely basis and that unneeded outputs are properly destroyed. Procedures include documenting who is authorized to receive outputs and carefully destroying unneeded reports and storage media.
- R:base PASSWORDs can be used to enforce data processing rights and authorities.
- There are three types of R:base PASSWORDS:
  - There is one OWNER password for each database.
  - Each database table may have an RPW (read password) and an MPW (modify password).
- R:base PASSWORDS are created in the DEFINE mode.
- Users provide their password to R:base with the USER command.
- Backup copies can be made with the R:base COPY, RELOAD, and UNLOAD commands.
- The recovery process has two steps:
  - Restoring from the backup copy
  - Repeating processing since the backup was made
- Use the COPY command to restore the database from backup copies made with the COPY or RELOAD commands.
- Use the R:base RUN or INPUT command to restore the

database from backups made with UNLOAD DATA or UNLOAD ALL without the AS ASCII clause.

- Use the R:base LOAD command to restore the database from backups made with UNLOAD DATA AS ASCII.

REVIEW QUESTIONS

Group I Questions

13.1
List two examples (not already mentioned in the text) of valuable data. How would you measure the value of the examples you listed?

13.2
What are the two basic threats to data?

13.3
How can data be accidentally lost or damaged?

13.4
How can data be intentionally lost or damaged?

13.5
List five basic categories of controls.

13.6
How does management's attitude affect data security?

13.7
What can management do to protect data?

13.8
How can a system which is menu-driven be more secure than one that is not?

13.9
Explain how training can affect data security.

13.10
Explain what the term *incompatible functions* means. How can this situation be avoided?

13.11
What does *backup and recovery* mean? How does it work?

13.12
Write an explanation of the following for someone who knows nothing about computing:

 a. Input controls

 b. Processing controls

 c. Output controls

Group II Questions

13.13
Find out if your state has a computer crime law. When was it enacted? What does it say about stealing data?

13.14
Find an example of an incident in which data was stolen. How was it stolen? If the incident did not involve a microcomputer, could it have? How could the theft have been prevented?

▍PROJECT

Design the processing rights and responsibilities for the GTPLAIN database. Make whatever assumptions you believe are appropriate. Based upon the processing rights and responsibilities determined by you, determine appropriate R:base passwords to enforce them.

CHAPTER 14

Natural Language Processing with CLOUT

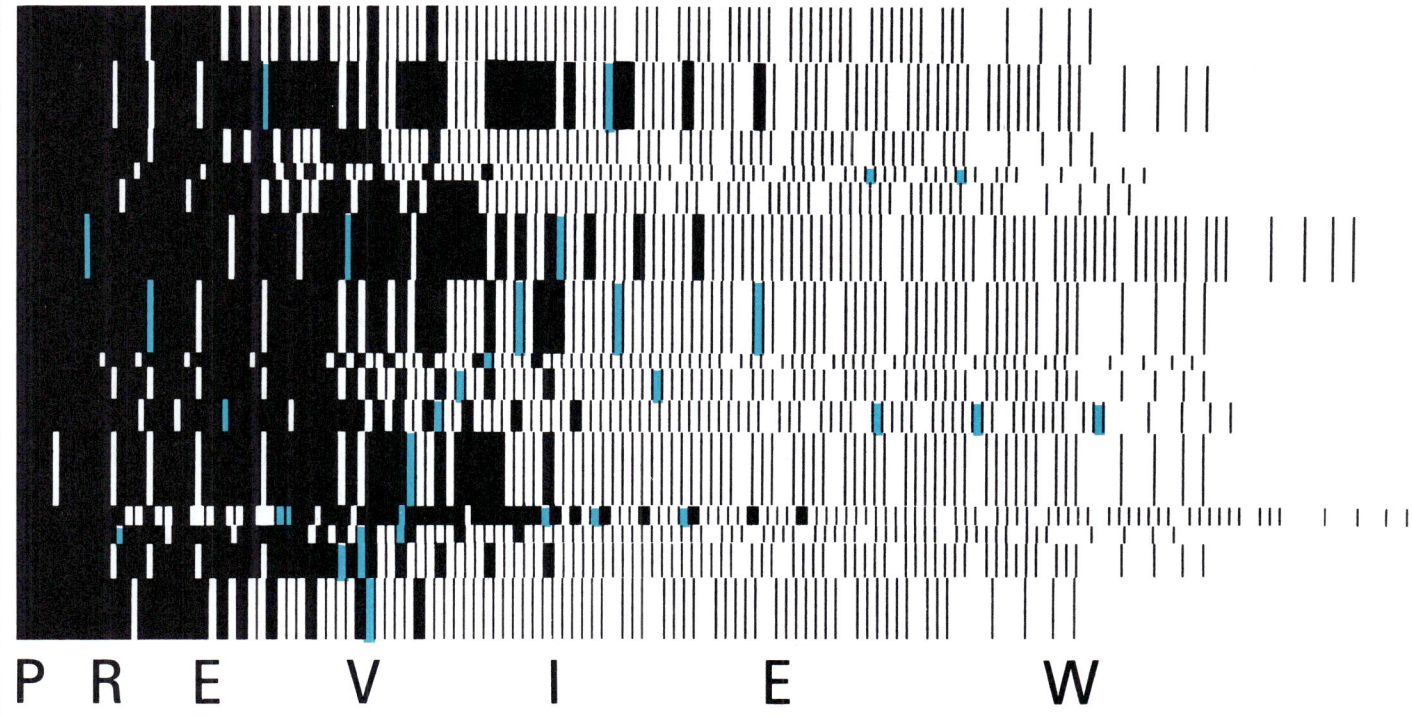

PREVIEW

Natural language processing involves the translation of normal, everyday language into a formal language that can be processed by computer. The translation of normal English into BASIC program statements is an example of a natural language transformation. Natural language is a branch of artificial intelligence and is in its infancy. Human language is so complex and so riddled with ambiguity that current natural language products often make serious errors and misinterpretations. Even still, there are impressive productivity gains to be made through the use of some existing natural language products. In this chapter, we will study one such product, called CLOUT (Conversational Language Option). CLOUT is a trademark of Microrim, Inc.

CLOUT, which is a product sold separately from R:base, accepts natural language queries expressed about data stored in an R:base database. It translates these queries into a series of retrieval actions and produces a list of data as output. CLOUT has no capability for defining databases or for storing, changing, or deleting data. CLOUT is designed to process already existing R:base databases.

CLOUT can deal with much more ambiguity than

can R:base or similar products. Even if questions are poorly formulated and incomplete, CLOUT will do its best to provide some sort of sensible response. The advantage of CLOUT is that it can be used by people who have little or no training. In a sense, CLOUT provides its own training. CLOUT is especially useful for answering *ad hoc,* one-of-a-kind questions. CLOUT's flexibility enables the user to obtain answers to questions without knowledge of the underlying database structure.

In this chapter, we will illustrate the general categories of questions that CLOUT can answer and then describe some of CLOUT's special features. We will also show several ways to increase the likelihood of accurate communication with CLOUT.

THE POWER OF CLOUT

CLOUT is an exceedingly powerful program. CLOUT learns. After you spend a short time with CLOUT, it will begin to talk your language. Furthermore, you will begin to talk CLOUT's language. Observing a typical CLOUT interaction, it is difficult to determine who is training whom. As you use CLOUT, you will probably be amazed at its power. You will most likely project human characteristics onto CLOUT. Most people find it hard to believe they are conversing with only a program and a machine.

There is a danger in all of this. CLOUT appears to understand more than it really does. Therefore, CLOUT will make surprising mistakes. When using CLOUT, you'll want to remember that CLOUT models human language, which is full of ambiguity. (Of course, it's ambiguity that gives our language its power and helps facilitate creativity.)

When you make an ambiguous statement to CLOUT, CLOUT will do its best to understand what you mean. CLOUT will also provide an answer. The answer, however, will be in response to the question *CLOUT thinks* you asked, and it may not be the answer to the question *you think* you asked.

Here's an example. Suppose you are processing employee data and you ask:

WHO HAS LESS THAN AVERAGE SALARY IN CALIFORNIA?

This is an ambiguous statement. It could mean:

- Of the employees living in California, who has less than the total average salary?

    OR

- Of the employees living in California, who has less than the average California salary?

    OR

- Which employees (living anywhere) earn less than the average California salary?

When you ask this query, CLOUT will respond with an answer, say "Jones and Parks." You will not be able to determine from the answer which of the meanings CLOUT used.

The situation is something like speaking with a new employee. At first, your communication may be confused. The phrase "fully allocated expense" may mean one thing to you and something else to the employee.

Many people in such a situation decide to phrase their questions carefully. A good interviewer may begin with broad, general questions that are likely to be clearly understood. The interviewer then asks more specific questions, checking the answers against one another. When answers appear inconsistent, the interviewer looks for differences in meaning. "No, I don't think you understood my question," is a typical response.

A similar process should be used with CLOUT or other natural language products. Begin with broad, general questions and proceed to more specific questions. Always be on the lookout for inconsistent responses. Such responses will be the only clue you get that you and CLOUT have misunderstood one another.

For example, if you type in the queries below, CLOUT might respond with the answers at right:

SHOW THE AVERAGE SALARY	$2,114
SHOW THE AVERAGE SALARY IN CALIFORNIA	$2,362
HOW MANY EMPLOYEES EARN LESS THAN THE AVERAGE SALARY IN CALIFORNIA	314
HOW MANY EMPLOYEES EARN LESS THAN $2,362	472

The last two queries may appear the same to you, but CLOUT will provide different answers. CLOUT will assume the fourth query refers to all employees while the third one refers only to employees in California.

This sort of misunderstanding is common among

FIGURE 14-1
Initial CLOUT screens

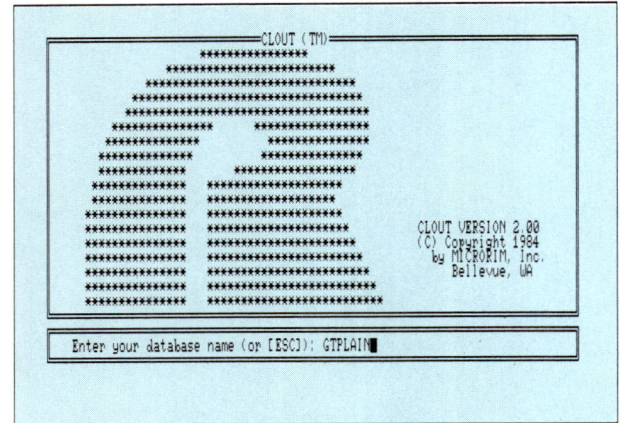

FIGURE 14-2
CLOUT main menu

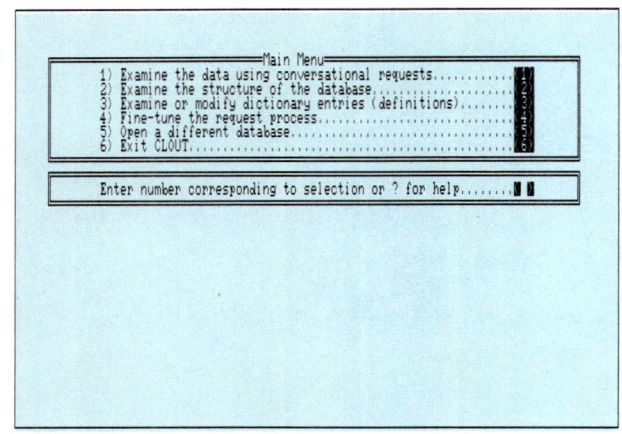

FIGURE 14-3
CLOUT fine-tune menu

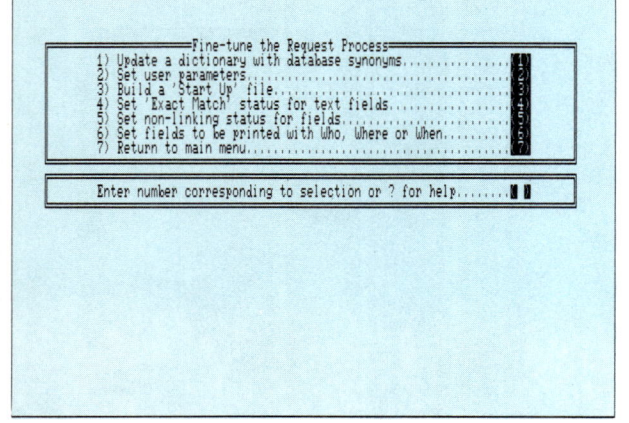

people. The fact that CLOUT is capable of it means that CLOUT models human language well. It also means that you need to be on the alert for this possibility.

USING CLOUT

The best way to become familiar with CLOUT is to use it. Begin by working with a small database and process it until you and CLOUT get to know each other. For the following examples, we will use GTPLAIN. You will learn much more from this chapter if you execute the instructions on your computer as you read.

To use CLOUT, you need the files CLOUT.EXE and CLOUT.DAT on your drive (or in your directory). Once they are loaded, type:

CLOUT

Once it is ready, CLOUT will ask you for the name of your database. Since we're using the GTPLAIN database, type:

GTPLAIN

(See Figure 14-1.)

Defining Synonyms

The first CLOUT menu is shown in Figure 14-2. You can type [1] to start asking questions, or you can take other actions. Type [4] for fine tuning. CLOUT responds with the menu shown in Figure 14-3. Enter [1] to define synonyms.

Read the text that CLOUT displays (Figure 14-4). At this point, CLOUT will lead you through each of your tables. For each column, you have a chance to define one or more synonyms. If you are following this discussion on your computer with the GTPLAIN database, then you should now define the synonyms in Figure 14-5. You can always delete synonyms, so don't be afraid to make a mistake.

Once you have defined synonyms, type [7] to return to the main menu (Figure 14-2). Now enter [1] to begin asking CLOUT questions.

Asking Questions

There are seven categories of questions you might want to ask CLOUT:

- Requests to display data
- Requests to display data with qualifications

- Queries requiring arithmetic functions
- Queries requiring processing with subgroups
- yes/no questions
- Multilevel questions
- Queries involving more than one table

FIGURE 14–4a
Instructions for defining synonyms—part 1

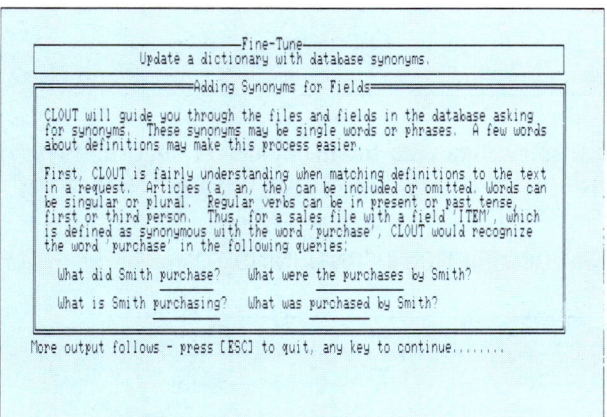

FIGURE 14–4b
Instructions for defining synonyms—part 2

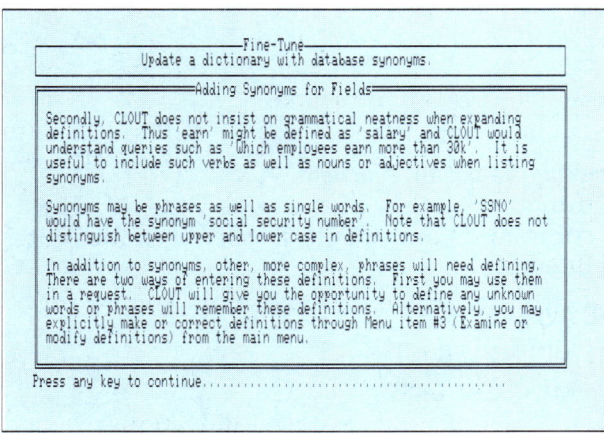

FIGURE 14–5
Synonyms defined for GTPLAIN

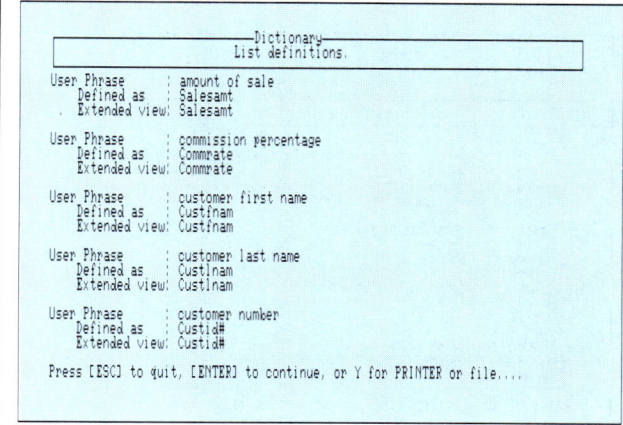

FIGURE 14–5
Synonyms (continued)

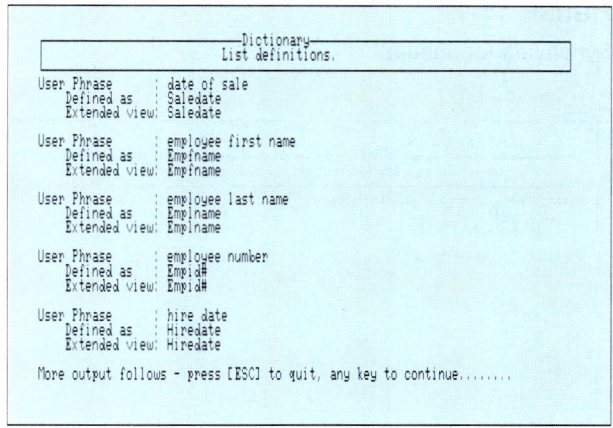

FIGURE 14–5
Synonyms (continued)

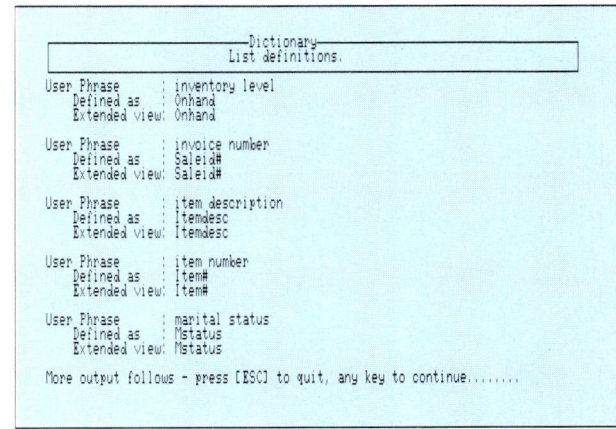

FIGURE 14-5
Synonyms (continued)

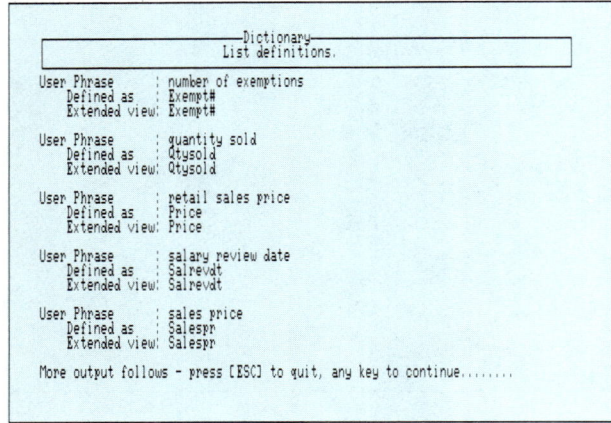

FIGURE 14-5
Synonyms (continued)

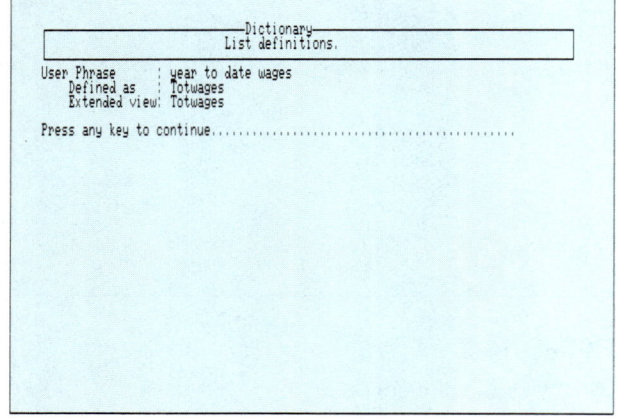

Requests to Display Data The first kind of question asks CLOUT simply to display data from a table. For example, when you type:

SHOW INV ITEM DESCRIPTIONS

CLOUT gives the following response:

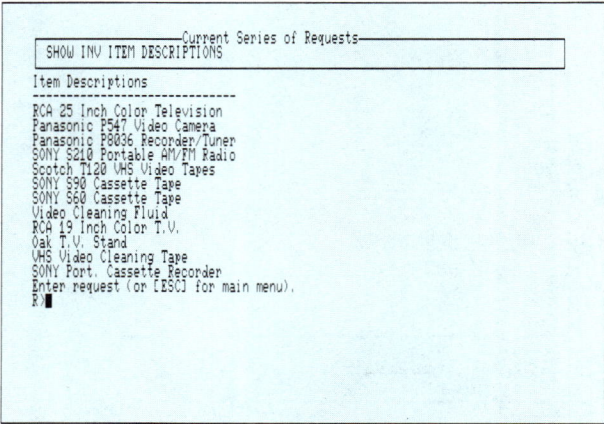

Requests to Display Data with Qualifications A second type of query displays relational data, but with a restriction. Here is an example:

SHOW ITEM DESCRIPTIONS CONTAINING SONY

Queries Requiring Arithmetic Functions A variety of arithmetic functions are available with CLOUT. The following commands and CLOUT responses illustrate the possibilities:

WHAT'S THE AVERAGE COST
WHAT'S THE MINIMUM COST
WHAT'S THE MAXIMUM COST

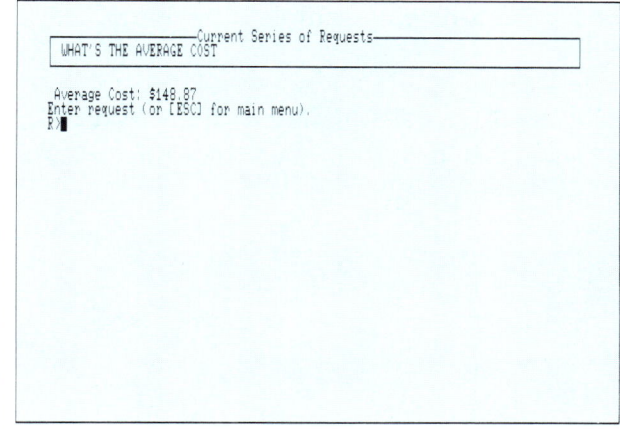

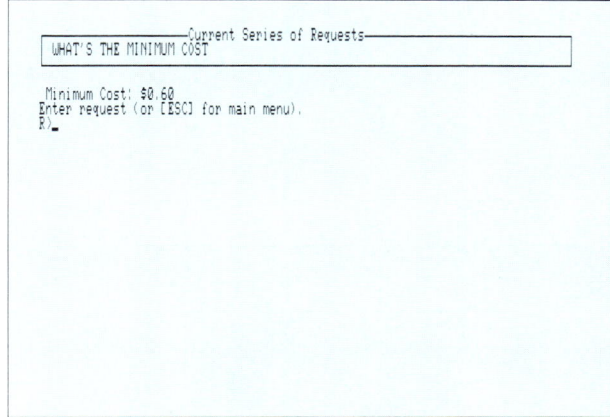

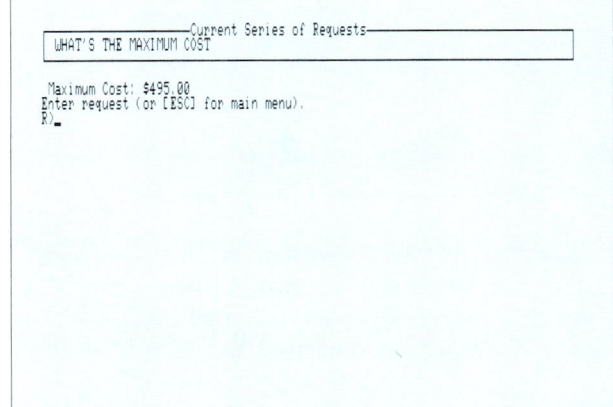

CLOUT can also compute the standard deviation and correlation coefficient of two columns.

Queries Requiring Processing with Subgroups CLOUT will compute arithmetic functions on subgroups of data as well. Consider the following sample queries and responses:

SHOW THE AVERAGE AMOUNT OF SALE BY ITEM NUMBER
SHOW THE MAXIMUM AMOUNT OF SALE FOR EACH EMPLOYEE NUMBER

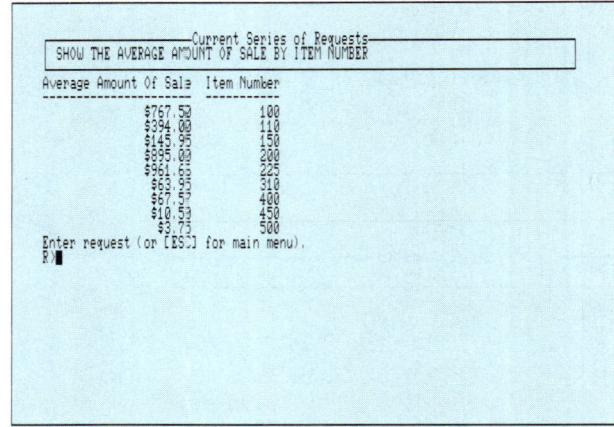

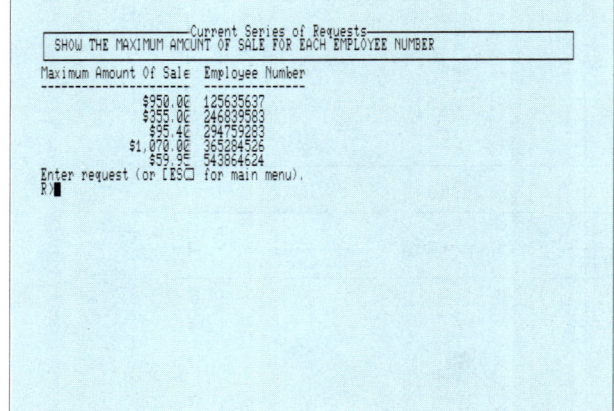

Yes/No Questions CLOUT will respond to some yes/no questions. The response is sometimes unnerving. For example, one user wanted to see a list of inventory items where the decription contains the word "video":

ARE THERE ANY ITEM DESCRIPTIONS WHICH CONTAIN "VIDEO"?

CLOUT responded:

YES!

In general, CLOUT will respond to questions of the form ARE THERE ANY ____? CLOUT will not respond to questions like DO ALL ITEM DESCRIPTIONS CONTAIN "VIDEO"? Instead, CLOUT will ask you to reformulate your question.

Multilevel Questions It is possible for CLOUT to consider a question as a continuation of a prior question. For example, suppose we repeat the query:

ARE THERE ANY ITEM DESCRIPTIONS WHICH CONTAIN "VIDEO"?

When CLOUT replies:

YES!

we can ask:

WHICH ONES?

CLOUT will then respond:

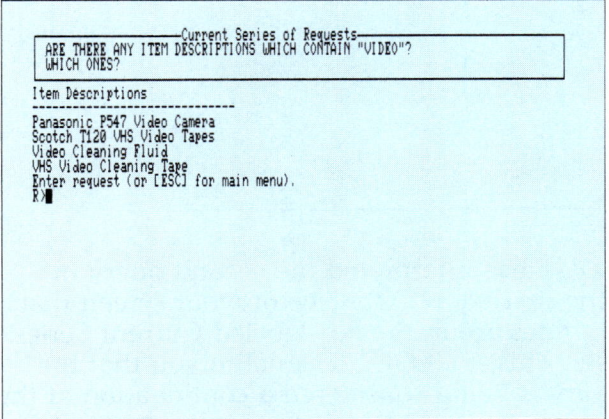

Observe that CLOUT correctly assumed that the phrase WHICH ONES? was not a question in its own right, but rather a continuation of the prior question.

Consider another two-level query and see how CLOUT responds:

SHOW TRANSACTIONS FOR ITEM NUMBER 500

Notice that CLOUT does not recognize the word *transactions* and asks for a synonym. Type "COMPSALE" (Figure 14–6). In this way, CLOUT "learns" from you as you work with it.

FIGURE 14–6

CLOUT asks for a synonym for "transactions"

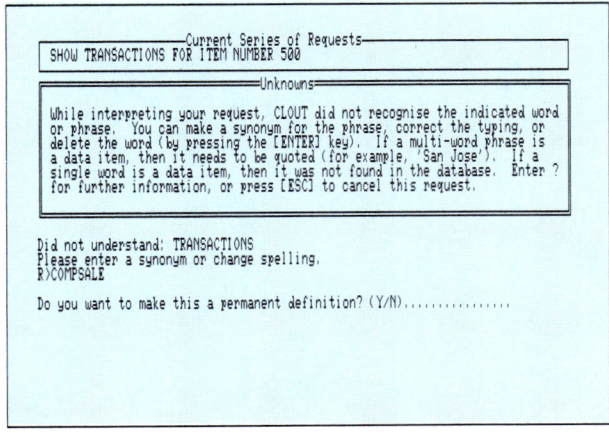

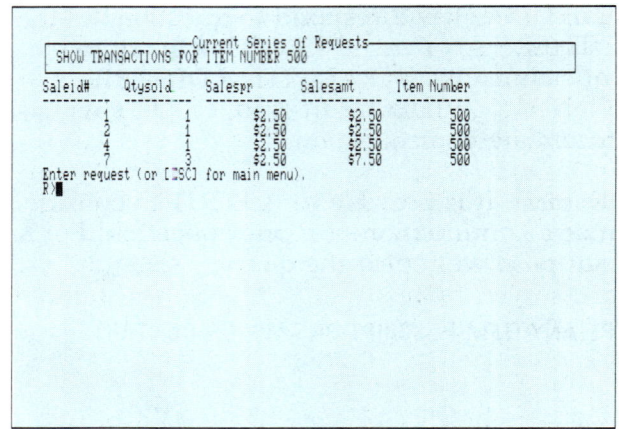

SHOW ONLY ITEM NUMBER AND AMOUNT OF SALE

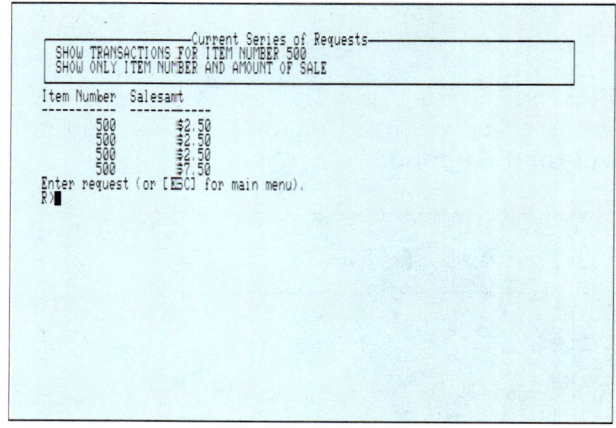

Here, CLOUT has interpreted the second query in terms of the first query. Observe on your screen that both query lines are in the box labeled Current Series of Requests. This is CLOUT's signal to you that the second query is being considered a continuation of the first query.

In general, CLOUT will consider a query to be a continuation if a pronoun or other reference-type word occurs in a phrase before any term or expression to which the pronoun could refer. Expressions like JUST THOSE UNDER FIVE and LIST HIS SALARY will be considered continuations of prior queries.

If CLOUT incorrectly interprets a question as a continuation, press [ESC] and rephrase your question. Similarly, if CLOUT does not take your question as a continuation, you can press [ESC] and rephrase your question in one line.

Queries Involving More Than One Table When you ask questions that involve data from more than one table, CLOUT will attempt to find a link connecting the two tables. Such a link will consist of pairs of columns arising from the same data.

For the GTPLAIN database, there is a link between CUSTOMER and SALE. CustID# in CUSTOMER arises from the same domain as CustID# in SALE. Consequently, CLOUT can join the two tables on CustID#. Similarly, there are links between SALE and COMPSALE (SaleID#), SALE and EMPLOYEE (EmpID#), and COMPSALE and INV (Item#).

If we ask CLOUT a question like WHAT IS THE SALARY OF ALL EMPLOYEES WHO HAVE SALES TO TOWNSAN? CLOUT will attempt to find a path from CUSTOMER to EMPLOYEE. It will first find a link between CUSTOMER and SALE (CustID#) and then a link between SALE and EMPLOYEE (EmpID#). CLOUT will look for paths that involve up to five relations.

Pathfinding and joining is invisible to the user; it happens automatically. Consider the following queries and responses:

SHOW THE ITEM DESCRIPTION FOR SALES TO GOLDSTEIN

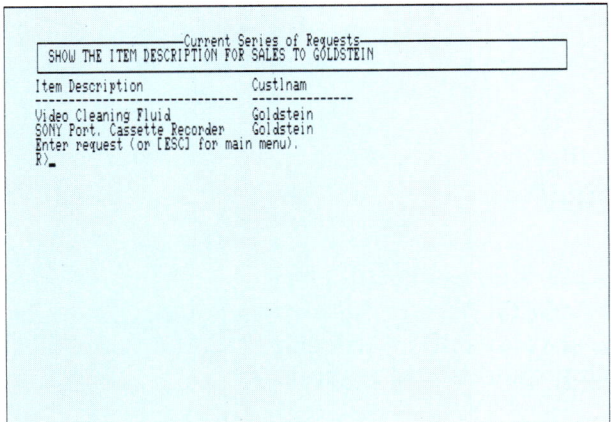

To answer this question, CLOUT joined SALE with CUSTOMER using CustID#. Here's another example:

WHAT IS THE AVERAGE AMOUNT OF SALES FOR GREG

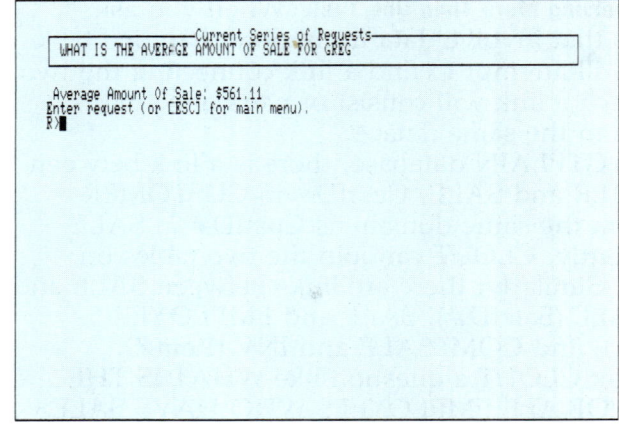

CLOUT'S SPECIAL FEATURES

The best way to learn CLOUT is to use it, but if that's all you do, you may never learn about some of CLOUT's special features. These features can be very useful. This section discusses several of them:

- High and low values (top/bottom)
- Sorting
- Search by partial value
- Fuzzy values
- Who/where/when
- Exact match
- Start-up files
- Help facility

High and Low Value (Top/Bottom)

You can ask CLOUT to present rows having the highest or lowest values of a particular attribute. Consider the following queries and responses:

SHOW THE TOP EMPLOYEE FIRST NAME BY AMOUNT OF SALE

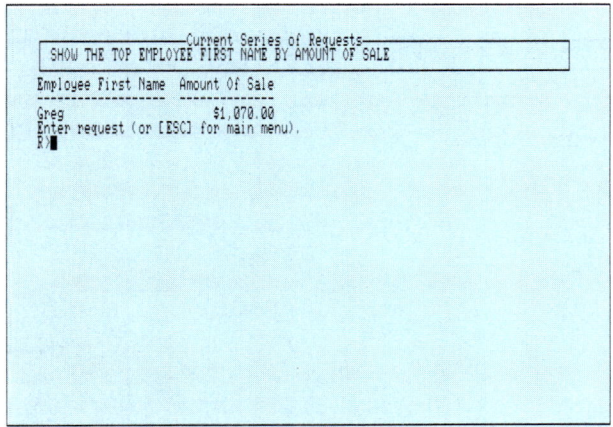

SHOW THE TOP EMPLOYEE FIRST NAME BY TOTAL AMOUNT OF SALE

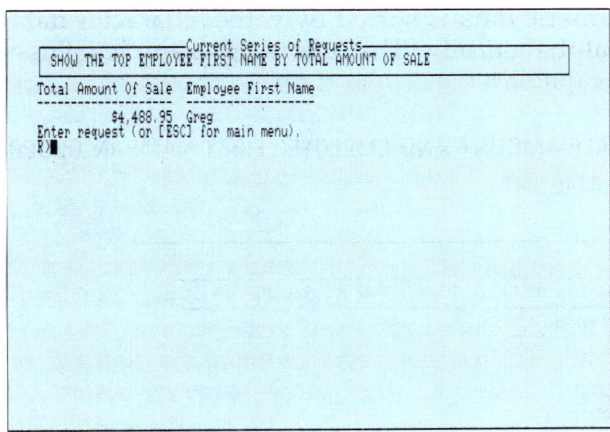

Observe from this example that either a single value of a column or an arithmetic function (total, average) of a column can be used to select the data to be displayed. Here is another example:

SHOW EMPLOYEE FIRST NAME OF THE BOTTOM 2 EMPLOYEES BY AVERAGE SALE AMOUNT

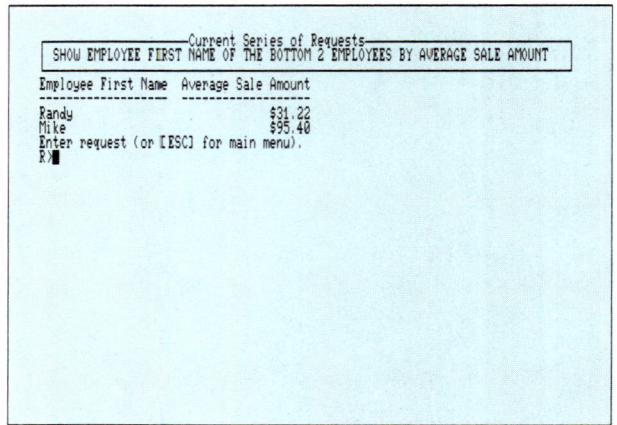

Sorting

CLOUT can present data in sorted order. The data can be in ascending or descending order by up to ten attributes. Numeric data is sorted by value; character data is sorted alphabetically. The following examples illustrate this capability:

SHOW SALE AMOUNT AND EMPLOYEE FIRST NAME IN ORDER OF SALE AMOUNT

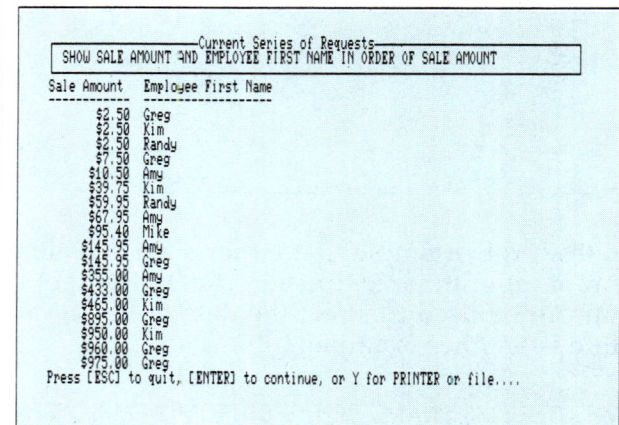

SHOW SALE AMOUNT AND EMPLOYEE FIRST NAME IN ORDER OF EMPLOYEE FIRST NAME AND SALE AMOUNT

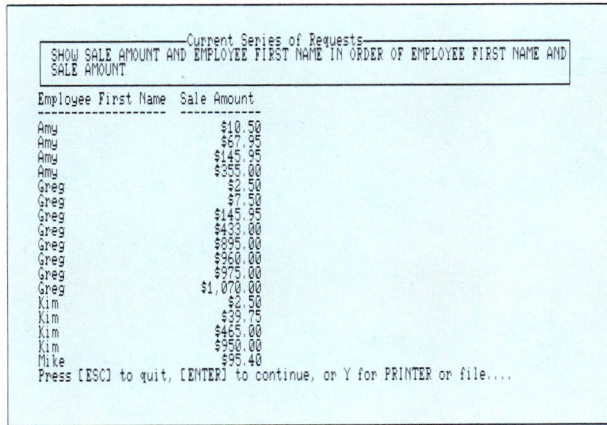

SHOW ITEM DESCRIPTION AND COST IN DESCENDING ORDER OF ITEM DESCRIPTION

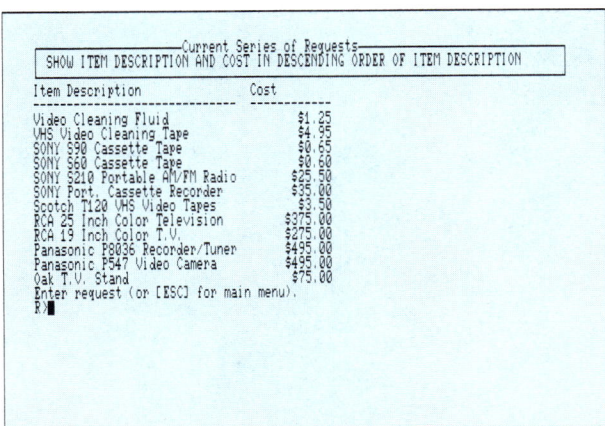

The columns must all be sorted in ascending or descending order. CLOUT is unable to sort one column (or group of columns) in ascending order and another column (or group) in descending order.

Searching by Partial Value

CLOUT will find rows with attributes having a specified character or character string. The character(s) can be at the beginning, at the end, or in the middle of the value. For example:

SHOW THE AVERAGE SALE AMOUNT, EMPLOYEE LAST NAME WHERE EMPLOYEE LAST NAME ENDS WITH L

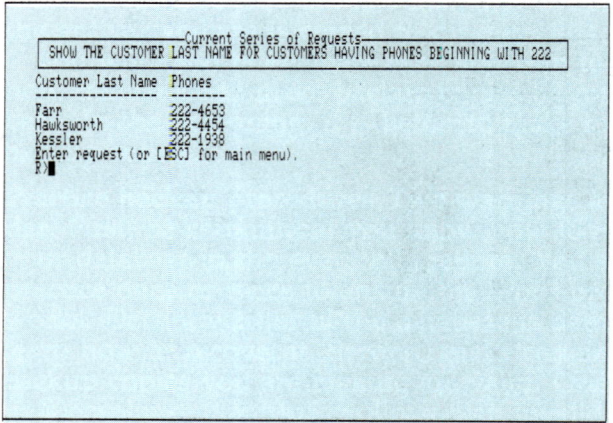

SHOW THE CUSTOMER LAST NAME FOR CUSTOMERS HAVING PHONES BEGINNING WITH 222

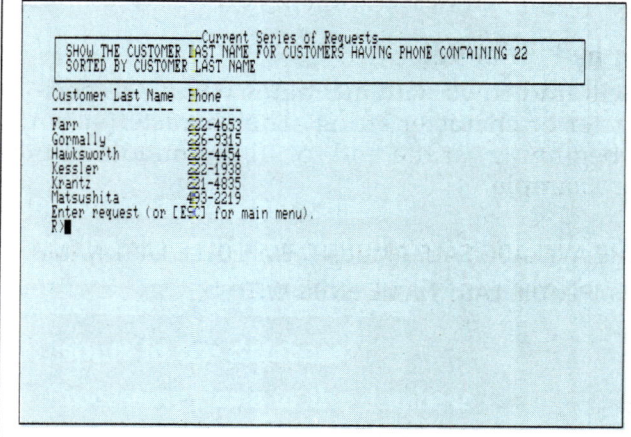

SHOW THE CUSTOMER LAST NAME FOR CUSTOMERS HAVING PHONE CONTAINING 22 SORTED BY CUSTOMER LAST NAME

Fuzzy Values

CLOUT does not require that values be exact. For example, you can ask CLOUT to show amounts equal to about 100. In this case, CLOUT will present data that rounds or truncates to 100. The number of zeros indicates to CLOUT how precise the answer should be. Thus, about 100 is more fuzzy than about 110.

Additionally, CLOUT understands the letter *K* to mean about 1000, and the letter *M* to mean about one million. Thus, amount equal to 5K means amount equal to about 5000, and sales equal to 4M means sales equal to about 4 million.

Dates and times can also be fuzzy. You can ask CLOUT to show orders in February, or orders on the 1st, or orders in 1984. Also, 12 o'clock means between 12 and 1, and 12:30 means between 12:30 and 12:30:59.

Who/Where/When

CLOUT allows the user to associate column names with the words *Who, Where, and When*. To do this, select "Fine tune the query process" from the main menu, and then select "Set fields to be printed with Who, Where or When" from the next menu. From there, CLOUT will ask you to specify columns that correspond to each of these words.

For the GTPLAIN database, we associated the columns EmpFName and EmpLName with *Who*, the column HireDate with *When*, and Addr1 with *Where*. Once these associations were specified, CLOUT could readily process queries such as:

WHO HAS SALARY OF ABOUT $1K

```
┌─────────────────────Current Series of Requests─────────────────────┐
│ WHO HAS A SALARY OF ABOUT $1K                                      │
└────────────────────────────────────────────────────────────────────┘

Empfname        Emplname        Salary
--------        --------        ------
Randy           Morgan          $1,500.00
Becky           Vick            $1,800.00
Stan            Abel            $1,650.00
Jean            Heather         $860.00
Anne            Holly           $860.00
Paige           Crystal         $860.00
Kim             Abel            $860.00
Greg            Abel            $975.00
Mike            Johnson         $1,750.00
Brian           Kleese          $500.00
Amy             Kleese          $500.00
Jerry           Matheson        $1,785.00
Enter request (or [ESC] for main menu).
R>
```

WHEN WAS STAN HIRED?

```
┌─Current Series of Requests──────────────┐
│ WHEN WAS STAN HIRED?                    │
└─────────────────────────────────────────┘
Hiredate  Empfname
--------  --------
11/14/80  Stan
Enter request (or [ESC] for main menu).
R>_
```

Associating columns with these pronouns makes it easier for CLOUT to understand what you want. CLOUT's answers will also be more specific. For example, if *When* is not defined as Hiredate, here's how CLOUT will answer the query above:

```
┌─Current Series of Requests──────────────┐
│ WHEN WAS STAN HIRED?                    │
└─────────────────────────────────────────┘
Empid#:    42278345E
Emplname:  Abel
Hiredate:  11/14/80
Salary:    $1,650.00
Commrate:  0.05000
Salrevdt:  11/18/85
Mstatus:   Married
Exempt#:   4
Totwages:  $3,300.00
Empfname:  Stan
Enter request (or [ESC] for main menu).
R>_
```

Exact Match

CLOUT will make every attempt to find matches for values that you specify in a query. If there is not an exact match, CLOUT will strip *s*, *ed*, and *ing* from the end of a value, and it will make possessive forms (Abel's) nonpossessive (Abel). All of the following queries will obtain the same response:

SHOW THE SALARY OF THE EMPLOYEES WHERE
EMPLOYEE LAST NAME EQ ABELS
SHOW THE SALARY OF THE EMPLOYEES WHERE
EMPLOYEE LAST NAME EQ ABELED

SHOW THE SALARY OF THE EMPLOYEES WHERE
EMPLOYEE LAST NAME EQ ABELING
SHOW THE SALARY OF THE EMPLOYEES WHERE
EMPLOYEE LAST NAME EQ ABEL'S
SHOW THE SALARY OF THE EMPLOYEES WHERE
EMPLOYEE LAST NAME EQ ABELS'

In some cases, this flexibility is inappropriate: sometimes we want an exact match or no match at all. For example, values of CustID# should match exactly. Without specific action on the user's part, CLOUT will accept the following query, even though it is so strange that CLOUT should generate an error message:

SHOW PHONE WHERE CustID# EQ 233542069ing

To prevent this situation, we can define CustID# to be an "exact match" column. When it is defined this way, CLOUT will look for exact matches only.

To define a column as exact match, enter the "Fine tune the query process" module, and select "Set 'exact match' status for text fields." CLOUT will then direct you to name the fields for which you want only an exact match. Once this is done for CustID#, CLOUT responds to the above query as follows:

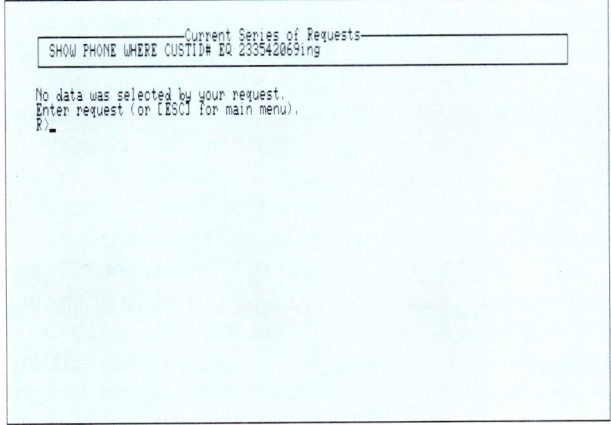

Start-up Files

When you start CLOUT, it normally will ask for the name of the database you want to process and then display the main menu. For occasional or unsophisticated users, this may be inappropriate. You may want to specify the database name on their behalf. If so, you can build a start-up file that will name the database to process and optionally skip the main menu. The user will be able to start CLOUT and then ask questions without any other initial activity.

To build a start-up file, select "Fine tune the request process" from the main menu. Next, select "Build a start up file." CLOUT will direct you from there.

Be aware of a danger in using start-up files: The end-user will not know which database is being processed. The end-user might think he or she is processing last month's invoices when this month's invoices are actually being queried. CLOUT will provide start-up files, but you must make sure the end-user knows what data is being processed.

Help

CLOUT has a help facility similar to the R:base help facility. To enter this module, simply type help or enter [?] whenever CLOUT is asking for input. The help menus will direct you from there.

IMPROVING YOUR COMMUNICATION WITH CLOUT

CLOUT is a very persistent program. When you give it a query, it will do just about everything except turn your computer upside down to try to figure out what you want.

CLOUT, the Determined Assistant

To understand CLOUT's determination, consider an analogy. Suppose you want to locate Don Abernathy in the Los Angeles Coliseum during a football game. You ask an assistant to find Mr. Abernathy. If your assistant had CLOUT's determination, here's what would happen: First the assistant would search available lists of participants. The assistant would search rosters of officials, rosters of athletes, rosters of coaches, and so forth. If that search were unsuccessful, the assistant would consider the possibility that you had misspelled Abernathy's name. The person would think of other ways of spelling Don Abernathy and check the rosters again. Also, the assistant would remove common endings like -s, -es, 's, -ed, and -ing and check again. Then the assistant would page the audience for Don Abernathy.

If all this were unsuccessful, the assistant would take a deep breath, walk to section 1, row A, seat 1 and ask the person sitting there if he or she is Don Abernathy. If not, the assistant would go to the next seat and ask again. The assistant would continue in this way, asking all 104,000 people if necessary.

If none of these actions successfully located Don Abernathy, the assistant, in an almost embarrassed fashion, would ask if you could give a little more data about Don. With the additional data, the assistant would go through the process again. It would continue in this way until you get what you want, or until *you* give up.

CLOUT is a very determined assistant.

How to Help CLOUT
There are several ways that you can reduce the amount of work CLOUT must do.

Getting Acquainted First, CLOUT learns about you and your vocabulary as you ask it questions. One way to help is to let CLOUT get to know you in a small stadium. Take CLOUT out to the local sandlot before you take it to the L.A. Coliseum. Further, when you do take CLOUT to larger stadiums, take the vocabulary you have built along with you.

More directly, when you first use CLOUT, start with a small amount of data. Construct a test database that has the same design as your production database. Fill the test database with a limited amount of data, say five or ten rows per table. Next, use the "Fine tune the query process" menu to specify synonyms and provide definitions (discussed below). Then, ask the questions that you will ask your production database.

While you are doing this, CLOUT will be storing data about the way you communicate in a file named XXXXXXXX.LEX. (The name of your text database will replace the *X*'s. For the GTPLAIN database, CLOUT builds a file name GTPLAIN.LEX.)

After you have asked questions of the test database, copy your LEX file to the device and directory (if appropriate) that contain your production database. When you do the copy, rename the LEX file to conform to the name of your database. Thus, if the test database is TEST and the production database is GTPLAIN, then the following copy command should be used:

COPY TEST.LEX GTPLAIN.LEX

WARNING: If anyone else is using CLOUT with GTPLAIN, they will have already developed a file named GTPLAIN.LEX. The above copy command will destroy their file. Since your co-worker will be understandably upset, don't do this. Instead, you will have to combine your file with your co-worker's file by unloading and reloading your LEX file. See the CLOUT documentation for details on how to do this.

Phrasing Your Questions Although CLOUT will accept a question phrased in almost any fashion, there are ways you can structure your questions to make it easier for CLOUT to understand what you want. First, when stating conditions (EMPLOYEE LAST NAME EQ ABEL), phrase your questions so that the column name and the value you want it to have are clearly related. Although the next two queries are logically equivalent, it will be easier for CLOUT to process the second one:

SHOW EMPLOYEE FIRST NAME FOR ABELS
SHOW EMPLOYEE FIRST NAME FOR EMPLOYEE LAST NAME EQ ABEL

Also, when stating a series of conditions, do not mix the order of columns and their values. Do not say column equals value (Employee last name EQ Abel) and later value equals column (Abel EQ Employee last name). Such a construction is not parallel and will confuse CLOUT. The next two questions are supposed to be logically equivalent, but CLOUT will answer them differently:

SHOW SALES AMOUNT WHERE EMPLOYEE FIRST NAME EQ KIM AND ABEL EQ EMPLOYEE LAST NAME
SHOW SALES AMOUNT WHERE EMPLOYEE FIRST NAME EQ KIM AND EMPLOYEE LAST NAME EQ ABEL

Defining Synonyms Another way to help CLOUT is to define as many synonyms as possible before you start asking questions. To do this, select "Fine tune the query process" from the main menu and then select "Update a dictionary with database synonyms."

If you have used CLOUT, you may have noticed that when CLOUT does not understand a term, it will automatically give you a chance to define a synonym. This feature is so convenient that you may have decided you do not need to define synonyms with the "Update a dictionary with database synonyms" menu.

This is not a valid conclusion. Realize that CLOUT will search the entire database before it gives up and asks you to define a synonym. In terms of the L.A. Coliseum analogy, CLOUT will have searched 104,000 seats before you get a chance to define the synonym. Thus, you can save CLOUT considerable processing by defining synonyms before you start.

When defining synonyms, think about other words that can describe the property measured by each attribute. Think about both nouns and verbs. For example, consider that the attribute *amount* represents money paid for a service. What other nouns have the same meaning? *Fee, revenue, money, earnings, income,* and *cost* are possibilities.

What verbs could represent this property? *Charge, bill, pay, earn,* and *credit* might be used. In addition to the verb itself, CLOUT will recognize regular verb forms. If you define *bill* as a synonym, CLOUT will automatically recognize *billed* and *billing.* CLOUT will not recognize an irregular form such as *"paid."* If *paid* needs to be recognized, it should be added to the list of synonyms. By the way, unlike Mrs. Gazernenplatz in the third grade, CLOUT will accept *payed.*

Specifying Definitions In addition to providing synonyms for column names, you have the option of defining meanings for terms and phrases. To do this, select "Examine or modify dictionary entries" from the main menu. CLOUT will ask you to type the term you wish to define and then to specify the meaning of that term.

There are two types of definitions. For the first type, you are telling CLOUT to substitute one set of words for another. For example, for GTPLAIN, we defined the term *revenue summary* to mean "total sales amount grouped by name." Type:

SHOW THE REVENUE SUMMARY

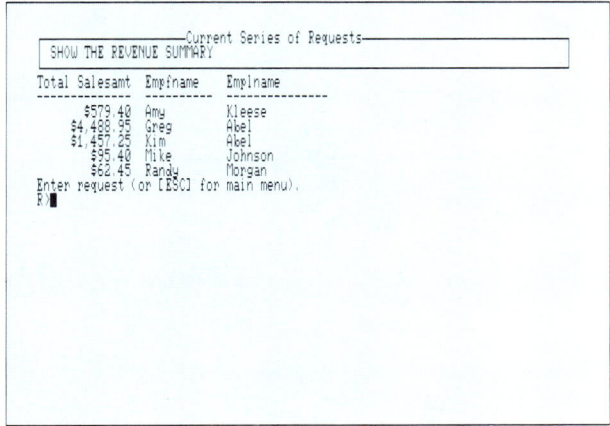

Internally, CLOUT responded by substituting TOTAL SALES AMOUNT GROUPED BY NAME for the words REVENUE SUMMARY.

The second type of definition is more flexible. To understand this type, consider the following problem: Suppose we frequently need to display the average sales amount and standard deviation sales amount for each employee. Sometimes we need the average and standard deviation total sales for Stan, sometimes we need these statistics for Kim, and sometimes we need them for another employee.

To do this, we need a phrase with a variable employee name. For example, we want the phrase STATS FOR XXX to mean AVERAGE SALES AMOUNT AND STANDARD DEVIATION SALES AMOUNT FOR EMPLOYEE FIRST NAME EQ XXX. When we use the definition, we will supply a value for XXX and we want CLOUT to use that value. Thus, when we say STATS FOR GREG, we want CLOUT to substitute AVERAGE SALES AMOUNT AND STANDARD DEVIATION SALES AMOUNT FOR EMPLOYEE FIRST NAME EQ GREG.

To specify definitions of this type, we identify the variable portion with an "at" sign [@] in both the term and in the definition of the term. For the above example, we would define

STATS FOR @A

The name of the variable is arbitrary. We could say STATS FOR @X or STATS FOR @TT. However, we must use whatever name we pick in both the statement of the term to be defined and in the definition of the term.

Once STATS FOR @A is defined, the following commands would be correctly executed:

STATS FOR GREG

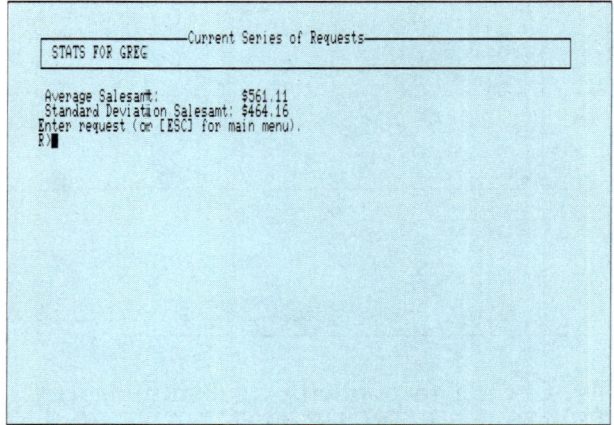

STATS FOR KIM

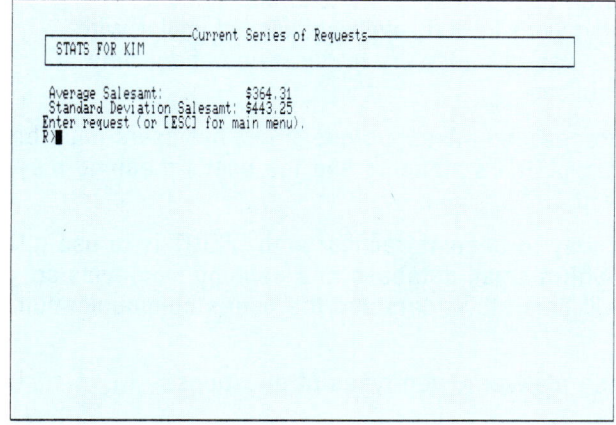

Limiting Database Searches As described above, CLOUT will search the database for unknown terms. To save time and processing, you can limit the total number of rows that CLOUT will search. CLOUT has a default limit of 500 rows. Unless you change this limit, CLOUT will search no more than 500 rows when looking for an undefined term.

To change the default limit, select "Fine tune the query process" from the main menu and then select "Set user parameters." Finally, select "Set limit for unknown search."

You can set the limit to whatever value you think is appropriate. Be aware, however, that setting the value to zero has a special meaning to CLOUT. If the limit is set to zero, CLOUT will search the entire database. If you want the minimum amount of searching, set the limit to 1.

SUMMARY

- CLOUT is an application of artificial intelligence technology. With CLOUT, even people unfamiliar with computers can get answers to questions about data in their databases.

- CLOUT processes ambiguous questions, but users must be aware that CLOUT's meaning and the user's meaning may be different.

- The best way to become familiar with CLOUT is to use it, starting with a small database and defining synonyms so CLOUT will begin to understand the user's communication style.

- CLOUT can answer seven types of questions:
  - Requests to display data
  - Requests to display data with qualifications
  - Queries requiring arithmetic functions
  - Queries requiring processing with subgroups
  - Yes/no questions
  - Multilevel questions
  - Queries involving more than one table

- CLOUT has many special features including the ability to:
  - Present rows having the highest or lowest values of a particular column (top/bottom)
  - Present data sorted in ascending or descending order
  - Search by partial value to find rows with attributes having a specified character or character string
  - Understand fuzzy values
  - Associate column names with *Who, Where, and When*
  - Limit searches to "exact match"
  - Construct start-up files for occasional or unsophisticated users
  - Help the user at any point

- CLOUT will persistently attempt to answer your questions, even if it means searching the entire database. To help CLOUT communicate efficiently, users can:
  - Get acquainted with CLOUT slowly, starting with a small database
  - Phrase questions clearly and logically
  - Define synonyms before asking questions

- Specify definitions for terms and phrases being used
- Limit the number of rows for CLOUT to search

REVIEW QUESTIONS

The questions in this section assume the following database:

CUSTOMER (Cust#, Custname, Custaddr, Custphon)
ORDER (Order#, Cust#, Sp#, Ord-date, Amt)
SALEPRSN (Sp#, Spname, Store)

14.1
Show a valid natural language query to display data.

14.2
Show a valid natural language query to display data with qualifications.

14.3
Show a valid natural language query which will require one or more of the arithmetic functions.

14.4
Show a valid natural language query that will require processing of subgroups.

14.5
Show a valid example of a yes/no query.

14.6
Show a valid natural language query that is split into two questions.

14.7
Show a valid natural language query involving more than one table.

14.8
Show examples of queries on this data using the following CLOUT features:
a. Present rows having the highest or lowest values of a particular column (top/bottom)
b. Present data sorted in ascending or descending order
c. Search by partial value to find rows with attributes having a specified character or character string
d. Understand fuzzy values
e. Associate column names with *Who, Where, and When*
f. Limit searches to exact match

14.9
Suppose you frequently need to know the total and average sales for a particular customer. Show an example of a CLOUT definition that will provide the data you want for a customer, say, Jones, when you type: SALES FOR JONES

CHAPTER 15

Database Processing on Local Area Networks

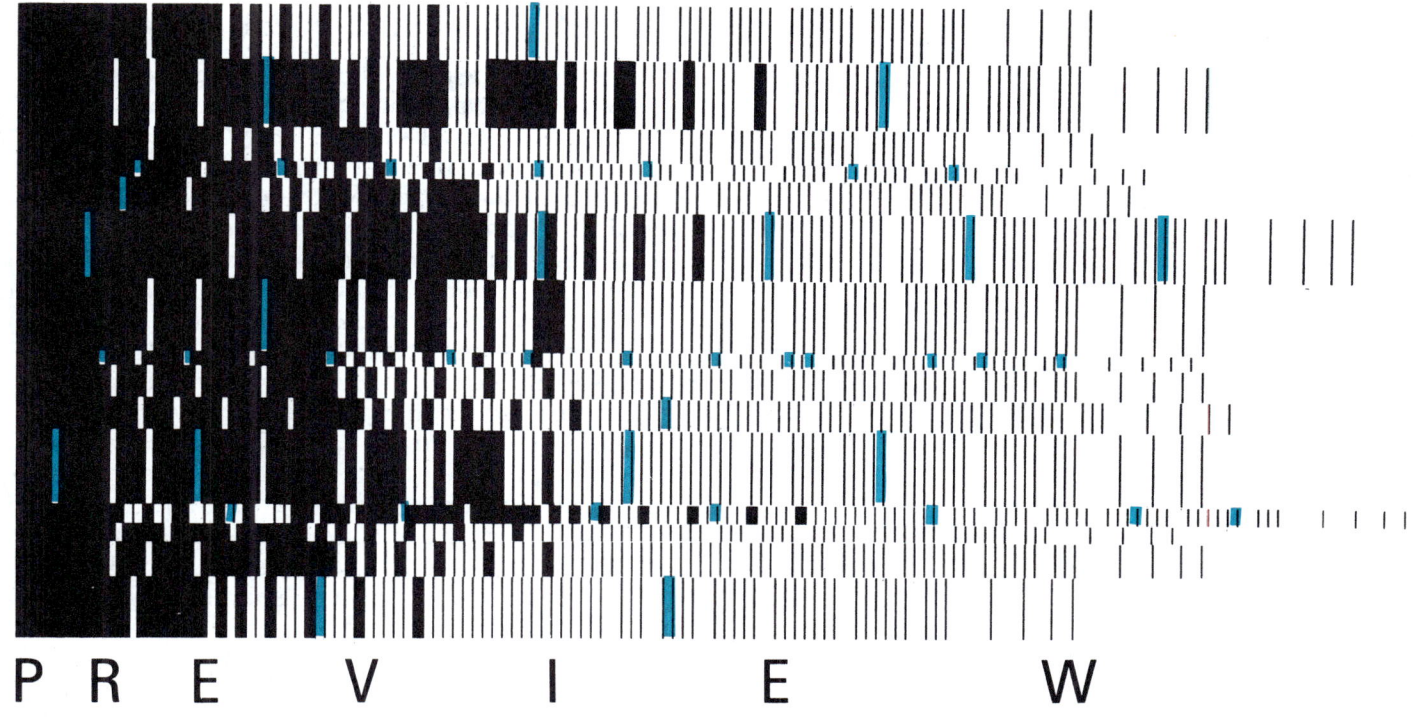

P R E V I E W

This chapter discusses the design and implementation of effective local area network (LAN) database applications. By *effective,* we mean systems that realize the benefits of LAN processing while avoiding the pitfalls. First we will discuss fundamental concepts of database processing on local area networks. Then we present design considerations when building database applications on LANs. Next, we will describe the design of a multi-user database application for Great Plains Music and Video. The last two sections concern implementation. First, the characteristics of R:base 5000 Multi-user, a version of R:base 5000 for use on LANS, will be described, and finally, the implementation of a multi-user database for Great Plains will be presented.

DATABASES AND LOCAL AREA NETWORKS

A local area network is a collection of microcomputers connected via short distance communication lines. Although the definition of *short distance* varies according to the brand of local area network in use, a good rule of thumb is that the micros on the network must reside within the same (regular-sized) building.

There are two primary benefits of local area networks. First, such nets allow users to *communicate* with one another. An account clerk at one micro, for example, can send messages to another clerk on the network. The second benefit is *resource sharing*. For example, a group of users can buy an expensive laser printer and connect it to the LAN. To use the printer, the users transmit documents from their local computers, across the network, to the laser printer. In this way, one such printer can serve the needs of a group of users. Other types of hardware, such as plotters and large disk drives, can also be shared in this way.

In addition to hardware, databases can also be shared across a LAN. Consider the loan department of a small bank. The department has three clerks who need to know the names and other data about customers having loans with the bank. Although each of the clerks could keep a complete copy of all customer data on his or her own micro, this action would result in much duplicated data.

As we have mentioned, data duplication has two major disadvantages. First, it wastes file space. Second, and far more important, data duplication results in integrity problems. Whenever a customer moves, his or her address would need to be changed on three databases. Invariably, the system will fail at some point, and one or more of the changes will not be made. When this occurs, the bank has a data integrity problem.

An alternative for the bank is to store customer data in a single database and allow the clerks to access the data across a local area network. This strategy will eliminate the data duplication and can result in an effective and useful system. Unfortunately, sharing a database on a LAN also introduces new problems and pitfalls.

Local Area Network Architecture

An example of a local area network is shown in Figure 15–1. This network has four computers, each with its own disk capacity. In this network, the computers can send, receive, or relay messages. Relaying is necessary when the computers are not adjacent to each other in the network. For computer A to send a message to

FIGURE 15–1
Example of local area network

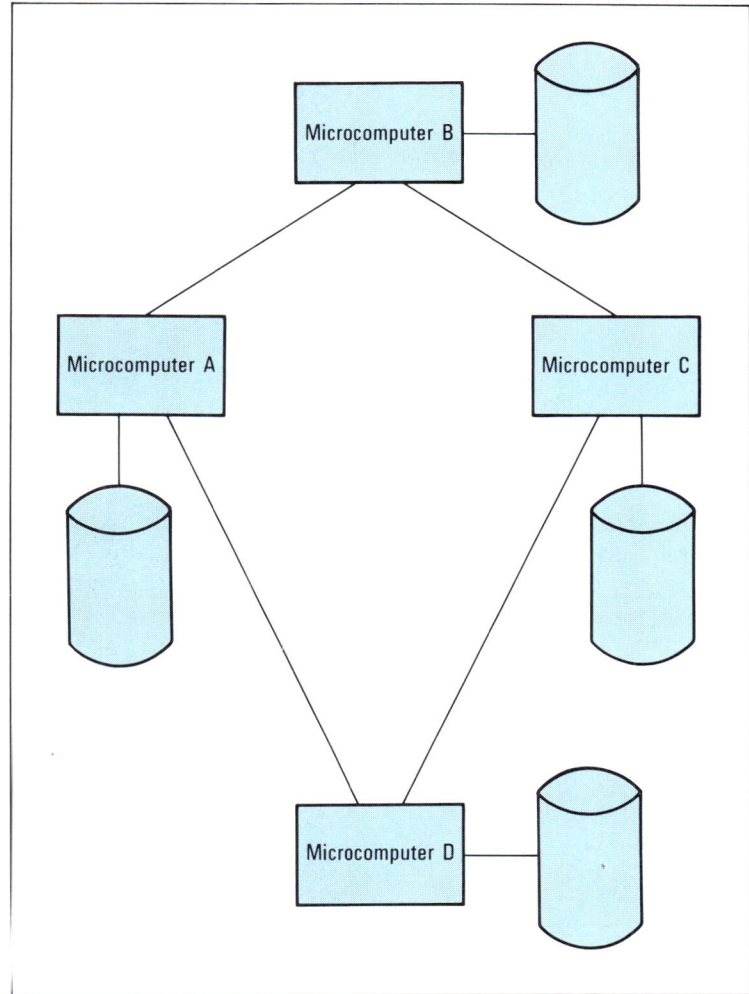

computer C, for example, it first sends the message to B, and B relays the message to C. (Alternatively, computer D could relay the message as well.)

Figure 15–2 depicts memory within these computers. Three programs are shown: an application program (AP), the network operating system (NOS), and the local operating system (OS). The application program calls on the network operating system to send or receive messages across the network. It calls on the local operating system for all other operating system functions, such as displaying data on the terminal screen, processing data on local disk or other devices, and the like.

FIGURE 15–2

Example of software in local area network system. AP = application program. NOS = network operating system. OS = operating system.

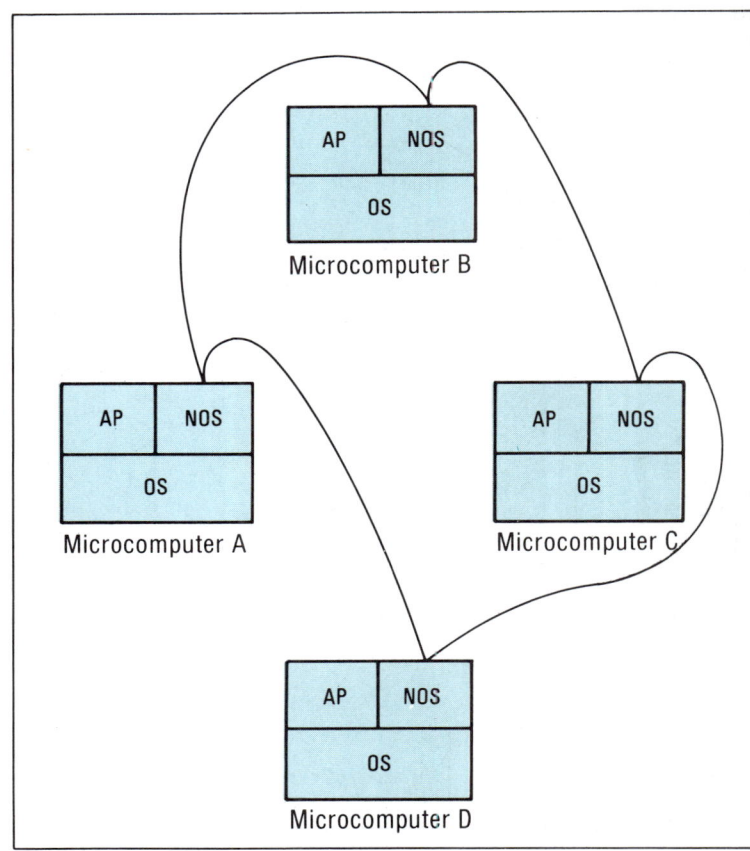

The network operating systems communicate with one another. They send, receive, and relay messages. They perform error-checking to ensure they receive complete messages. They determine which nodes are active and which are not, and so forth.

Just as there are a variety of local operating systems (MS/DOS, concurrent CP/M, XENIX), so, too, there are a variety of network operating systems (DOS 3.1, 3COM/3+ or Ethershare, Novell NetWare). The processing methodology of these operating systems varies; not all of them have equivalent features and functions. Some are faster than others, some provide more services than others, and some are more popular than others. Since knowledge of the specifics of network operation is unnecessary for the design and implementation of effective database applications, however, we will not consider the subject in this book. See reference 8 in the bibliography for more information.

The computers in a local area network operate as co-operating colleagues. No computer has control over another. Rather, each computer is independent. When it receives a message, it can process the message or not. Furthermore, note that the microcomputers operate simultaneously. While computer A is processing a spreadsheet, for example, computer B can be processing a database application, *at the same instant in time.*

Database Processing on Local Area Networks

Figure 15–3 depicts a typical local area network with database applications. Node A is running a DBMS processing a local database. Node B is running a spreadsheet application, while node C is running a DBMS that is processing the database located on node D. Finally, node D is running the DBMS that is processing the shared database.

In this scenario, neither application on nodes A or B needs access to the network, and all of their operating system interaction will be with the local operating system. The applications on nodes C and D, however, will call on the network operating system to perform input and output on the shared database.

It is clear from Figure 15–3 why node C needs to access the network operating system for data. You may wonder, however, why node D needs access to the network operating system. After all, the database is located on node D's disk and could be processed via the local operating system. The answer to this question is that the network operating system will coordinate node D's requests with those from node C. If node D were to access the database files directly through the local operating system, these requests could interfere with requests from node C.

Database Processing on Concurrent Operating Systems

The architecture shown in Figure 15–3 is not the only way of providing multi-user database processing. Figure 15–4 shows another style that was first developed for mainframe and minicomputers. In this alternative architecture, the microcomputer which maintains the database acts as a centralized master node. It controls all of the processing of the database. The other microcomputers become slaves of this master and submit requests for processing against the database. The master decides if and when to honor the requests.

The advantage of the concurrent architecture is control. The master computer knows what processing is under way and can order processing to minimize con-

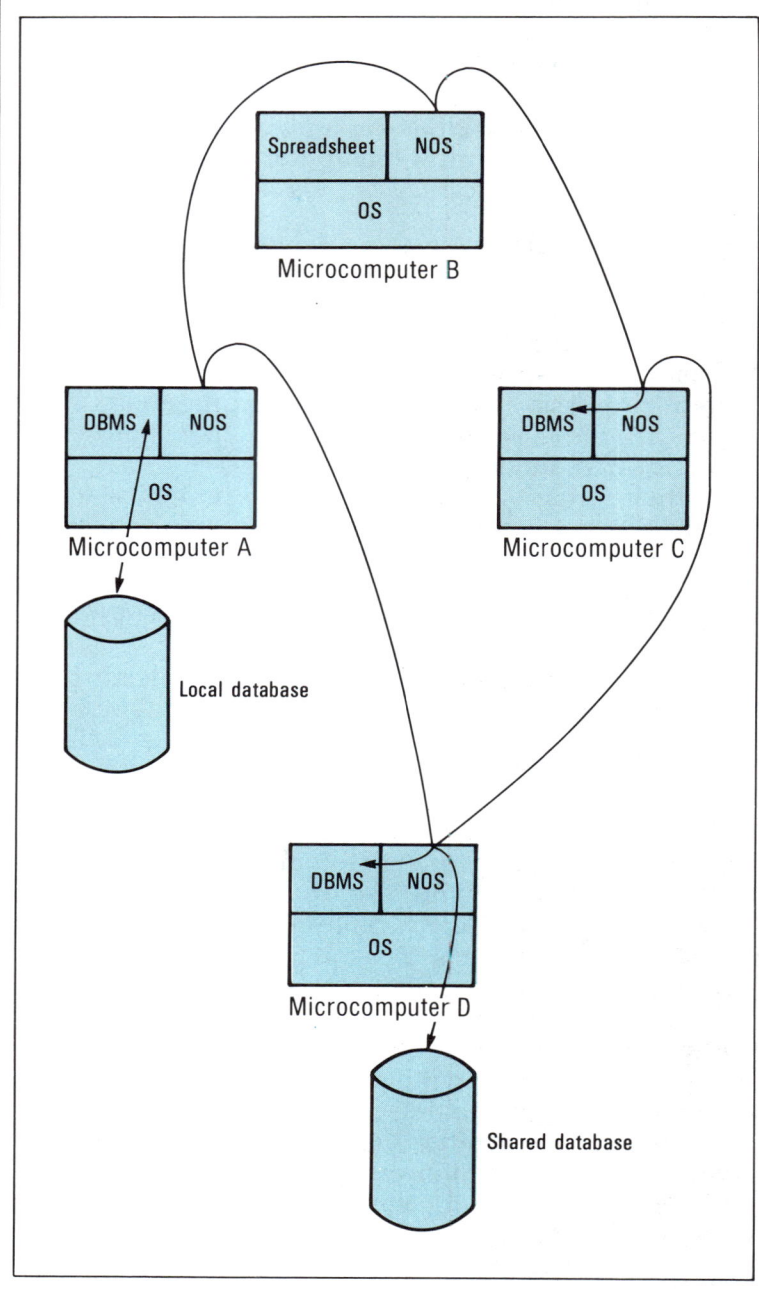

FIGURE 15–3

Sharing a database on a local area network

flict. The disadvantage of this architecture is performance. The master computer can become a bottleneck: if more requests are submitted than it can handle, some of the micros will need to wait. This waiting will

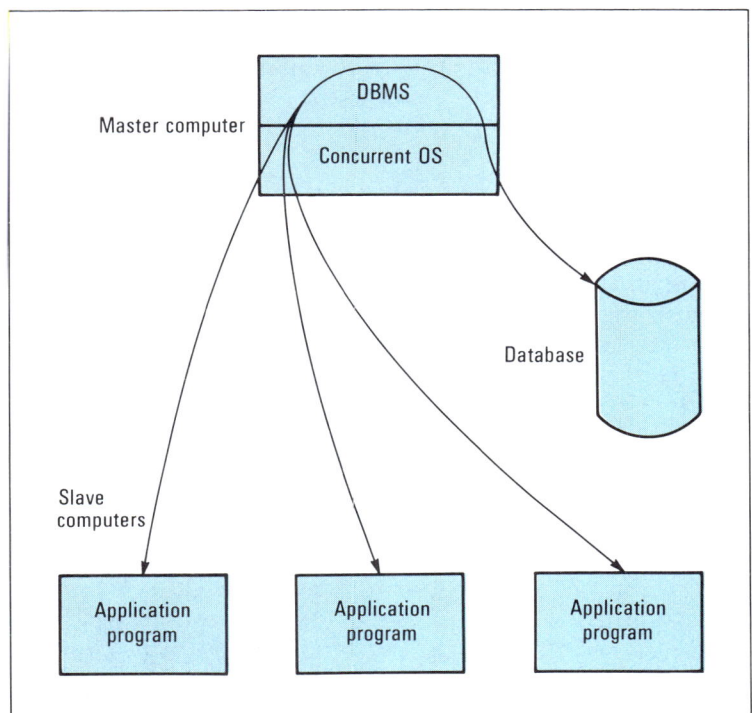

FIGURE 15–4
Database processing on concurrent operating system

occur even though the micro slaves possess sufficient capability to process the database themselves. In essence, this architecture turns the microcomputers into terminals. The CPUs of the micros are underutilized.

Such processing has been done for many years on mainframe and minicomputers. The technology is well known and understood. We will not consider it further in this book. See reference 12 in the bibliography for more information.

DESIGN CONSIDERATIONS FOR DATABASE APPLICATIONS ON LANs

In this section we will consider characteristics of LAN-based database applications. First we will describe one of the great pitfalls of multi-user processing, the *concurrent update problem*. Then we will discuss alternative strategies for maintaining a shared database. Next backup and recovery procedures will be described, and finally we will illustrate the need for database administration.

The Concurrent Update Problem

To understand the concurrent update problem, consider the database application illustrated in Figure 15-3. Suppose that this application maintains loan processing records for a bank. Further suppose that both nodes C and D change the database. In particular, assume that both nodes need to change the record for customer 1234: node C wants to change the customer's address and node D wants to update the customer's account balance.

To effect these changes, assume node C reads customer 1234's record and then node D reads the same record. The user at node C then keys in the new customer address and sends the changed record back across the network to node D, where it is written to the database. Next, the user at node D keys in the new customer balance and has it written to the database as well. Both changes have been made, but, unfortunately, only one of them has been recorded on the database. Node C's change has been lost!

What happened? When node D wrote its record to the database, it did not have the current record, since node C had changed the customer's address. That address change was overwritten by node D.

Certainly, a chain of events like the one described here is rare. Seldom do two nodes attempt to change the same record at exactly the same time. Unfortunately, rare or not, this chain of events cannot be allowed to happen. If it is allowed, then over time, the database will be filled with errors, and the users will lose confidence in it.

A variety of methods have been devised for avoiding or preventing the concurrent update problem. By *avoiding* we mean designing the system so that two users cannot update the same record. By *preventing* we mean that when two users attempt to update the same record, the DBMS will not allow the update. Consider each of these methods in more detail.

Avoiding the Concurrent Update Problem There are several methods for avoiding the concurrent update problem. The first, and simplest, is to restrict updating to a *single node*. Other nodes on the network may only read the database. This strategy can be implemented in two ways. First, users can take turns with the computer which is authorized to make updates. They can either wait in line on a first come, first served basis or they can agree on a schedule.

An alternative approach is to collect all requests for changes to the database into a *batch*. These requests can be sorted or otherwise organized and then processed. One person can be trained to make updates or several users can participate. Further, the batch processing can be scheduled to take place at night or at other times when reading activity is low.

A second method for avoiding the concurrent update problem is to update the database *sequentially*. For the example in Figure 15–3, node C could be authorized to update the database in the morning while node D could be authorized to make updates in the afternoon. When more than two nodes are processing the database, of course, the schedule would need to be more complicated. Sequential updating works best with a formal schedule. It is generally too inefficient for users to wander around the office trying to find out if anyone else is updating the database. Even if the DBMS can inform a user that someone else is updating, it will be difficult to know when that person is finished, or if someone else is waiting. Thus, sequential updating is generally scheduled.

A third way of avoiding concurrent update is *partitioned processing*. With this method, the database is divided into pieces and batch or sequential updates are processed against each piece. For example, suppose the loan processing database has three tables: CUSTOMER, ACCOUNT, and HISTORY. The database could be broken into three pieces, one table in each piece. Using batch-updating strategy, a single computer could be authorized to update each table. Although updates would occur concurrently, they would not interfere with one another since the updates would be against different tables.

Partitioning the database by table is infeasible for some applications. For the bank, for example, if customer balances are stored in the CUSTOMER table, then an update to ACCOUNT will necessitate an update to CUSTOMER. For this situation, a different partitioning will need to be found. One possibility is to partition the database by account number: accounts with numbers from 1000 to 5000 could form a partition, accounts with numbers from 5001 to 10,000 could form a second partition, and so forth. With this method, updates to both CUSTOMER and ACCOUNT could be allowed, but conflict among concurrent updates would be avoided since no two users would be updating accounts within the same range.

Preventing the Concurrent Update Problem All methods of *preventing* the concurrent update problem involve some form of *resource locking*. The basic notion is this: a lock is placed on data to be changed before it is read. The lock prevents other users from reading and updating the locked data. When the update is completed, the lock is released.

Consider an example. Suppose a user wants to change the address for customer 1234. First, a lock is placed on that customer's data. If, when the lock is requested, another user has that data, then the user requesting the lock is forced to wait. When the data becomes available, the lock is granted. The user then makes the change to the customer's address and releases the lock.

Lock levels Locking strategies vary in several ways. First, they vary by *level*. Some DBMS products place very broad locks; a lock against the entire database is an example. A more narrow lock is to lock an entire table. A smaller lock is against a single row of a table, and the smallest lock is against a column within a row.

The level of lock allowed is determined by the capabilities of the DBMS. Some products allow only broad locks, while others allow more narrow ones. In general, the narrower the lock, the less lock contention (when one user must wait for another to finish). In turn, less lock contention usually means more throughput. This is not always true, however. The overhead of placing and releasing many narrow locks may generate so much work for the DBMS and produce so much traffic on the network that throughput actually goes down. The specific result depends on the DBMS, the network, and the application.

Lock source Another way locks vary is by *source*. Some DBMS products invoke locks automatically on behalf of the user. Other products require the user (or programmer) to invoke the lock. Still others allow both. Locks which are invoked automatically are called *implicit locks* while those which are manually invoked are called *explicit locks*.

Obviously, it is easier for the user or programmer if the locks are invoked implicitly. If this is to be done, however, the DBMS must invoke a lock anytime it appears that a user might change a record. Further, the lock must be held until the DBMS can definitely determine that the user has finished any update activity. This strategy necessitates many locks that are held a long time, and performance can be a problem. Therefore, explicit locks are sometimes preferred. The choice regarding which is better depends on the application.

Lock type There are two fundamental types of locks. *Exclusive locks* prevent access of any type. No reads, adds, changes, or deletions are allowed when an exclusive lock is in place. *Shared locks* prevent adds, changes, or deletions, but allow reads to continue to occur. As with other lock characteristics, the proper choice depends on the application. Locking characteristics are summarized in Figure 15–5.

The deadly embrace Resource locking creates the potential for a problem often called the *deadly embrace.* The problem occurs as follows: User A places a lock on a record, say, account 123. User B places a lock on a different record, say, invoice ABC. User A now decides she needs invoice ABC. Accordingly, she requests a lock for that record, and is placed in a waiting line (sometimes called the *wait state* or a *waiting queue*). Now, for the coup de grace, user B decides that he needs account record 123. Accordingly, he requests a lock for that record and is also placed in the wait state. At this point, user A holds record 123 and is waiting for record ABC while user B holds record ABC and is waiting for record 123. This waiting game will go on until the computer wears out or doomsday, whichever occurs first.

There are a variety of solutions for this situation. Some rely on avoiding the deadly embrace while others cure it by eliminating one of the user's requests. The specifics of this are beyond the scope of this book, however. You should be aware that it can occur, and when you develop a multi-user application, be certain you understand how your particular DBMS will solve this problem. See reference 12 in the bibliography for more information.

Backup and Recovery

Multi-user systems pose special problems for backup and recovery. For a single-user system, backup can be accomplished by periodically saving the database files and keeping track of the changes made since the last backup. When a failure occurs, the database is restored from the saved files and the changes are reapplied to the database.

For a multi-user system, the situation is not so straightforward. The problem concerns ordering. How can we be certain that the changes are reapplied in the correct order? For example, suppose that a company keeps a parts inventory on a multi-user database. Users access the inventory data, determine if parts are available, and, if so, reduce the parts in inventory and produce shipping documents. Suppose that on a given morning, users A and B both want the same last widget from inventory. Both users attempt to place locks on the widget record and one of them is first. Assume it is A. Now, later in the day, the database fails; perhaps the problem is a hard disk crash. The

FIGURE 15–5
Summary of database locking facilities

- Lock levels
  Database
  Relation
  Row
  Data-item
- Lock sources
  Explicit
  Implicit
- Lock types
  Shared
  Exclusive

disk is repaired or replaced and the database is restored from the saved files. The users begin reprocessing their workload. This time, however, assume that B gets the lock on the widget record before A (this can happen since A and B won't process their workloads at precisely the same speed they did in the morning). In this case, the database will indicate that user B's customer got the widget, but the physical shipping documents prepared in the morning will indicate that A got the widget.

This may seem like a trivial problem. After all, won't A and B talk with one another? They will, but they will also be busy reprocessing many documents. Furthermore, out of the dozens or hundreds of documents to reprocess, A and B won't know which ones conflict.

Unfortunately, at the present time, microcomputer DBMS products do not offer much help. In the mainframe environment, backup and recovery systems have grown to be very sophisticated. Customers such as banking institutions have insisted on it. Mainframe products provide automatic rollback, rollforward, transaction journaling, and so forth (see reference 12). Ultimately such technology will be incorporated into microcomputer DBMS products as well. Meanwhile, designers of multi-user systems need to be aware of this problem, and build systems accordingly.

For example, consider the problems of users A and B and the inventory application. A and B need to know the order in which documents were processed and recorded in the database. To do this, their application should produce a journal of transactions. This journal shows, in time sequence, when transactions were started, when they were finished, and what their outcome was. During recovery, A and B can use the journal to guide their recovery actions.

Over the next few years, DBMS backup and recovery support will undoubtedly improve. Meanwhile, multi-user database application designers must be aware of the need for transaction logs and other measures to restore a database to the same condition it had prior to a failure. It is too late to think of these matters after a database has been ruined! See Chapter 12 for additional information.

Database Administration

Multi-user database applications have a particular need for strong database administration. Users of such applications must share their database, and since time immemorial, when groups of people are required to share *anything*, problems develop. These applications are more likely to be successful if someone is identified as having responsibility for database administration, and, as summarized in Figure 15–6, if that person exercises strong control in three areas: processing, backup and recovery, and structure change.

Processing Control In the previous section we discussed problems that can occur in multi-user applications. All of the methods for avoiding concurrent update problems involved the scheduling of computers and processing. For these methods to be effective, the schedules and processing limitations must be adhered to. Little is gained if procedures and schedules that are carefully designed to avoid update conflicts are ignored.

One of the functions of the database administrator is to ensure that such procedures are followed. When they are not followed, the database administrator must take corrective action. Users may need further instruction to explain the procedures, or they may need to be convinced of the necessity of having such procedures. Perhaps the procedures are inappropriate or ineffective for some users. If so, such procedures may need to be changed. The point is that someone must ensure procedures are followed. Otherwise, people being people, the procedures will gradually fall into disuse and the integrity of the database will be lost.

Backup and Recovery Control As indicated in the previous section, backup and recovery for multi-user applications is crucial. Backup procedures cannot be allowed to become lax, and someone must be thoroughly trained to supervise recovery processing. These functions fall to the database administrator.

If there is a long time between failures (which there should be), the need for backup data will not be apparent. Users will tend to ignore their backup responsibilities. The database administrator must ensure that this does not occur. He or she must observe backup preparation and ask the users to produce records indicating that backups have been made. This may seem obvious or unimportant, but many a group has been caught off-guard by failure.

The database administrator is the group's expert on recovery. After a failure, the DBA will need to participate and supervise recovery processing. He or she ensures that standard procedures are followed. Additionally, the correct course of action is often unclear and the DBA has the ultimate say in what is to be done. Further, after a recovery operation, the DBA

FIGURE 15–6
DBA responsibilities for local area network applications

- Processing control
  Batch
  Sequential
  Partitioned
- Backup and recovery
  Manage backup activities
  Supervise recovery
  Change procedures as necessary
- Structure changes
  Coordinate changes
  Notify users
  Resolve conflicts

has responsibility for modifying the standard backup and recovery procedures for greater effectiveness.

Structure Control As the database is used, application requirements will change. The business may change, new products or services may be developed, or management may alter the way in which business is transacted. Further, the users will identify new and improved ways of accomplishing their jobs. As this occurs, there will be a need to change both application programs and the database structure.

Changes to application programs are generally easier than changes to the database. A change to such a program will affect only the users of that program. A change to the database structure could well affect all users.

As mentioned in Chapter 12, the DBA is the focal point for changes to the database structure. He or she notifies all users of an impending change so that they have a chance to object to or, at least, adapt to the change. Adding a new column to a table, for example, may necessitate changes to screens and reports. The users need a chance to make and adapt to these changes before the database structure is actually altered.

Microcomputer DBMS products provide great flexibility. Although this flexibility is often welcome, it can also be a curse. In a multi-user application, it simply will not do for one user to make a change to the database structure without coordinating the change with others. The DBA serves as the focal point for this coordination.

A MULTI-USER DESIGN FOR GREAT PLAINS MUSIC AND VIDEO UNLIMITED

To illustrate the design and implementation of a multi-user database, consider the situation of Great Plains Music and Video. Suppose that Great Plains' business grows to the extent that one microcomputer is simply inadequate. Great Plains needs the computer to process sales transactions, and, during critical business periods, one keyboard is inadequate. Further, during business hours, a clerk needs to change inventory data as shipments arrive, orders are written, and products are discontinued. Customer data also needs to be modified both during and outside of business hours. Thus, Great Plains decides to acquire and install a local area network with three microcomputers. Their system is illustrated in Figure 15–7.

According to this design, one of the computers

FIGURE 15-7
Local area network system for Great Plains Video

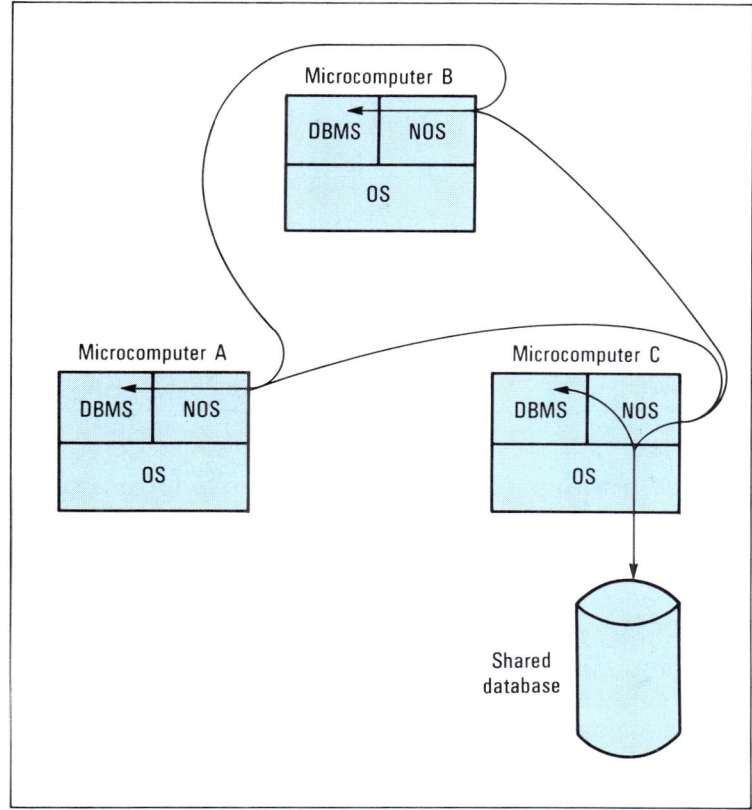

(node A) will have a 30 megabyte hard disk and will manage the database. This computer will also be used to process the database during periods of high sales volume. Since this computer will have both workloads, it will have a faster CPU than the other two machines. The other computers will process the shared database via the local area network.

The design for Great Plains' database was developed in Chapter 5. For convenience, the final design shown in Figure 5-8 is repeated here in Figure 15-8. Observe that there are five different tables: CUSTOMER, INVENTORY, SALE, COMPONENT/SALE, and EMPLOYEE.

The first task for the designers of the multi-user system is to determine what type of concurrent access is required. The designers interviewed Great Plains personnel and arrived at the conclusions summarized in Figure 15-9. The EMPLOYEE relation contains very sensitive data, such as salaries and total wages. Man-

FIGURE 15-8

Database structure for Great Plains

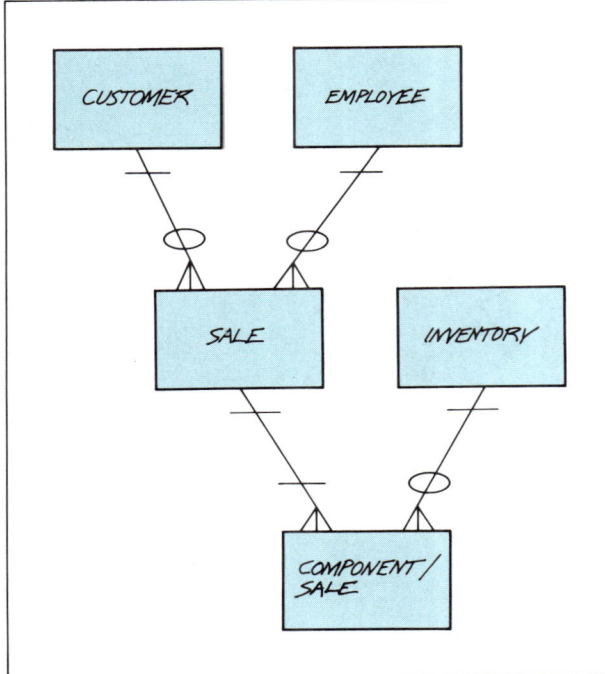

CUSTOMER (<u>Customer identification number</u>, Customer name, Customer address, Customer phone)

INVENTORY (<u>Item number</u>, Item description, Units, Quantity on hand, Cost, Price)

SALE (<u>Sales identification number</u>, Customer identification number, Social security number, Date)

COMPONENT/SALE (<u>Item number</u>, <u>Sales identification number</u>, Quantity sold, Sales price, Sales amount)

EMPLOYEE (<u>Social security number</u>, Employee name, Hire date, Salary, Commission rate, Salary review date, Marital status, Exemptions, Total wages)

FIGURE 15-9

Summary of processing restrictions for Great Plains shared database application. NAV = not available on LAN. SCHEDULE = single-user update according to a schedule. LOCK = concurrent update; control via locking. NAL = not allowed.

	Employee	Customer	Inventory	Sale and Component Sale
READ	NAV	ALL	ALL	ALL
ADD	NAV	ALL	SCHEDULE	ALL
CHANGE	NAV	LOCK	SCHEDULE	NAL
DELETE	NAV	SCHEDULE	SCHEDULE	NAL

agement wants only a few individuals to have access to this data. When the system only involved one micro, this was easy to control visually. With several micros, such visual control will be difficult, if not impossible, and management decided that it did not want the EMPLOYEE data available on the LAN system. Consequently, the design calls for all EMPLOYEE data to be unavailable. Management will process this data in the single-user mode when the network is inactive during nonbusiness hours.

With regard to CUSTOMER, all micros need unrestricted access to read, add, and change data during sales processing. Both read and add can be performed concurrently without problem. This is not the case for concurrent changes, however. The designers decide to control these changes by preventing concurrent update with locks. (The designers already know that Great Plains will use R:base 5000 Multi-user and that this product will support such locking. If this were unknown, the designers would need to find out or leave the control methodology open until implementation.)

Management wants to be very careful about deleting CUSTOMER data. They want to be sure all accounts are fully paid and that there are no special reasons (public relations, future marketing, and so forth) for keeping a customer's data on file. Therefore, management decides that only they will delete customer data, and they will do so by gathering deletions into batches and processing them during off-business hours.

Concurrent processing of INVENTORY data is different from that for CUSTOMER. All employees are allowed to read this data, but only Great Plains' inventory clerks are allowed to add, change, or delete it. Further, for consistency's sake, the clerks must have control over the entire table when they are making changes. This is necessary for implementing actions such as changing quantities on hand. If two or more products are being ordered, all changes need to be completed before any access to the INVENTORY data is allowed. Thus, concurrent access for INVENTORY will be controlled via exclusive locks *on the entire table.*

Changes to SALE and COMPONENT/SALE are always made at the same time. Recall that when a sale is recorded, a new SALE row is created and that new COMPONENT/SALE rows are created for each item in the sale. Thus, the combination of the new SALE row with the corresponding new COMPONENT/SALE rows represents a sales invoice.

As shown in Figure 15–9, all employees are allowed to read and add new SALE and COMPONENT/SALE rows. There will be no conflicts due to concurrent processing since all sales identification numbers are assigned by the system; every addition will involve different rows. Additionally, to provide adequate accounting control, the designers decided that neither changes nor deletions would be allowed for these tables. When a legitimate adjustment needs to be made to an invoice, this will be done by creating a second invoice that corrects the error. In accounting terminology, such invoices are called *compensating transactions.* Controls such as this prevent employees from temptations such as eliminating the invoices of friends or relatives.

We will now consider the implementation of this design using R:base 5000 Multi-user.

IMPLEMENTING A MULTI-USER DATABASE WITH R:BASE 5000 MULTI-USER

R:base 5000 Multi-user is a special version of R:base 5000 designed for use on local area networks. The major difference between the standard and multi-user products is that Multi-user includes features and functions for concurrency control. (A second difference is a legal one. The license for a single-user system prevents its use on a local area network. This restriction is intended to prevent organizations from installing the single-user product on a network server and sharing that single copy on several machines. In contrast, the license for the multi-user product specifically allows such usage.)

Figure 15–10 summarizes the locking capabilities of

FIGURE 15–10

Summary of R:base 5000 locking

	DATABASE	TABLE		DATA-ITEM
EXPLICIT LOCKS		SET LOCK COMMAND		
IMPLICIT LOCKS	PACK UNLOAD	Structure change commands EDIT ALL DELETE ROWS	CHANGE ASSIGN	EDIT USING

R:base 5000. The columns of this table represent three lock levels: database, table, and data-item. The rows represent explicit and implicit lock types.

Explicit Locks

As you can see from this figure, R:base 5000 Multi-user allows only one type of explicit lock: a lock at the table level. This lock is invoked by the R:base command:

R> SET LOCK table[s] — name ON [or OFF]

Valid examples of this command are:

R> SET LOCK EMPLOYEE ON
R> SET LOCK EMPLOYEE, INVENTORY ON
R> SET LOCK FOR EMPLOYEE, INVENTORY OFF

As you can see, more than one table can be locked at a time. Since this is the case, two users can put themselves in the deadly embrace. An example scenario is: User A locks table R1; user B locks table R2; user A attempts to lock table R2; user B attempts to lock table R1. After a certain period of time (which can be set by the user, but the particulars are beyond the scope of this text), R:base will note that the users have been inactive and will give them a chance to abort their second lock requests. Unless the users are malingering, one of them will eventually give up and the embrace will be broken.

With this type of locking scheme, there are two easy

ways to prevent the deadly embrace. First, users can lock all the tables they want in a single request. If this is done, no lock will be granted until all are granted. Thus, user A should lock both R1 and R2 in the same request. If user A has R1 and later decides R2 is needed, he or she should first release R1 and then issue the lock for R1 and R2. When R1 is released, user B will be given control of R1 and will finish processing. Then user A will be given control of both R1 and R2.

A second way to prevent the deadly embrace is for the users to agree to invoke all locks in a certain order. For example, they could agree always to invoke the locks in alphabetical order according to table name. Thus, R1 must be locked before R2, CUSTOMER must be locked before INVENTORY, and so forth. If either of these strategies is followed, no deadly embrace can occur.

Implicit Locks

As shown in Figure 15–10, R:base 5000 provides a variety of implicit locks. When either of the commands PACK or RELOAD is used, the entire database is locked. This is done because these two commands reformat the entire database, and they must be completed before any other activity can commence. Further, the DEFINE command will also cause the entire database to be locked, at least until R:base can determine what changes will be made to the database structure.

A table will be implicitly locked by R:base when any command is issued that changes the table structure. For example, the CHANGE COLUMN command will cause the whole table to be locked until the change is complete. Additionally, changes that involve more than one row at a time will also cause the entire table to be locked. Examples of this are the EDIT ALL (for browsing) and DELETE ROWS commands.

The CHANGE and ASSIGN commands are shown midway between the Table and Data-Item columns in Figure 15–10. The reason for this is that both of these commands will lock the entire table when starting their operation. Once started, the lock on the entire table will be modified so that CHANGE, ASSIGN, and EDIT USING can be processed concurrently.

Locking with EDIT USING is different from locks we have described so far. Recall that the EDIT USING (a form) command is used to display a single row of a relation for the purpose of changing it. When the command is issued, R:base will display the named form on the screen and fill in the fields with values of the row selected by the user. An example of this command is:

R> EDIT USING EMP-FORM WHERE EMP-NUM EQ 12345

When a form is defined, the user specifies the table to be displayed and edited. For this example, when form EMP-FORM was defined, the user specified table EMPLOYEE. Thus, the command above will cause R:base to display the form named EMP-FORM and fill in the blanks with the values of employee 12345 in the EMPLOYEE table.

When EDIT USING is issued, R:base Multi-user does not actually lock the row. Instead, it sends the row to the user for editing and keeps a copy of this data. When the user has made changes and is ready to store those changes in the database, R:base reads the row and compares the current values of any data-items changed by the user with the values of those data-items which it originally sent to the user. If the values are the same, then no other user has changed those items and the row is written to the database. If the values are different, then someone else has changed the data-items while the user was editing. In this case, the row is returned to the user with the message that someone else changed the same data-items and the user is given another chance to edit.

Consider an example. User A issues the EDIT USING command shown above. When it is issued, R:base on user A's computer obtains employee 12345's data from the shared database. It sends one copy to the screen for editing and keeps a second copy. When user A finishes editing, R:base reads the data from the shared database a second time. It compares the current values of employee 12345's data with the values that were sent to user A. If any of the values which user A has changed have been changed by someone else while user A was editing, then R:base sends the row back to user A and notifies her that someone else changed the same data-items. User A can then make her changes again, or make some other changes.

This scheme protects against losses due to the concurrent update problem while at the same time allowing maximum throughput. With concurrency control at the data-item level, conflicts will seldom occur. At the same time, this scheme involves only a few locks, so locking overhead is low.

With this introduction to R:base Multi-user, we will now consider the implementation of Multi-user at Great Plains.

A MULTI-USER DATABASE APPLICATION AT GREAT PLAINS MUSIC AND VIDEO

Except for considerations regarding locking, R:base 5000 Multi-user operates identically to R:base 5000. All commands, forms, reports, and command files that work with R:base 5000 work with the multi-user product as well. Since this is so, the application which has been developed for Great Plains in earlier chapters can be carried over to the multi-user database. The only changes that need be made concern locking and concurrency control; we must implement the processing constraints summarized in Figure 15–9.

So far in this chapter, we have been using the table names developed for the database design. As explained previously, R:base table names must be eight characters or less, so the names developed in the design had to be altered. In this section we will switch to the R:base names developed in Chapters 6 through 10.

EMPLOYEE Processing

EMPLOYEE data is to be unavailable on the multi-user database. This could be accomplished in one of two ways. First, EMPLOYEE data could simply be removed from the database and stored in a database of its own. This second database would not be made available on the LAN. Another alternative is to place both READ and MODIFY passwords on the EMPLOYEE table. The first alternative is more secure but also more cumbersome. In this case, Great Plains management decided to place passwords on the EMPLOYEE table. This was done using the process described in Chapter 13.

CUSTOMER Processing

Considering the CUSTOMER table, R:base will automatically implement the desired processing of READ, ADD, and CHANGE commands. By default, READ will be allowed for all users. Adding poses no problem since the users will be adding different customers rows. Control over changes will be handled via the EDIT USING command. As described in the last section, if users attempt to concurrently change the same data-item, R:base will detect this situation and require the changes to be rekeyed.

Observe, too, that the CHANGE and ASSIGN commands can be used to make changes in this table. This would most likely be done in a command file. If these commands are used, however, performance on the network may suffer since CHANGE and ASSIGN lock the entire table during a portion of their processing.

One approach for Great Plains would be to try command files that include CHANGE or ASSIGN and observe performance. If performance is unacceptable, the command files could be eliminated and all changes implemented using only the EDIT USING command.

Unfortunately, R:base does not provide a facility to implement the constraint that only management can make CUSTOMER deletions. A MODIFY password is too restrictive; it would prevent additions and changes as well. Further, if the users employ the EDIT USING command, one of the options is to delete the row. Thus, the only way to prevent CUSTOMER deletions is through manual procedures. All employees must be instructed not to make such changes. Further, management may want to prepare special backups of CUSTOMER just in case a deletion is made by accident. Another solution would be to develop command files that implement a delete passwood.

INV Processing

The processing constraints on INV data are that all users are to be able to read the data, but only certain users may add, change, or delete data. Further, when changes are under way, the entire table is to be locked.

These constraints are easily implemented in R:base. A MODIFY password is placed on the INV table to prevent unauthorized users from changing it. Additionally, before any of the inventory clerks change this table, they can issue an explicit lock on INV with the following command:

```
R> SET LOCK INV ON
```

This command will prohibit others from reading or changing the INV table. When the clerk is finished with his or her changes, the lock must be set off. If the user closes the database without releasing the lock, R:base will automatically turn it off. Since the users will only lock one table, the deadly embrace cannot occur.

These commands could be inserted into all of the command files which the clerks use. This would be a wiser course of action since the clerks might forget to set the locks manually themselves.

SALE and COMPSALE

The processing constraints on SALE and COMPSALE are to allow all users to read and add rows, but no one is to be allowed to change or delete rows. These constraints cannot be implemented with R:base in a straightforward fashion. Passwords cannot be used because a MODIFY password is too restrictive; it would eliminate the addition of rows. Additionally, if users employ EDIT USING commands with these tables, R:base will give them the opportunity to change or delete data. This violates the constraints.

The best approach for this situation is to develop special command files for processing SALE and COMPSALE. Users must be instructed to employ these command files whenever a sale transaction occurs. The users must be further instructed *not* to use any other R:base command or command file when processing SALE or COMPSALE data.

Summary of the Great Plains Implementation

The implementation of a multi-user database application for Great Plains can be accomplished without much difficulty. By and large, the applications developed for the single-user database can be used. Passwords need to be added to EMPLOYEE and CUSTOMER relations. Further, explicit locks need to be added to command files that process the INV relation.

Unfortunately, the controls over the deletion of CUSTOMER data and over the change and deletion of SALE and COMPSALE data are weak. In both cases, users who are familiar with R:base commands, particularly EDIT USING, DELETE ROWS, ASSIGN, and CHANGE, will be able to violate the processing constraints if they want to.

Given this situation, the best solution may be to develop custom command files for all processing and never teach any R:base commands to the users. In this case, all processing would be done via programs that the users never see. As long as the users do not learn R:base commands, none of the constraints can be violated. Another important control is to make backup copies of all data periodically and to reconcile any differences between the current database values and the data on the backed-up files. This action would detect any unauthorized activity.

These control weaknesses are not that severe. The implementers of the application should make management aware of them, however.

SUMMARY

- A local area network is a collection of microcomputers connected together via a short-distance (within the same building) communications line. LANs allow micros to communicate with one another and they allow users to share resources, such as expensive peripherals and databases.

- A database application on a LAN involves three software components: the local operating system, the network operating system, and the DBMS.

- Microcomputers support multi-user databases in two modes: local area network and concurrent operating system. In the LAN mode, the micros operate as cooperating colleagues. In the concurrent mode, the node storing the database operates as a master and the other computers operate as slaves.

- Multi-user databases are subject to the concurrent-update problem in which two users process the same row at the same time. In this case, the updates of one of the users can be lost. There are two ways of solving this problem. It can be avoided by scheduling batch, sequential, or partitioned updating, or it can be prevented by locking.

- Locks vary by level, source, and type. Lock levels can be broad, such as the entire database, or narrow, such as a data-item. Lock sources can be explicit (issued by the programmer or user) or implicit (issued by the DBMS). Lock types are shared and exclusive. With a shared lock, concurrent reading is allowed. With an exclusive lock, no concurrent access of any type is allowed.

- When locks are used, the deadly embrace can occur. This situation develops when two users are each waiting for a resource that the other user has locked. The manner in which the deadly embrace is resolved depends on the features of the DBMS.

- Backup and recovery is critical for multi-user applications. Unfortunately, microcomputer DBMS products do not yet provide comprehensive backup and recovery facilities. End-users must take special precautions during recovery to compensate for the DBMS.

- Multi-user database applications require strong and effective database administration. Particular emphasis must be placed on the control of processing, backup and recovery, and structure changes to the database.

- R:base 5000 Multi-user provides a variety of locks to support the processing of shared databases. Explicit locks are available for locking tables. Implicit locks are applied at the data-item, table, and database levels, depending on the command being processed.

- Multi-user database design and implementation considerations are illustrated in the application for Great Plains Music and Video.

REVIEW QUESTIONS

15.1
Describe two disadvantages of duplicated data. Which is the more serious and why?

15.2
Name and describe the function of three types of software involved in database processing on LANs.

15.3
Describe an example of the concurrent update problem as it might pertain to a database used in class scheduling.

15.4
Describe three ways the concurrent update problem can be avoided.

15.5
Describe three different lock levels.

15.6
Describe two sources of locks.

15.7
Describe two types of locks.

15.8
Why is backup and recovery crucial for multi-user applications? Describe a situation in which it would be difficult to reprocess transactions in their original order. Why does this matter?

15.9
Describe special considerations for database administration on local area network database applications.

15.10
Explain, in your own words, the processing restrictions for EMPLOYEE, CUSTOMER, and INVENTORY tables in the Great Plains example database.

15.11
Describe R:base 5000 Multi-user explicit locking facilities.

15.12
Describe R:base 5000 Multi-user implicit locking facilities.

15.13
How does R:base 5000 control concurrent processing at the data-item level for EDIT USING commands?

Appendix A

Sharing Data Between Computers

Computers are increasingly sharing data. Keying data manually is both slow and error-prone. Once we have keyed data into computer A, it makes little sense to key the same data into computer B. Rather, we prefer to have computer A send the data to computer B in electronic form.

The transfer of such data involves three fundamental systems as illustrated in Figure A–1. First, the manager of the data (we assume a DBMS here, although this could be a file processing system such as VSAM) on computer A must extract data from local files and send that data to communications software. The communications software packages the data and delivers it to the physical equipment for transmission according to a communications protocol. Finally, the physical equipment transmits the data from computer A to computer B.

On the receiving computer, these operations take place in reverse order. The data is received by the equipment and delivered to the communications programs. These programs coordinate with the communications programs on the first computer to ensure that all of the data is accurately received. Finally, the data is delivered to the DBMS on the receiving computer.

This chapter is concerned only with the DBMS portion of Figure A–1. Specifically, we will consider the ways that R:base can receive and send data. We will also discuss the conversion of data from hierarchical and network DBMS products to R:base. Finally, guidelines will be provided for conversion of databases managed by IMS, IDMS, TOTAL (IMAGE), and ADABAS.

FIGURE A–1
Sharing data between computers

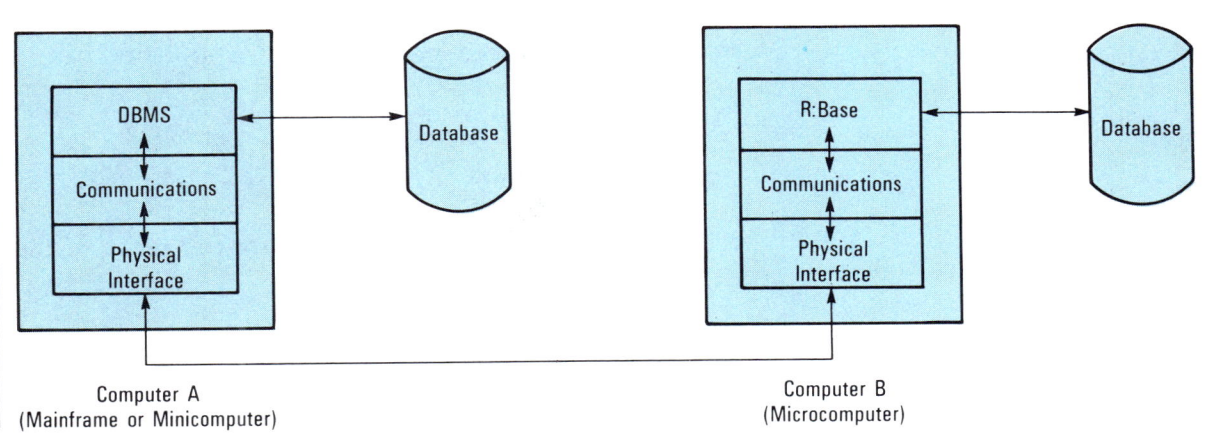

FIGURE A–2
CUSTOMER table

Table: CUSTOMER
Read Password: NO
Modify Password: NO

#	Name	Columns Type	Length
1	F-name	TEXT	5 characters
2	L-name	TEXT	10 characters
3	Custnum	TEXT	4 characters
4	Phone	TEXT	8 characters

FIGURE A–3a
Fixed-format example for CUSTOMER table

Column	Content
1–5	F-name
11–20	L-name
25–32	Phone
37–40	Custnum

FIGURE A–3b
Sample CUSTOMER data in fixed format

1/	11/	Column 25/	37/
Mary	Jones	236-0089	100
Fred	Parks	345-9987	200
Don	Abernathy	325-0098	300
Sally	Freedman	325-9887	400

MASS TRANSFERS OF DATA TO AND FROM R:BASE

R:base can receive and send data in batches. Each batch must contain data for one and only one table. Tables can be sent in their entirety or a subset of the rows can by transmitted. R:base assumes that data is transmitted row by row. Thus, data for the first row is transmitted, then data for the next row, and so forth. A complete row can be sent or only some of the columns of a row can be sent.

Receiving Mass Inputs

R:base has two ways of receiving a batch of data: fixed format ASCII or delimited ASCII (ASCII = American Standard Code for Information Interchange). To understand these, consider the sample CUSTOMER table in Figure A–2. This table has four columns defined as shown. Suppose that you wish to receive a large number of CUSTOMER rows—say 1000—and that these rows have been stored on a file named CUST.DAT. The format of the data in this file determines whether the data will be input as fixed format or delimited ASCII.

Input Via Fixed Format ASCII Data that is to be input as fixed format must be highly structured. Specifically, each and every column must occur in a fixed position within the data record. Figure A–3a shows one way that CUSTOMER data could be structured in the file CUST.DAT. F-name is located in positions 1 through 5; L-name is located in positions 11 through 20; Phone is located in positions 25 through 32; and Custnum is located in positions 37 through 40. Notice that every row of data in Figure A–3b conforms to this convention.

For R:base to read this file, we need to create an R:base form to describe the location of each column in the input record. The form will contain a single line that specifies column locations. It will have no heading; in fact, it will have no text at all.

To define such a form, type:

FORMS

R:base will respond with a request for the name of the form. We used:

CEXAMPLE

Next, R:base requests the name of the table to receive the input. Type:

CUSTOMER

Since the form has no text, choose "Locate" to indicate the column locations in the form. For this form, we started F-name in column 1, L-name in column 11, Phone in column 25, and Custnum in column 37 (Figure A–4). Observe that we marked the end of each column with an E at the end of each column location.

At this point, data can be loaded into CUSTOMER from the fixed file with the following command:

ENTER CEXAMPLE FROM CUST.DAT

Recall that CEXAMPLE is the name of the form and CUST.DAT is the name of the file containing the data.

Input Via Delimited ASCII Files The second way R:base can receive data is from a delimited ASCII file. Whereas column values must occur in specific locations for fixedformat files, column values in a delimited ASCII file can occur anywhere in the record. The only restriction is that the column values must appear in the same order in every record. Thus, if the order of the first record is F-name, L-name, Custnum, Phone, then the order of columns for all other records must be the same.

You may be wondering, with all this flexibility, how R:base distinguishes the value of one column from the value of another. R:base assumes that column values are separated, or delimited, by either spaces or commas. Thus, R:base would find four values in the following record:

Don Abernathy   300   325-0098

When this record is read, the value of F-name is Don, the value of L-name is Abernathy, the value of Custnum is 300, and the value of Phone is 325-0098. The values in the next record could occur in different locations, as long as the order of the columns remained the same.

If you wanted to load 1000 rows of data into the CUSTOMER table, you must create a file having the format shown above. Suppose we do this on the file CUST.DAT. To input the data into CUSTOMER, we would type the following R:base command:

LOAD CUSTOMER FROM CUST.DAT AS ASCII

When this command is executed, the data in the file will be added to the CUSTOMER table. Since we have

FIGURE A–4

Definition of format to input CUSTOMER data

```
E[dit form], L[ocate attributes], Q[uit]:

S  E     S       E   S     E    S E
```

not mentioned any column names in the LOAD command, R:base assumes that columns will occur in the order in which they were defined in the table. For the example in Figure A–2, columns will be read in the order F-name, L-name, Custnum, Phone.

If the data in the file occurs in a different order, we can instruct R:base to read columns in the proper order. For example, if the data were written to the file in the order L-name, F-name, Phone, Custnum, then the following LOAD command would be used:

LOAD CUSTOMER FROM CUST.DAT AS ASCII USING +
L-name F-name Phone Custnum

You may be wondering what happens if the data contains a blank or a comma. For example, suppose we have a customer whose first name is Mary Jo? To input data containing blanks, we put the data value in quotes as follows:

"Mary Jo" Abernathy   300   325-0098

Similarly, if a data item has commas, it must also be enclosed in quotes.

In some cases, it may be undesirable to put quotes around data values that have blanks or commas. In this case, other characters can be selected as the delimiter between column values. This is easy to do and you can find the particulars in the R:base documentation.

Output from R:base

R:base can also write data in both fixed and delimited ASCII formats.

Output as Fixed Format To generate a file having a fixed format, you define a one-line report similar to the one-line form used for fixed format input. This one-line report has no headings, no footings, and no text. It is simply a report body: each line of the report contains the values of a single row of a table.

For example, suppose you want to output the CUSTOMER table in the following fixed format: L-name starting in column 1, F-name starting in column 11, Phone starting in column 21, and Custnum starting in column 31. To generate this file, create a one-line report, CUSTOUT, with the columns located in the predetermined positions. The report should have no headings or footings. Also, the page length must be set to zero so that R:base will not place page delimiters in the output file.

CUSTOUT can be used to produce a fixed format file. For example, suppose we want to construct a file having all CUSTOMERs with Custnum values less than 600. Further suppose we name this file CUST1.DAT. The following commands will generate the file:

    OUTPUT CUST1.DAT
    PRINT CUSTOUT WHERE Custnum LT 600
    OUTPUT TERMINAL

The output command instructs R:base to send output to the file name CUST1.DAT. The PRINT command then fills the file. The second OUTPUT command redirects output to the terminal. If we wanted all of the CUSTOMER data to be output, we would simply omit the WHERE clause from the PRINT command.

Delimited ASCII Format Producing a delimited ASCII output file is very simple. Suppose we want all the CUSTOMER data to be output in delimited ASCII form (that is, with column values separated by blanks) in a file named CUST1.DAT. The following R:base commands will do this:

    OUTPUT CUST1.DAT
    UNLOAD DATA FOR CUSTOMER AS ASCII
    OUTPUT TERMINAL

DATABASE CONVERSIONS

DBMS products can be classified in three broad categories: relational, hierarchical, and network. In this section, we will summarize the action necessary to convert data from a DBMS in one of these categories to R:base.

DBMS products have their own terminology. To avoid complexity, we will use a standard set of terms in this section. The term *record* means a collection of data items relating to a single object; it corresponds to a *row in a table*. We will use the term *file* to refer to a collection of records; *file* corresponds to *table*. Thus, for example, when referring to IMS, we will discuss an IMS *record*; we actually mean an IMS *segment*, but we will avoid that term and all other DBMS-unique terminology.

Relational to R:base Conversions

Since R:base is itself a relational DBMS, the conversion of data from a relational DBMS to R:base is straightfor-

FIGURE A–5a
One-level hierarchy

FIGURE A–5b
Multiple-level hierarchy

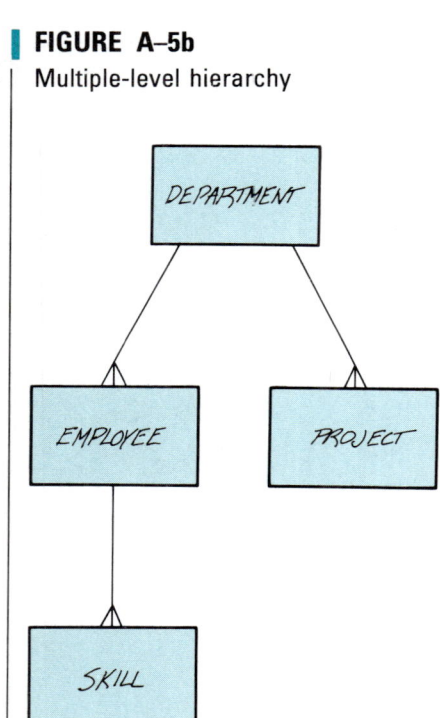

ward. Each table to be transmitted is unloaded from the source DBMS and sent to R:base. The structure of the tables in both the source DBMS and R:base should be the same.

One difference concerns RULES. R:base is unique in its ability to define and enforce RULES. Most other DBMS products do not have this feature. Therefore, rules are often embedded in application programs or other facilities. If this is the case, you will need to determine what rules actually exist on the source DBMS data and define those RULES to R:base.

Hierarchical to R:base Conversions

Hierarchical DBMS products such as DL/1, IMS, and System 2000 model data as hierarchies, or trees. Relationships among records are one-to-many, and each record has at most one parent. Figure A–5 shows examples of two hierarchies. In Figure A–5a, DEPARTMENTs have many EMPLOYEEs, but an EMPLOYEE works in a single DEPARTMENT. Thus, the relationship from DEPARTMENT to EMPLOYEE is one-to-many.

Figure A–5b shows a multilevel hierarchy. DEPARTMENTSs have two types of subordinate records: EMPLOYEE and PROJECT. EMPLOYEE, in turn, has SKILL records as subordinates.

To represent these structures with R:base, we need to express the relationships in data. Specifically, in Figure A–5a, we need to ensure that DEPARTMENTs can be combined with the appropriate EMPLOYEEs using either R:base JOIN or R:base INTERSECT commands.

As we saw in previous chapters, for R:base to JOIN or INTERSECT two tables, the tables must have linking columns arising from the same domain. To model the one-to-many relationship between DEPARTMENT and EMPLOYEE, EMPLOYEE must contain a unique identifier of the DEPARTMENT in which the EMPLOYEE works. Thus, when the EMPLOYEE data is unloaded, the key from DEPARTMENT must be added to the EMPLOYEE record (assuming that such a key is not already a part of the EMPLOYEE record).

Figure A–6a shows a relational version of the structure in Figure A–5a. DEPARTMENT and EMPLOYEE are each represented by tables. The relationship between DEPARTMENT and EMPLOYEE is represented by adding the key of DEPARTMENT to EMPLOYEE.

Figure A–6b shows a relational version of the structure in Figure A–5b. DEPARTMENT, EMPLOYEE, PROJECT, and SKILL are all represented by tables. The relationship between DEPARTMENT and EMPLOYEE is represented as just described. The relationship be-

FIGURE A–6a
Relational representation of Figure A–5a

DEPARTMENT Relation

Dept. no				
100				
200				
300				
400				
500				

EMPLOYEE Relation

Emp. no				Dept. no
1000				100
2000				200
3000				100
4000				200
5000				300
6000				100

FIGURE A–6b
Relational representation of Figure A–5b

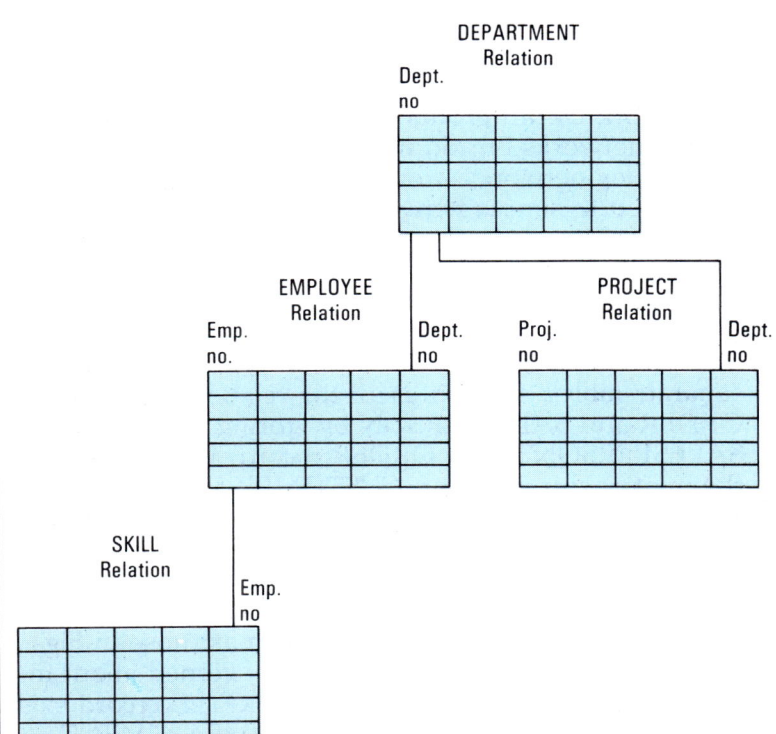

tween DEPARTMENT and PROJECT is represented by storing the key of DEPARTMENT in PROJECT. The relationship between SKILL and EMPLOYEE is represented by storing the key of EMPLOYEE in SKILL.

In Figure A–6b, SKILL contains the key of its parent

FIGURE A–7a
Simple network relationship

FIGURE A–7b
Complex network relationship

(EMPLOYEE), but not the key of its grandparent (DEPARTMENT). For some applications, it may be desirable to store both the keys of both the parent and the grandparent (and possibly of other generations as well) in the record. If so, these keys should be added when the data is unloaded.

Network to R:base Conversion

The third classification of DBMS products is network systems. Unlike the hierarchical DBMS, these systems easily allow records to have more than one parent. The most notable examples of network systems are products that conform to the CODASYL DBTG model. IDMS, IDS II, and DMS-1100 are examples of such systems.

Two types of networks are possible. Figure A–7a shows a simple network. Here, ORDER records have two parents: a CUSTOMER parent and a SALESPERSON parent. This network is called a simple network because the parents are different types of records. Figure A–7b shows a complex network. Here, SUPPLIERs have more than one parent (suppliers can supply many parts), but the parents are of the same record type.

Network DBMS products allow the representation of simple networks but do not allow the representation of complex networks. Complex networks must be decomposed to simple networks before they can be represented. Therefore, we need only be concerned with the transformation of simple networks to tables.

To transform a simple network, we represent each record type by a table. For Figure A–7a, we represent SALESPERSON, CUSTOMER, and ORDER by three separate tables. We represent the relationship between ORDER and SALESPERSON by storing the key of SALESPERSON in the ORDER record. We represent the relationship between CUSTOMER and ORDER by storing the key of CUSTOMER in the ORDER record. This transformation is shown in Figure A–8.

A Note about RULES

When we make transformations such as those in Figures A–6 and A–8, we need to be concerned about interrelation constraints. Can an EMPLOYEE record exist in the database if its corresponding DEPARTMENT record does not exist in the database? Similarly, can an ORDER record exist if its corresponding SALESPERSON record does not exist?

If such existence is to be prohibited, we must define appropriate R:base RULES. The RULES should be defined before the data is loaded into R:base. R:base will then enforce the RULES as the data is loaded. By the

FIGURE A–8
Relational representation of a simple network (Figure A–7a)

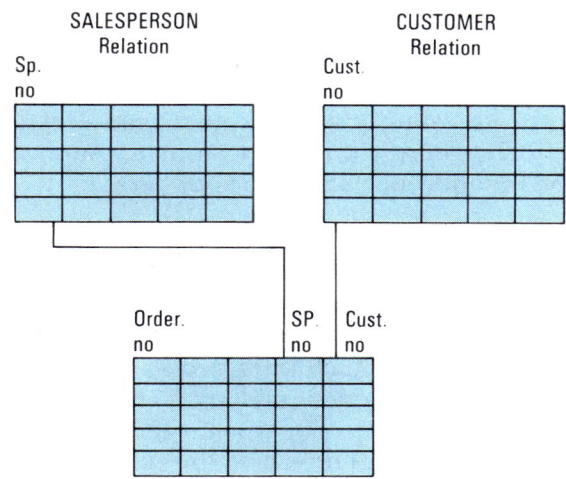

way, if such interrelation rules are defined, all parent records (DEPARTMENT, SALESPERSON, CUSTOMER) must be loaded before the children (EMPLOYEE, ORDER). If children are loaded first, R:base will not permit any of the parent records to be loaded.

GUIDELINES FOR CONVERTING DATA TO R:BASE

Converting data from a DBMS to R:base depends very much on the particular DBMS product that processes the source database. This section presents a few suggestions for several popular DBMS's.

IMS and DL/1

IMS and DL/1 data should be converted according to the general guidelines in the previous section. Each segment can be represented in R:base as a table. The key of parent segments must be stored as part of the child's table.

IMS and DL/1 support the representation of complex networks (many-to-many relationships) via paired logical pointers. If the data to be unloaded has such a structure, a table will need to be created that represents the intersection of the two segments.

For example, if the many-to-many relationship between PART and SUPPLIER is represented with paired logical pointers, the fact that a particular part is supplied by a particular supplier will have to be recorded in a table. In this case, three tables would be transmitted to R:base. One table would have PART data, one would have SUPPLIER data, and one would have intersection data (data about the relationship between PART and SUPPLIER).

Suppose we call the third table SOURCE. The columns of SOURCE are the key of PART and the key of SUPPLIER. If PART A is supplied by SUPPLIER 100, then a row with the values (A,100) would need to be stored in SOURCE. There would be a similar row for every valid combination of parts and suppliers.

IDMS and CODASYL Systems

Converting from IDMS and other CODASYL systems is relatively straightforward. Each record type is defined as an R:base table. Sets are represented by storing a key of the parent in the child record as discussed in the last section. If a set is defined, but a child record is not in any occurrences of that set, then a null value should be defined for the key of the parent column.

A row is placed in a set by replacing a null value in the child with the key of the parent. Thus, manual set insertion status can be simulated. Automatic insertion status can be simulated by defining a rule that prevents records with null values in the parent key column from being stored.

Mandatory set retention status can be simulated with the same rule. Not allowing a record to have a null value in the parent key column forces a record to always belong to a set.

TOTAL and IMAGE

The easiest way to convert TOTAL and IMAGE databases to R:base is to define a table for each master and variable record. Further, the key of each master must be stored in the variable records as illustrated in the previous section.

Such a straightforward conversion will work, but it does not undo the contortions that are sometimes placed in TOTAL or IMAGE databases because of the one-level limitation for relationships. The structure in Figure A–5a, for example, would have to be redefined and somewhat contorted to be stored using TOTAL or IMAGE. Since the relational model does not require these contortions, it is desirable to remove them from the database when the data is converted. Unfortunately, it is not possible to provide a generalized way of doing this. Be forewarned, however, that a one-for-one conversion from master and variable files to tables may look quite strange to the end-user.

ADABAS

Conversions from ADABAS are in most cases quite easy. Each ADABAS record can simply be stored as a table. Since ADABAS represents relationships by common values of keys, all of the data necessary to represent relationships will already be part of the record.

A conversion problem may occur regarding repeating groups. The rows of a table are supposed to be of fixed length. If the source database has repeating groups, these groups will need to be removed. They can be moved to a new table, and the key of the record that contained the repeating group can be stored with the repeating group data in the new table.

Bibliography

1. Atre, S. *Data Base, Structured Techniques for Design, Performance, and Management.* New York: John Wiley, 1980.
2. Brooks, F. P. *The Mythical Man-Month.* Reading, MA: Addison-Wesley, 1975.
3. Codd, E. F. "A Relational Model of Data for Large Shared Databanks." In *Communications of the ACM,* Vol. 13, No. 6, June 1970.
4. DeMarco, Tom. *Structured Analysis and System Specification.* New York: Yourdon Press, 1978.
5. Dolan, Kathy. *Business Computer Systems Design.* Santa Cruz, CA: Mitchell Publishing, 1983.
6. Fagin, Ronald. "A Normal Form for Relational Databases That Is Based on Domains and Keys." In *Transactions on Database Systems,* Vol. 6, No. 3, September 1981.
7. Finkelstein, Clive. "Information Engineering." Reprinted from *Computerworld,* May 11, 1981, May 25, 1981, June 1, 1981, June 8, 1981, and June 15, 1981.
8. IBM Corporation. *IBM PC Network Program User's Guide.* Armonk, NY: International Business Machines Corporation, 1984/1985.
9. Inmon, William H. *Effective Data Base Design.* Engelwood Cliffs, NJ: Prentice-Hall, 1981.
10. Jackson, M. A. *Principles of Program Design.* Orlando, FL: Academic Press, 1975.
11. Knuth, Donald E. *The Art of Computer Programming: Fundamental Algorithms.* Reading, MA: Addison-Wesley, 1968.
12. Kroenke, David M. *Database Processing: Fundamentals, Design, Implementation.* Chicago: Science Research Associates, 1983.
13. Lyon, John K. *The Database Administrator.* New York: John Wiley, 1976.
14. Microrim, Inc. *Clout Users' Manual.* Bellevue, WA: Microrim, Inc., 1984.
15. Microrim, Inc. *R:base 5000 Users' Manual.* Bellevue, WA: Microrim, Inc. 1985.
16. Orr, Kenneth T. *Structured Requirements Definition.* Ken Orr and Associates, 1981.
17. Page-Jones, Meilir. *The Practical Guide to Structured Systems Design.* New York: Yourdon Press, 1980.
18. Peters, Lawrence J. *Software Design: Methods and Techniques.* New York: Yourdon Press, 1981.
19. Yourdon, Edward, and Constantine, Larry L. *Structured Design.* Engelwood Cliffs, NJ: Prentice-Hall, 1979.

Index

A

Accidental loss to data, 255
Alternation, 211
Application EXPRESS, 100, 196
　building applications with, 196
　database definition with, 100
Application programs, 12, 14
Asking CLOUT questions, 282
Assigning passwords, 266
Attribute, 41–42, 100

B

Backup, 9, 11, 14, 267
Backup and recovery, 260–261, 317
BASIC, 12
Bit, 12
Breakpoint, 180
Building employee awareness, 257
Byte, 12

C

Careful destruction of reports, 264
Careful destruction of storage media, 264
Central processing unit, 15
Changes to the database, 11
Characteristics of database tables, 40
Checks of batch totals, 263
CHOOSE command, 217, 221
Choosing links, 85–86
CLEAR ALL VARIABLES command, 220–221
Clerical users, 10
CLOSE command, 268
CLOUT startup files, 297
COBOL, 12
Column, 41–42, 100
Command file, 194, 210
Comments in command files, 213
Completed Great Plains database design, 93, 102, 123, 170
Components of information management systems, 9–10
COMPUTE command, 112–113, 183
Computed variables, 175
Concatenated string variables, 174
Concurrent update, 314
Concurrent-user systems, 240
COPY command, 268

D

Data archives, 243
Data as an asset, 254
Data duplication, 7–8
Data model, 38, 42
Data model design, 45–46
Data types in R:base, 101
Database, definition of, 11–12, 100, 122
Database administration, 236, 318
Database administrator, selection of, 248
Database application, 194
Database configuration control, 246
Database control, 238
Database design, 45, 48, 313
　deciding what facts are important, 82
　describing the relationships, 78
　designating the key columns, 83
　evaluating the design, 93
　listing the objects, 76
　local area networks, 313
　problems from poor design, 56
　recording the relationships, 84
　relationship constraints, 79–81
　types of relationships, 79–81
Database management system, 6
Database planning, 238
Database processing, 4, 6, 11
　advantages 7–8
　disadvantages, 8–9
Database tables, 40
DBMS, 6, 8, 12–14, 71
DBMS utilities, 13–14, 71
Deadly embrace, 317
Decision makers, 10
DEFINE command, 122
Defining CLOUT synonyms, 282
Defining R:base FORMS, 129
Defining R:base REPORTS, 133, 168
　define report, 135, 171
　edit report, 135, 170
　locate data items, 135, 176
　mark report sections, 137, 178
　save report, 139, 182
　set lines per page, 138, 182
Definition of responsibilities, 259
DELETE ROWS command, 269–270
Dependencies, splitting, 70
Dependency, 59, 63
Design, 45
Difference, 148, 150–152, 158
DISPLAY command, 218
Documentation of reports, 264
Documented processing schedule, 263
Domain, 61, 63
Domain/key normal form, 59, 63

E

EDIT command, 113
Employee accountability, 259
Employee checks and balances, 264
Employee training, 257
Enforcing database restrictions, 71, 126
ENTER command, 132
ERASE command, 268
Evaluating database design, 63
Exact match with CLOUT, 296

F

Field, 12, 41–42
File, 12, 41–42

File processing, 4, 11
FILLIN command, 221, 223–224
FORMS, 129
FORTRAN, 12
Function of database administration, 238
Fuzzy values with CLOUT, 295

G

Great Plains Music and Video Unlimited, 22

H

Hardware, 14–15
HELP command, 114, 116

I

IF-THEN-ENDIF, 218–219, 221, 225
Implementation of local area networks, 323
Inclusion constraints, 70, 79
Information management system, 4
INPUT command, 269–270
Input controls, 263
Integrated processing, 4, 6–7
Internal program documentation, 213
INTERSECT command, 152, 194
Intersection, 148, 150–151, 154, 162
Intertable constraints, 70, 79–81
Iteration, 211

J

Join, 43–46, 148, 154, 156, 161
JOIN command, 156

K

Key, 60, 63, 83–85

L

Limiting database access, 260
Limiting database searches with CLOUT, 303
Limiting physical access, 260
Links, 85–87
LIST command, 131
LOAD command, 216, 270
LOAD WITH PROMPTS command, 105, 128
Local area networks:
　architecture, 308
　database administration, 318
　database processing, 311
　definition, 308
Locking, 315
Locking with R:base, 324
Lookup variables, 173

M

Management controls, 256
Menu, 194
Menu-driven database application, 195, 211

Modification anomalies, 58, 63, 71
Monitoring error reports, 258

N
Natural language processing, 279
Natural language queries, 13
NEWPAGE command, 221, 224–225
NEXT command, 227–228

O
OPEN command, 104, 194, 268
Operating system, 14
Operations scheduling, 242
Organizational controls, 258
OUTPUT command, 221, 223–224, 269–270, 272
Output controls, 264

P
PACK command, 268
Partial values with CLOUT, 293
Pascal, 12
PAUSE command, 222, 224–225
People, 10
Physical models, 38
Placing links, 87
   many-to-many relationships, 90–91
   one-to-many relationships, 89
PRINT command, 140, 183
Printing an R:base REPORT, 140, 182
Procedures, 10
Processing controls, 263
Processing rights and responsibilities, 238
Program/data independence, 8, 11
Programming language interface, 12
Programs, 12
PROJECT command, 152, 158, 194
Projection, 42, 44–45, 148, 151–154, 156, 160–161
PROMPT command, 115
Protecting the database, 256

Q
Query/update, 13
QUIT command, 219, 221

R
R:base 5000 Multi-user, 323
R:base commands:
   CHOOSE 217, 221
   CLEAR ALL VARIABLES, 220–221
   CLOSE, 268
   COMPUTE, 112–113, 183
   DEFINE, 122
   DELETE ROWS, 269–270
   DISPLAY, 218
   EDIT, 113
   ENTER, 132
   FILLIN, 221, 223–224
   FORMS, 129
   HELP, 114, 116
   IF-THEN-ENDIF, 218–219, 221, 225
   INPUT, 269–270
   INTERSECT, 154, 194
   JOIN, 156
   LIST, 131
   LOAD, 216, 270
   LOAD WITH PROMPTS, 105, 128
   NEWPAGE, 214, 219, 221, 224–225
   NEXT, 227–228
   OPEN, 104, 194, 268
   OUTPUT, 221, 223–224, 269–270, 272
   PACK, 268
   PAUSE, 222, 224–225
   PRINT, 140, 183
   PROJECT, 152, 158, 194
   PROMPT, 115
   QUIT, 219, 221
   RELOAD, 267–268
   REMOVE, 153, 158, 194, 270
   RENAME COLUMN, 156
   REPORTS, 133, 168
   RETURN, 222, 224–225
   RUN, 195, 204, 219, 221, 226, 228, 269
   SELECT, 105–111, 115, 151, 194
   SET, 219, 221, 224
   SET DATE, 102, 183, 225, 228
   SET POINTER, 225–228
   SET VARIABLE, 183, 214–216, 221, 224–225, 227–228
   SHOW VARIABLE, 215, 225, 228
   SORTED BY clauses in 110–111, 114
   SUBTRACT, 158–159
   UNLOAD, 269–270
   WHERE clauses in, 106–109, 111, 113–114, 152–153, 183, 194
   WHILE/ENDWHILE, 216, 221
   WRITE, 221, 224–225
R:base data types, 101
R:base global variables 171, 214
R:base passwords, 265
R:base RULES, 124
RBASE.DAT file, 204
RBEDIT, 194
Record, 12, 41–42
Recovery, 9, 11, 14, 271
Relation, 41–42, 63, 100
Relationship constraints, 79
Relationships in the database, 12, 79
RELOAD command, 267–268
REMOVE command, 153, 158, 194, 270
RENAME COLUMN command, 156
RENAME command, 268
Reordering R:base report variables, 176
Report writing utilities, 13
REPORTS command, 133, 168
Resource controls, 259
Restriction, 62–63
Restrictions, enforcement, 71, 126
RETURN command, 222, 224–225
Row, 41–42, 100
RULES in R:base, 124
RUN command, 195, 204, 219, 221, 226, 228, 269

S
Screen utilities, 13
Security, 15
SELECT command, 105–111, 115, 151, 194
Selection, 43, 45, 148, 151–154, 160–161
Selection of database administrator, 248
Separation of duties, 258
Sequence, 211
Sequential-user systems, 239
SET command, 219, 221, 224
SET DATE command, 102, 183, 225, 228
SET POINTER command, 225–228
SET VARIABLE command, 183, 214–216, 221, 224–225, 227–228
SHOW VARIABLE command, 215, 225, 228
Single-user systems, 239
SORTED BY clause, 114
Sorting with CLOUT, 292
Splitting dependencies, 70
Steps in database design, 48, 49, 76
SUBTRACT command, 158–159
Supervisor review of processing reports, 264
System failure, 10
System variables, 172

T
Table, 41–42, 63, 100
Technical users, 10
Threats to data, 254
Transaction count, 263
Tuple, 41–42, 100

U
Union, 148–149, 151, 158, 162
Union compatible, 148
UNLOAD command, 269–270
Unloading critical data, 260

V
Verification of keyed data, 263
Video Rental Information Management System, 23
Video Rental System:
   changing member data, 27
   main menu, 23

W
WHERE clause, 106–109, 111, 113–114, 152–153, 183, 194
WHILE/ENDWHILE command, 216, 221
Who/Where/When with clout, 295
WRITE command, 221, 224–225